THE CATHEDRAL

o

THE CATHEDRALS
OF
GREAT BRITAIN

THEIR HISTORY AND ARCHITECTURE

BY

P. H. DITCHFIELD, M.A., F.S.A.

Fellow of the Royal Historical Society, Rector of Barkham

WITH NUMEROUS ILLUSTRATIONS

BY

HERBERT RAILTON, J. A. SYMINGTON, H. M. JAMES,
H. CRICKMORE, ETC.

1902

London : J. M. DENT & COMPANY
Philadelphia : J. B. LIPPINCOTT COY.

PREFACE

IN this volume I have attempted to give an architectural description of all the cathedral churches of England, Wales, and Scotland, together with a brief history of each see. In order to include any adequate account of each church and bishopric in one volume of portable size, which may be of use to visitors in their travels, much compression has been necessary, but it is hoped that nothing of importance has been omitted which might be useful to those who would read aright the architectural history of our great churches. On account of their immense importance in the history of Gothic art, it has been thought well to include in this volume some account of the churches of Westminster and Beverley. At the close of each history of a cathedral will be found a record of the principal building dates and dimensions, and also a brief account of the chief places and churches of interest in the city or neighbourhood which it is advisable to visit.

I desire to express my grateful thanks to all who have kindly assisted in the preparation of this work, to the deans and canons-in-residence who have often guided me by their counsel during my study of their cathedrals, and also to the vergers who have readily afforded me much valuable help. More especially do I wish to thank the Deans of Lincoln, Ely, Chester and Gloucester, Canon Tristram of Durham, Bishop Anson of Lichfield, and Archdeacon Richardson of Southwell, for their courtesy and kindly interest. I have also to record my obligations to the work of many previous writers. The works of Freeman, Rickman, Britton, Willis, Winkle, and the Diocesan histories published by S.P.C.K. have been consulted, as well as the special monographs on each cathedral, which are too numerous to mention. Prior's *Gothic Art* has been of the greatest possible assistance, Addis's *Scottish Cathedrals and Abbeys*, and also the very valuable and indispensable handbooks published by the late Mr. John Murray. I have found the volumes of Bell's Cathedral Series most useful when visiting the buildings of which they treat, and Messrs. Isbister's volumes written by the deans of our cathedrals contain picturesque and attractive accounts of the historic buildings. To all these works I desire to acknowledge my great indebtedness. And lastly I have to record my grateful thanks to the artists who have enriched these pages with their charming drawings, and to Mr. Dent, the publisher of this work, for much encouragement, valuable advice, and able direction, without which this volume would have lacked whatever of merit it may possess.

P. H. DITCHFIELD.

BARKHAM RECTORY,
September 8, 1902.

CONTENTS

LIST OF ILLUSTRATIONS

LIST OF PLANS

Cathedrals of Great Britain

THE ARCHITECTURE OF THE CATHEDRALS OF GREAT BRITAIN

WE are endeavouring to follow the traces of the handiwork of the great master-builders who have filled the English Isle with so many noble shrines, to mark the growth and development of the various styles and modes of building, and to endeavour to interpret their meaning. The story of the rise and fall of English Gothic art has a fascination that is all its own; and with the intention of endeavouring to realise its high aims, its strength and beauty, and to understand its true spirit, we will start on our pilgrimage to those fanes which it has reared to the honour and glory of the Most High. And as we watch the rise and progress of English Gothic art, we shall note that it is no exotic, no alien welcomed to our shores; but a true English native art, born in the brains and faith of our English forefathers, and nourished here with a nation's whole-hearted affection. French writers on architecture are accustomed to state that our English Gothic came from France, and that each stage and change were wrought by the influence of foreign masons and were borrowed from them. There could not be a greater error. The Anglo-Norman style was developed quite as much in this country as in Normandy, which was then a province of England. We shall see that English Gothic sprang into being in the choir of Lincoln. No foreign mason taught our English masons the secret of their art. Even Westminster, most French of all our buildings, and designed by a foreigner, is, in the language of Sir Gilbert Scott, "a great French thought expressed in excellent English." And while we have a style peculiarly our own, the Perpendicular of the fifteenth century, at that period the French with

A

their Flamboyant tracery were only imitating the flowing lines of our fourteenth-century Decorated. And as we study more carefully these examples of English Gothic art, we shall admire the great unknown toilers who built so surely and so well, who put their hearts and lives, affections and religion into their work; we shall reverence the relics of their handiwork which time has spared and love them exceedingly.

For the convenience of classification, mediæval architecture has been divided into four distinct styles or periods, and we must again chronicle the oft-told story of their varied peculiarities.

I. The Norman style commenced in the reign of Edward the Confessor, whose work at Westminster (the sub-structure of the dormitory and the lower part of the walls of the refectory with the ornamental arcade) is declared to be the earliest example of the Norman style in England. This style prevailed to the time of Henry II., when a period of transition set in, and the style began to approximate to that of the succeeding century. The main characteristics of the Norman style are—cylindrical massive piers, round-headed arches, a great variety of mouldings such as zigzag, billet, double-cone, pellet, lozenge, beak-head, etc., small and narrow windows splayed only on the inside, buttresses slightly projecting from the wall. Some of the best examples of this style are the naves of Ely, Gloucester, Durham, and much Norman work is seen at Winchester, Exeter, Canterbury, Chester, Peterborough, Norwich, Rochester, Chichester, Oxford, Worcester, Wells and Hereford.

II. The Early English style began with the thirteenth century, in the reign of King John, the choir of Lincoln being the earliest example. Wearied with the Romanesque uncouth details of Norman art, the English masons were feeling after and finding a more excellent way, and discovered the beauties of Gothic architecture. This style flourished until the time of Edward I.; during his reign another period of transition set in, and this style gradually developed into the Decorated.

Its main characteristics are lighter and more elegant forms of construction and decoration, pointed arches, often shaped like a surgeon's lancet, whence they derive their name, deeply undercut mouldings, dog-tooth ornament, piers formed of columns with detached shafts united under one capital, and bound together by a band, bell-shaped capitals, stiff-leaved foliage, trefoiled arches, plate-tracery. Early English work is seen in the choir of Lincoln, Worcester, Chichester, Salisbury, Exeter, Wells, Rochester, York (south transept), Southwell, Ripon, Ely, Peterborough, Durham ("nine altars"), Glasgow.

III. The Decorated style commenced in the fourteenth century, or a few years earlier, reached its zenith before the middle of the century, and ended with the reign of the third Edward. The period of transition between this style and the last is perhaps the era of the greatest beauty of English art. The characteristics of the style are, more elaborateness of detail and ornament, much larger windows with beautiful and complex tracery, heavier buttresses, piers with closely-joined shafts, not detached as before, sculpture closely imitating natural foliage, mouldings less deeply cut, the ball-flower ornament. Decorated work is very plentiful, and may be seen in the chapter-houses of Wells, Norwich, Winchester, Canterbury, also at York, Lichfield, Exeter, Carlisle, Lincoln, Southwell, and elsewhere. A period of transition again followed during the last half of the fourteenth century, during which the style developed into the Perpendicular.

IV. The Perpendicular style prevailed during the fifteenth century and continued until the reign of Henry VIII., when the mediæval period ceased. This style is, as we have said, peculiar to England. In Scotland, where French influence was great, there are many examples of the Flamboyant style, which prevailed in France, and was scarcely known in England. This style is characterised by more elaborate and richer work, increased use of ornament and panelled decoration, peculiar window tracery (the mullions being carried straight up through the head of the window, while smaller mullions spring from the heads of the principal lights), much larger windows, depressed arches (Tudor arch), much heavier buttresses, mouldings carried up the piers and arches without any break or capital, cavetto (a wide and rather shallow variety), ogee, bowtell mouldings, the rose ornament, Tudor flower. The extensive use of panelling is always the hall-mark of the Perpendicular period. The choir of Gloucester is the earliest known example of this style, and King's College, Cambridge, St. George's Chapel, Windsor, and Henry VII.'s Chapel at Westminster, are the most perfect specimens of Perpendicular art.

Then followed the Renaissance period, when classical and Roman features were mingled with the latest English style. There was an attempt to revive the Gothic style in the time of James I., but the foreign influence was too strong, and not till the close of the eighteenth century did this revival take place. The love of Gothic art had never been quite extinguished in this country, and to the English people belongs the honour of restoring to its rightful place that style which has created so many superb and magnificent buildings instinctive of the faith and reverence which first called them into being.

In our cathedrals we have endless varieties of plan, construction, style and adornment, as well as in the associations connected with their histories. They derive their name from the Latin word *Cathedra* (Greek, Καθίδρα), signifying a seat, a cathedral church being that particular church of the diocese where the bishop's seat or throne is placed. If this church belonged to a monastery it was served by the monks, but many of our cathedrals were in the hands of secular canons, who were not monks, and should not be confused with the "regular" clergy. Monastic churches had always a complete series of monastic buildings—the cloister-court, the centre of a monk's life, around which were grouped the chapter-house, dormitory, refectory, infirmary, hospitium or guest-hall. Churches served by secular canons sometimes have a cloister, but this was added more as an ornament, and was not a necessity. The Reformation wrought many changes in our cathedrals. Out of the spoil of the monasteries Henry VIII. undertook to endow five new sees, and thus created the sees of Oxford, Peterborough, Chester, Gloucester and Bristol. These are called the cathedrals of the New Foundation, and with these are classed the monastic cathedrals which survived the shock of the Reformation, viz.: Canterbury, Winchester, Worcester, Rochester, Norwich, Ely, Durham, Carlisle. The cathedrals of the Old Foundation which survived, with some changes in their constitution, were York, London, Salisbury, Wells, Chichester, Hereford, Exeter, Lichfield and Lincoln, and the Welsh dioceses of St. David's, Llandaff, Bangor and St. Asaph. Episcopacy was finally banished from the Church of Scotland on the advent of William III.; hence the cathedrals in the northern country are so only in name. The Episcopal Church of Scotland has, of course, cathedrals, but most of these are modern. Since the Reformation in England, and especially in modern times, many new sees have been formed; these are Manchester, Liverpool, Ripon, St. Alban's, Southwell, Truro, Wakefield and Newcastle. The plan of our cathedrals is usually cruciform, formed by a nave with aisles, north and south transepts, central tower, choir and presbytery. Sometimes the plan is that of a double cross, there being a second or eastern transept towards the eastern end of the choir.

Our inspection of the exterior begins first by trying to obtain a good general view of the building. We notice the remains of the walls and gates which guarded the close, or precincts of the cathedral. Within these walls the bishop's power was supreme. If sanctuary was claimed by a fugitive from justice, here he was safe ; and the clergy and the serving-men were free from the ordinary law, and could be tried only by the ecclesiastics.

Then we notice the west front, usually a fine screen of stone-work, wherein are enshrined in niches weather-worn statues telling of the men of old who had done well in their days for their Church and realm.

Passing to the north we see the central tower, possibly Norman as high as the roof, with a superstructure of later times. The pitch of the roof may have been altered in later times from a high pitch to a flat one, and the marks of the old roof may often be seen on the tower walls. Just below the eaves is the range of clerestory windows. Flying buttresses connecting the buttresses of the outer wall with those of the inner are frequent and produce a very graceful effect. Niches for statues are often carved upon the buttresses. Curious grotesquely-carved heads, called gargoyles, look down upon us from the gutters of the roof. The tracery of the windows is no indication of the age of the walls, as they have frequently been inserted in place of others of an older period. The porch is a large structure, and sometimes has a chamber, called a parvise, over it. The object of this chamber cannot always be determined. Sometimes it was the abode of the sacristan, and occasionally it was set apart for the use of an anchorite or recluse. The monastic buildings are usually on the south side in Benedictine monasteries, but sometimes on account of the nature of the ground they are on the north.

On entering the church we view the nave, which is usually in three storeys—the main arcade, the triforium, which opens into a gallery or passage, and the clerestory. Sometimes the choir occupies two bays of the nave, but usually begins with the screen placed on the east side of the central tower. This screen was formerly the rood-screen, and a large crucifix stood on it; but at the Reformation all roods were destroyed, and sometimes the organ stands in its place.

Entering the choir we see before us the high altar with a fine reredos behind it, so called from the French *L'arrière-dos*, meaning " embroidered hangings." On the south of this is the piscina, consisting of a hollow basin with a stone-drain, wherein the priest cleansed the sacred vessels after using them in the Holy Eucharist. On the same side are the sedilia, or stone seats for the clergy, frequently with richly-carved canopies. Then there are the beautifully-carved stalls with fine tabernacle work, and the *sub-sellæ* or misereres (French, *miséricorde*) with their quaint carvings. It is a popular error, gravely perpetrated by some cathedral vergers and others, to suppose these misereres were a kind of ingenious trap for sleepy monks, who, when the heavy seat fell down with a loud bang, were detected in slumber and forced to do penance. They were so placed as a concession to human weakness in order that the monks or canons might lean against them during the long mediæval services, when sitting was not allowed. The eastern portion of the choir is called the presbytery.

We pass to the north aisle of the choir and proceed to the ambulatory, processional path, or retro-choir. Here, at the back of the altar, was the chief shrine, where the relics of some great saint were preserved under a gorgeous cover decorated with gold and silver and precious jewels, to which crowds of pilgrims flocked, and there prayed and gazed upon the wondrous shrine, and made their offerings. The steps and pavement leading to the shrine often still show by their worn condition the evidence of the tread of countless numbers of pilgrims. Near the shrine was a watching chamber, where a monk stayed to guard the shrine and its treasures.

Eastward of the ambulatory is usually the Lady Chapel, where the altar of the Virgin stood ; and here, and in other parts of the church, are numerous chantry chapels, sometimes built on to the church, or in the church itself, containing effigies of the founders and altar tombs, where masses were said by specially-endowed chantry priests for the repose of the souls of the deceased and their families. Some effigies of knights and warriors have their legs crossed. It is another popular error to suppose that this fashion of representing the deceased had anything to do with the Crusades. Beneath some portion of the church we find a crypt with the remains of numerous altars, where masses were said for the souls of those who lie buried here.

A door on the south side of the church leads to the cloister-court; immediately on the left as we traverse the east walk we see the slype or passage leading to the monks' cemetery. Another door from this walk leads to the chapter-house, where the monks assembled daily to arrange the affairs of the monastery, enforce its discipline, assign the duties of the day and transact other business. On the same side of the cloister was the dormitory; the refectory was on the south; the uses of the buildings on the west side varied in different houses.

As we see our cathedrals now, the view that meets us differs much from that which would have greeted us in mediæval times. Then all was ablaze with colours. Through the beautiful ancient glass the light gleamed on tints of gorgeous hues, on rich tapestries and hangings, on walls bedight with paintings, and every monument, pier and capital were aglow with coloured decorations. We have lost much, but still much remains. At the Reformation the avaricious courtiers of Henry VIII. plundered our sacred shrines, and carried off under the plea of banishing superstition vast stores of costly plate and jewels, tapestry and hangings. In the Civil War time riotous fanatical soldiery wrought havoc everywhere, hacking beautifully-carved tombs and canopies, destroying brasses, and mutilating all that they could find. Ages of neglect have also left their marks upon our churches; and above all, the hand of the ignorant and injudicious "restorer" has fallen heavily on these legacies of Gothic art, destroying much that was of singular beauty, and replacing it by the miserable productions of early nineteenth-century fabrication.

But in spite of all the evils that have been wrought, in spite of Puritan iconoclasm and Reformation violence, in spite of natural decay, eighteenth-century lethargy, and the intemperate zeal of unwise and tasteless modern restorers, our cathedrals still preserve much of their ancient beauty and attractiveness. They are standing witnesses to the greatness of the masons and builders who fashioned and perfected our English Gothic art, "an art that was created here in this land according to our native instincts, and in accord with the sober dress of our skies and the simple pleasantness of our scenery."[1] A man cannot fail to love that English art, whether he has been born amongst it like ourselves, or has come wonderingly on its simplicity from all the grandeur over seas.

[1] *History of Gothic Art in England*, by E. S. Prior.

ST. PAUL'S CATHEDRAL

THE great Cathedral of St. Paul has abundant claims to the love and veneration of every Englishman. Situated in the heart of the city of London, it has ever been associated with the religious, social and civic life of the people; and as the great national Cathedral of England all the principal events in our country's annals have been connected with St. Paul's. Without doubt it is the finest and grandest building in London, if not in the world. Comparing it with St. Peter's at Rome, we find that its dimensions are, of course, much smaller, though its grace and beauty are in no way inferior to the magnificent conception of Michael Angelo. It is the shrine of our national heroes, the *chef d'œuvre* of a great genius; its massive dome surmounted by a golden cross greets the traveller returning from beyond seas; its walls have echoed with the strains of high thanksgiving on the occasion of national victories and blessings, when kings and queens have come in solemn state to render thanks to Him who is the King of kings and Lord of lords. Just as Westminster was ever the church of the king and the government, so St. Paul's was the church of the citizens.

The prominent place which St. Paul's takes in the national and social life of England, in the great functions of Church and State, and in promoting the religious life of the people, is worthy of its best traditions, and at no time during its long history has it taken a higher place in the affections of the nation.

THE OLDER CATHEDRALS OF ST. PAUL'S

The present Cathedral, erected by the skill and genius of Sir Christopher Wren, is the third sacred edifice built upon this site. Indeed, Camden and certain early fanciful historians tell us of a Roman temple dedicated to Diana which they assert once stood here, erected during the time of the Diocletian persecution upon the site of an early Christian church. It is, however, certain that when Sir Christopher sank his foundations for the present building, he found beneath the interred bodies of mediæval times several Saxon stone coffins,

8

and at a still lower depth Celtic and Roman remains, showing that the site had been set apart as a cemetery from very early times.

The earliest church of which we have sure records was erected in Saxon times by good King Ethelbert of Kent in the year 610. St. Mellitus, the companion of St. Augustine, was the first English Bishop of London,[1] who came there in order to convert the East Saxons. Siebert, their king, joined with his uncle, Ethelbert, in building the Cathedral church, and the former probably founded the monastery of St. Peter called Westminster on Thorney Island, a place then "terrible from its desolate aspect—a mass of marsh and brushwood."

But the Londoners loved their Paganism, and took not kindly to the new faith. The men of the "emporium of many nations" clung to their worship of Wodin and Thor, and not even the wise words of Mellitus in the new Cathedral could win them. It was the original design of Pope Gregory, who sent Augustine to our shores, to make the Cathedral of London the Metropolitan Church of England—a design which Augustine could not carry out on account of the violent opposition of the Pagan-loving people. Hence Canterbury was elevated to the position of the Metropolitan Church. Thirty-eight years passed away. At length the fiery spirit of the Londoners was subdued after three great missionary efforts, and they gradually learned the story of the cross. The Cathedral was beautified by Bishop Cedd, brother of St. Cedd or Chad of Lichfield, and Sebbe, King of Essex, and was fortunate in having St. Erkenwald as the fourth Bishop of London, who wrought great wonders and attracted many converts, restoring wealth and honour to his Cathedral. To his memory a golden shrine was erected which was much frequented by pilgrims. Saxon kings gave of their wealth to the endowment of the Cathedral, and many rich lands were granted to it, as the ancient charters bear witness.

Fire has always been a great foe to St. Paul's. A very destructive conflagration raged in 961 A.D., and again in 1086 the Cathedral was wholly destroyed. We have no means of knowing what kind of architecture characterised this earliest fane, but probably it possessed round arches of stone, massive piers, and the usual characteristics of the Saxon style.

[1] There were some British Bishops of London. One of these, Restitutus, was present at the Council of Arles in A.D. 314, and Geoffrey mentions Theon, Bishop of London, amongst those who fled into Wales during the Saxon invasion.

The energy of the English people is evident to all who study our national annals. When any alarming catastrophe occurs, immediately they arise to repair the disaster. As it was in the seventeenth century when the Great Fire swept over London and laid the city low, so it was in the eleventh. The Saxon church had no sooner been reduced to a heap of ruins than the Norman builders began to rear another noble pile. Bishop Maurice was the designer of this great edifice, which existed until the time of the Great Fire, though it was greatly injured by a fire in 1136.

A very noble church it must have been, with its walls ablaze with colour, richly-canopied tombs, pictures and frescoes, books, and vestments glittering with gold, silver and precious stones. It was the largest Cathedral in England.

Old pictures tell us that it was cruciform, with a high tower and spire in the centre. The nave was long and noble, built in Norman style, having twelve bays. William of Malmesbury describes it as being " so stately and beautiful that is was worthily numbered amongst the most famous buildings." At the west end were two towers for bells, and sometimes used as prisons. The central tower had flying buttresses. Besides the high altar there were seventy or eighty chantries, with their own altars all ablaze with rich draperies. St. Paul's was also very rich in relics, among the number of which were two arms of St. Mellitus, a knife of our Lord, some hair of Mary Magdalene, blood of St. Paul, milk of the Virgin, the hand of St. John, the skull of Thomas à Becket, the head of King Ethelbert. But " the pride, glory and fountain of wealth " to St. Paul's was the body of St. Erkenwald, covered with a golden shrine, behind the high altar. Dean Milman states that in the year 1344 the offerings made by pilgrims alone amounted to £9000. The choir was rebuilt in 1221, and the Lady Chapel added in 1225. There was a very large east window, and a rose window over it. Buttresses crowned with pinnacles and adorned with niches supported the walls. The interior view, judging from Hollar's engraving, must have been very fine. The pillars and arches were Late Norman. The choir consisted of twelve bays and was finished about the end of the thirteenth century. We have few records to tell us about the details of the building of this old St. Paul's. In 1312 the nave was paved with marble, and two years later a spire of wood was raised to the height of 460 feet, then the highest in the world. This was damaged and ultimately destroyed by lightning.

ST. PAUL'S FROM CHEAPSIDE

THE PRECINCTS

We will now examine the precincts of the Cathedral. A wall surrounded the vast space which extended from Carter Lane on the south to Creed Lane and included Paternoster Row. This wall had six gates, the site of two of which is marked by St. Paul's Alley and Paul's Chain. The Bishop's Palace occupied the north-west corner of this space, and on the north were some cloisters decorated with mural paintings representing the Dance of Death, a favourite subject of mediæval painters, of which Holbein's conceptions are best known. This cloister was on the site of Pardon Churchyard, where a chapel was founded by Gilbert à Becket, the father of St. Thomas of noted memory. The chapter-house stood on the south side of the Cathedral, and was a very beautiful structure, so beautiful that Protector Somerset coveted the materials for his palace in the Strand, and took down and removed them.

At the north-east corner of the precincts stood the famous Paul's Cross, the scene of so many famous preachings and strange events, where folk-motes were held, Papal bulls promulgated, Royal proclamations made, excommunications and public penances declared, and sometimes riots and tumults excited. Paul's Cross played a very prominent part in the history of old London. Near the Pardon Churchyard once stood the Parish Church of St. Faith, called the Chapel of Jesus ; but this was destroyed, and the parishioners received in lieu of it a church in the crypt of the Cathedral. Fuller, remarking on this and on the existence of the Parish Church of St. Gregory on the Thames side of the Cathedral, quaintly observed, " St. Paul's may be called the Mother Church indeed, having one babe in her body and another in her arms."

St. Paul's was the centre of the life of London. Its great bell summoned the London citizens to their three annual folk-motes at Paul's Cross, where all the municipal business of the city was transacted, disputes settled, grievances stated and rights vindicated. Very turbulent and jealous of their liberties were these good citizens, and even the sovereign will of kings and queens must bow before the noisy clamours of the burghers of London. The bell of St. Paul's, like that of its famous brother " Roland " at Ghent, seemed endowed with a human voice when it summoned the multitudes to their meeting - place at the Cross, and declared in loud tones the will of the people.

Historical Events

The citizens might well love to have their church in their midst, for the ecclesiastical power was very strong, and often enabled them to defy the will of tyrannical kings or troublesome barons. In the time of the Conqueror, Bishop William of London obtained from the king a renewal of their privileges of which the monarch had deprived them. In gratitude for this benefit, the mayor, aldermen and livery companies of London used to visit the tomb of the good bishop in grand procession, in order to pray for his soul, and to commemorate his great services.

In the reign of Stephen civil war raged, and the country was divided into hostile camps, one siding with the king and the other with the Empress Maud. The citizens of London were not doubtful in their opinions. They rang the great bell of St. Paul's, summoned their folk-mote, and loudly declared that it was the privilege of the citizens of their great city to elect a sovereign for England, and with one voice supported Stephen.

Thomas à Becket, Archbishop of Canterbury, was a favourite of the citizens, though hated by his sovereign. Gilbert à Becket, his father, had a shop in Cheapside on the site of Mercers' Hall, whither the fair Saracen is said to have followed him from the Holy Land, where he had gone on a Crusade. He built a chapel in the churchyard of St. Paul, and his son, the famous archbishop, was well known to the citizens. Gilbert Foliot, Bishop of London, however, had taken the side of the king, Henry II., in the fatal quarrel, and aroused the anger of the prelate. A curious scene took place in consequence in old St. Paul's. A priest was celebrating mass, when a man approached, thrust a paper into his hand, and cried aloud, " Know all men that Gilbert, Bishop of London, is excommunicated by Thomas, Archbishop of Canterbury." The news spread fast among the citizens. Foliot at first attempted to defy the dread sentence ; but he knew something of the nature of the citizens of London, and wisely bowed before the decree, which the people were quite willing to enforce.

St. Paul's was the scene of a memorable council in the reign of Richard Cœur de Lion, who was crusading in Palestine. The bishops, together with the king's brother John, met in the nave and condemned Longchamp to resign the office of justiciary, and to surrender the castles which he held in the name of the king. During this reign a factious demagogue, William Fitz-Osbert, equally distinguished by the length of his beard and the vehemence of his eloquence, called the people together at Paul's Cross, and excited them to rebel against their oppressors. Bishop Hubert, however, calmed the multitude on the eve of a formidable rising. The people deserted their leader, who took refuge in St. Mary-le-Bow Church, which was set on fire, and Fitz-Osbert suffered death at the hands of the hangman. Thus from the tyranny of a Royal favourite, and from that of a mob orator, the people were saved by the influence of the Church in St. Paul's Cathedral.

A still greater service did St. Paul's render to England. Here was assembled a grand concourse of bishops, abbots, deans, priors and barons, to withstand the oppressive lawlessness of King John. Here Magna Charta was first devised. Here, at the instigation of Archbishop Langton, the barons and chief men swore to maintain the principles of the Charta, and to protect the liberties of Englishmen.

St. Paul's also set itself in opposition to the authority of the Pope; and when a Papal legate sought to enthrone himself in St. Paul's, he was openly resisted by Cantelupe, Bishop of Worcester. Boniface of Savoy, "the handsome Archbishop," brought with him fashions strange enough to English folk. His armed retainers pillaged the markets, and he felled to the ground, with his own fist, the prior of St. Bartholomew, Smithfield, who presumed to oppose his visitation. He came to St. Paul's to demand first-fruits from the Bishop of London, but deemed it advisable to wear armour beneath his robes. He found the gates of the Cathedral closed against him; but he fared better than two canons of the Papal party, who were killed by the citizens a few years later when they attempted to enter St. Paul's. London was aroused by these Italian priests, and the citizens at length besieged Lambeth Palace and drove the obnoxious archbishop beyond seas.

Again and again the tocsin sounded, as St. Paul's bell rang clear and loud, and the citizens seized their weapons and formed their battalions beneath the shadow of the great church. Now it was to help Simon de Montfort against the king; now to seize the person of the obnoxious Queen Eleanor, who was trying to escape by water from the Tower to Windsor, and who was rescued from their hands by the Bishop of London, and found refuge in his palace. Now the favourites of Edward II. excited their rage, especially the Bishop of Exeter, the king's regent, who dared to ask the Lord Mayor for the keys of the city, and paid for his temerity with his life.

An incident which shows the attachment of the people to their church and bishop occurred in the reign of the third Edward. Wycliffe was summoned by Bishop Courtenay to appear before a great council at St. Paul's. But the reformer did not come alone ; to the surprise of his accusers he arrived attended by a large following of friends, among whom were John of Gaunt and Lord Percy. These powerful supporters of Wycliffe attacked the bishop with angry words.

News was flashed among the citizens that John of Gaunt had threatened their bishop and vowed to drag him out of the church by the hair. They gathered together in angry crowds, and would have slain the duke and sacked his palace, the Savoy, in the Strand, if the bishop had not interfered on behalf of his enemy. Wycliffe and Lollardism did not then find much favour with the people of London.

There were reformers within the Church who were quite as eager to correct abuses as those outside the fold. Among these was Bishop Braybroke of London, who lived in the time of Edward IV. He contended for the sanctity of the sacred building, inveighed against the practice of using it as an exchange, of playing at ball within the precincts or within the church, and of shooting the pigeons which then as now found sanctuary at St. Paul's.

The chronicles of the Cathedral tell the story of the troublous times of the Wars of the Roses. We see Henry IV. pretending bitter sorrow for the death of the murdered Richard, and covering with cloths of gold the body, which had been exhibited to the people in St. Paul's. We see Henry V. returning in triumph from the French wars, riding in state to the Cathedral, attended by " the mayor and brethren of the city companies, wearing red gowns with hoods of red and white, well-mounted and gorgeously horsed, with rich collars and great chains, rejoicing at his victorious returne." Then came Henry VI., attended by the bishops, the dean and canons, to make his offering at the altar. Here the false Duke of York took his oath on the Blessed Sacrament to be loyal to the king. Here the rival houses swore to lay aside their differences, and to live at peace. But a few years later saw the new king, Edward IV., at St. Paul's, attended by great Warwick, the king-maker, with his bodyguard of 800 men-at-arms. Strange were the changes of fortune in those days. Soon St. Paul's saw the exhibition of the dead body of the king-maker, and not long afterwards that of the poor dethroned Henry, and Richard came in state here amid the shouts of the populace. After the defeat of the conspiracy of Lambert Simnel, Henry VII. celebrated a joyous thanksgiving in the Cathedral, and here, amid much rejoicing, the youthful marriage of Prince Arthur with Catherine of Arragon took place, when the conduits at Cheapside and on the west of the Cathedral ran with wine, and the bells rang joyfully, and all wished happiness to the Royal children whose wedded life was destined to be so brief.

THE REFORMATION AND AFTER

At the dawn of the Reformation period we will pause in order to try and realise what kind of scenes took place daily in the great Cathedral, and what vast numbers were employed on the staff. The members of the Cathedral body in the year 1450 included the following :—The Bishop, the Dean, the four Archdeacons, the Treasurer, the Precentor, the Chancellor, thirty greater Canons, twelve lesser Canons, about fifty Chaplains or Chantry-Priests and thirty Vicars. Of inferior rank to these were the Sacrist, the three Vergers, the Succentor, the Master of the Singing School, the Master of the Grammar School, the Almoner and his four Vergers, the Servitors, the Surveyor, the twelve Scribes, the Book Transcriber, the Bookbinder, the Chamberlain, the Rent-collector, the Baker, the Brewer, the Singing-men and Choir Boys, of whom priests were made, the Bedesmen and the poor folk. In addition to these must be added the servants of all these officers—the brewer, who brewed in the year 1286, 67,814 gallons, must have employed a good many ; the baker, who ovened every year 40,000 loaves, or every day a 100, large and small ; the sextons, grave-diggers, gardeners, bell-ringers, makers and menders of the ecclesiastical robes, cleaners and sweepers, carpenters, masons, painters, carvers and gilders. One can very well understand that the Church of St. Paul alone found a livelihood for thousands.

The inventory of church goods belonging to the Cathedral in 1245 exists, and is worth studying. It enumerates sixteen chalices, five of gold and the rest of silver-gilt. A chalice of Greek work had lost its paten, but retained its reed (*calamus*), a relic of the time when the deacon carried the chalice to the people, and each one drank of its hallowed contents through a long narrow pipe, which was usually fastened on a pivot to the bottom of the cup of the chalice. Amongst other curiosities of the inventory are three *poma*, or hollow balls of silver, so contrived as to hold hot water or charcoal embers for the warming of the hands of the celebrant during mass.

Of shrines and relics we have already spoken. There were three episcopal staves, and also a precentor staff of ivory with silver-gilt and jewelled enrichments, and a *baculus stultorum* for use at the profane travesty called the feast of fools. Among the mitres were two for the boy-bishop's use on St. Nicholas Day. There were thirty-seven magnificent copes, and forty-four others, and thirty-four specially fine chasubles.

The inventory of 1402 supplies some curious information as to the manner in which the numerous and costly vestments were arranged when not in use. In the treasury, on the west, stood a wardrobe, *armariolum*, in which were twenty-four *pertica*, pegs, or rods, or frames, from which the copes and chasubles could be suspended, one *pertica* holding from three to six copes. The vestments were arranged according to colour. Three other wardrobes were also stored with goodly vestments, and there were twenty-six in daily use. The total is 179 copes, fifty-one chasubles and ninety-two tunicles, and the colours were red, purple, black, white, green, yellow, blue, red mixed with blue.

We have remarked that St. Paul's was the centre of the social life of the people in olden days, which led to some abuses.

Francis Osborn says, " It was the fashion in those days, and did so continue until these, for the principal gentry, lords and courtiers, and men of all professions, to meet in St. Paul's by eleven of the clock, and walk in the middle aisle till twelve, and after dinner from three to six, during which time they discoursed of business, others of news."

Shakespeare represents Falstaff in *Henry V.* as having " bought Bardolph in Paul's " ; and Dekker thus speaks of the desecration of the sanctuary, " At one time in one and the same rank, yea, foot by foot, elbow by elbow, shall you see walking the knight, the gull, the gallant, the upstart, the gentleman, the clown, the captain, the apple-squire, the lawyer, the usurer, the citizen, the bankrout, the scholar, the beggar, the doctor, the idiot, the ruffian, the cheat, the Puritan, the cut-throat, highman, lowman and thief ; of all trades and professions some ; of all countries some. Thus while Devotion kneels at her prayers, doth Profanation walk under her nose in contempt of Religion."

Here lawyers received their clients ; here men sought service ; here usurers met their victims, and the tombs and font were mightily convenient for counters for the exchanges of money and the transaction of bargains, and the rattle of gold and silver was constantly heard amidst the loud talking of the crowd.

Gallants enter the Cathedral wearing spurs, having just left their steeds at "The Bell and Savage," and are immediately besieged by the choristers, who have the right of demanding spur-money from anyone entering the building wearing spurs.

Nor are the fair sex absent, and Paul's Walk was used as a convenient place for assignations. Old plays are full of references to this practice.

Later on the nave was nothing but a public thoroughfare, where men tramped carrying baskets of bread and fish, flesh and fruit, vessels of ale, sacks of coal, and even dead mules and horses and other beasts. Hucksters and pedlars sold their wares.

Duke Humphrey's tomb was the great meeting-place of all beggars and low rascals, and they euphemistically called their gathering "a dining with Duke Humphrey."

Much more could be written of this assembly of all sorts and conditions of men, but we have said enough to show that the Cathedral had suffered greatly from desecration and abuse. Indeed, an old writer in 1561 declared that the burning of the steeple in that year was a judgment for the scenes of profanation which were daily witnessed in old St. Paul's. He writes, "No place has been more abused than Paul's has been, nor more against the receiving of Christ's Gospel ; wherefore it is more marvel that God spared it so long, rather than He overthrew it now. From the top of the spire at coronations, or at other solemn triumphs, some for vain glory used to throw themselves down by a rope, and so killed themselves vainly to please other men's eyes," and much more to the same effect.

But the strictness of the worthy divine did not altogether cure the evils against which he railed. Eight years later the first great lottery was drawn before the west doors. There were 10,000 lots at ten shillings each, and day and night from January 11 to May 6 the drawing went on. The prizes were pieces of plate, and the profits were devoted to the repair of the havens of England.

So profitable was the lottery that another took place here in 1586, the prizes being some valuable armour.

At the dawn of the Reformation we see Henry VIII. in all the pomp and glory of mediæval pageantry riding in state to the Cathedral to be adorned with a cap of maintenance and a sword presented to him by the Pope. There was no sign yet of any breach of alliance between the Roman Pontiff and him whom he honoured with the title of "Defender of the Faith." Lollardism in spite of some burnings spread, and the western tower of the Cathedral earned the name of the Lollards' Tower, as several were imprisoned there.

Wolsey, the great cardinal, in the height of his prosperity often came to St. Paul's, and very gorgeous were the scenes which took place there, when thanksgiving for the peace between England, France and Spain was celebrated, when Princess Mary was betrothed to the Dauphin of France, and Charles V. proclaimed emperor. But signs of trouble were evident. Bishop Fisher thundered forth invectives against the works of Luther, which were publicly burnt in St. Paul's Churchyard. A few years later there was a burning in the Cathedral of heretical books in the presence of the cardinal, who caused some of Luther's followers to march round the blaze, throw in faggots, and thus to contemplate what a burning of heretics would be like, and be thankful that only their books and not their bodies were condemned to the flames.

During this troubled time and in Mary's reign, St. Paul's was often used as a place of trial for heretics, but Paul's Cross was a fruitful breeding place for the principles of the Reformation. Here Latimer, Ridley, Coverdale, Lever, and a host of others used to inveigh against the errors of Rome and deny the authority of the Pope. Here they exhibited the Boxley Rood, with all the tricks whereby it was made to open its eyes and lips, and seem to speak. The crowd looked on, and roared with laughter, seized the miraculous Rood, and broke it in pieces. And then a strange thing happened in the Cathedral. One night all the images, crucifixes and emblems of Popery were pulled down. Terrible havoc was wrought, chalices and chasubles, altars and rich hangings, books and costly vestments, were all seized and sold, and helped to increase that vast heap of spoil which the greedy ministers of Edward VI. gathered from the wasting of the Church's goods. Tombs were pulled down, chantries and chapels devastated, cloisters and chapter-houses removed bodily to Somerset House by Protector Somerset for the building of his new palace, and all was wreckage, spoliation and robbery.

Then came the fitful restoration of the "old religion," and many riots ensued, many ears were nailed to the pillory nigh Paul's Cross; many Protestants condemned in the Cathedral to the fires at Smithfield, and many horrors enacted which Englishmen like not to remember.

With the coming of Elizabeth more peaceful times ensued, but the Cathedral was in a sorry condition. Desecration reigned within. Then in 1561 the spire caught fire, blazed and fell, destroying parts of the roof. The clergy and citizens soon set to work to repair the damage, but the glory of "old St. Paul's" had departed, and its ruinous condition was the distress of rulers and the despair of the citizens and clergy.

Elizabeth often visited the Cathedral, and troubled Dean Nowell by her plainly-spoken criticisms. Felton was hung at the bishop's gates for nailing a Papal bull to the palace doors, which declared the queen to be a heretic and released her subjects from their allegiance. This attempt of the Pope to dethrone the Virgin Queen was not very successful. Some other conspirators suffered for their crimes in the following reign in the precincts, four of the gunpowder conspirators being hung, drawn and quartered before the west doors. Here also Garnet, the Jesuit, shared a like fate.

King James attempted to restore the Cathedral, but his efforts came to nothing. Charles I. did something, and from the designs of Inigo Jones built a portico at the west end, and made some other improvements, but the troubles of the Civil War intervened, and the money which had been collected by Archbishop Laud and the generosity of the citizens of London was seized by the Parliament and converted to other and baser uses.

THE CIVIL WARS

Desolation reigned supreme in the once glorious church when Puritan rage had vented itself on its once hallowed shrines and sacred things. Cromwell's troopers "did after their kind." Whatever beautiful relics of ancient worship reforming zeal had left were doomed to speedy destruction. In the western portico built in the last reign shops were set up for sempstresses and hucksters; Dr. Burgess, a Puritan divine, thundered forth in his conventicle set up in the east of the building ; and the rest of the Cathedral was turned into a cavalry barracks.

The conduct of the rough soldiers created great scandal. They played games, brawled and drank in the church, prevented people from going through the nave, and caused such grievous complaints, that an order was passed forbidding them to play at ninepins from six o'clock in the morning to nine in the evening.

The *Mercurius Eleneticus* of 1648 waxes scornful over the misdeeds of these rough riders, and scoffs sarcastically : " The saints in Paul's were last week teaching their horses to ride up the great steps that lead to the Quire, where (as they derided) they might perhaps learn to chant an anthem ; but one of them fell and broke his leg, and the neck of his rider, which hath spoilt his chanting, for he was buried on Saturday night last, a just judgment of God on such a profane and sacrilegious wretch."

The famous Cross in the churchyard, which according to Dugdale, " had been for many ages the most noted and solemn place in this nation for the greatest divines and greatest scholars to preach at, was, with the rest of the crosses about London and Westminster, by further order of the Parliament, pulled down to the ground."

After the Great Fire

With the restoration of the monarchy came the restoration of the Cathedral. Dr. Wren, the great architect, was consulted, plans were discussed, Wren prepared himself for the great work, and all was in readiness, when the Great Fire broke out, and completed the ruin which had already begun. It, however, paved the way for the erection of the grand church which will ever be associated with the genius of its great architect.

Both the diarists, Pepys and Evelyn, speak of the melancholy spectacle of the great ruin. Pepys laments over the " miserable sight of Paul's church, with all the roof falling, and the body of the nave fallen into St. Faith."

And Dryden sings :—

> " The daring flames press'd in and saw from far
>   The awful beauties of the sacred quire :
> But since it was profaned by civil war
>   Heaven thought it fit to have it purged by fire."

Evelyn, in his diary, describes his visit to the church before the

THE WEST FRONT

fire with Dr. Wren, the bishop, dean and several expert workmen. "We went about to survey the general decay of that ancient and venerable church, and to set down in writing the particulars of what was fit to be done. Finding the main building to recede outwards, it was the opinion of Mr. Chickley and Mr. Prat that it had been so built *ab origine* for an effect in perspective, in regard of the height; but I was, with Dr. Wren, quite of another judgment, and so we entered it: we plumbed the uprights in several places. When we came to the steeple, it was deliberated whether it were not well enough to repair it only on its old foundation, with reservation to the four pillars; . . . we persisted that it required a new foundation not only in regard of the necessity, but that the shape of what stood was very mean, and we had a mind to build it with a noble cupola, a form of church-building not as yet known in England, but of wonderful grace. . . ."

Then came the Great Fire, so graphically described by Evelyn. He writes: " The stones of Paul's flew like granados, the melting lead running down the streets in a stream, and the very pavements glowing with fiery redness, so as no horse or man was able to tread on them, and the demolition had stopped all the passages, so that no help could be applied."

This Great Fire roused again the energy and indomitable spirit of Englishmen. They beheld without alarm the ashes of their houses, and the destruction of their great city. They felt that the eyes of Europe were upon them. A new city was to be built worthy of their nation, worthy of the great centre of the commerce of the world. But to restore St. Paul's was a stupendous work. Some were for rebuilding on the old walls. Pepys describes the ruins: " I stopped at St. Paul's, and then did go into St. Faith's Chapel, and also into the body of the west part of the church; and do see a hideous sight of the walls of the church ready to fall, that I was in fear as long as I was in it; and here I saw the great vaults underneath the body of the church." And again: " Up betimes, and walked to the Temple, and stopped, viewing the Exchange, and Paul's, and St. Faith's, where strange how the very sight of the stones falling from the top of the steeple do make me sea-sick."

They began to repair the west end for service against the advice of Wren, and Dean Sancroft was obliged to confess to the architect,—

" What you whispered in my ear at your last coming here is

come to pass. Our work at the west end of St. Paul's is fallen about our ears."

At last the order was given to take down the walls, clear the ground, and proceed according to the plans of Wren. He was thwarted and distressed by the interference of many. His original design was to build it in the form of a Greek cross, but to this the clergy objected, and a Latin cross was decided upon.

In 1674 the workmen began to clear away the old ruins, no light task, but in the end it was accomplished, the first stone of the new Cathedral being laid on June 21, 1675. In October 1694 the choir was finished, and on December 2, 1697, Divine service was performed for the first time in the new edifice. It was a special thanksgiving for the Peace of Ryswick, a peace which settled our Dutch William more securely on the throne of England. His Majesty wished to attend the service, but it was feared that amongst the vast crowds there might be too many Jacobites, and he was persuaded to remain at his palace. Bishop Compton preached a great sermon on the occasion from the text, " I was glad when they said unto me, we will go into the House of the Lord."

Thirteen years elapsed before the highest stone of the lantern on the cupola was laid by Wren's son, and the magnificent building was completed by the skill, genius and determination of one man, whose memory deserves to be ever honoured by all Englishmen.

The men of his own day did not treat him worthily. During the building of the Cathedral he was beset by all the annoyances jealousy and spite could suggest, and at the end of his long and useful career, by the intrigues of certain German adventurers, he was deprived of his post of Surveyor-General after the death of Queen Anne. He retired to the country, and spent the few remaining years of his life in peaceful seclusion, occasionally giving himself the treat of a journey to London, in order that he might feast his eyes on that· great and beautiful church which his skill had raised.

His was the first grave sunk in the Cathedral, and it bears the well-known inscription, than which none could be more fitting :—

LECTOR, SI MONUMENTUM REQUIRIS CIRCUMSPICE.

THE EXISTING CATHEDRAL—EXTERIOR

The new St. Paul's is without doubt the grandest building in London. Perhaps the finest view is obtained from the approach by

Ludgate Hill, and the grandeur of its majestic dome is most impressive. The style is English Renaissance. We will begin our survey with the *West Front*, which was erected last, and therefore bears the stamp of Wren's matured genius. There are two storeys. In the lower there is a row of Corinthian columns arranged in pairs, and in the second storey a similar series. On the triangular pediment above is a carving of the Conversion of St. Paul, while a statue of the saint crowns the apex, the other statues representing SS. Peter and James and the four Evangelists. Two towers stand, one on each side of the front, and complete a superb effect. These contain a grand peal of twelve bells, one of which, called Great Paul, fashioned twenty years ago, is one of the largest in the world. Rich marbles, brought from Italy and Greece, adorn the pavement.

Proceeding to the *north side* we note the two-storied construction, the graceful Corinthian pilasters,[1] arranged in pairs, with round-headed windows between them ; the entablature ; and then, in the second storey, another row of beautiful pilasters of the Composite order. Between these are niches where one would have expected windows ; but this storey is simply a screen to hide the flying buttresses supporting the clerestory, as Wren thought them a disfigurement. The walls are finished with a cornice, which Wren was compelled by hostile critics to add, much against his own judgment. There are some excellently-carved festoons of foliage and birds and cherubs, which are well worthy of close observation. The *North* and *South Fronts* have Corinthian pillars, which support a semi-circular entablature. Figures of the Apostles adorn the triangular-shaped head and balustrade. The Royal arms appear on the north side, and a Phœnix is the suitable ornament on the south, signifying the resurrection of the building from its ashes.

The south side is almost exactly similar to the north. The east end has an apse.

The magnificent *Dome* is composed of an outward and inward shell, and between these there rises a cone-shaped structure which supports the lantern, crowned with its golden ball and cross. The arrangement of this is most complex, and is a witness to the marvellous skill of the architect. Above the row of Composite columns is a gallery, which affords a good view to those who are anxious to climb. Above the actual dome is the Golden Gallery,

---

[1] A pilaster is a column attached to a wall.

and then the lantern, roofed with a dome bearing the ball and cross.   The whole height is 365 feet.

INTERIOR OF THE BUILDING

The view on entering the Cathedral at the west is most impressive.   The magnitude of the design, the sense of strength and stability, as well as the beauty of the majestic proportions, are very striking.   Over the doors we see carvings of St. Paul at Berea.   A gallery is over the central doorway, and here is a good modern window.

The nave has a large western bay with chapels, three other bays, and a large space beneath the west wall of the dome.   It has three storeys, the lofty arches, a storey which in a Gothic church would be termed the triforium, and a clerestory.   Grand Corinthian pilasters are attached to the massive piers, with wonderfully-wrought capitals, which support the entablature.   The arches spring from smaller pilasters joined to the larger ones.   Great arches springing from the triforium piers span the nave, and between these arches are dome-shaped roofs.   High up there are festoons of carving.   The aisles have three large windows, and Composite pilasters adorn the walls and support the vault.   The north chapel at the west end is the Morning Chapel, and is adorned with mosaics and modern glass, in memory of Dean Mansell (1871).   The south chapel is called the Consistory, and once held Wellington's monu-

ment, to which the marble sculptures refer. Here is an unusual *Font* of Carrara marble.

The *Dome* is supported by immense and massive masonry. Above the arches a cornice runs round, supporting the *Whispering Gallery*. Then the dome begins to curve inward. Above is a row of windows, set in groups of three, separated by niches recently filled with statues of the Fathers, and then the dome is completed and painted by Sir James Thornhill with scenes from the life of St. Paul. These are too faint and too far distant to be easily observed. The painter nearly lost his life through stepping backward in order to see the effect of his brush, and nearly fell from the scaffold. His companion just saved his life by flinging a brush at the painting, and Thornhill rushed forward to rescue his work, and thus his life was saved.

The *Pulpit* is made of rich marble, and the lectern was made in 1720. The modern *mosaics* are of unique interest, and add much to the beauty of the Cathedral. To Sir William Richmond the credit of this work is mainly due, and for some of earlier portions to Mr. G. F. Watts, R.A.

The *Transepts* have good windows, representing (north) the twelve founders of English Christianity, and south, the first twelve Christian Saxon kings, and also a window in memory of the recovery from illness of His Majesty Edward VII. when Prince of Wales.

The *Choir* has some wonderfully-carved stalls by the famous Grinling Gibbons, and these bear the names of the prebendaries attached to the Cathedral, with the parts of the Psalter which each one had to say each day, an arrangement similar to that at Lincoln.

Woodwork
South Choir Aisle

The *Reredos* is a noble example of modern work, and is worthy of close examination. Behind it is the Jesus Chapel, containing a monument of Canon Liddon. The mosaic decorations of the choir are the work of Sir William Richmond, and are worthy of the highest praise.

Monuments

One feature of St. Paul's especially endears it to us, and that is that there lie all that is mortal of many of our national heroes. Westminster is richer in its many monuments of great poets and writers; but the makers of the Empire and most of our distinguished painters are entombed in the "citizens' church." We can only point out the tombs of the most illustrious.

Nave (North Aisle)—
Wellington (d. 1852), the hero of Waterloo.
Gordon (d. 1890), slain at Khartoum.
Stewart, General (d. 1880), who tried to rescue Gordon.
Melbourne, Viscount (1848), Queen Victoria's first Prime Minister.

North Transept—
Sir Joshua Reynolds (1792), by Flaxman.
Rodney, Admiral (1790), the hero of Martinique.
Picton (1815), slain at Waterloo.
Napier, General (1860), author of *Peninsular War*.
Ponsonby, General (1815), killed at Waterloo.
Hallam, the historian (1859).
Johnson, Samuel (1784).

South Transept—
Nelson, Admiral.
Sir John Moore (1806), killed at Corunna.
Turner, Joseph, R.A. (1851), painter.
Collingwood, Admiral (1810), Colleague of Nelson.
Howe, Admiral (1799), Colleague of Nelson.
Howard, John (1790), the prison reformer, the first monument erected.
Lawrence, General (1857), killed in Indian Mutiny.
Cornwallis, General (1805), fought in American War and in India.

South Choir Aisle—
Dean Milman (1868).
Dean Donne (1631), monument removed here from old St. Paul's.
Bloomfield, Bishop (1856).
Jackson, Bishop (1885).
Heber, Bishop (1826), of Calcutta.
Liddon, Canon (1890).

The *Crypt* contains the Parish Church of St. Faith, Wellington's funeral car fashioned from captured cannon, and his tomb, Nelson's tomb (the coffin is made from the wood of one of his ships—the tomb is sixteenth-century work and was made for Cardinal Wolsey), the grave of Wren with its famous inscription, and many illustrious painters sleep in the *Painters' Corner*, amongst whom our modern artists Leighton and Millais rest with Reynolds, Lawrence, Landseer and Turner.

DIMENSIONS

Total length	460 ft.
Length of nave . . .	200 ft.
Width of nave . . .	100 ft.
Height of nave . . .	89 ft.
Length of choir . .	160 ft.
Height of cross on dome . .	363 ft.
Height of west towers . .	222 ft.
Area	59,700 sq. ft.

Style—English Renaissance.

BUILDING DATES

Begun June 21, 1675.
Cathedral finished 1710.

A West Front
B Central West Doorway
C C Nave
E E North and South Aisles
    of Nave
F¹ Bell Tower
F² Dean's Stair
G Morning Chapel
H Consistory Court
    containing Font
J K North and South
    Transept

L Dome
M Choir
N O North and South Choir Aisles
P Jesus Chapel
Q Minor Canons' Vestry
R Dean's Vestry
S Staircase leading to Library,
    Whispering Gallery, etc.
T Staircase leading down to Crypt
V Victoria Jubilee Inscription, 1897
W Lectern
X Pulpit

MONUMENTS

1 Wellington
2 Gordon
3 Viscount Melbourne
4 Sir Joshua Reynolds
5 Admiral Rodney
6 Sir Thomas Picton
7 General Napier
8 General Ponsonby
9 Henry Hallam
10 Samuel Johnson
11 Nelson
12 Sir John Moore

MONUMENTS

13 J. M. W. Turner
14 Admiral Collingwood
15 Admiral Howe
16 John Howard
17 General Lawrence
18 General Cornwallis
19 Dean Milman
20 Dean Donne
21 Bishop Blomfield
22 Bishop Jackson
23 Bishop Heber
24 Canon Liddon

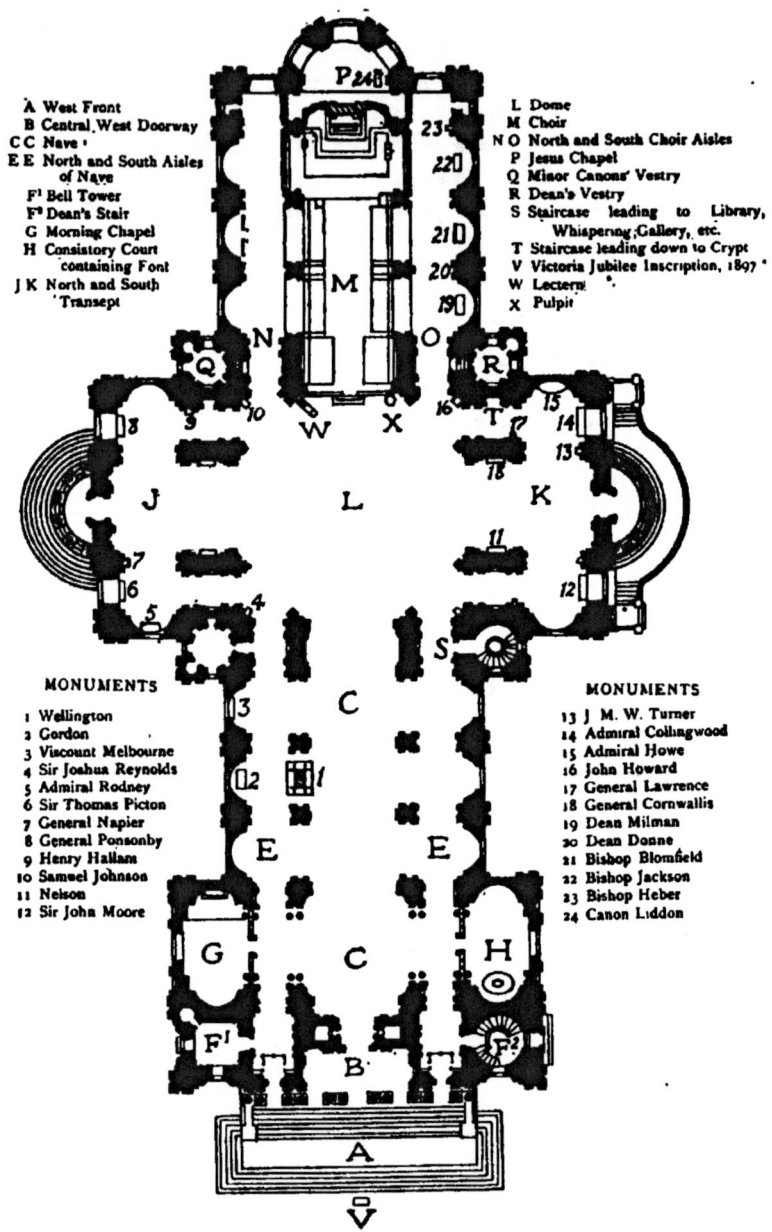

PLAN OF ST. PAUL'S CATHEDRAL

WESTMINSTER ABBEY

THE famous Abbey Church of Westminster, though not a cathedral, must be included in our chronicle of the chief ecclesiastical buildings in this country. It is the coronation church of the sovereigns of England, the final resting-place of many, the national tomb-house of our heroes and great men, as well as a triumph of Gothic architecture of singular beauty and attractiveness. For one brief space at the time of the Reformation there was a Bishop of Westminster, but the see did not long continue, and it is for other reasons that Westminster must find a place in this volume. In early Saxon times a chapel dedicated to St. Peter was built by Siebert in the seventh century on an island rising from the marshy ground bordering the Thames. It was called Thorney, and the eastern portion of the water in St. James's Park is a part of the arm of the Thames which encircled the sanctuary of the monks and the palace of the Anglo-Saxon kings. Here was established by Dunstan a colony of Benedictine monks. In the charters of Edgar (951) the original boundary of Westminster is clearly defined, though this charter is esteemed doubtful by Kemble, and the importance of Westminster gradually increased. Edward the Confessor took a particular interest in the place, and began his building of the Abbey in 1050. On Childermas Day (the Feast of the Holy Innocents) 1065 the choir was finished and consecrated, and on " Twelfth Mass Eve " the king died and was buried here. The Bayeux tapestry depicts the scene of this Royal funeral, and gives a representation of the church. The earlier church still remained as the nave of the new choir. A few fragments of Edward's work remain beneath the pavement of the present choir. The work progressed while William Rufus was building his Royal palace, and at the time of his death the transepts and first bay of the nave were completed, the first conspicuous example of a great Benedictine church in England. Henry I. and Matilda were crowned here with much pomp, and all the monarchs since the time of the Conqueror. Early in the days of Henry III. a new lady chapel was built, and this inspired the artistic soul of the young king, who determined to build an abbey worthy of the honour of God in the best and newest style of architecture. He was a Frenchman in feeling, and had passed many days at the Court of St. Louis. So his new monastic church must be fashioned in the French style; his monks must speak French, and he chose a French model for his architecture, for the plan of his church with its French *chevet*, and for the radiating chapels of the choir. But in spite of this French design our Westminster remains "a great French thought expressed in excellent English"; it is like "one of Chaucer's lays, a sweetly English poem inspired by a French romance," and is the most finished product of the Early English of the first half of the thirteenth century. Its French peculiarities may be seen in the narrowness and height of the bays of the choir, its plan with regard to the radiating chapels, and in the tracery of the windows. The work began in 1245 with the east end, and all the building as far as the fourth bay of the nave was finished in 1269. The noble re-founder was buried in his glorious minster. Edward I. brought here the coronation stone of the Scottish kings, and had it placed in the new throne which he fashioned to enclose it. In the fourteenth century much building was done to perfect the monastery. In the time of Richard II. the reconstruction of the old nave was in progress, and Henry V. took much interest in it. His father died in the Jerusalem Chamber. The building of the nave continued, and the well-known Whittington, "thrice Lord Mayor of London," in 1413 helped forward the work by liberal contributions. The Tudor badges in the vaulting of the last bays show the later character of that portion of the building. Henry VII. built the beautiful and famous chapel at the east end in place of the Lady Chapel built in 1220, which is such a perfect example of the best Perpendicular work. It was finished about 1520.

At the dissolution of monasteries Westminster shared the fates of the rest, and the last abbot, Benson, became the first dean, and for a brief space there was a bishop. Protector Somerset turned his greedy eyes upon the noble minster, and was with difficulty induced to refrain from plundering it overmuch. Indeed, he had thoughts of pulling it down, but was propitiated by bribes of some manors and many loads of Caen stone for the building of his new palace, Somerset House. The services were of course changed, and many goodly treasures sold; during the brief reign of Mary the Roman Catholic ritual was restored, and the Confessor's shrine

DEAN'S YARD, WESTMINSTER, IN 1730

re-erected; but Elizabeth turned out Abbot Ferkenham, and constituted Westminster a collegiate church with a dean and twelve prebendaries. The remains of poor Mary Queen of Scots were brought here by James I. and laid side by side with Queen Elizabeth. Here in the gatehouse Sir Walter Raleigh was imprisoned. Soon the tumults of the Civil War arose, but Westminster happily escaped the fury of the Puritans. The noted Westminster Assembly was called together in Henry VII.'s Chapel in 1643, for the purpose of " settling the government and liturgy of the Church of England and clearing of the doctrine from false aspersions and interpretations." This Assembly took upon itself to denounce the Book of Common Prayer and to substitute the Directory for Public Worship. Many restorations of the fabric have taken place since the Restoration of the monarchy. Sir Christopher Wren was a wonderful architect, but he was scarcely the man to tamper with an ancient and beautiful Gothic building. He set to work to rebuild the western towers, which were finished after his death in 1739. New stone-work has been erected in place of the old in most of the exterior of the Abbey, and Sir Gilbert Scott and Mr. Pearson were responsible for the restoration of the north front of the north transept. The complete story of the Abbey of Westminster would tell of all the pageants and coronation festivals which have taken place therein, to which another has just been added when King Edward VII. and his queen were crowned; it would tell of the last solemn rites of monarchs and great men, poets, sages and generals who sleep within the hallowed precincts. But the story must be left to others, and we will now examine the details of this ancient pile which is so closely connected with all the chief events in English history.

THE EXTERIOR

The *West Front* is flanked by two towers 225 feet high, built by Wren, and finished by his pupil, Hawksmoor, about 1740. In the centre of the front is the great Perpendicular window, beneath which is a row of niches. The entrance porch has a groined roof. The nave is remarkable for its length and height. On the north side we notice that there is a wealth of buttresses. Strong buttresses support the aisle walls, and from these flying buttresses stretch across to the walls built on the central arcade. The four eastern buttresses comprise the part of the church finished by

Henry III.; the rest of the nave, with the exception of Wren's towers, was built during the last half of the fourteenth century and the beginning of the fifteenth. The figures in the niches are modern.

The *North Front* is new, designed by Sir G. Scott and Mr.

THE NORTH FRONT

Pearson. It·is very elaborate work, and much of it is beautiful, but it does not seem to harmonise with the rest of the building. There is a large rose window; on each side tall buttresses crowned with turrets and covered with niches.   There is an arcade of open-work below, and then some deeply-recessed Early English windows, and below three doorways under one string-course, the centre one having a high gable. This door is divided by a pier having a finely-carved figure of the Virgin and Child. The tympanum is divided into three panels. In the highest is Our Lord in glory surrounded by angels, and below Him are the Twelve Apostles, while in the lowest tier are figures representing Art, History, Philosophy, War, Legislation and Science, with the builders of the Abbey, Edward the Confessor, Henry III. and Richard II. The niches are filled with figures of persons in some way connected with the Abbey. The *Choir* is in the form of an apse, with radiating chapels, planned on the model of the French *chevet*, according to the taste of Henry III., which he had cultivated during his sojourn in France. The *Lady Chapel* at the east end, commonly called Henry VII.'s Chapel, is one of the noblest examples of the best Perpendicular work in the kingdom, and ranks with St. George's Chapel, Windsor, and King's College, Cambridge. The monastic buildings are on the south side of the Abbey, and will be approached from the interior.

THE INTERIOR

The view of the interior is very impressive. Standing at the west end of the nave we cannot fail to admire the magnificent beauty of this noble shrine. This *Nave* of twelve bays, with its clustered columns, its beautiful triforium, and its lofty and firmly-proportioned roof, soaring to the height of 101 feet, is very striking. A close inspection will show the difference between the piers of the portion finished by Henry III. and the newer work of the fourteenth century. The tracery of the triforium openings is very fine. The *Choir-Screen*, which crosses the nave at the eighth pier, is modern, and also the pulpit. The west window is Perpendicular, and has some Georgian glass containing figures of the Patriarchs. Much architectural beauty has been sacrificed for the sake of ponderous monuments, but many of these have much interest, and for many visitors will prove the most attractive features of the Abbey. A list of the most important monuments will be found at the close of our account of the Abbey.

The north-west tower contains the monuments of distinguished members of the Whig party, and has in the window some ancient glass. The south-west tower was formerly the Baptistery. The architecture of the aisles has suffered much from the erection of stupendous monuments. The gallery at the west of the south aisle was erected at the same time as Henry VII.'s Chapel by Abbot Islip, and is known as the *Abbot's Pew*. The door at the east end is Late Early English. The *South Transept* is known as the *Poets' Corner*, on account of the memorials of the votaries of the muses which stand here. The architecture is of very beautiful design in the style of Early English, when it was merging into Early Decorated. In the south wall is the entrance to the Chapel of St. Faith, the door of which was once covered with the skins of Danes. Two tiers of trefoiled arches are above this, and higher still the triforium, the spandrels of the arches being enriched with sculpture. There is no west aisle. Chaucer's tomb will attract most visitors. In the chapel are some ancient paintings of the Crucifixion, St. Faith, and a kneeling monk.

The *Choir*, which has been the scene of so many solemn and memorable services, has no ancient woodwork. The stalls were erected about the middle of the last century. The altar and reredos are modern. There are some large figures, and a mosaic of the Last Supper. Here the coronations of our monarchs take place. The pavement is interesting, as it was brought from Rome by Abbot Ware in 1268, and beneath it he rests with other abbots of Westminster. The sedilia are thirteenth-century work, and were decorated with paintings. The figures of King Siebert, the first founder, and of Henry III., the munificent re-founder, remain. Above the base of the tomb of Anne of Cleves, one of Henry VIII.'s many wives, is a remarkable painting of Richard II., and behind it some ancient tapestry. A record of the interesting tombs here will be found later. *Edward the Confessor's Chapel* is a mausoleum of Royal personages, wherein our monarchs have been laid to rest, a portion of the building which always possesses a solemn and pathetic interest. Here is the shrine of the "miracle worker," the pious but weak last Saxon king, St. Edward. It was fashioned in 1269 by order of Henry III., the artificer being one Peter, a Roman citizen. The style of the oldest part, the base of the shrine, is of a Byzantine character. The upper part was probably made by Abbot Feckenham in Mary's reign, in imitation of that which was destroyed in Reformation times. It is difficult to imagine what must have been the splendour of this wondrous shrine when it was adorned with gold and gems, ere the greedy commissioners of Henry VIII. despoiled it of its treasures. Henry III., Eleanor of Castile, in whose honour her loving husband, Edward I., raised the Eleanor crosses wherever her body rested

Holy Corner

on its last journey to the Abbey, Edward I., and other monarchs rest here. *Henry V.'s Chantry* is a splendid piece of ornate Perpendicular work, with elaborate sculptured figures representing St. George, St. Denys, and the story of the hero's life, his fights, his coronation, his court. The effigy has been much mutilated. Above the tomb is the monarch's achievement, his shield, saddle and helmet, which were borne in his funeral procession. The coronation chairs have especial interest at this time, especially the famous throne of Edward I., which has under the seat the coronation stone of Scone, brought by him from Scotland. Legends tell us that this stone was the veritable stone used by Jacob as a pillow when he dreamt that wondrous dream at Bethel. There is also the throne of William and Mary, and Edward III.'s sword and shield.

In the *South Ambulatory* are three chapels, dedicated to SS. Benedict, Edmund and Nicholas, all of which have interesting monuments which will be noticed later. We now enter *Henry VII.'s Chapel*, the most perfect example of the Perpendicular style at its best in the country. At the entrance are beautiful bronze doors covered with designs symbolical of the titles of the Royal founder. It is impossible to describe in words the richness and beauty of the interior of this noble chapel. Washington Irving wrote : "The very walls are wrought into universal ornament, encrusted with tracery and scooped into niches, crowded with statues of saints and martyrs. Stone seems, by the cunning labour of the chisel, to have been robbed of its weight and density, suspended aloft as if by magic, and the fretted roof achieved with the wonderful minuteness and airy security of a cobweb." The vault is very beautiful with fan-tracery. The banners of the Knights of the Order of the Bath hang over their stalls. The misereres are wonderfully carved, and are worthy of close examination. The black marble tomb of the founder is considered to be the best example of the Renaissance style in England. It was fashioned by Torregiano. Very numerous monuments are found here, which will be described later. The tombs of Mary Queen of Scots and of Queen Elizabeth have especial interest. Oliver Cromwell's body once lay in the most eastern chapel, but the Royalists at the Restoration wrought vengeance on his corpse, and on that of other regicides, and did not suffer them to remain in these hallowed precincts.

Returning we traverse the *North Ambulatory*, from which open the Chapels of SS. Paul, John Baptist, Erasmus and Abbot Islip.

St. Erasmus was a Bishop of Campania, martyred in the time of the Diocletian persecution. His chapel has a fine, Late Decorated doorway. Abbot Islip died in 1532, and had previously adorned this chapel for his tomb, of which only the base remains. A curious eye will discern his rebus. In the upper chapel are preserved some remarkable wax effigies of deceased monarchs and others, which were used in ancient times in funeral processions. Charles II., Elizabeth, William and Mary, Anne, Duchess of Richmond, General Monk, and a few others have survived the wreck of time.

The *North Transept* resembles the south and is remarkable for its noble architecture. It is part of Henry III.'s construction. The carving is rich and beautiful, especially the famous sculptures of the *censing angels*, which are best seen from the triforium. On the east are the three Chapels of SS. John the Evangelist, Michael and Andrew, which are now filled with monuments.

We will now visit the *monastic buildings*, which may be entered from the south aisle of the nave. The east walk of the cloisters was finished in 1345, and the south and west walks a few years later under the rule of Abbot Litlington. The north walk is a century earlier. From the east walk we enter the *Chapter-House*. The doorway is remarkably fine, with its sculptured figures in the mouldings. This is one of the finest and largest chapter-houses in England, and was built by Henry III. in 1250. Its plan is octagonal. There is a central, slender, clustered shaft from which the vaulting springs. This vault is a restoration. The windows have beautiful tracery, and are filled with modern glass. The old paintings representing the Second Advent are very interesting. This room has been devoted to many uses. Here the House of Lords used to meet, and here the Records were once kept. The Chapel of the Pyx, a fine Early Norman structure, where "the trial of the Pyx" took place, is not open to the public. Above this and the vestibule was the dormitory, now the library and schoolroom of the famous Westminster School founded by Henry VIII. The cloisters have many monuments. On the south-east lies the little cloister formerly the infirmary, approached by a passage from the east cloister. The refectory was on the south side of the cloister-court, and on the west was the abbot's house, now the Deanery. Permission should be obtained to see the famous *Jerusalem Chamber*, probably so called from the tapestry which once hung here. Here Henry IV. died, which fact Shakespeare mentions in his play, *Henry IV.*, and many other historical scenes have these walls witnessed.

HENRY V.'S CHANTRY

Kings Buried in Westminster Abbey

Siebert, King of the East Saxons.	Edward V.
Edward the Confessor.	Henry VII.
Henry III.	Edward VI.
Edward I.	James I.
Edward III.	Charles II.
Richard II.	William III.
Henry V.	George II.

List of Monuments

St. Edward's Chapel, or the Chapel of the Kings—

Edward the Confessor.	Edward I.
Henry III.	Eleanor of Castile.
Henry V.	Queen Philippa.
Edward III.	Richard II. and Queen.

Queen Editha and Queen Matilda (good Queen Maud) are buried here.

Henry VII.'s Chapel—

Mary Queen of Scots.	Henry VII. and his Queen.
Queens Elizabeth and Mary.	James I. No monument.

In the " Stuart Vault " are buried—
Elizabeth, Queen of Bohemia, and Prince Rupert.
Lady Arabella Stuart, Anne Hyde, and several Royal children.

In the " Royal Vault " are buried—

Charles II.	Queen Anne.
Queen Mary II.	Prince George of Denmark.
William III.	

Under the Nave of the Chapel are buried—
George II. and Caroline of Anspach.
Edward VI. The old altar by Torregiano under which he was laid has been of late years restored.

In " Oliver's Vault " were originally buried—
Cromwell, and other leaders of the Commonwealth; the only body that has remained undisturbed is that of the Protector's daughter, Elizabeth Claypole.

A small sarcophagus contains the bones supposed to be those of Edward V. and the Duke of York.

D

In this Chapel are also buried—

Addison, to whom a statue was raised in 1809 in the *Poets' Corner*.

George Villiers, Duke of Buckingham, an immense tomb.

Nave and Choir—

Charles James Fox.

Henry Fox, Lord Holland.

Major-General Charles George Gordon, bronze bust.

William Pitt.

William Wordsworth, seated statue.

John Keble, bust.

Frederick D. Maurice, bust.

Charles Kingsley, bust.   } Baptistery.

Matthew Arnold, bust.

Dr. T. Arnold, bust.

William Congreve.

Major John André.

Charles Robert Darwin, medallion portrait.

(Sir John Herschell, buried next to Darwin).

Ben Jonson (buried here—monument in Poets' Corner).

Sir Charles Lyell, bust.

Sir Isaac Newton.

Buried here are—

David Livingstone,

Robert Stephenson,

Dean Trench,   } without monument.

Sir George Gilbert Scott,

Lord Lawrence, bust.

Sir James Outram (a bas-relief of Relief of Lucknow).

Colin Campbell, Lord Clyde.

Dr. Isaac Watts.

John and Charles Wesley (buried elsewhere).

Admiral Sir Cloudesley Shovel.

Sir Godfrey Kneller, the only painter commemorated in the Abbey.

William Wilberforce, seated figure.

Henry Purcell, tablet.

(Sir William Sterndale Bennett buried here.)

INTERIOR FROM CHAPEL OF ST. JOHN

North Transept—
> William Pitt, Earl of Chatham.
> Viscount Palmerston, statue.
> Sir Robert Peel, statue.
> Lord Beaconsfield, statue.
> Gladstone (no monument yet erected).
> Warren Hastings (buried elsewhere).
> Richard Cobden, bust (buried elsewhere).

Poets' Corner—
> John Dryden, bust.
> H. Wadsworth Longfellow, bust.
> Abraham Cowley.
> Geoffrey Chaucer.
> Lord Tennyson, bust.
> Robert Browning (no monument).
> Michael Drayton.
> Ben Jonson, monument bears same inscription as stone above
>   grave.
> Edmund Spenser.
> Samuel Butler (buried elsewhere).
> John Milton.
> Thomas Gray (buried elsewhere).
> Matthew Prior.
> Thomas Campbell.
> Robert Southey (buried elsewhere), bust.
> S. Taylor Coleridge (buried elsewhere), bust.
> William Shakespeare.
> Robert Burns (buried elsewhere), bust.
> James Thomson (buried elsewhere).
> John Gay (buried ?).
> Oliver Goldsmith, medallion (buried elsewhere).
> Sir W. Scott, replica of bust at Abbotsford.
> John Ruskin, medallion.
> George Frederick Handel, statue.
> Jenny Lind Goldschmidt, portrait head.
> W. Makepeace Thackeray (buried elsewhere), bust.
> Joseph Addison (buried in Henry VII.'s Chapel).
> Lord Macaulay, bust.
> William Camden.
> David Garrick, full-length figure.

Among those buried here without monuments are—
Sir John and Francis Beaumont.
Sir John Denham.
Dr. Samuel Johnson (monument at St. Paul's).
Richard Brinsley Sheridan.
Charles Dickens.
Sir William Davenant.
Richard Hakluyt.
Thomas Parr.
Queen Anne, Richard III.'s wife, is believed to be lying here.

Monuments to Dr. Busby and Dr. Robert South.
Portion of tomb of Anne of Cleves.

Within the rails of the Choir are three old tombs—
Aveline, Countess of Lancaster, married to Henry III.'s son, Edmund Crouchback.
Aymer de Valence, Earl of Pembroke, cousin to Edward I., employed as general in wars in Scotland.
Edmund Crouchback, Earl of Lancaster.

South Ambulatory—
Supposed tomb of King Siebert.

Chapel of St. Edmund—

William de Valence, Earl of Pembroke (father of above), half-brother to Henry III. This is the only existing example in England of an effigy in Limoges enamel work.
Lord Lytton, black marble slab.

North Ambulatory—
General James Wolfe.

Chapel of St. Paul—
James Watt, statue.

Islip Chapel—
Remains of Islip's tomb form a table by the window.

St. John's Chapel—
Sir John Franklin.

St. Andrew's Chapel—
Sir Humphrey Davy (buried elsewhere), tablet.
Mrs. Siddons, statue.
John Kemble, statue.

Among those who are buried in the Cloisters are—
Thomas Betterton, actor.
Mrs. Bracegirdle, actress.
Aphra Behu.
Samuel Foote.

A tablet in the Cloisters has been put up in memory of seven of the Queen's Westminster Volunteers killed in South Africa, 1900.

Monument to Dean Stanley (Henry VII.'s Chapel).

Archbishop Tait, bust (Poets' Corner).

Window commemorative of—
George Herbert.
William Cowper.

DIMENSIONS

Length of nave	166 ft.
Breadth of nave	38 ft.
Breadth of nave and aisles . .	71 ft.
Height of nave and choir . .	101 ft.
Length of choir . . .	155 ft.
Breadth of choir . . .	38 ft.
Length of whole church . .	511 ft.
Height of central tower . .	151 ft.
Height of west towers . .	225 ft.
Area	46,000 sq. ft.

PRINCIPAL BUILDING DATES

1050-1100—Fragments beneath pavement of choir, Chapel of the Pyx.

1245-1269—Choir and four eastern bays of nave, transepts, chapter-house, and north and part of east walk of cloister.

1330-1350—Cloisters, south and west walks.

1350-1512—West parts of nave, Henry VII.'s Chapel, abbot's pew, Henry V.'s Chantry, Jerusalem Chamber.

1739-1741—West front.

Modern—North front of north transept.

A West Entrance
B Nave
C C North and South Aisles
D Choir
E E North and South Transept
F Central Doorway, North Transept
G Central Tower
H H North and South Ambulatory
I Altar
J Chapel of St. Paul
K Chapel of St. John Baptist
L Chapel of St. Erasmus
M Chapel of Abbot Islip
N Chapel of St. Benedict

O Chapel of St. Edmund
P Chapel of St. Nicholas
Q Chapel of St. John the Evangelist
R Chapel of St. Michael
S Chapel of St. Andrew
T Henry VII.'s Chapel
U Chapel of St. Faith
V Chapter-House
W Chapel of the Pyx
X Cloister
Y Jericho
Z Jerusalem Chamber

1 Shrine of the Confessor
2 Tomb of King Edward I.
3 Tomb of King Henry III.
4 Tomb of Queen Eleanor
5 Tomb of King Henry V.
6 Tomb of Queen Philippa
7 Tomb of King Edward III
8 Tomb of King Richard II.
  and Queen Anne of Bohemia
9 Tomb of Sebert
10 Tomb of Aveline, Duchess
   of Lancaster
11 Tomb of Aymer de Valence
12 Tomb of Edmund Crouchback
13 Tomb of Queen Anne of Cleves
14 Tomb of William de Valence

15 Tomb of John of Eltham
16 Tomb of King Henry VII.
   and Queen Elizabeth of York
17 Tomb of Ludovic Stuart,
   Duke of Richmond and Lennox
18 Tomb of Dean Stanley
19 Cromwell Vault
20 Sheffield Vault
21 Tomb of George Villiers,
   Duke of Buckingham
22 Tomb of Lady Margaret Beaufort
23 Tomb of Mary Queen of Scots
24 Tomb of Lady Margaret Stuart
25 Tomb of Queen Elizabeth
26 Tomb of Children of James I.
27 The Poet's Corner
28 The Coronation Chairs
29 Dining Hall
30 Court
31 Entrance to East Cloister
32 Entrance to West Cloister
33 Site of Edward the Confessor's
   Building

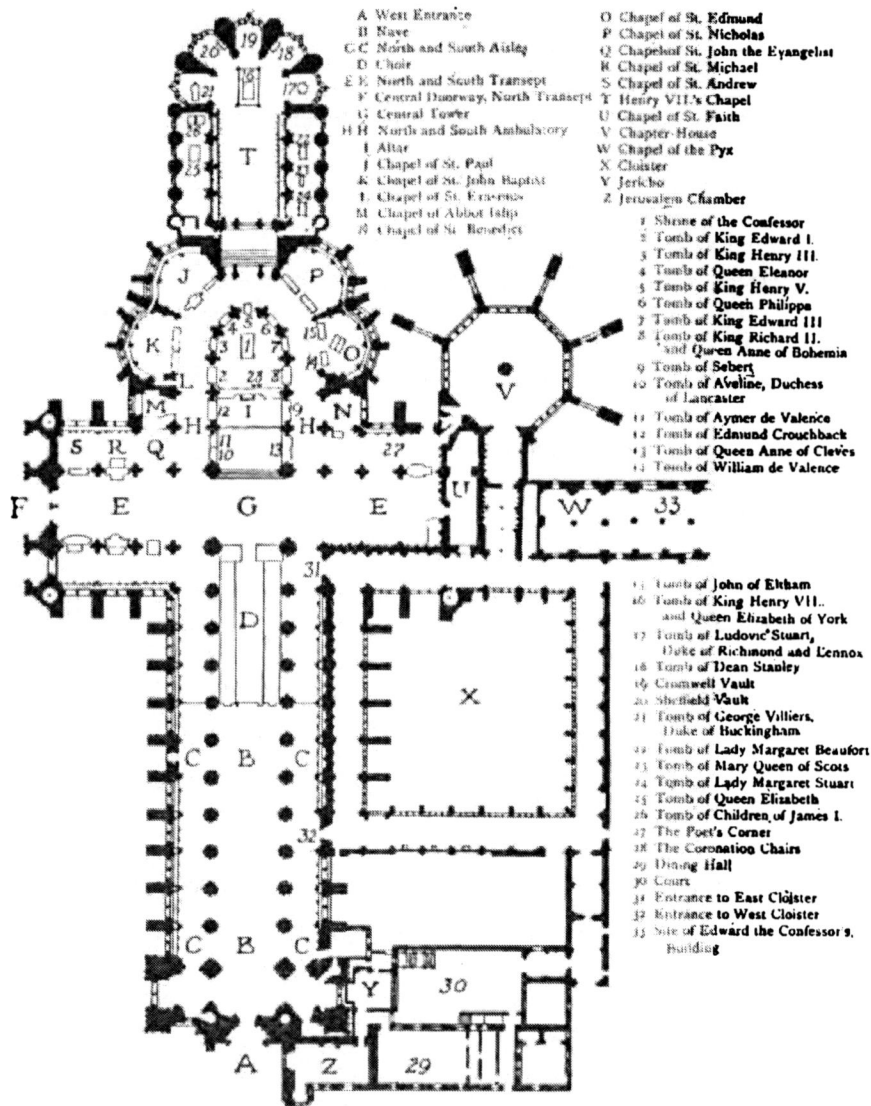

PLAN OF WESTMINSTER ABBEY

ROCHESTER CATHEDRAL

THE city of Rochester has a distinguished past. It lies on the great high road to London, the Old Watling Street. Hence, all the great and Royal visitors passed through Rochester, and few events of historical importance which occurred in the Kentish corner of England were unconnected with this city. It was a Roman station. The Saxons called it *Hvof-Cestre*. Ethelbert founded the Cathedral here in 604, and this first raised it to importance. Athelstan established a mint here, and at the beginning of the tenth century it was one of the principal ports of the kingdom. This was the cause of its undoing, as the Danes found it a convenient landing-place, and pillaged and ravaged the city. A Norman castle was built by Bishop Gundulf, of whom we shall hear more later. This fortress, of which there are extensive remains, has been frequently besieged. It was granted by the Conqueror to Odo, Bishop of Bayeaux, who was faithless to William and was besieged in this castle. Again, King John and Simon de Montfort, and Wat Tyler, all tried the strength of this mighty fortress. Many scenes of mediæval pageantry took place here. In the time of Henry III. a grand tournament was held here, and gay was the city with the presence of contending knights and squires and all the pomp of ancient chivalry. It were vain to name all the Royal visitors who have sojourned here. Here at the Restoration came the " Merry Monarch," and here, when the fortunes of the Stuarts were very low, came James II. in his secret flight, and embarked from Rochester on his fatal journey to France. The story of the city is full of interest; but its Cathedral was the primary cause of its greatness, and thither we must wend our way, and try to read its history.

The see was founded by Ethelbert at the instigation of Augustine in 604, Justus, one of the followers of the Apostle of the English, being its first bishop. He was the builder of the earliest church, some foundations of which have been recently discovered. Here the great missionary of the north, Paulinus, came, the Apostle of the North of England, having been driven away from Northumbria, and was bishop here till 644, when Ithamar succeeded, the first native bishop of the English Church. The church was dedicated to St. Andrew. Danish invasions caused much destruction. Siward, formerly Abbot of Abingdon, was the last Saxon prelate who preserved his see when the Conqueror came. But the chroniclers tell of the miserable condition of the church, " wretched and empty, destitute of all things within and without." In 1076 came Gundulf of Bec to preside over the fortunes of the harassed see, and he wrought vast changes. He introduced Benedictine monks, who replaced the secular canons, rebuilt the Cathedral, and, not content with that, erected a castle here, and built parts of Dover Castle and the Tower of London. Soon after his death Ernulf, whose work at Canterbury we shall see, became bishop here, and carried on his great building operations, erecting the dormitory, chapter-house and refectory.

In 1130, in a grand assembly of bishops, nobles, and in the presence of the king, Henry I., the Cathedral was consecrated.

As with many other cathedrals, fire wrought havoc in the sacred fane, especially in 1138 and 1177. The later Norman builders added much to the perfection of the church, carving the capitals of piers of the nave, recasing them, and building the west front, which Gundulf does not seem to have accomplished. After the fires the building was renewed, especially in the monks' quarters, which had suffered much. Another great misfortune was the plundering and devastation of the church by King John after his capture of the castle; but happily an event occurred which helped to fill the treasury of the monks, and enabled them to adorn their minster. One William of Perth, a baker by trade, who was of a pious mind, undertook a pilgrimage to the Holy Land, but was killed by robbers near Chatham, and buried here. Miracles were said to have been wrought at his tomb; the fame thereof spread; and crowds of pilgrims began to frequent St. William's shrine, and bring costly offerings. William de Hoo was sacrist and prior at the beginning of the thirteenth century, a most active builder, who rebuilt the choir and aisles, using much of the old Norman work. This choir was used for the first time in 1227. Another great builder was Richard de Eastgate, sacrist, who constructed a new west transept, and began the construction of the central tower. His work was continued, and before the century was completed there was a new south transept, and the piers finished for bearing the tower.

Bishop Glanville (1185-1214) was much hated by the monks,

and continuous disputing arose. "He came from Northumbria," says a monk, "and is a proof of the saying that out of the north proceedeth all evil."

In 1264 Simon de Montfort and the barons besieged Rochester, and on Good Friday "the satellites of the devil entered the Church of St. Andrew with their drawn swords, and, striking fear and horror into its children and those also who had taken refuge in it, crucified them together with the Lord, Who suffereth in His elect. Moreover, they plundered the gold and silver and precious things. Some of the monks they imprisoned all the night, and armed men on their horses rode about the altars, and dragged thence with impious hands certain persons who had fled to them. The holy places—the chapels, cloisters, chapter-house, infirmary—were made stalls for their horses, and filled with filth and uncleanness."

Walter de Merton was bishop here in 1274-1278. He was the noble founder of Merton College, Oxford, and from his rules which he framed for his institution it is evident that he liked not monks. At one time it seems to have been the intention of the builders to pull down the nave and rebuild it in Gothic style, but in the fourteenth century the monks seem to have given up the idea, and joined the new work with the Norman.

The affairs of the monastery did not always go very smoothly. We have noticed some disputes between the bishop and the monks, and in the fourteenth century there were endless quarrels between the monks and the citizens. The latter had the altar of St. Nicholas in the body of the nave near the screen for their use. Their access to it the monks tried to control, and scenes of violence resulted. So the monks encircled the precincts with a wall, and enclosed the choir with strong gates and screens, and subsequently built a church for the parishioners.

Bishop Haymo de Hythe (1319-1352) contributed large sums to the restoration of his Cathedral. He built the central tower and raised a campanile, in which he placed four bells, named Dunstan, Paulinus, Ithamar and Lanfranc. He also built the door leading to the chapter-house. Several alterations were made in Perpendicular times, new windows inserted, and the Lady Chapel built in the unusual position on south of the nave, and the fabric of the Cathedral finished. At the dissolution of monasteries the monks were turned adrift, and the New Foundation called into being, consisting of a dean, prebendaries, minor canons, choristers, together with a grammar school.

At the Civil War the Cathedral fared better than many. The soldiers changed the position of the altar and broke the rails, and profaned the church by using it as a stable and a tippling place, while saw-pits were made here, and carpenters plied their trade.

At the Restoration all churchmen set about repairing their cathedrals, and the citizens of Rochester lagged not behind. Much money was spent on the fabric, and many repairs effected. In the eighteenth century Sloane was the architect who rebuilt the steeple. Very extensive alterations were made at the beginning of the nineteenth century, under the direction of Cottingham, which were drastic, and Sir G. Scott and Mr. Pearson have both been at work on the Cathedral, whose restorations we will examine when we inspect the Cathedral. The Bishopric of Rochester since the Reformation has been occupied by several remarkable men. Bishop Fisher, a learned, brave and saintly man, was doomed to death on the scaffold by Henry VIII. (1535), and Barlow, Buckeridge, Warner and Atterbury were all men who achieved fame in their times.

THE EXTERIOR

The best view can be obtained from the castle. The *West Front* is a fine example of Norman work, with the exception of the large Perpendicular window, and the modern imitation of Norman work. It is a mistake for architects to destroy the accretions of centuries, and to substitute a reproduction of what they imagine to have been the original design. Mr. Pearson had the audacity to take down the fifteenth-century north turret, and to erect a bran-new Norman turret in its place. The front, as we see it, consists of a centre flanked by turrets, and two wings, which form the ends of the aisles. First we notice the beautiful west door, which is one of the finest Norman doorways in the kingdom. It has five orders, and is of elaborate design and profusely adorned with mouldings, the capitals being richly carved. On the fourth shaft on each side are two curious figures, supposed to represent Henry I. and his queen. In the tympanum is the Saviour, with angels and the evangelistic emblems, and below small mutilated figures of the Apostles. The old doors were said to have been covered with the skins of Danes, but these have disappeared, and the new ones have no trace of the epidermis of our destructive visitors. The great west window was inserted about 1470. Rows of Norman arcading adorn the front. Two modern statues of Bishops Gundulf and

John have been placed in the niches on each side of the doorway. The turrets are octagonal, that on the west being modern, and built by Mr. Pearson on the model of that on the south, in place of a Perpendicular one erected at the same time as the window. The north tower has been quite recently erected in imitation of the ancient design, and the south tower raised to its original height.

The *Nave* is for the most part Norman. The clerestory is Perpendicular, also the windows in the north aisle. The *North Transept* is Early English, but has been re-roofed at a much higher pitch by Sir G. Scott, who added the pinnacles and circular windows. On the east of this is *Gundulf's Tower*, built by the founder of the Norman church and probably intended for purposes of defence, and as a treasury. It seems that the only entrance to it was from the top, a bridge connecting it with a staircase in the neighbouring transept. It was afterwards used as a belfry. The north side of the choir shows its Early English character, and the presence of the dog-tooth ornament bespeaks its style. There is, however, much modern work. The high gables that call loudly for corresponding roofs were built by Scott, and perhaps some generous visitor will be willing to grant their silent appeal. The south side of the presbytery adjoins the chapter-house and library, built in the eighteenth century in place of the noble Norman chapter-house, the ruins of which still remain. The monastic buildings stood in an unusual position on the south side of the choir, and were mainly constructed by Ernulf. Gundulf's cloisters were on the south of the nave in the usual place for a Benedictine abbey, but these have entirely disappeared. In the ruins of Ernulf's monastic buildings there is much fine Norman work, zigzag and billet mouldings, his favourite diaper which is found at Canterbury, and a curious carving of the sacrifice of Isaac. Parts of the wall of the dormitory and the refectory, with a lavatory, remain. The south side of the choir and the choir transept were much restored by Cottingham in 1825. A fine Decorated window has been inserted in the south wall of the choir transept aisle. The *South Transept* is Late Early English work. On its west side is the Lady Chapel, erected in the Perpendicular style about 1500.

The lower part of the central tower, which is hardly worthy of the Cathedral, was built by Bishop Haymo de Hythe (1319-1352); all above the roof was erected by Cottingham in the restoration of 1825.

The remains of the old wall which surrounded the precincts are still in existence. The Prior's Gate was built about the middle of the fourteenth century; and the other remaining gates are College Gate, and the Deanery Gate, both of which belong to the time of Edward IV.

THE INTERIOR

We enter the *Nave* by the beautiful west doorway and are at once impressed by the fine Norman character of the building. Much of it is the work of Gundulf, the first Norman bishop, the companion of Lanfranc, who fashioned his rising church after the model of Canterbury, and has thus left us a copy of the appearance of that church ere it was refashioned by later builders. The two eastern bays are Early Decorated. The clerestory is Perpendicular work, and the flat timber roof was erected at the same time. The later Norman builders, Bishops Ernulf and John (1115-1137), greatly improved the appearance of Gundulf's nave. They finished the west end, recased the piers, and carved the zigzag mouldings and the capitals, and seem to have added a new triforium or enriched the old arcade with diaper work. There is no triforium gallery, as it opens both into the aisles as well as into the nave. The fine interior of the west doorway will be noticed, and also another Norman doorway in the south-west corner. The windows in the north aisle are Perpendicular. The font is modern, and also the pulpit, stalls and lectern. On the south of the south aisle is the Late Perpendicular Chapel of St. Mary, usually called the Lady Chapel. It was restored in 1852. Here the consistory court used to meet. It is now used as a chapel for the grammar school. The *South Transept* is of later date than the corresponding north transept; its style is Late Early English, when the style was merging into Early Decorated. The architect was Richard de Waldene, sacrist. Above in the south wall there are five single-light windows, and below three double windows, and the extensive use of Purbeck marble in the shafts will be noticed. Banded shafts of marble cluster around the great tower-piers. Cottingham erected the present ceiling in 1840. It will be noticed that the Purbeck marble shafts on the two western tower-piers stop some distance from the ground, and a block of intrusive masonry obtrudes itself on the west of the northern one. Various conjectures have been made concerning the object of this. Possibly it formed part of a stone rood loft, or served as a buttress to the arch. The *North Transept* is Early English, the work of Richard de Eastgate, sacrist. The dog-tooth ornament is seen in the clerestory. The carved corbels, representing monastic heads, are finely executed. In the recess on the east side there is a piscina which marks the site of an altar.

The *Monuments* in the nave and transepts are not important. That of Richard Watts in the south transept is worthy of notice. He entertained Queen Elizabeth at his house called Satis,[1] and erected a hostel for six poor travellers, "not being rogues or proctors," which in later times has been immortalised by Charles Dickens, as a tablet sets forth. Near it is the monument of Sir Richard Head, who sheltered the fugitive monarch James II. when he fled from his kingdom. The glass is all modern.

The *Choir Screen* has been restored in memory of Dean Scott, who, with Dean Liddell of Christ Church, Oxford, compiled the well-known Greek Lexicon. The doorway is ancient Decorated work; the figures are (beginning on the north side) St. Andrew, Ethelbert, St. Justus, St. Paulinus, Gundulf, William de Hoo, Walter de Merton, Bishop Fisher, all of whom were connected with the See of Rochester. As at Canterbury, we ascend several steps to gain the choir, rendered necessary by the height of the crypt below. All the work before us in the choir is Early English, but fashioned on the old Norman walls. It was finished sufficiently for use in 1227, in the year of the accession of Henry de Sandford to the bishopric, and is the work of William de Hoo. The choir aisles are separated from the choir by stone walls. Shafts of Purbeck marble support the vault. Some of the brackets of Early English foliage which support the shafts are beautifully carved. Some of the windows in the presbytery and south choir transept are later insertions, and are Decorated. Sir G. Scott wrought drastic changes here, and substituted two tiers of lancets instead of a large east window, brought the altar away from the extreme east end and designed a new reredos. He made new stalls, using much of the old woodwork. Some fine old fourteenth-century painting he discovered behind the old stalls, which he carefully reproduced, and designed a new throne, pulpit and reredos. Amidst so much that is new and beautiful in its way, it is pleasant to discover some ancient work. The sedilia are Perpendicular, and an Early English piscina and aumbrey are observable behind the altar. There is a

---

[1] When the queen was departing he apologised for his poor entertainment, but she replied "*Satis*" ("sufficient"), from which august reply Watts named his house.

curious and interesting mural painting on the north wall representing the *Wheel of Fortune,* which is probably a thirteenth-century production.

The *North Choir Transept* (Early English) contains the tomb of St. William, to whom we have already referred, and whose shrine brought much gain to the treasury. The tomb is of Purbeck marble, with a floriated cross. A flat stone marked with six crosses in the centre of the transept is said to be the site of the shrine. The steps leading to this transept from the north choir aisle are much worn by the feet of pilgrims. Here is also the tomb of Walter de Merton (1274-1277) of Early Decorated design, the founder of Merton College, Oxford. The slab is modern; an alabaster effigy made in 1598 now is placed in the adjoining recess. Here is also the tomb of Bishop Lowe (1467). In the aisle (St. John Baptist's Chapel), are tombs of Bishop Warner (1666), the founder of the college for widows at Bromley, who occupied the see during the Commonwealth period; of Bishop John de Sheppey (1360), the sculpture of which is worthy of the highest praise. It was long hidden away in the wall, and remained so for centuries, until the restorations of 1825 brought it to light.[1] Here also is a very ancient statue said to be the figure of Gundulf. In the chancel or sacrarium are the tombs of Bishop Gilbert de Glanville (1214), a shrine - shaped monument with medallions containing mitred heads; Bishop Lawrence de St. Martin (1274), of Early Decorated design; at extreme east, Sir W. Arundel (1400) and his lady; and on the south side the supposed coffin of Bishop Gundulf; Bishop Inglethorp (1291), a thirteenth-century coffin, and another in the south choir transept (name unknown). The glass in this part of the church is all modern.

The *doorway into the Chapter-House* is one of the great glories of the Cathedral. It is Late Decorated work, and was probably erected during the episcopate of Haymo de Hythe (1319-1352). Cottingham restored it in 1830, and made the left-hand figure into a grave and reverend bishop holding a model of a cathedral and a crozier. It is probably correct that in a more recent restoration the figure should have been made into that of a female. It is meant to signify the Christian Church, just as the right-hand figure represents the Jewish Church, blindfolded, and leaning on a broken reed and holding a reversed table of the Law. The two seated figures on the right and left sides represent the four doctors—SS. Jerome, Augustine,

[1] Authorities differ as to whether the colouring is ancient or modern. Mr. Palmer, in his recent and valuable history of the Cathedral, pronounces in favour of the latter; but Mr. St. John Hope considers it to be ancient.

Ambrose and Gregory, while above appear angels who have rescued a pure soul from purgatorial fires. The crocketed ogee arch and the diaper work above are worthy of attention ; the door is modern.

The *Chapter-House and Library* occupy a room which is a modern addition. The library has some treasures, amongst which may be mentioned *Textus Roffensis*, a collection of records, gifts and privileges of the Cathedral, compiled under the direction of Bishop Ernulf (1115-1124). It has passed through many perils, having been stolen, restored, borrowed, lost in the Thames, recovered, and we trust its dangers are now over.

Custumale Roffense, another valuable MS. of the thirteenth century, a great collection of *Bibles*, including Coverdale's, Cranmer's or the Great Bible, and the Bishops' Bible. Above the choir transepts are two chambers called the Treasury, where the church plate is kept, and the Indulgence Chamber.

Following the course of the pilgrims, we proceed down the flight of steps to the south choir aisle, or Chapel of St. Edmund. There is the mutilated tomb of Bishop John de Bradfield (1278-1283). Following the second flight of steps we come to the *Crypt*, which extends under the whole choir and is one of the most perfect in the kingdom. The western part is Early Norman, and has massive piers and cushion capitals. The rest is Early English. The altars in the crypt were numerous, and traces of them remain, as shown by the piscinas. The crypt was extensively decorated with mural paintings, and some traces of them may still be seen.

DIMENSIONS

Total length, 306 ft. ; length of nave, 126 ft. ; width of nave, 65 ft. ; length of choir, 147 ft. ; length of west transept, 120 ft. ; length of east transept, 88 ft. ; height of tower, 156 ft. ; height of vault, 55 ft. ; area, 23,300 sq. ft.

DESCRIPTION OF ARCHITECTURE

Norman—Most of the nave and part of crypt and old chapter-house.

Early English—The choir and transepts.

Decorated—Chapter door and some windows at east end.

Perpendicular—Clerestory of the nave, west window, Lady Chapel.

Modern — Tower, chapter-house and library, roof of west transept and north-west tower.

CANTERBURY CATHEDRAL

IN the minds of readers of English history Canterbury must always rank first amongst our cathedrals on account of the wealth of historical associations connected with it. The story of Canterbury is the story of England, and every record of our annals abounds with allusions to it, or to the distinguished prelates connected with it. It is the metropolitan church of the southern province, and is regarded with veneration as the Mother Church not only of England, but of all the churches in America and the colonies of the British Empire.

There was probably a Roman or Romano-British church here; when Augustine converted King Ethelbert to Christianity the monarch gave him his palace together with an old church which stood near it. This was on part of the site of the present Cathedral. We need not record again the tangled story of the conversion of the English, or the names of all the successors of Augustine. The first seven were buried in the Monastery of St. Augustine, now St. Augustine's College, Archbishop Cuthbert (d. 758) being the first to be interred in his own Cathedral. Archbishop Odo (942-959) known as "the Severe" on account of his endeavour to restore discipline among the clergy, although born a heathen Dane, was a zealous prelate, and set himself to restore the ruinous condition of his Cathedral. For three years the work of building progressed. The eleventh century brought the Danish ravages, and with fire and sword the Pagan hosts attacked Canterbury and murdered the archbishop, Alphege. His successor, Living or Leofing, was held captive by the Danes for some time, but sought safety beyond seas, and lived to crown Canute. The Cathedral was restored by the next prelate, Egelnorth, but a fire destroyed it in 1067, and it was not till Norman times that a complete restoration was attempted. Lanfranc, the first Norman archbishop, finding the church utterly dilapidated, destroyed the old fabric and built a noble minster. We have a description of the old Saxon church in the writings of Eadmer, a monk of Canterbury: "At the east end of the church stood the high altar, which enclosed the body of St. Winifred. This was of rough stone cemented together. A little before that was an altar where Mass was said daily; in which altar St. Alphege enclosed the head of St. Swithun, and many other relics which he brought with him from Winchester. Descending hence by several steps was the crypt. At the foot of these steps was a descent into a vault which went under the east part of the church; and at the east end of it was an altar, wherein was enclosed the head of St. Fursius. From hence by a winding passage, at the west end, was the tomb of St. Dunstan, separated from it by a wall. His body was buried deep in the ground before those stairs, and over him was a tomb erected in the form of a lofty pyramid. The hall or body of the church was separated from the choir. About the middle of the hall were two towers jutting out beyond the walls—that on the south had an altar dedicated to St. Gregory; and from this tower was a passage, the principal porch of the church, anciently called Stuthdore, a large and capacious portico. The tower on the north side was erected to the honour of St. Martin, having a passage to it from the cloisters. The end of the church was adorned with the oratory of the Blessed Virgin. In the eastern part of it was an altar, consecrated to her, which enclosed the head of a saint."

Lanfranc also built the monastic buildings. The saintly Archbishop Anselm, who succeeded Lanfranc, took down the east end and rebuilt it with great magnificence. His chief architect was Ernulf, the prior, afterwards Bishop of Rochester. Prior Conrad succeeded, who finished the choir, which was hereafter known as "the glorious choir of Conrad." Gervase, a monk of Canterbury, describes this church, which had a central tower, a nave supported on each side by eight pillars, two western towers with gilt pinnacles, a rood-screen, surmounted by a great cross with figures of SS. Mary and John. He concludes that the dedication of this church was "the most famous that had ever been heard of on the earth since that of the Temple of Solomon."

This church was the scene of the murder of Thomas à Becket, which convulsed the land, and here Henry II. did penance before the tomb of the archbishop slain at his instigation. In 1174 a fierce conflagration raged and destroyed the beautiful choir, and at the sight of the ruins, Gervase tells us, the people were mad with grief, and beat the walls and tore their hair, blaspheming the Lord and His saints. The task of rebuilding was at once commenced, and William of Sens was appointed architect. He laboured for four years, and then falling from a scaffold was so much injured that he was obliged to return to France. An English William then took over the superintendence of the work. It is not stated that he was a pupil of William of Sens, or was in any way influenced by French models. In 1184 the choir was finished, and soon new cloisters were added. In 1304 the choir was beautified and a new pulpit erected by Prior d'Estria, who added the great bell called Thomas. In 1376 Archbishop Sudbury took down the western transepts and the nave, and began the rebuilding of the former in the Perpendicular style, the work being continued by Prior Chillenden during the rule of Archbishop Courtenay, the oppressor of Lollardism. The cloisters and chapter-house were finished at this time. Archbishop Arundel (1396-1414), who was addicted to burning heretics, also added greatly to the beauty of the church, and his successor, Chichele, spent vast sums on the church, founded a library, and began the spire on the west tower. In 1449 Prior Goldstone built the beautiful chapel of the Virgin called the Dean's Chapel, and another prior of the same name in 1495 began the great central tower, or Angel Steeple, when Archbishop Morton ruled, whose rebus is inscribed upon it. The same prior also built the Christ Church Gate in 1517. The troublous times of the Reformation followed, and we find Cranmer occupying the archiepiscopal throne, who was ultimately doomed to the stake at Oxford. Fanatical reformers wrought terrible havoc in the Cathedral. The magnificent shrine of Becket, to which millions had flocked to pay their devotions, was entirely destroyed, and numerous other costly shrines shared its fate. Archbishop Laud attempted to restore the beauty of the sanctuary, and erected a fine altar with reredos; but soon the pikes of the Puritans and their wild savagery reduced the interior of the Cathedral to a ruinous desolation. The usual scenes of mad iconoclasm were enacted, windows broken, altars thrown down, lead stripped off the roof, brasses and effigies defaced and broken. A creature nicknamed "Blue Dick" was the wild leader of this savage crew of spoliators, who left little but the bare walls and a mass of broken fragments strewing the pavement.

Since then numerous alterations and restorations have taken place. At the Restoration of the monarchy Bishop Juxon of London, who attended Charles I. on the scaffold at Whitehall, was made Archbishop of Canterbury, and he and Archbishop Sheldon, his successor, did much to restore the fabric and remove the traces

of Puritan fanaticism. Archbishop Tenison (1694-1716) removed the old stalls and substituted pews. He covered Prior d'Estria's screen with wainscotting, and erected a fine throne with carving by Grinling Gibbons. Queen Mary also added to the beauty of the Cathedral by sundry costly gifts. In 1834 a new north-west tower was built. In 1872 a fire broke out in the roof, but happily no very extensive damage was done, and five years later Sir G. Scott began his restorations, which have removed some of the faults committed in the early eighteenth-century alterations.

THE EXTERIOR

The best views are obtained from the mound in the Dane John (or Donjon—probably a fortified earthwork of Norman times) approached by St. George's Terrace, adjoining the Cattle Market, from the green or outer court of the monastery, and from the village of Harbledown. The *West Front* is flanked by two towers. That on the north was built in 1840, as the former one, called the Arundel, was in a dangerous condition; that on the south, called the Dunstan, was finished by Prior Goldstone (1449-1468), and is in the Perpendicular style, with characteristic panelling. A large window is in the centre of the front, and two smaller windows for the aisles, and above, in the gable, another window with elaborate tracery. The *South Porch* was built by Prior Chillenden about 1400. Erasmus tells us that he saw figures of Becket's murderers here, but these have disappeared. The niches have been filled with modern figures. Proceeding along the south side of the church, we notice the Perpendicular style of the nave and aisles, the work of Prior Chillenden, which replaced the old Norman nave. There is a close resemblance between this and Winchester, which was being constructed at the same time. All that remains here of Lanfranc's nave is the lowest base of the aisle walls. The south-west transept is of the same date as the nave and has a large window on the south front with three tiers of panels over it, and an elaborate turret at the south-west corner. The south-east transept is Late Norman, the work of William of Sens and William the Englishman. Here we have Norman round-headed windows with arcades, also a circular window, and on the west a Norman turret capped with a short spire. Proceeding eastwards we see Anselm's Tower, and on the extreme east the corona, the work of English William. On the west Henry IV.'s Chantry, St. Andrew's Chapel, corresponding to that of St. Anselm, the treasury, and the range of monastic buildings, consisting of library, chapter-house and cloisters, which we will examine later. A wall surrounded the precincts, the principal gate being that called *Christ Church* Gate, erected by Goldstone in Perpendicular style in 1517.

THE INTERIOR

We enter the *Nave* by the south porch. Lanfranc's nave was entirely removed in 1380 on account of its ruinous state, and the present nave erected by Prior Chillenden, who was employed and supported by Archbishops Sudbury, Courtenay and Arundel. As we have said, it resembled Winchester, built at the same time, but it is lighter in character, as here the piers were built anew, and not cased with Perpendicular work as at Winchester. The height of the floor of the choir necessitated a lofty flight of steps leading to it from the nave; and this is a peculiar feature of this Cathedral and of much beauty. The nave is very lofty, being 80 feet high. The great west window contains the fragments of old glass which have been brought together here. The rest of the stained glass is modern and hideous. In the north aisle are monuments of Adrian Saravia, the friend of Hooker (1612), Orlando Gibbons, organist to Charles I., Sir John Boys (1614), founder of a hospital, Archbishop Sumner (1862), who crowned Queen Victoria, and memorials of military men who died for their country. In the south aisle are monuments of Dr. Broughton, Bishop of Sydney, and Dean Lyall (1858).

The central tower is supported by original Norman piers, cased with Perpendicular work at the time when the nave was built. The vault and all the upper part of the tower above the roof were erected by Prior Goldstone (1495-1517), and also the arches, which act as buttresses and bear the Prior's rebus, three golden bars. The screen is fifteenth-century work and is remarkable for its beauty; formerly the figures of our Lord and the Twelve Apostles occupied the upper niches, but these fell victims to Puritan iconoclasm. The devastators spared, however, the figures of the kings in the lower tier.

The *North-West Transept*, or Chapel of the *Martyrdom of Becket*, claims our close attention, as the event which occurred here filled Christendom with amaze.

The martyrdom of Thomas à Becket took place on Tuesday,

29th December 1170. Early in the morning the four barons had an interview with him, pretending to come on a peaceful visit with messages from the king. They were shown into the room in the palace where the archbishop usually remained. Some high words passed between them and they departed; in the evening they entered the Cathedral, armed. While the archbishop was ascending the steps, Sir Reginald Fitzurse entered the door of the church, clad in complete armour, and, waving his sword, cried, "Come hither, servants of the king!" The other conspirators, Sir Hugh Morvill, Sir William Tracey and Sir Richard le Breton, immediately followed him, armed to the teeth, and brandishing their swords. It was already twilight, which within the walls of the dimly-lighted church had deepened into the blackest obscurity. Becket's attendants entreated him to fly to the winding staircase which led to the roof of the building, or to seek refuge in the vaults underground. He rejected both of these expedients and still stood to meet his assailants. "Where is the traitor?" cried a voice. There was no answer. "Where is the archbishop?" "Here I am," replied Becket; "but here is no traitor. What do ye in the House of God in warlike equipment?" One of the knights seized him by the sleeve; he pulled back his arm violently. They then advised him to go with them, as though they repented of the evil design. They called upon him to absolve the bishops. He refused; and Fitzurse, drawing his sword, struck at his head. The blow was intercepted by the arm of one of the monks who stepped forward to protect him, but in vain. A second blow descended, and while the blood was streaming from his face some one of his assailants whispered to him to fly and save himself. Becket paid no heed to the speaker, but clasped his hands and bowed his head, commending his soul to God and the saints. The conspirators now fell upon him with their swords and quickly despatched him. One of them is said to have kicked the prostrate body, saying, "So perishes a traitor." The deed thus accomplished, the conspirators passed out of the town without hindrance, but no sooner had they done so than the news spread throughout the city and the inhabitants, in the utmost excitement and indignation, assembled in crowds in the streets and ran towards the Cathedral. Seeing the body of their archbishop stretched before the altar, men and women began to weep, and while some kissed his hands and feet others dipped linen in the blood with which the pavement was covered. It was declared by the people that Becket was a martyr, and although a Royal edict was published forbidding anyone to express such an opinion, the popular feeling still manifested itself. Some soldiers attempted to seize the corpse, but the monks, who had received an intimation of the design, buried it hastily in the crypt of the Cathedral.

Since that eventful scene the transept has been rebuilt. The stones around us, except it be the pavement, did not witness that bloody deed. When the nave was rebuilt by Chillenden this part of the church was much transformed. Portions of the old Norman walls built by Lanfranc remain, but the main character of the building is Perpendicular. The door is the same by which the murderers entered, part of the wall, and probably the pavement, wherein is a small square piece which marks the actual spot where Becket fell. The great window was given by Edward IV., and has figures of his queen, his daughters, and the two princes who were murdered in the Tower. The west window is modern, and represents scenes from the life of Becket. There are monuments here of Archbishop Peckham (1292), the oldest in the Cathedral, and Archbishop Warham (1532), who crowned Henry VIII., and was the opponent of Wolsey and the friend of Erasmus. A door at the east end of this transept leads to the *Dean's Chapel*, formerly the Lady Chapel, built by Goldstone in Perpendicular style. The monuments here are to Dean Fotherby, Dr. Bargrave, Dean Boys with his books, and Dean Turner, a favourite of Charles I.

The daily crowd of pilgrims who visited the scene of the martyrdom in mediæval times used to pass on to the shrine of St. Thomas by the north choir aisle, on their way to his shrine, and we will follow in their steps. In this aisle we see much of the original Norman work of Archbishop Anselm's choir, erected under the supervision of Prior Ernulf. William of Sens added many architectural details and made some alterations, but he seems to have intended to preserve the special features of the earlier work. The roof was, however, raised, and the clerestory of Ernulf's building converted into the triforium windows of William of Sens. The latter brought with him the use of the chisel, the former carving his ruder ornamentation by means of an axe. William also introduced the pointed arch. Here is the monument of Archbishop Tait. Three "squints" will be observed in the west wall. Two apsidal chapels are at the east end, dedicated to SS. Stephen and Martin. In the aisle there is some ancient glass of thirteenth-century work, which is of extreme beauty, also an old desk with ancient

Bible. An ancient mural painting should be noticed, representing the conversion of St. Hubert. Next we visit the *Chapel of St. Andrew*, now the vestry, which has some traces of colour decoration. It was built by Prior Ernulf, and was formerly the sacristy, where relics of Becket were preserved in a chest, together with a quantity of vestments. Beyond this, to the north, was the treasury, which was well protected by a massive door. The treasures of costly plate and jewels at Canterbury were of enormous value. In the aisle on the south side there is the splendid tomb of Archbishop Chichele (1443), whom Shakespeare represents in *Henry V.* as instigating the war with France, and who was the founder of All Souls', Oxford. Also there are monuments of Archbishop Howley (1848) and Archbishop Bourchier (1486).

Up lofty steps, climbed by pilgrims on their knees, we ascend to the *Retro-Choir*, the work of William the Englishman, the successor of William of Sens. *Holy Trinity Chapel* occupies the centre, where stood the wondrous shrine of Becket. Architecturally it is interesting as showing the triumph of English achievement over the foreign influence, and the gradual development of the English Gothic style; and historically it is fascinating as being the goal of pilgrims from all quarters of the land. The famous shrine has entirely disappeared, owing to the cupidity of Henry VIII. and his commissioners. Some idea of what it was like is given by a representation of it in one of the windows of the chapel. There was a stone base with marble arches, and above the shrine covered with a wooden canopy, "which at a given signal was drawn up, and the shrine then appeared, blazing with gold and damasked with gold wire, and embossed with innumerable pearls and jewels and rings, cramped together on this gold ground." One great diamond or carbuncle was as large as a hen's egg, called the *Regale of France*, and presented by Louis VII. All the monarchs and nobles in mediæval times came here to worship, and crowds flocked from all quarters "the holy blissful martyr for to seek"; the pavement is worn by their knees; cripples begged to rub their limbs against the pillars of the holy shrine, and perchance were healed— faith plays a wondrous part in many a cure—and Chaucer sings of the tales and doings of the not always very austere Canterbury pilgrims. The windows of this chapel contain some of the best thirteenth-century glass in existence. They record miracles wrought by Becket. Above the shrine is a gilded crescent, concerning which many theories have been suggested, none wholly satisfactory.

In this chapel is the monument of *Edward, the Black Prince* (1376), who fought at Creçy and Poictiers, one of the bravest of our national heroes. The effigy is of brass and was once gilded, and represents the prince in full armour. The head rests on a casque, and the features of the Plantagenets are distinctly traceable. Above the tomb is a canopy, having on it a representation of the Trinity, and above that are the remains of dress and armour actually worn by the prince—his helmet, a shield, a velvet surcoat, gauntlets, and the scabbard of the sword. On the tomb is an inscription in Norman French which, translated, tells: "Here lies the most noble Prince Edward, eldest son of the most noble King Edward III., Prince of Aquitaine and Wales, Duke of Cornwall and Earl of Chester, who died on Trinity Sunday, the 8th of June 1376. To the soul of whom God grant mercy.—Amen." Then follow some verses written by the prince, which begin :—

Tomb of the
Black Prince

" Tu que passez ove bouche close pur la ou c'est corps repose,
    Entent ce qe te dirray, sicome te dire la say,"

and proceed to contrast the riches and glory of this present life with the mouldering and decay of death. Below are seen shields of arms which bear those of France and England, and the ostrich or Prince of Wales's feathers, with the motto *Houmont Ich diene*. Both Welsh and German origin is claimed for the motto. Dean Stanley preferred the latter, and stated that *Houmont* meant *high-spirited*, while the latter words signify *I serve*.

Another interesting tomb is that of Henry IV. (1413), and his second wife, Joan of Navarre (1437). The tomb was opened in 1832, and the body of the dead king discovered in wonderful preservation. He founded the chantry near his tomb. Some vestments taken from a tomb are preserved in this chapel. Other memorials are those of Dean Wotton, by Bernini; Cardinal Coligny, whose brother fell in the massacre of St. Bartholomew, and who was poisoned by his servant; Archbishop Courtenay, the oppressor of the Lollards, who is represented in archiepiscopal robes, with his mitre and crosier.

The *Corona* at the extreme east end is a beautiful piece of work, accomplished by English William. It is in the form of a circular apse, and has a triforium and clerestory. For some obscure reason it has been popularly called "Becket's crown," possibly from the presence here of some relic of the martyr. Here were the shrines of Archbishop Odo and St. Wilfrid of York, and here is the tomb of Cardinal Pole, archbishop in the time of Mary, a plain brick monument, plastered over with the inscription: "The body of Cardinal Pole."

Turning to the *South Choir* aisle, which resembles the north, we see the *Chapel of St. Anselm*, formerly that of SS. Peter and Paul. It resembles that of St. Andrew, and was built by Ernulf, and probably restored after the great fire. Behind the altar was buried the great Anselm, one of the most saintly and renowned prelates who ever occupied the see of Augustine. The south window is Decorated, inserted by Prior d'Estria in 1336. There is a monument here of Archbishop Simon de Mepham (1333), whom we shall hear of again at Exeter, when his visitation was resisted by the arrogant Bishop Grandisson; and also of Archbishop Bradwardine (1349). Above this chapel is the *Watching Chamber*, where a monk was stationed to guard the shrines. Proceeding along the aisle on the right are monuments of Archbishop Sudbury (1381), beheaded in the Wat Tyler rebellion; Archbishop Stratford (1348) and Archbishop Kemp (1454).

The *South-East Transept* is similar to the northern one. The walls are the work of Ernulf. It is to William of Sens, however, that we have to attribute the architectural details. There are apsidal chapels dedicated to SS. John and Gregory, the remains of Archbishop Winchelsey's tomb (1313); and the "patriarchal chair," erroneously called "St. Augustine's." In the aisle on the left are two tombs said to be those of Archbishop Hubert Walter, who accompanied Richard I. on a Crusade, and Archbishop Reynolds (1327), the friend of Edward II.

The *South-West Transept* was rebuilt at the same time as the nave by Chillenden. On the east of this is the *Warrior Chapel*, dedicated to St. Michael. Its style is Perpendicular, *circa* 1370, and was probably erected by Chillenden. Here is the monument of Stephen Langton (1228), who wrested from King John the Magna Charta. The position is curious, only the head of the tomb appearing through the wall. Other monuments are those of John Beaufort, Earl of Somerset, half brother of Henry IV. (1409), and Thomas of Clarence, second son of the same king, killed in battle in 1421, erected by the widow of both; Lady Thornhurst (1609) and Sir Thomas, Sir John Rooke, one of the heroes of the capture of Gibraltar, and some military trophies and memorials.

The *Crypt* is one of the finest in England, built before 1085. There is here some very fine Norman work, the western portion was constructed mainly by Ernulf, though there is some of the work of Lanfranc also here. The carving was executed after the stones were set in their places, and we can see that some of the carving was left unfinished, the designs having been roughly traced out. The portion of the crypt east of the Trinity Chapel is the work of English William (1178-1184). The Chapel of Our Lady Undercroft is enclosed by some Late Perpendicular open stone-work, and was very magnificent. Only privileged pilgrims were allowed to see the wealth of precious stones and costly ornaments with which this wondrous shrine was adorned. In the crypt is the monument of Lady Mohun of Dunstar (1395), the chantry founded by the Black Prince, St. John's Chapel, the tomb of Isabel, Countess of Athole (1229). Here Becket's body was hastily buried by the monks after his murder ; it remained here for fifty years, and was resorted to by the crowds of pilgrims, and here Henry II. endured his penance, receiving five strokes of a rod from each bishop and abbot present, and three from each of the eighty monks, and remaining all the night fasting, resting against one of the pillars. Queen Elizabeth gave the Flemish refugees the use of the crypt both as a place of worship and as a home for their industry. Here they plied their busy looms, and in their moments of leisure wrote inscriptions on the walls. The descendants of these settlers still live in Canterbury, and use part of the crypt as their chapel.

THE MONASTIC BUILDINGS

Canterbury was a Benedictine monastery. We enter the *Cloisters* from the north transept, which are mainly Perpendicular in style, though occupying the site of the old Norman buildings, and containing remains of earlier work. Chillenden, the builder of the nave, is responsible for all the Perpendicular work. The *Chapter-House* was rebuilt on Norman lines late in the thirteenth century, and re-ceiled and re-windowed in the fourteenth by Chillenden. The ceiling is composed of panels of Irish oak. Unfortunately a severe restoration in 1897 has somewhat vulgarised its former beautiful features. At the east end there is the beautiful priors' sedilia, with glass mosaics on the spandrels of the throne. After the Reformation the chapter-house was used for preachings, and acquired the name of the sermon-house. On the north of the garth was the refectory, the entrance to which may be seen, and also the remains of the monks' lavatory.

Passing along we see the Priors', now known as the Green Court, a large open space surrounded with the remains of the domestic buildings of the monastery. The Deanery, previously part of the priors' lodgings, is on the east, and the south was also occupied by the dormitory and refectory, with kitchens. On the west is the Porter's Gate, a Norman structure, with curious ornamentation. The very interesting late *Norman Staircase* leading to the hall of the

Grammar School should be examined. Returning, we traverse the passage north of the chapter-house, and come to the *Lavatory Tower*—erroneously called the baptistry—of Late Norman construction, built by Prior Wibert for supplying the various buildings with water, and adjoining this is the *Library*, which possesses a fine collection of books. A very interesting MS. is the charter of Eadred (949 A.D.), written by Dunstan; there is an ancient portrait of Queen Edgiva (late fourteenth century). The remains of the infirmary and the garden of the monastery may also be seen; and an arched doorway in Palace Street is all that remains of the once famous Archbishop's Palace, which was inhabited by so many distinguished prelates, and the scene of so many events in English history. It was destroyed during the Commonwealth period.

Dimensions

Total length . . .		522 ft. (inside, 514 ft.)
Length of nave . .		178 ft.
Width of nave . .		71 ft.
Length of choir . .		180 ft.
Height of nave . .		80 ft.
Height of central tower .		235 ft.
Height of west tower .		130 ft.

Principal Building Dates

Nave (1378-1411), Prior Chillenden.
Choir (1174-1184), William of Sens and English William.
Choir-screen (1304-1305), Prior d'Estria.
Towers of St. Andrew and Anselm, Prior Ernulf.
Retro-choir and corona (1178-1184), English William.
Crypt, west part (1070-1109), Lanfranc and Ernulf.
Crypt, east part (1178-1184), English William.
Central tower (1495), Prior Goldstone.

1 Doorway to Cloisters from the North Aisle of the Nave
2 Entrance to St. Michael's or Warriors' Chapel
3 Entrances to the Virgin or Deans' Chapel
4 General Entrance to Crypt
5 Doorway to Cloister
6 Archbishop Warham's Mt.
7 Archbishop Peckham's Mt.
8 Staircase to Upper Parts of Church
9 Stairs to Crypt
10 Lady Holand's Monument
12 Stairs through the Walls
13 Organ Screen
14 Archbishop Walters' Mt.
15 Archbishop Reynolds' Mt.
16 Kempe's Monument
17 Stratford's Monument
18 Sudbury's Monument
19 Mepham's Monument
20 Black Prince's Monument
21 Courtney's Monument
22 Chatillon's Monument
23 Theobald's Monument
24 Pole's Monument
25 Dean Wotton's Monument

26 Henry IV.'s Monument
27 Henry IV.'s Chantry Chapel
28 Bourchier's Monument
29 Chichell's Monument
30 Stairs to Crypt, and to the Upper Galleries, etc., of the Transept
31 Font and Circular Room
32 Library
33 Chapter-House
34 Cloisters Square

A Western Porch and Doorway
B South Porch and Doorway
C C Nave
D D South Aisle
E E North Aisle
G North-Western Tower
H South-Western Tower
J South End of Transept
K Martyrdom, or North End of Transept
L Space beneath Great Tower
M Choir
N South Aisle
O North Aisle
P South End of E. Transept
Q North End of E. Transept
R Presbytery
S Altar
T Trinity Chapel
U U Aisles of same
W Becket's Crown
X Anselm's Chapel
Y Vestry
Z Treasury

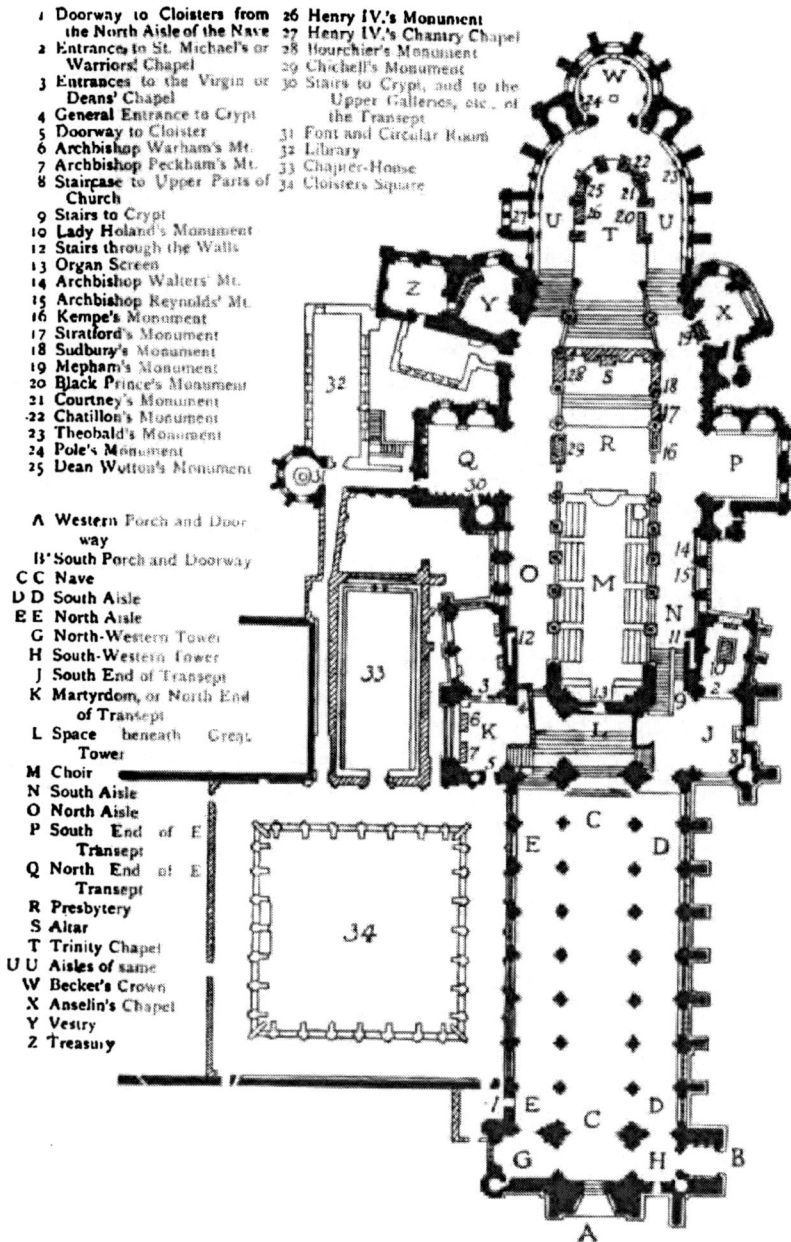

PLAN OF CANTERBURY CATHEDRAL

OTHER CHURCHES AND OBJECTS OF INTEREST

St. Martin's Church, traditionally said to be the oldest church in the kingdom, is certainly of great antiquity. A large number of Roman bricks are built up in the walls. It contains a stone coffin, in which it is said that Queen Bertha lies, the wife of King Ethelbert, converted by Augustine, but this is improbable. The font is Saxon, and it is, according to tradition, which is not very reliable, the font in which Ethelbert was baptised.

St. Augustine's College for Missionaries was formerly the Monastery of St. Augustine. The earliest house was dedicated to SS. Peter and Paul, said to have been founded by Augustine. Dunstan enlarged it, and added the founder's name to the dedication. It became very rich and important. The buildings were destroyed by the Danes, but they arose again in greater glory, and at the dissolution of monasteries the house became a Royal palace. The buildings are well worthy of a visit.

St. Dunstan's Church.

The *West Gate,* built by Archbishop Sudbury, *temp.* Richard II.

Holy Cross Church.

St. Peter's Church.

St. Thomas's Hospital for Entertainment of Pilgrims.

The remains of the old *Chequers Inn* at the south-west corner of Mercery Lane, can be traced, and a portion of it is incorporated in the house known as Grafton House. There are some fine old houses in this street, anciently called *La Merceri,* each stone projecting outwards, so as almost to meet at the top, typical of an old English city street.

WINCHESTER CATHEDRAL

THE city of Winchester, the ancient capital of England, the Caer Gwent of the Britons, the Venta Belgarum of the Romans, the Royal city of Alfred the Great and of William the Conqueror, was a place of vast importance in the annals of England. Under Cnut it was the capital of a kingdom stretching across the seas to Scandinavia, and under the Normans a large part of France was in subjection to it. Here kings were born and Royal weddings celebrated with great pomp in its grand Cathedral. If Royal patronage could have preserved the glories of ancient Winchester, it would have remained the capital of England; but London was the centre of the commercial activity of the country, and in the end Winchester was forced to yield supremacy to its more powerful rival.

Its ecclesiastical history is no less important. A British church here is said to have been destroyed during the Diocletian persecution (A.D. 266) and restored subsequently and dedicated to St. Amphibalus, the martyr. Heathendom returned with the Saxons, until they were converted by St. Berinus, and by the baptism of King Kynegils the triumph of Christianity was assured. He built a new Cathedral, which was again rebuilt by Bishop Ethelbold (980) and consecrated by Dunstan, and this church remained until the Norman builders came with the Conqueror, and began, under his kinsman, Walkelin, to erect that stately fane which we are now about to visit.

Winchester is unlike Salisbury, which was, for the most part, completed in one period of architecture; the former was the work of several builders at different eras. A large part of the Early Norman Cathedral remains; the crypt and transepts and the core of the walls being all Norman work. The eastern aisles and chapels are the work of Bishop de Lucy (1189-1204), built in the Early English style, during the troubled reigns of Richard I. and John; the noble nave was begun by Bishop Edingdon in 1345, and not finished until the time of Waynflete, in 1496, while the dawn of the Reformation saw the building of the side aisles of the presbytery and the east part of the Lady Chapel. The celebrated William of Wykeham, Bishop of Winchester, Chancellor of

85

Edward III., the founder of the Colleges of Winchester and New (Oxford), was the chief architect of the nave.

We approach the Cathedral by an avenue of stately elms, and reach the west door. The best exterior view is obtained from the north side of the close. The tower is low massive Norman work, built in the time of the first Henry, the first tower having fallen, as some said, because William Rufus, the bad king, was buried beneath it. The west front has been recently restored. It is evidently Perpendicular work, and was probably constructed by Bishop Edingdon.

On entering we are struck by the grandeur and impressiveness of this noble nave: Winchester is the largest Cathedral in England. The whole church is 556 feet in length, and nearly 400 feet of magnificent stone-vault is visible from the west doorway. This nave presents some architectural problems. The style is evidently Perpendicular work of the fourteenth and fifteenth centuries, but the builders of that period transformed much of the original Norman work, which still remains in the piers and walls, into that of the later style. They did not rebuild, but transformed, adding new mouldings, casing, and concealing, though not obliterating, the ancient Norman features. We can trace the work of the successive builders. Bishop Edingdon entirely rebuilt the west front and extreme west portion. Examine the two west windows of the north aisle, and compare them with the third, the work of William of Wykeham, and notice their heavy and less graceful appearance. Wykeham was responsible for the complete transformation of the nave, but lived only long enough to complete the south side. Notice the thickness of the piers. This was caused by casing the Norman piers with Perpendicular stone-work, and the balcony above the arches was necessitated by the work of reconstruction. Wykeham's successor, Cardinal Beaufort (uncle of Henry V., the "rich Cardinal," as men called him, one of Joan of Arc's judges, but withal not so base a man as Shakespeare depicts), continued, and Bishop Waynflete, the founder of Magdalen College, Oxford, completed that magnificent structure which we now see. On each side of the west door are bronze statues of Charles I. and James I. by Le Sueur.

On the bosses of the roof we see some armorial bearings; the lily (the arms of Magdalen College) is the device of Waynflete, and the arms of Wykeham, Beaufort, John of Gaunt and Richard II. (white hart chained) are there represented.

The Minstrels' Gallery or tribune, erected by Edingdon, is at the west end of the north aisle, and the oldest piece of iron grill-work in England of very good design is seen in a neighbouring door. The font is Norman work, the sculptures representing scenes from the life of St. Nicholas of Myra, together with doves and the salamander. The chantry chapels on the south side of the nave are extremely interesting : (1) Bishop Edingdon's Chantry (1345-1366), (2) William of Wykeham's Chantry, which is very beautifully designed. We see the effigy of the distinguished prelate with two angels holding the pillow under his head, and three monks at his feet praying for his soul. Some modern statues have been added at the east end and an ingenious cronogram. In the south aisle there are two monuments by Flaxman (Henrietta North and Dr. Warton), and one to the once famous Bishop Hoadley, the founder of the Bangorian controversy, which shows the Magna Charta by the side of the Bible and the cap of liberty contending with the pastoral staff. Some heroes of the Crimean War are also commemorated. There are memorials of Mrs. Montagu, the founder of the "Blue Stockings," and of Jane Austen.

The pulpit is Jacobean, and was brought here from New College, Oxford. The screen separating the nave from the choir is modern. The bronze figures of James I. and Charles I. formed part of an older screen erected by Inigo Jones. Cromwell's soldiers wrought havoc here as in many other churches and cathedrals. They broke the windows and woodwork, desecrated shrines, and paid much attention to this statue of their king.

On entering the choir we find ourselves immediately beneath the tower, which, as we have observed, is Late Norman work, and notice the immense piers which support it. The former tower having fallen, the builders were determined not to have a similar misfortune, and therefore built these piers abnormally strong and massive. The ceiling was erected in the time of Charles I. (1634), and bears medallions of that ill-fated monarch and his queen. Beyond the tower we see the piers and arches and clerestory of the presbytery, which belong to the Late Decorated period. The noble reredos belongs to the fifteenth century, and has been recently restored, the vacant niches being again filled with statuary. In the centre is the figure of our Lord upon the Cross, with the Virgin and St. John. On each side of the altar are SS. Hedda and Ethelwolf, and in the spandrels of the two doorways some ancient sculptures of the life of the Virgin. Above are figures of SS. Swithun and Berinus, and above the doors SS. Benedict and Giles, and SS. Stephen and Lawrence. In the highest row are SS. Peter and Paul and the four Latin doctors. There are numerous smaller statues of kings and prelates. The whole appearance of the screen is very magnificent.

The woodwork of the stalls is the most perfect in the kingdom, and was constructed in the closing years of the thirteenth century. The carved foliage is remarkable for its grace and elegance. Notice the carved heads and the monkeys and other animals playing amidst the branches. The *Misereres* are interesting, and are earlier than the canopies. The pulpit was presented by one "Thomas Silkstede, prior," whose name it bears.

In the centre of the presbytery we see the supposed tomb of William Rufus, who was accidentally killed by an arrow when hunting in the New Forest. His ashes, however, do not rest beneath this stone, but are preserved in the chests above the screen, together with the bones of Canute and some Saxon prelates. Cromwell's soldiers rifled the tomb and found therein a chalice, which sacred vessel was usually placed in the coffins of bishops and therefore could not have belonged to the grave of the red-haired monarch. Bishop Fox (1500-1520) did much for this part of the Cathedral. He placed the glass in the east window, which has been much modified. Glass painting at this period had attained its highest perfection as an art, and in its original condition this window must have been unrivalled. The stone screens on each side of the presbytery were also erected by Fox, and six mortuary chests containing the bones of Saxon kings and bishops are placed upon them. Amongst the bones of other illustrious men are deposited in a mingled state the mortal remains of Kynegils, Ethelwolf, the father of Alfred the Great, Egbert, Canute, and many others. The soldiers of Cromwell played havoc with these bones of kings, and scattered them about the Cathedral, hence it is impossible to be certain that these chests actually contain the mortal remains of those whose names they bear. The vault of the presbytery is wooden, and the bosses are interesting.

Behind the reredos is the feretory or place for the shrines of patron saints, with a stone platform at its east end on which formerly stood the shrines of St. Swithun[1] and St. Berinus.

---

[1] St. Swithun became bishop in 837; he was "a diligent builder of churches in places where there were none before, and a repairer of those that had been destroyed before." In modern times his name is best known as a weather prophet; according to the tradition that if it is fine or wet on St. Swithun's day (July 15th) the same weather will last for the next forty days. The legend arose from the moving of his body from the lowly grave in the churchyard to its golden shrine in the Cathedral being delayed on account of continued rain.

WINCHESTER CATHEDRAL

Pilgrims used to pass in procession before these shrines along the stone passage. A collection of fragments of carved work is shown here.

We now visit the north transept and find ourselves in the earliest portion of the Cathedral, built by Bishop Walkelin in the old Norman style. The windows were inserted in the Decorated period, and the ceiling belongs to the last century. The transepts have aisles on the east and west sides and also at each end, over which is a gallery. This is not common in England. At St. Alban's there is a similar arrangement, and in several Normandy churches. The Norman work of the transepts is of two periods. The earlier part by Walkelin (1070-1098) is distinguished by the smaller piers and plain groined vaulting; the later (1107) by the ribbed vaulting and larger piers. When we visit Ely Cathedral we shall notice the similarity of design, the transepts of that building having been erected by Simeon, Walkelin's brother. Under the organ-loft is the Chapel of the Holy Sepulchre. Notice the curious mural paintings representing the Passion of our Lord which date from the thirteenth century, and the Decorated canopies built against the Norman piers.

We now enter the north aisle of the presbytery and proceed to the extreme eastern portion of the Cathedral. Here seven chantries and chapels are seen which record the memory of illustrious prelates. " How much power and ambition under half-a-dozen stones ! I own I grow to look on tombs as lasting mansions, instead of observing them for curious pieces of architecture," wrote Walpole. Almost all the east end was built by Bishop Godfrey de Lucy (1189-1204) at the beginning of the Early English period and is of exquisite design. The north chapel is called that of the Guardian Angels, and is so named from figures of angels in the vaulting. There is a bronze figure of the Earl of Portland here, the treasurer of Charles I. Notice the figure holding a heart. It represents Bishop Ethelmar, half-brother of Henry III., who died in Paris but directed that his heart should be conveyed to this Cathedral.

The Lady Chapel has work of divers periods—north and south walls Early English (De Lucy), east wall and window with small eastern parts of north and south walls Perpendicular (Prior Hunton, 1470-1498, and Prior Silkstede, 1498-1524). The rebuses of these two priors on the vault are curious: T. *Hun* and a ton ('Thomas Hunton), and i and *Por* for Prior; T. *Silk* and a horse

(Thomas Silkstede). Mural paintings by the latter prior representing the legends of the Virgin adorn the walls. The panelling is the work of Bishop Fox.

The south chapel (Early English) is the Chantry of Bishop Langton, who died of the plague in 1500, just before he was translated to the Archbishopric of Canterbury. The woodwork of the stalls is very beautiful. The pikes of Cromwell's soldiers wrought havoc here, and we notice that just above the height they could reach with their weapons the woodwork is uninjured. Mediæval artists were fond of puns and rebuses, and here we have Langton's name represented by a *long* (or musical) note with a *ton*, and a *vine* and *ton* for Winton or Winchester. Winton is also represented by a dragon coming from a ton, referring to Solomon's warning against the wine that is red which biteth like a serpent, etc. An object of much interest is preserved here—Queen Mary's chair upon which she sat when she was married to Philip of Spain in the Lady Chapel. On that occasion there was much feasting and rejoicing in Winchester, though the nation liked not the Spanish marriage, and much ill came to England through that ill-starred connection. De Lucy's tomb in the centre of the retro-choir looks upon the noble work which he built for his beloved Cathedral. On the north of the central aisle is the Chantry of Waynflete, the founder of Magdalen College, Oxford ; on the south that of Cardinal Beaufort. Both were much injured by the soldiers. Between these is the effigy of a knight in armour, Sir A. de Gavaston, the father of the favourite of Edward II.

Notice the wall at the back of the feretory, with its beautiful tabernacle work of Decorated period, under which images once stood. The names of the worthies appear below. " The Holy Hole " formerly led to the crypt but has now been closed. On the north side of this wall is Bishop Gardiner's Chantry, who was the leader of the Roman Catholic party at the Reformation and was styled the " Hammer of Heretics." He took a leading part in the Marian persecutions. On the south side is the Chantry of of Bishop Fox (1500-1528), the founder of Corpus Christi College, Oxford, who bore the pelican as a device.

The south wall of the south aisle of the presbytery is Late Perpendicular work. Another instance of heart burial is recorded on the wall opposite, that of Bishop Nicholas of Ely (1280), and an inscription tells of the burial of Richard, son of William the Conqueror, who was killed while hunting in the New Forest.

We now enter the south transept, the architectural features of which are similar to those of the north transept. Silkstede's Chantry should be visited. This worthy prior loved a rebus, and here carved a skein of *silk* to represent his name, also the letters THOMAS appear on the screen, the MA being formed differently from the rest to represent his patroness, MARY the Virgin. Isaac Walton's tomb is here, the author of the *Angler*. There are some good mural paintings. The monument of Bishop Wilberforce forms a conspicuous object in the transept. Adjoining Silkstede's Chapel is the Venerable Chapel, with a fine screen. On the west side are the chapter-room and the old treasury. Passing through the chamber on the south we enter the slype.

The library has some treasures, notably a Vulgate of the twelfth century

The Cathedral
West Front.

and some valuable MSS. The crypt is entirely Norman work, except the east part, which is Early English. The cloisters and old chapter-house were destroyed in 1563. The Deanery was formerly the home of the prior; its entrance belongs to the time of

Henry III., and the hall within the house to the fifteenth century. Over the dean's stables is a long room which was probably the guest-house for pilgrims; rude carvings can be seen on the beams of the roof probably made by the pilgrims.

DIMENSIONS

Total length, 556 ft.; length of nave, 262 ft.; width of nave and aisles, 88 ft.; height of vault, 78 ft.; area, 53, 480 sq. ft.

PRINCIPAL BUILDING DATES

1079-1093—Transepts, crypt and cores of piers and wall; 1120—central tower rebuilt; 1202—retro-choir and eastern chapels; 1320—presbytery rebuilt; 1360—west front and two bays of nave; 1394-1486—nave reconstructed; 1487—east end of Lady Chapel; 1520—alterations in presbytery by Bishop Fox.

Other objects of interest in Winchester—

The *School*, founded by William of Wykeham: the *Hospital of St. Cross*, founded by Henry de Blois in 1136; *Hyde Abbey*, the resting-place of the body of Alfred the Great; the *County Hall*, with the so-called Round Table of King Arthur; *Wolvesey Castle*, the ancient episcopal palace.

A Central Western Porch and
    Doorway
B B Side West Doors. Entrances
    to North and South Aisles
    of Nave
C Nave
D North Aisle
E South Aisle
F Choir
G Presbytery
H Sanctuary
J North Transept
K South Transept
L South Aisle of Choir
M North Aisle of Choir
J N Retro-Choir and Aisles
O Feretory
P Lady Chapel
Q Site of Cloisters
R Bishop Langton's Chapel
S Chapel of the Guardian Angels

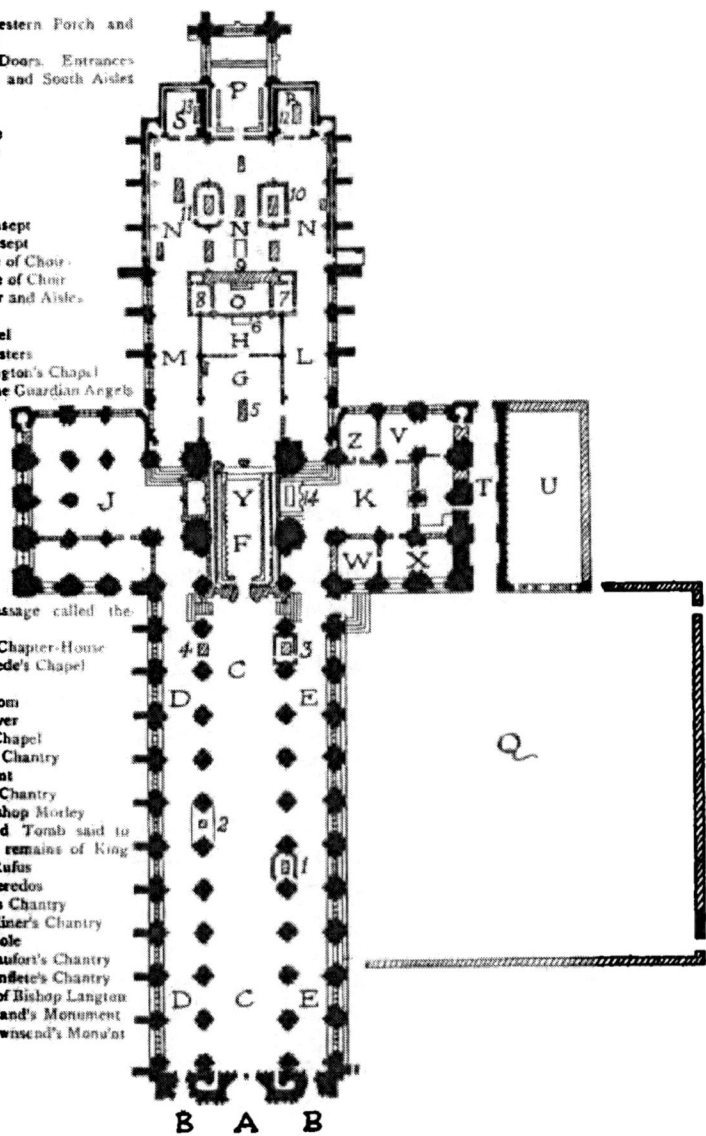

T Arched Passage called the
    Slype
U Site of Old Chapter-House
V Prior Silkstede's Chapel
W Treasury
X Chapter-Room
Y Central-Tower
Z Venerable Chapel
1 Wykeham's Chantry
2 Norman Font
3 Edingdon's Chantry
4 Tomb of Bishop Morley
5 Coffin-shaped Tomb said to
    cover the remains of King
    William Rufus
6 Altar and Reredos
7 Bishop Fox's Chantry
8 Bishop Gardiner's Chantry
9 The Holy Hole
10 Cardinal Beaufort's Chantry
11 Bishop Waynflete's Chantry
12 Altar Tomb of Bishop Langton
13 Earl of Portland's Monument
14 Sir Isaac Townsend's Monu'nt

PLAN OF WINCHESTER CATHEDRAL

CHICHESTER CATHEDRAL

CHICHESTER, like most of our cathedral cities, has a long history dating back to the time of the Romans. The Roman town stood on the line of the road now known as Stane Street, and seems to have been a populous place where trade was carried on, and not merely a military station. A marble slab discovered in 1713 (preserved at Goodwood) bears an inscription which tells us much of the Roman city and runs as follows: *Neptuni et Minervæ templum pro salute domus divinæ ex auctoritate Tib. Claud. Cogidubni r. leg. aug. in Brit. collegium fabror. et qui in eo a sacris sunt d. s. d. donante aream Pudente Pudentini fil.* Much has been made of this inscription, that there was a temple here dedicated to Neptune and Minerva, that there was a large body of craftsmen who built this temple, and that Chichester was the seat of King Cogidubnus mentioned by Tacitus as possessing independent authority in Britain.

When the Pagan Saxons under Ælla came they destroyed the place. "Ælle and Cissa," says the chronicle, "beset Anderida [1] and slew all that were therein, nor was there afterwards one Briton left," and overran the coast, establishing the kingdom of the South Saxons, or Sussex. Then Cissa, having captured the old Roman city, made it the capital of his kingdom, calling the place *Cissan-caestre*, or the fortress of Cissa, now corrupted to Chichester. This was at the close of the fifth century. Shut in by the great forest of Anderida, these South Saxons retained their Paganism long after the advent of Augustine and the conversion of other parts of the country. St. Wilfrid was shipwrecked on their coast, but they fiercely attacked the crew of the vessel, which escaped with difficulty from the perilous coast owing to the prayers of the saint. Thirty years later he returned and converted them to Christianity. A famine raged owing to long draught. He taught them to fish in the sea, and so won their confidence, and on the day when their chiefs came to be baptised rain fell and the famine ceased. The Island of Selsey or Seal's Island was given to the saint, where he founded a monastery and became the

[1] The modern Pevensey.

first bishop of the South Saxons. Until the conquest Selsey remained the seat of the bishopric. The last Saxon prelate, Ethelric, though he was a learned, and moreover a very aged man, received harsh treatment from William I. He was deprived of his bishopric and imprisoned. Then came Stigand, who moved the bishop's throne to Chichester, and made the minster Church of St. Peter's Monastery his Cathedral. The waves of the sea now roll over the site of the Early Saxon church. Ralph de Luffa, the third Norman prelate (1091-1123), began the building of the present Cathedral. Fire played havoc with the newly-erected church in 1114, four years after its completion, but Ralph again set to work to restore it. It was consecrated in 1148, twenty-five years after his death. He was a noble bishop, and accomplished much for his diocese and for the Church of England in the time of the tyranny of Norman kings. Fire again raged in 1186, which prepared the way for the alterations and improvements of the transitional builders who were developing the beauties of English Gothic. Bishop Seffrid, the second who bore that name, was the director of the work, which shows the purist style of the twelfth century. The triforium, the upper storey of the western towers (the present north-west tower is a modern imitation of the south-west tower) and the lower storey of the central tower are mainly his work. This bishop had the doubtful honour of crowning King John. Bishop Neville (1224-1244) designed and began to build the spire, and the Lady Chapel was partly constructed by Bishop Gilbert de St. Leofard (1288-1304). John de Langton, bishop (1305-1336), who was a skilful architect, finished the retro-choir and the south wing of the transept. By this time the Cathedral had assumed much of its present form. The apsidal chapels in the choir had been made to assume the more English form of square-ended buildings. The thirteenth-century bishops who accomplished all this excellent work were remarkable men. Bishop Simon Fitz Robert (1204-1207) obtained many benefactions for his see, and grants of stone from the Isle of Purbeck for the beautifying of his church. Richard Poore, the noble builder of Salisbury, was here for two years, and Bishop Neville worked hard during his episcopacy for his church, and built a palace for his see in London which stood on the site of Lincoln's Inn. St. Richard de Wych was an excellent bishop (1245-1253), who reformed his diocese with some severity, and ordered his flock to contribute liberally to the building fund of his Cathedral. "St. Richard's Pence" afterwards became a fruitful source of income. Bishop

Gilbert de St. Leofard followed in his steps, and, as we have said, built the main parts of the Lady Chapel, which is of Decorated style. The work of the fourteenth century was rather that of adornment than of construction. We find Bishop Langton (1305-1337), the suppressor of the Templars, inserting a beautiful window in the south transept, and building the chapter-house. A little later a noble reredos was erected behind the altar, the choir stalls added, and some changes made in the window tracery. The founder of Merton College Library, William Read, was bishop here in 1369-1385. Lollardism was rampant in the diocese, and Bishop Robert Rede (1397-1415) took strong steps to uproot the obnoxious teaching. The beginning of the fifteenth century saw arising the detached bell tower, called Raymond's Tower, the only existing detached belfry in the kingdom. Some of the Bishops of Chichester at this time fared ill. Bishop Moleyns (1446-1450), who helped Henry VI. to marry Margaret of Anjou, was murdered by some sailors at Portsmouth, and his successor, Peacocke (1450-1459), was tried on account of his supposed heretical opinions and deprived. Bishop Storey (1478-1503) was the builder of the famous Market Cross and the Grammar School. Bishop Sherbourne (1508-1536) who favoured not the " new Religion," employed the Bernardi, an Italian family who had previously settled in Flanders, to decorate his church, and we shall see some of their work in the Cathedral. Then came the trouble of the Reformation period, when altars were destroyed, shrines pillaged of their gold and ornaments, and the whole church ransacked of its treasures. Further spoliation and destruction were wrought by the Parliamentary soldiers under Waller, who " plundered the Cathedral, seized upon the vestments and ornaments of the church, together with the consecrated plate serving for the altar; they left not so much as a cushion for the pulpit, nor a chalice for the Blessed Sacraments; the common soldiers broke down the organs, and dashing the pipes with their pole-axes, scoffingly said, 'Hark, how the organs go!' . . . On the Tuesday following, after the sermon, possessed and transported by a Bacchanalian fury, they ran up and down the church with their swords drawn, defacing the monuments of the dead, hacking and hewing the seats and stalls, and scraping the painted walls. Sir William Waller and the rest of the commanders standing by as spectators and approvers of their barbarous impieties." Bishop King was prelate at this time; his palace and goods were destroyed, and he was treated with cruel indignity. In the seventeenth-century the north-west tower fell, and the central tower was

Chichester

so insecure that the upper part of the spire was removed and rebuilt by Wren. Since then several attempts at reparation have been made. At length in 1860 a terrible disaster befell, and the central tower and spire collapsed. It was rebuilt by Sir G. Scott with much care, and may be said to be an exact copy of the old, and in addition to other improvements the north-west tower has been rebuilt.

THE EXTERIOR

The best views may be obtained from the city wall to the north, also from West Street and East Street, and a fine distant prospect is observed from the Goodwood Downs. We will begin our inspection as usual with the *West Front*, which consists of a gable with windows and porch, flanked by two towers. The upper part of the north-west tower is a recent construction, made in imitation of the south-west tower, and built on the ruins of the former tower. The south tower is of Norman workmanship, the upper part being Early English, and also the plain and heavy buttresses at the south-west corner. The basement and next storey are part of the original work of Bishop Ralph, and the rest of Bishop Seffrid II. The west porch is plain and deep, with double buttresses at the corners. The doorway consists of a wide arch, under which are two smaller ones divided by a single clustered column. These have been restored in imitation of the ancient design. The interior of the porch is very beautiful Early English work, the arcading of quatrefoils being very effective. The monuments have evidently been placed there in later times. Above the porch are three Early English windows, and above these a large modern window, and in the gable are two small Early English windows. The cross above is modern.

The *Bell Tower*, the only instance in England of a detached belfry, though not unusual abroad, is a massive and plain building, 120 feet high. The upper storey is octagonal and low, and resembles the great west tower of Ely, but is much inferior. Both these towers were built about the same time, at the beginning of the fifteenth century, and are in the Perpendicular style. The north side of the nave exhibits in the clerestory the round-headed windows of the original Norman church. The parapet is fourteenth-century work. Flying buttresses connect the clerestory with the outer wall. The windows of the chapels are Early Decorated, and were erected during the reign of Edward III. One of them is modern. The *North*

Porch is Early English work, and the dog-tooth ornament is observable in the arches. It has a parvise. The *North Transept* on west side has some of the original Norman wall and Norman windows, and on the north end there are thirteenth-century buttresses with octagonal turrets, a large window and a rose window over it. On the east side there are some Early English windows. Proceeding eastward we pass the Chapels of St. Edmund and St. John Baptist, of Early English design, with some Perpendicular windows, the same style prevailing in the presbytery. Flying buttresses support the main walls. The old Norman church ended in an apse, and traces of the curve can still be observed, and other remains of twelfth-century work can be seen. Two of the windows are Perpendicular in style, but have been much restored. The low Lady Chapel projects at the east end. Two western bays are twelfth-century work, the two eastern bays being added by Bishop Gilbert de St. Leofard at the end of the thirteenth century, and are Late Decorated. Much restoration has been found necessary here. Early English work prevails in the chapel on the south side. The south wall of the choir aisle has several points of interest and several styles of architecture are shown here. A consecration cross can be seen in one of the bays. The south transept is very similar to the north, and on the west of it is the sacristy. Norman walls are on the north and east, and Early English on south and west. On the south side of the Cathedral are the *Cloisters*, which are curiously shaped. The Paradise is not square, the east walk being longer than the west. These cloisters are fifteenth-century work, having Perpendicular windows and flat roof. The south side of the nave is interesting, and resembles somewhat the north side. The arches of the windows in the aisles are Early Decorated, the tracery is modern. In the fourteenth century the buttresses were strengthened and enlarged, the parapet added. The Norman wall and windows remain in the clerestory, though later tracery has been inserted in two of these. The south porch leading to the west cloister has been much restored. The doorway in the south-west tower is Norman, and is adorned with chevron moulding, and beautifully designed. The window over it is also of the same date.

THE INTERIOR

The interior is more imposing than the exterior. The best view is perhaps obtained from north-east corner of the nave. The width of the nave is the first peculiarity which we notice. It has double aisles on each side of the nave, a peculiarity shared only with Manchester, and some parish churches, such as Abingdon, Taunton and Coventry. There are some grand effects of light and shade, and the nave is well proportioned, and has a quiet dignity which is all its own. There are eight circular arches, supported by seven flat piers, isolated and flanked by half columns of cylindrical character with plain capitals and cable moulding. Purbeck marble is extensively used in the string-courses and capitals of the vaulting shafts. The triforium preserves its Norman character. Here are the Norman circular arches, containing two smaller arches resting on single shafts. The surface of the stone in the head is hatched as at Rochester. There is a striking analogy between Chichester and Peterborough, both in the nave and choir. Both were destroyed by fire, and both rebuilt about the same time. The main arcade and triforium are the work of Bishop Ralph de Luffa (1091-1124).

Bishop Seffrid II. (1180-1204) rebuilt the clerestory, and made it loftier than the triforium. The style is Early English. It will be noticed that the middle arch of the windows is round and higher than the side arches, which are pointed. The windows are separated by small shafts of Petworth marble, and the capitals are carved with leaves of palm trees. The Cathedral is dedicated to the Holy Trinity, and the builders seem to have wished to express symbolically the threefold nature of the Deity by the triplicity of the work. Triple clustered shafts appear everywhere. The vaulting is of stone, and is a little later than Seffrid's work. Alarmed by the fires, the architect determined to build a stone and chalk roof instead of wood. In the sixteenth century this vaulting was painted in gaudy colours by Bishop Sherbourne.

Two storeys of the south-west tower are original Norman work, with rude cushion capitals, and formed part of the first church finished by Bishop Ralph. This is used as a baptistry, and has a modern font, an imitation of that at Shoreham.

In the *South Aisle* are the Chapels of St. George and St. Clement. The latter has been restored in memory of the last good bishop, Durnford. The figures placed in the old wall arcade are SS. Anselm, Clement and Alphege. The old piscina and aumbrey remain, as also in the other chapel. The chapels were added in the second half of the thirteenth century. The *North Aisle* resembles the south. Here were the Chapels of St. Anne, St.

Theobald or the Four Virgins, and SS. Thomas and Edmund.
The screen, pulpit and lectern are all modern, and also the glass.
The *monuments* here are :—in the south aisle, Bishop Durnford
(1895), and Captain Cromwell (Flaxman) ; and in the north aisle,
Poet Collins, Richard Fitz-Alan, Earl of Arundel and his wife
[the earl was a supporter of the Duke of Gloucester, uncle of
Richard II., and was beheaded in 1397], an unknown lady, sup-
posed to be Countess of Arundel (1270). This tomb is of
Decorated design, and is beautifully executed.

The *North Transept* was once the Parish Church of St. Peter
the Great. The main walls are part of Bishop Ralph's Norman
church, and there are Norman windows on the west and arches of
the same style on the east. These open into the old Chapel of St.
John Baptist and St. Edmund, which has now been converted into
the *Library*. The north and east walls are Early English, the
vaulting is very beautiful, the ribs being ornamented with zigzag.
The library has some early MSS., but is not particularly rich in its
treasures. Entering the north choir aisle we see the monuments of
Bishop Storey (1503), the builder of the Market Cross ; Bishop
King (1670), who suffered much from the Parliamentary soldiers ;
Carleton (1685) ; Grove (1691) ; Otter (1840), and an early
slab of thirteenth century representing a heart burial. Formerly an
inscription could be deciphered which told in Norman French:
" Here lies the heart of Maud." At the end of this aisle is the Chapel
of St. Katherine. This eastern end of the aisle is all Early English
work. Here are preserved the paintings of the Bishops of Chichester
and Kings of England made by Bernardi, which were much injured
by the soldiers and restored by an indifferent artist. The *Retro-
Choir* is early thirteenth century, and has a fine vault which in style
resembles that of some French churches. The piers are curious,
and the shafts are further detached from the main piers than in any
other known example. The capitals are most beautifully carved.
The triforium is ornamented with rich tracery and carving and
clustered shafts of Purbeck. It somewhat resembles Ely, the work
of Bishop Hotham in 1235. The clerestory is later. Here
stood the magnificent shrine of St. Richard, the glory of Chichester,
and the resort of pilgrims. This St. Richard de la Wyche, who
was the friend of Becket, died in 1245. He was remarkable for his
zeal and charity. On his death his body was found wrapped in a
shirt of horse hair and bound with rings of iron. Miracles being
reported to have taken place at his tomb, he was canonised. The

Lady Chapel in Norman times extended two bays eastward, and was extended by two bays by Bishop Gilbert de St. Leofard at the end of the thirteenth century (1288-1305). It was formerly used as the library, and Willis speaks of it as "having nothing to recommend it except a good collection of books." The east window has five lights, and all the windows have been restored.

The vaulting is good and the fittings are modern. In the vault is a beautifully-painted design by Bernardi (1519). The *South Choir Aisle* resembles the north. The Chapel of St. Mary Magdalene is at the east end, which has been restored. St. Richard's head was preserved here as a precious relic. Some modern paintings here represent scenes from the life of St. Richard and our Lord. Passing by the door into the cloisters we see on the north the tombs of Dean Hook (1875), and Bishop Daye (1552); and on the south, Bishop Sherbourne (1536). Here are two carved panels of very early character, which legendary lore tells were brought from Selsey when the bishop's stool was transferred to Chichester. It is quite possible that they

The Presbytery.

are Saxon, and the style of art has a Byzantine appearance. The subjects are the Raising of Lazarus and Our Lord at Bethany with Mary and Martha. A door on the left leads to the vicar's vestry, and then we come to the *South Transept*, which resembles the north. The walls on both west and east are Norman. On the south is a very beautiful window inserted by Bishop Langton (1305-1337), one of the finest Early

Decorated windows in England. The glass is modern and hideous. The paintings here on the back of the choir stalls are interesting. They are the work of Theodore Bernardi, an Italian artist, who settled in Flanders and afterwards came to England, and with his son lived at Chichester. Bishop Sherbourne employed him to decorate his Cathedral. The paintings here represent the foundation of the see at Selsey by Caedwalla, and the foundation of four prebends by the bishop and Henry VIII. The soldiers much injured the paintings, which were restored by Bishop Mawson, who employed an inferior artist and thus destroyed much of their merit. The saintly Bishop Richard has a monument here. On the east is the Chapel of St. Pantaleon, a Nicomedian martyr, which retains its piscina. It is now used as the canons' vestry. On the west is the entrance to the *Sacristy*, a large room, now used as a music room, with a vaulted ceiling. Above this is the old consistory court where heretics were tried. Lollards were often examined and condemned here, and behind the seats there is a sliding door leading to what is commonly known as the Lollards' prison. It was probably either a treasury or evidence chamber. Langton's tomb, the builder of the beautiful window, is below that fine structure. He died in 1336.

The *Choir* is long and narrow and has been much restored. The design is Early English, though much of the old Norman piers was retained. The carving in the triforium is very beautiful. The screen is modern. The stalls were erected in Bishop Sherbourne's time, and are of carved oak and inferior to many. The dean's and precentor's stalls are new. The old throne was much defaced by the soldiers under Waller. A new one was given by Bishop Mawson (1740-1754) and this has given place to a modern one. The reredos and altar are modern.

DIMENSIONS

Total length	393 ft.
Length of nave	155 ft.
Width of nave	90 ft.
Height of nave	61 ft.
Length of choir . . .	115 ft.
Length of transept . . .	131 ft.
Height of spire . . .	277 ft.
Area	28,000 sq. ft

BUILDING DATES

Norman (Twelfth Century)—South-west tower and part of west front, piers of nave and triforium, part of transepts, parts of walls of choir aisles and piers of choir, and parts of Lady Chapel. The upper part of south-west tower late twelfth century.

Early English (Thirteenth Century)—Remodelling of the nave and choir, chapels, porches, and Lady Chapel begun.

Decorated (Fourteenth Century) — Retro-choir and south window in south transept. Lady Chapel finished.

Perpendicular (Fifteenth Century)—Bell tower, choir walls, paintings, cloisters.

Modern—Tower and spire and north-west tower.

SALISBURY CATHEDRAL

SALISBURY is one of the finest examples of Early English architecture in England. It was built for the most part in one style and at one period, and therefore does not present to us that varied conglomeration of the art of different ages which we see in most of our ecclesiastical edifices. The story of its building is full of interest, and we must look for the original home of the Salisbury diocese on the wind-swept fortified heights of Old Sarum, where Bishop Herman fixed his episcopal seat in Early Norman times. The early history of the sees of Southern England is somewhat complicated. When the Story of the Cross was first proclaimed here, and the savage Saxons became Christianised, the whole of Wessex and Sussex were comprised in the see of Dorchester, a small village in Oxfordshire. This huge bishopric was then divided into the two sees of Winchester and Sherborne. Then Selsey (afterwards Chichester) was taken out of Winchester, which diocese was again divided, and Ramsbury formed. Out of the diocese of Sherborne, Wells and Crediton were constituted, and then Bishop Herman in 1058 united the sees of Ramsbury and Sherborne, and formed the diocese of Salisbury, fixing his seat at Old Sarum, the Saxon town of Searobyrig. On this hill fortress seven prelates ruled, amongst whom were the saintly Osmund (1078-1099), who completed the first Cathedral, of which no stone remains, and compiled the famous "Use of Sarum," the model of all service-books in the South of England; Bishop Roger (1102-1107), a most powerful prelate and castle-builder; Jocelyn de Bohun (1142-1184), the opponent of Becket; Hubert Walter (1188-1193), a crusading bishop, the companion of Richard Cœur de Lion; Herbert le Poer or Poore (1194-1216), and then his brother or kinsman, Richard Poore (1217-1228), the founder of the present Cathedral. Various reasons are assigned for the transference of the see. Old Sarum lacked water. It was a lofty, barren height, swept by every wind of heaven, and "when the wind did blow they could not hear the priest say Mass." But the real reason was the quarrel between the clergy and the soldiers who guarded the castle of the king. On one occasion, when during Rogationtide the ecclesiastics went in solemn procession to the Church of St. Martin, on their return they found the gates closed against them, and had to remain without shelter during a long winter's night. Similar insults frequently being offered them, the bishop and his clergy determined to seek a new home. Whither should they go? Legends tell us of the arrow shot at random from the heights of Old Sarum, of the bishop's mysterious dream, wherein the Virgin appeared and told him to seek for the spot Mœrfield, of his talking with the Abbess of Wilton, and her reply that he had plenty of land of his own without seeking to spoil her. At any rate the bishop gave the land for his new Cathedral out of his own domain, and he began to build the stately edifice which we now see. The first stones were laid on the feast of St. Vitalis, April 28, 1220; one Elias of Dereham was the master-mason, and the work progressed rapidly until Bishop Poore was translated to Durham in 1228. There his "Chapel of the Nine Altars" attests to the love of building which he acquired at Salisbury, and the similarity of the styles of architecture. His successors continued to build with much zeal, and in the time of Bishop Giles de Bridport (1257-1262) the church was consecrated by Archbishop Boniface, of Savoy, in the presence of Henry III. and his court. The church was now complete. Only forty-six years were spent in its building—a marvellous achievement. The monastic buildings were begun by Bishop Walter Delawyle (1262-1270). As yet the tower was not so high as it is now, and there was no spire; but the fourteenth century had scarcely begun before the two upper storeys were added, and the lofty spire, which forms such a glorious crown of this beautiful structure. It was the work of the mason, Richard of Farleigh, who was at the same time engaged on work at Bath and Reading. In the time of Bishop Wyvil (1329-1375) Edward III. granted permission to fortify the close, and to use the stones from the Cathedral of Old Sarum for this purpose. Hence in the walls which surround the close we see Norman carvings which once adorned the ancient edifice. Of this Bishop Fuller says that "it is hard to say whether he was more dunce than dwarf, more unlearned or unhandsome, insomuch that Walsingham tells us that had the Pope ever *seen* him (as he no doubt *felt* him in his large fees) he would never have conferred the place upon him." His curious brass tells of his recovering for his see the Castle of Sherborne and the Chase of Bere, of which the bishopric had been wrongfully despoiled. Prominent among its bishops was Robert Hallam (1408-1417), who was present at the Council of Constance, which saw the burning of Huss and Jerome of Prague, and strove hard to avert their fate. Bishop Ayscough (1438-1450) was murdered by the rebel followers of Jack Cade at Edingdon. Bishop Beauchamp (1450-1481) built the great hall of the palace, and his chantry (destroyed by Wyatt). Here one of the unhappy Woodvilles, brother of Edward IV.'s queen, was bishop (1482-1485), and he had the unhappiness of seeing his brother-in-law, the Duke of Buckingham, beheaded at Salisbury, just before the battle of Bosworth (*cf.* Shakespeare's *Richard III.*). Cardinal Campeggio was bishop just before the Reformation, and after Wolsey's disgrace was deprived of his see. There are no records to show what damage was done during that stormy period, but probably the niches of the west front were deprived of many of their images at this time, the windows broken, and the treasury shorn of its plate and relics. One of the best of the Salisbury bishops was Jewel, the author of the *Apology of the Church of England* (1560-1571), who built the library over the cloisters. During the Civil War Ludlow's soldiers were quartered here, and garrisoned the belfry, but they seem to have behaved with extraordinary mildness. The Cathedral had powerful protectors, and when some of Waller's men carried off some church goods, the Parliament ordered that these should be restored. Bishop Seth Ward (1667-1688), one of the founders of the Royal Society, did much to repair his Cathedral, and restored the palace, which was ruinous, having been bought by one Van Ling from the Parliament, and partly converted into cottages. Unhappily the arch-destroyer, Wyatt, was turned loose on the building at the end of the eighteenth century, who wrought vast and irreparable destruction, which it is pitiable to see. Since his day there have been many efforts to obliterate his work; vast sums have been spent, and the Cathedral restored to much of its ancient glory and beauty.

THE EXTERIOR

As we enter the Cathedral precincts we are at once struck with the wondrous beauty and charm of this peaceful close, which surrounds, with its circling green sward, the magnificent Gothic pile. All writers have vied with each other in singing the praises

of this grand achievement of Gothic art, and nowhere can we gain a better view of the grand proportions of this church, with its noble spire, than from the south-east or north-east corner of the close. Around us are the venerable walls of the fortifications, erected in the time of Edward III., who granted a license for this purpose, and gave leave to the bishop to pull down the walls of Old Sarum, in order to provide the stone. Embedded in the wall we find some stones with Norman carving, which bespeak their former location in the Norman buildings on the old stronghold of Sarum. The grand *Spire* is the highest in England (400 feet). The tower on which it stands is Early English as far as the first storey; the two higher storeys were added in the early part of the fourteenth century, and are Early Decorated. The whole structure is magnificent. On each side there is an arcade, richly canopied, and having double windows. At each angle there is a turret, with a small crocketed spire, and from a mass of richly-decorated pinnacles the great spire rises. In the capstone still remains a small leaden box containing a fragment of decayed silk or fine linen, doubtless a relic of the Virgin. The spire has sometimes caused anxiety, and has been strengthened by metal bands, but the Early English substructure has sustained with wonderful constancy the weight of the two higher storeys and the spire which the somewhat venturesome builders of the time of Edward III. forced them to bear.

The *West Front* it is the fashion to abuse. It has been censured for its " parcellings " and " raggedness." Professor Freeman denies the honesty of such fronts, because they extend beyond the walls of the aisles and nave, and are what the professors of "true principles " call " shams." Such criticisms fail to recognise the real object of such screens, which was to set forth a chronicle in stone of the history of the church, and people the niches with figures of the great men and benefactors, the saints and heroes, whose memories are here enshrined. It is no " sham," and we must try to imagine it as it really was, not shorn of half its beauties, bereft of its images, or supplied with the works of modern art which do not always harmonise with their surroundings. Inferior it may be to the fronts of Wells or Lincoln, but it still possesses many merits, and is certainly impressive. It was the last completed portion of the Cathedral, as in the mouldings we see the ball-flower which is the sign-manual of the Decorated period. There is a central portion with a gable and buttresses, and a compartment on each side flanked by small towers with small spires. There are five storeys.

In the lowest there is a triple porch, deeply recessed with canopies. The west window is large, and is a triplet divided by slender clustered shafts. There are about 100 niches which have been filled with some of the best examples of modern art by Mr. Redfern. Above all we see our Lord in glory, to whom all the others are offering their praise.

Mr. Armfield in his *Legend of Christian Art* gives us the following detailed account of the various figures in the west front and the meaning of their several emblems :—

The Tier of Angels.—The celestial hierarchy have been divided into three classes, each class containing three grades. The first class consists of Seraphim, Cherubim and Thrones ; the second of Dominions, Powers and Authorities ; the third of Principalities, Archangels and Angels, Angels being thus the lowest order of celestial creation.

The Tier of Old Testament Worthies.—David, with the harp ; Moses, carrying the Tables of the Law ; Abraham, with the knife in his hand ; Noah, with the ark in his left hand ; Samuel ; Solomon, with the sceptre in his right hand and the Church in his left hand.

The Tier of Apostles.—St. Jude, with the halberd ; St. Simon Zelotes, with the saw ; St. Andrew, with the cross ; St. Thomas, with the builder's square ; St. Peter, with the keys in his right hand ; St. Paul, with the sword in his right hand ; St. Luke and St. John. The figures of St. Peter and St. Paul are restorations of ancient figures which had been mutilated. St. James the Less, with the fuller's club ; St. James the Greater, with the pilgrim's staff ; St. Bartholomew, with the knife ; St. Matthias, with the lance.

The Tier of the Doctors, Virgins and Martyrs.—St. Ambrose, Bishop of Milan ; St. Jerome, in a Cardinal's hat ; St. Gregory the Great, with the tiara of the Papacy ; St. Augustine, Bishop of Hippo, in Africa ; St. Augustine, of Canterbury ; St. Mary the Virgin, St. Barbara, St. Catherine, St. Roch, St. Nicholas, St. George, the patron Saint of England ; St. Christopher, St. Sebastian, St. Cosmo, St. Damian, St. Margaret, St. Ursula, St. John the Baptist ; St. Stephen, the proto-martyr ; and the four virgins—St. Lucy, St. Agatha, St. Agnes and St. Cecilia.

The Tier of Worthies distinctively belonging to the English Church.—Bishop Giles de Bridport, bishop of the diocese at the time of the consecration of the Cathedral ; Bishop Richard Poore, founder of the present Cathedral; King Henry III., the monarch who granted the Charter for the building of the Cathedral; Bishop Odo; Bishop Osmund, who built the first Cathedral of Sarum; Bishop Brithwold; St. Alban, holding sword and cross; St. Alphege, Archbishop of Canterbury; St. Edmund, king and martyr; St. Thomas of Canterbury. A mutilated figure on the west side of north turret is probably that of St. Berinus. We notice several consecration crosses on the walls of the church.

The *North Porch* is large and massive, and has a parvise in the upper storey. On the inside there is a double arcade with foliated arches, and the pinnacles on each side of the gable are very fine. The *Nave* presents a perfect example of Early English workmanship. Notice the regularity of the masonry, which is one of its great peculiarities. The stones run in even bands throughout. The aisle windows have two lights; the clerestory has triple lancets, and each pair is flanked by flying buttresses. The fronts of the transepts are graced by beautifully-designed windows and are divided into four storeys. The porch on the north side was removed by Wyatt. The east front of the choir is a fine arrangement of lancets. There is great similarity between the north and south sides of the Cathedral. On the north side of the Lady Chapel formerly stood the Hungerford Chapel, ruthlessly destroyed by Wyatt; the Beauchamp Chapel on the south side shared the same fate. Bishop Beauchamp erected the flying buttresses on the south of the choir in 1450. The gates of the close are:—High Street Gate, built at the same time as the walls; St. Anne's Gate, and Harnham Gate, of which little remains. On the south of the nave is the cloister-court, which we will visit after seeing the interior. Salisbury possessed at one time a separate belfry at the north-west corner of the close. It was entirely destroyed and removed by Wyatt. The *Palace* is on the south-east. It was commenced by Poore. The hall was built by Bishop Beauchamp in the fifteenth century.

THE INTERIOR

Entering the building by the west door we obtain a grand view of the interior. The beautiful clustered columns of the fine arches, wrought of Purbeck marble, the fine triforium and clerestory, the distant view of the choir, all combine to make a very impressive scene. The oft-quoted lines tell us that

"As many days as in one year there be,
  So many windows in this church we see ;
  As many marble pillars here appear
  As there are hours throughout the fleeting year ;
  As many gates as moons one year does view—
  Strange tale to tell ! yet not more strange than true."

The uniformity of the architecture in the first beauty of Gothic conception, the long rows of sepulchral monuments of warriors and bishops, and the noble proportions of the building, add greatly to the charm of this building ; and yet it lacks much of the beauty which once shone here. Little of its stained glass, which once shed wondrous light on all we see, has been saved from the wreck caused by Reformation zeal and the wanton destruction of Wyatt. The triforium with its flat-pointed arches, subdivided into four smaller ones, ornamented with trefoils and quatrefoils, alternating with cinquefoils and octofoils, greatly resembles that at Westminster. The clerestory windows are triple lancets. The vaulting is plain, the arches rising from clustered shafts with foliated capitals, and resting on corbel-heads. The west wall has a triple-lancet window, and beneath this is an arcade of four arches, each of which contains two sub-arches. In the west window has been collected fragments of old glass saved from the wreck. It is possible to discover the figure of our Lord in Majesty, the Virgin,

Zacharias in the Temple, the Adoration of the Magi. There is some Flemish glass also here. The glass in the west windows of the aisles is ancient (1240-1270), and we see here the arms of Bishop Jewell (1562) and John Aprice (1558). The aisles have double-lancet windows. There is a curious stone bench on each side of the nave, upon which the piers stand. This was so placed in order to distribute the great weight of the building resting on these piers, as the foundations were not laid upon any very firm ground, the nature of the soil being formerly marshy, and the situation liable to floods. This ingenious plan has evidently had the desired effect, as the building has stood for nigh 700 years. The nave contains a fine series of monuments which were arranged here by Wyatt in a barbarous fashion. This vandal was guilty of every enormity. Not only did he remove the monuments from their original positions, but he seems to have mixed up the effigies and put them on tombs to which they did not belong. Beginning at west end of south side, leaving the figure of Hibernia, which graces Lord Wyndham's monument (1745), we see the monuments of the following :—

1. Bishop Herman (1078), which was brought from Old Sarum.
2. Bishop Jocelyn (1184), which was brought from Old Sarum (the head is later than the rest).
3. Bishop Roger (1139), which was brought from Old Sarum. (There is some uncertainty about the identity of these.)
4. Incised slab to an unknown personage.
5. Bishop Beauchamp (1481), whose chantry was destroyed by Wyatt.
6. Robert, Lord Hungerford (1459), whose chantry was destroyed by Wyatt. Notice the plate armour and collar of saints, also sword and dagger.
7. Lord Stourton, hung in the market-place in 1556 for the murder of the Hartgills, accomplished in a brutal fashion. He was hung, as a concession to his noble birth, with a silken cord. The "wells" on each side allude to the six heads of the Stour river, which rise near the Stourton mansion.
8. Bishop de la Wyle (1271), mutilated. The base is made up of fragments of much later date.
9. William Longespée, first Earl of Salisbury of that name,

son of Henry II. by Fair Rosamond (1226). Notice the chain-armour and surcoat, shield with arms of Anjou, and the decoration of the tomb—silver diaper work. He fought in the Crusades and in France, and was present at the signing of Magna Charta.

Crossing to the north side we see the monuments of—

10. Sir John Cheyney (1509), standard-bearer of Henry of Richmond at battle of Bosworth, unhorsed by Richard III.

11.
12.} Walter, Lord Hungerford, and his wife.

13. Sir John de Montacute (1389), fought at Creçy and in Scotland under Richard II. Notice armour, especially gauntlets.

14. Chancellor Geoffrey.

15. Person unknown.

16. Longespée, Earl of Salisbury (1250), son of the above-mentioned earl, a Crusader killed by the Saracens. The fact that this is a cross-legged effigy does not prove that all cross-legged effigies represent Crusaders.

17. "Boy Bishop," the great attraction of the ordinary visitor and tourist. The ceremony of the boy bishop is well known. One of the choir boys was elected on St. Nicholas Day, and presided until Innocents' Day, and a special service and procession took place during his rule. The old idea was that this boy died during his brief episcopacy, and was thus honoured with an effigy. It is now generally believed that such small figures represent heart burials. In bygone times the body was usually buried at the place where the person died, and not infrequently the heart was conveyed to the special church associated with the family or life of the deceased. The library, however, contains the order of service of boy bishop, and the ceremony lingered on until the time of Elizabeth.

18. Person unknown.

Near the entrance is a monument to Dr. Turburville, an oculist of Salisbury (1696).

The *North Transept* is entered by a Perpendicular arch, by Bishop Beauchamp (1450-1481). It was designed to support the tower. The style of this transept resembles that of the nave.

The two-light windows, which take the place of the triforium on the north side, and the beautiful clerestory windows, with their slender pilasters, should be noticed. There is an eastern aisle, divided into chapels, which Wyatt robbed of their screens. The monuments here are :—Brass to John Britton, the eminent antiquary; James Harris, author of *Hermes*, by Bacon; Earl of Malmesbury, by Chantrey; W. B. Earle, by Flaxman; Bishop John Blythe (?) (1499); Sir R. Hoare, the Wilts historian, by Lucas; Richard Jefferies, the charming modern writer on country life; Walter and William Long, by Flaxman; Bishop Woodville (1484).

The *South Transept* resembles the north. Here are monuments of :—Bishop Mitford (1407), a fine tomb of white marble; Bishop Fisher (1825); Edward Poore (1780).

The *Choir-Screen* is good modern work, and replaced a patchwork structure of Wyatt's handiwork, made up of spoil taken from his destroyed chantries. The organ is modern.

The *Choir and Presbytery* differ in no way from the architecture of the nave. The east end is beautifully designed. At the base of the reredos are three arches, and above five arches, with cinquefoil headings, and above these a triplet window. The roof is painted with an interesting series of designs, which are modern reproductions of thirteenth-century work. First there are series of Old Testament saints, the Forerunner of our Lord being ranked with the prophets. Then come the Apostles, with the figures of our Lord and the Evangelists; and further east are representations of the months, which are curious and interesting. January is represented by a man warming his hands; February, a man drinking wine; March, digging; April, sowing; May, hawking; June, flowers; July, reaping; August, threshing; September, gathering fruit; October, brewing; November, timber-felling; December, killing a pig.

The *Choir Stalls* are a patchwork composition. There is some old Perpendicular work; some of the work is by Wren. Happily Wyatt's productions have been removed. The reredos is modern, is a very elaborate piece of work. All the other fittings of the choir are new. In the choir are the chantries of Bishop Audley (1524), a fine piece of Late Perpendicular work, which has a fan-vault and some traces of colour, and of Walter, Lord Hungerford (1429), removed here from the nave, and made into a family pew by Lord Radnor. The iron-work is good, and such chapels are rare, the Chantry of Edward IV. at Windsor being the finest of its kind.

In the *North Choir Aisle* and *Transept* there are two monuments of the *memento mori* type, the large tomb of a thirteenth-century bishop, either Bingham or Scammel, Bishop Wyvill (1375), Gheast (1576), and Jewell (1571), and the curious brass of Bishop Wyvill, who recovered for the see Sherborne Castle and the Bere Chase, seized by Stephen, and granted by Edward III. to the Earl of Salisbury. To decide the right the wager of battle was resorted to, and both bishop and earl chose a champion. The king, however, caused the matter to be settled amicably. The bishop is here shown in his castle, praying for his champion, and below are the hares and rabbits representing the chase. In this north-east transept is a fine Early Perpendicular lavatory, which is evidently not in its original position, part of an Early English screen, removed by Wyatt, and a curious aumbrey. In the aisle toward the east we see an effigy, said to be that of Bishop Poore, the founder of the Cathedral, and at the east end is the monument of Sir Thomas Gorges and his lady, who was a maid of honour to Queen Elizabeth. It is a cumbrous piece of work.

The *Retro-Choir* or processional path has beautiful clustered shafts and fine vault, and forms a graceful entrance to the *Lady Chapel*, a most perfect piece of Early English building, and the oldest part of the church. At the east end is a triple lancet, with another lancet on each side, filled with modern glass. There is a new altar here, and modern colouring adorns the walls and ceiling. The canopies of the niches under the windows on the north and south were brought here from the Beauchamp Chapel destroyed by Wyatt. Here in former days stood the shrine of St. Osmund, the second Norman bishop, the saintly man to whom the diocese and the English Church owe much. His tomb remains here, but his shrine was plundered and destroyed at the Reformation. At the east end of the south choir aisle is the stately tomb of the unhappy Earl of Hertford (1621), who married Catherine, the sister of Lady Jane Grey, and thus incurred Queen Elizabeth's resentment, and was imprisoned. The poor lady, when released from the Tower, was separated from her husband, and died of grief. He survived her sixty years. Near here are the modern tombs of Bishops Moberly and Hamilton, and the Perpendicular tomb of William Wilton, Chancellor of Sarum (1506-1523) The old sacristy, now the vestry, is on the south of this transept; above this is the muniment room, the ancient treasury. In the transept is the remarkable monument of Bishop Giles de Bridport (1262), under whose rule the church was finished. It is the most interesting tomb in the church. The carvings in the spandrels record the chief events in the bishop's life—his birth, confirmation, education, and possibly his first preferment, his homage, a procession (probably referring to the dedication of this church), his death, and the presentation of his soul for judgment. Here are monuments also of Canon Bowles (1850) ; Bishop Burgess (1837) ; Bishop Seth Ward (1689), Hooker, the famous divine ; Young, the father of the poet ; Isaak Walton, the son of the angler ; Bishop Davenant (1641) ; Mrs. Wordsworth, the wife of the bishop ; and a brass to Canon Liddon's memory. Further on are the monuments of Bishop Salcot (1557), and Sir Richard Mompesson and his wife (1627). Notice the inverted strengthening arches in both choir transepts.

Passing through the south transept we enter the *Cloisters*, which are considered to be "among the finest in England," and without doubt they can lay claim to be a great and beautiful architectural triumph. They are a little later than the Cathedral, having been begun directly after its completion, and finished during the rule of Bishop Wyvill, about 1340. The windows are finely constructed, and consist of double-arched openings, each arch having two sub-arches, while in the head is a large six-foiled opening. On the wall side is a blind arcade of graceful arches. An unfortunate restoration in 1854 did not improve the appearance of the cloisters. On the north side, between the cloister and the church, is the plumbery. The monuments here do not possess much interest. The *Library*, over part of the east walk, was built by Bishop Jewell, and contains about 5000 volumes, and a valuable collection of MSS. One of the most interesting is a Gallican version of the Psalter (969 A.D.), Geoffrey of Monmouth's Chronicles (twelfth century), a copy of Magna Charter (now in muniment room), and many others of much value and importance. The *Chapter-House* was built early in the reign of Edward I. It is a noble octagonal building, and can scarcely be surpassed by any other. The roof is modern. There is a central pillar, from which the vaulting springs. On each side there is a large window, resembling in tracery those in the cloisters. Below the windows is an arcade, and beneath this a stone bench, and at the east end a raised seat for the bishop and his officials. There is a remarkable series of sculptures above the arcade, which are extremely interesting and merit close study. The following are the subjects represented :—

West Bay

1. Description of Chaos.
2. Creation of the Firmament.

North-West Bay

3. Creation of the Earth.
4. Creation of the Sun and Moon.
5. Creation of the Birds and Fishes.
6. Creation of Adam and Eve.
7. The Sabbath.
8. The Institution of Marriage.
9. The Temptation.
10. The Hiding in the Garden.

North Bay

11. The Expulsion.
12. Adam tilling the Ground.
13. Cain and Abel's Offering.
14. Murder of Abel.
15. God sentencing Cain.
16. God commanding Noah to build the Ark.
17. The Ark.
18. Noah's Vineyard.

North-East Bay

19. The Drunkenness of Noah.
20. Building of the Tower of Babel.
21. The Angels appearing to Abraham.
22. Abraham entertaining Angels.
23. Destruction of Sodom and Gomorrah.
24. The Escape of Lot.
25. Abraham and Isaac journeying to the Mount.
26. The Sacrifice of Isaac.

East Bay

27. Isaac blessing Jacob.
28. Blessing of Esau.
29. Rebecca sending Jacob to Padan-aram.
30. Meeting of Jacob and Rachel.
31. Rachel introducing Jacob to Laban.
32. Jacob wrestling with the Angel, and Jacob's Dream.
33. The Angel touching Jacob's Thigh.
34. Meeting of Jacob and Esau.

South-East Bay

35. Joseph's Dream.
36. Joseph relating his Dream.
37. Joseph being placed in a Well.
38. Joseph sold into Egypt.
39. Joseph's Coat brought to Jacob.
40. Joseph brought to Potiphar.
41. Joseph tempted by Potiphar's Wife.
42. Joseph accused before Potiphar.

South Bay

43. Joseph placed in Prison.
44. The fate of Pharaoh's Baker and Butler.
45. Pharaoh's Dream.
46. Pharaoh's Perplexity.
47. Joseph taken from Prison, and interpreting the Dream.
48. Joseph ruling in Egypt.
49. The Brethren journeying into Egypt.
50. The Cup placed in Benjamin's Sack.

South-West Bay

51. The Discovery of the Cup.
52. The Brethren pleading before Joseph.
53. Jacob and Family journeying to Egypt.
54. The Brethren pleading before Joseph after the Death of Jacob.
55. Joseph assuring his Brethren of his Protection.
56. Moses in the Presence of God.
57. The Passage of the Red Sea.
58. Destruction of the Egyptians.

West Bay

59. Moses striking the Rock.
60. The Declaring of the Law.

In the vestibule the doorway is remarkable for its great beauty.

In the voussoirs of the arch is another series of sculptures representing moralities, the triumph of virtue over vice. We see Concordia trampling on Discordia, Temperantia pouring liquor down the throat of Drunkenness, Bravery trampling on Cowardice, Faith on Infidelity, Virtue covering Vice with a cloak, while Vice embraces her knee with one hand and stabs her with the other. Truth pulls out the tongue of Falsehood, Modesty scourges Lust, and Charity pours coin into the throat of Avarice. These sculptures are of the very highest class of art, and are among the most interesting remains of Early Gothic carving in the world. All the glass in the chapter-house is modern, and also the tiling. A fine old specimen of fourteenth-century furniture is seen in the ancient table preserved here.

DIMENSIONS

Total length	473 ft.
Length of nave . . .	229 ft.
Width	82 ft.
Height	84 ft.
Height of spire . . .	404 ft.

PRINCIPAL BUILDING DATES

Early English (1220-1260)—The main buildings of the church were completed at this time.
  (1262-1270)—Monastic buildings.
Decorated (1330-1350)—Two upper storeys of tower and spire.
Perpendicular (1460)—Arches supporting tower in north and south transepts. Flying buttresses on south side of choir.

Other buildings of interest in Salisbury—

The Guild Hall.
Market Cross, called the Poultry.
Churches of St. Martin, St. Edmund, St. Thomas à Becket.
In the neighbourhood are—
Old Sarum.
Stonehenge.

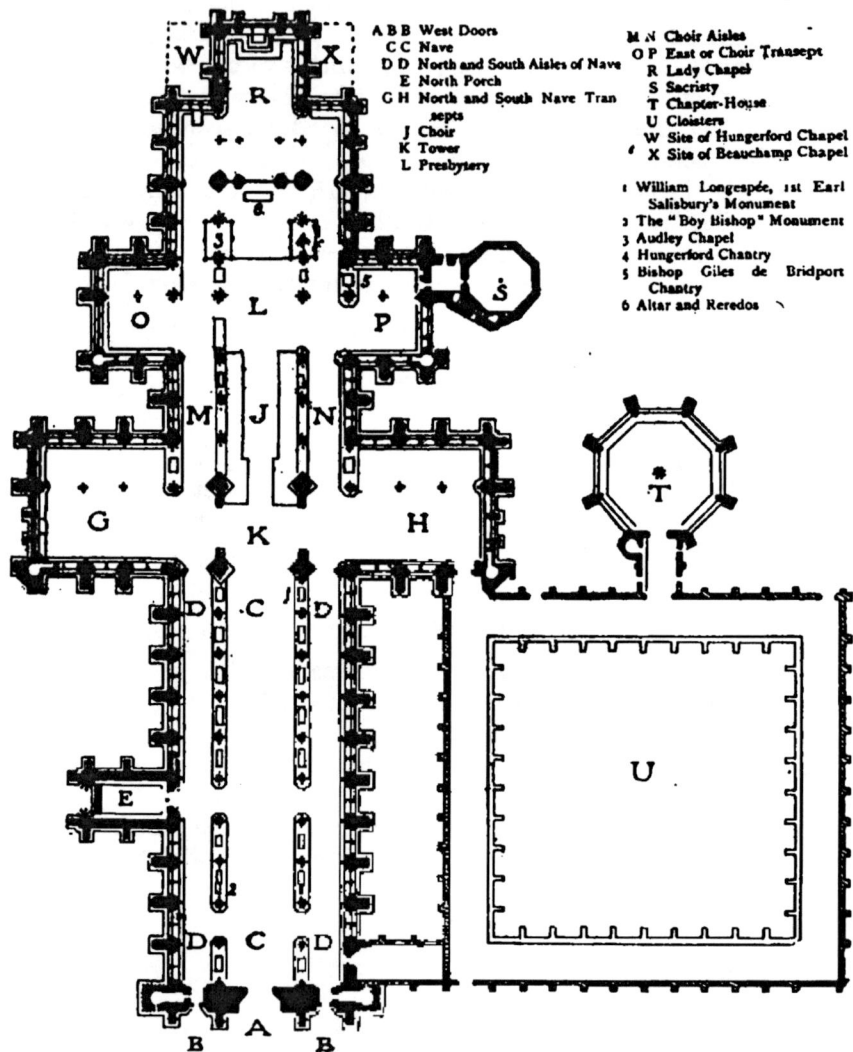

A B B West Doors
C C Nave
D D North and South Aisles of Nave
E North Porch
G H North and South Nave Tran
septs
J Choir
K Tower
L Presbytery

M N Choir Aisles
O P East or Choir Transept
R Lady Chapel
S Sacristy
T Chapter-House
U Cloisters
W Site of Hungerford Chapel
X Site of Beauchamp Chapel

1 William Longespée, 1st Earl
Salisbury's Monument
2 The "Boy Bishop" Monument
3 Audley Chapel
4 Hungerford Chantry
5 Bishop Giles de Bridport
Chantry
6 Altar and Reredos

PLAN OF SALISBURY CATHEDRAL

OXFORD CATHEDRAL

OXFORD is so full of varied interest that we must leave our readers to gain knowledge of its history from other sources, and confine ourselves to its Cathedral records. This see was one of those founded by Henry VIII. out of the proceeds of his spoliation of the monasteries. The Cathedral was originally the Church of the Priory of St. Frideswide. This lady was the daughter of Didan, the chief man of the town. At an early age she took the veil, and her father built for her a convent; but Algar, King of Mercia, wished to marry her, and swore that he would carry her off. She fled for refuge, and on her return to Oxford was gallantly defended by the men of her city against Algar, who was struck blind. She was buried in her convent, and many miracles were wrought at her shrine. Such was the beginning of what ultimately became the Cathedral of Oxford. Terrible was the scene which took place in this little church. The Danes were in Oxford. There was peace between the Saxon king, Ethelred, and their foes; but on St. Brice's Day, 1002, the folk of Wessex were excited to slaughter the Danes, who fled for sanctuary to the little church. The Saxons respected no more the sacredness of the building than the laws of hospitality, and set fire to the place and massacred the helpless Danes. The remains of this Early Saxon church are said to have been discovered, which we shall examine later.[1]

Ethelred, repenting of his crime, determined to rebuild the church, which he accomplished, and recent authorities assure us that the present church is in plan and main substance the Saxon church of Ethelred, erected in 1004, and not the later Norman church about which the older writers tell us. He seems to have established a community of secular canons. The work was interrupted by the later Danish invasions, and perhaps never finished. At anyrate it was ruinous in the time of the Early Normans kings.

[1] Mr. Micklethwaite considers these remains to have belonged to Ethelred's church.

In 1111 A.D., it was granted by either Roger, Bishop of Salisbury, or by Henry I., to Prior Guimond and his fellow canons. This prior began to restore the ruined church and monastery, but his successor, Robert de Cricklade (1141-1180), did most of the work, and restored the nave, choir, central tower and transepts. All the later Norman work is due to him. In 1180, in the presence of Henry II., his nobles and a goodly company of bishops, the relics of St. Frideswide were translated to a place of honour in the restored building on the north side of the choir, to which there was great resort of pilgrims on account of the miraculous healings which took place there. Fire played havoc with the city of Oxford in 1190, but the church escaped without much injury. The monastic buildings suffered, and the traces of fire can still be seen on the old Norman doorway in the cloisters. In the thirteenth century the Lady Chapel was built adjoining the north side of the choir, some of the old walls being used, the spire raised above the tower, the chapter-house and part of the Latin Chapel added, which was completed in the fourteenth century. A few Decorated details were added at this period, and windows in this style inserted. The fifteenth century witnessed sundry alterations in the cloisters, the building of St. Frideswide's latest shrine, the insertion of some Perpendicular windows, and the erection of the fine vaulting of the choir.

Then a mighty change dawned on the old monastery. Cardinal Wolsey obtained a bull from Pope Clement VII. for its suppression and determined to convert it into a college, which was designed to be the largest in Oxford. He played sad havoc with the fabric of the church. A great part of the nave he destroyed altogether in order to make room for his great "Tom Quad," so named after the famous bell which still rings each night at five minutes past nine, and is the signal for the closing of the gates of all Oxford colleges. Part of the old cloisters disappeared also. Wolsey contemplated the building of another church for his college, and indeed began its construction; but his fall in 1529 put an end to the carrying out of his great conception, and the college fell into the hands of King Henry VIII. Here the monarch established one of his newly-formed sees (the bishop's seat was first fixed at Oseney Abbey, just outside Oxford), and with characteristic parsimony applied the revenues of the college to the support of the see. The dean of the Cathedral is still the head of the college, and the canons are university professors. As was usual at this time, the Cathedral was shorn of all its costly ornaments, vestments, plate and other treasures, but the fabric remained intact.

Dean Brian Duppa in 1630 wrought much evil in the way of restoring his Cathedral, destroying the old glass and woodwork, tearing up the brasses, and "improving" the windows by cutting away the old tracery. He was rewarded for his zeal by being made Bishop of Salisbury. His loyalty to the fallen fortunes of his sovereign, Charles I., somewhat atones for his wanton destruction of much that was beautiful in Christ Church Cathedral. In the Civil War, Oxford was the great centre of the Royalists. Here King Charles held his court. Students flocked to his standard, and the Cathedral was the scene of several thanksgiving services on the occasion of victories. Cromwell's soldiers at length captured Oxford, and did some damage in the Cathedral, breaking much of the glass. Bishop Fell (1676-1686) was a munificent benefactor of the college. His father when dean had built the fine staircase to the hall with its fan-tracery vault, and commenced the buildings on north and west of the quadrangle. This Bishop Fell finished the buildings of the college together with the west belfry, designed by Sir C. Wren, but he does not appear to have done much for the Cathedral. Neglect and the hard hand of time wrought much mischief, and it seems to have been in a deplorable state when the restorations of the last half of the nineteenth century were inaugurated. To rescue it from its wretched condition Dean Liddell, whose name is familiar to every student of Greek, set himself with much energy, and the work was entrusted to Sir G. Scott. His restoration was carried out with much wisdom and careful regard for antiquity. The author of *Alice in Wonderland*, a fellow of the college, published a satirical pamphlet on *The Three T"s*, the tunnel, the tower (the third we forget), and compared the new entrance with a railway tunnel, representing a railway train emerging from the portal, and scoffing at the new tower, which arose above the grand staircase to the hall. But it is easy to criticise, and Sir G. Scott's work at Oxford compares favourably with most restorations, and for this posterity will thank him.

THE EXTERIOR

Oxford Cathedral is so hidden away behind the obtrusive walls of Wolsey's college that it is difficult to obtain any good exterior views. The best is that seen from the garden of one of the canons, to enter which permission may be obtained. The view from the cloister is also satisfactory. The principal entrance is from "Tom Quad" by the "tunnel," as Lewis Carrol termed the passage or porch situated a little to the north of the entrance to the hall. As we have said, the west front and the greater part of the nave were destroyed by Wolsey when he erected the college buildings. He also destroyed the west walk of the cloister, which we enter by a passage leading from the entrance to the hall. The cloisters are Perpendicular work of the latter part of the fifteenth century. The north walk was at one time converted into a muniment room, but has recently been restored to its original form, and has a modern imitation of the old vaulting. The old refectory stood on the south side, but has been converted into college rooms. Its large Perpendicular windows still remain looking on to the cloister. The entrance to the chapter-house is in the east walk, and a fine Norman doorway it is. It belongs to the later Norman period. It has four orders, richly ornamented with zigzag. A round-headed window is on each side of the door. The chapter-house is one of the best examples of the Early English style in the kingdom, and may be compared with those of Lincoln, Salisbury and Chester. The east end is very fine, and consists of an arcade of five arches which are double. Slender clustered shafts with capitals adorned with foliage support the inner arches. The three central arches are pierced for windows. Similar arcades are at the east end of north and south sides. The sculpture in this chamber is extremely fine. Grotesque corbels, carved capitals and the bosses in the vault, are all beautiful and interesting. One of the bosses represents the Virgin giving an apple to the infant Christ. There is also some old glass and interesting mural paintings. Diocesan meetings are held in this delightful room. The foundation stone of Wolsey's college at Ipswich is preserved here. In the room on the south are some fine paintings, an Elizabethan table and an old chest. Another door in this cloister leads to the old slype, a passage to the monastic burial-ground. On the left is St. Lucy's Chapel, mainly of Norman construction, the east window being much later. It is of Decorated character, and the tracery is flamboyant and of very beautiful design. The south choir aisle adjoins, and is part of the original church. The windows are modern imitations of Norman work. The windows in the clerestory of the choir are Perpendicular. The east end is modern, having been reconstructed by Scott. On the north side of the Cathedral, viewed from the canon's garden, we

Oxford Cathedral

see the north transept with its large Perpendicular window, erected
at the beginning of the sixteenth century, flanked by two turrets
crowned with pinnacles; the Latin Chapel of beautiful Decorated
design, erected in the fourteenth century, and the Lady Chapel, the
east wall of which is part of the old Saxon church, and Mr. Park
Harrison has discovered the remains of three Saxon apses which
are perhaps the remains of the earliest Saxon church, the Church of
St. Frideswide, built by Didan early in the eighth century.[1] A
Decorated window has been inserted here. We must now notice
the *Tower* and *Spire*, a beautiful feature of the Cathedral. The lower
storey is Late Norman, similar to the style of the nave; the belfry
and the spire are Early English. This spire ranks with that of
Barnock, Northants, and New Romsey, Surrey, as being one of
the earliest in the kingdom. It was restored by Scott. The
pinnacles at the angles of the tower are modern but accurate copies
of the ancient ones. The spire is octagonal, and is what is termed
a broach spire, *i.e.*, it rises from the exterior of the tower walls and
not from the interior of a parapet as in the later spires.

THE INTERIOR

Entering by the new porch from the quadrangle and passing
under the organ-screen we see a Cathedral, small, indeed, but possessing features of peculiar interest. In its main plan it is possibly
the church of Ethelred begun in 1004, but finished in Late Norman
times when Robert de Cricklade or Canutus was prior (1141-
1180).[2] The piers of the *Nave* are alternatively circular and
octagonal. There is a very unusual triforium. Arches spring
from the capitals of the piers, and in the tympana are set the
triforium arcade. From half capitals set against the piers spring
another series of arches at a lower level than the others we have
mentioned, and above the curve of these is the triforium arcade.
Very few examples of this curious construction are found in this
country. The carving of the capitals is graceful, and though it
differs somewhat from the stiff-leaved foliage of Early English style,
it somewhat resembles that character. The clerestory belongs to
the period of transition between Norman and Early English. The

[1] Mr. Micklethwaite believes these apses to have been part of Ethelred's
church.
[2] Although Mr. Park Harrison's theory is attractive, we are unable to accept
all his conclusions as to the pre-Norman character of the details of the church.

central arch of the triple windows is pointed, and the others, which are blocked up, round. The corbels and shafts which support the roof are Norman, but the brackets are Perpendicular, erected by Wolsey, who intended to build a stone vault. The present fine timber roof belongs to his time, or a little later. The stalls and seats are modern. The screen is Jacobean, above which is the organ, a fine instrument enclosed in a Jacobean case. The pulpit belongs to the same period and is very interesting, especially its grotesque carving. The central tower has fine and lofty arches, and its appearance has been improved by the removal of the ceiling which formerly existed here. A curious subterranean chamber was discovered here in 1856. It contained two aumbries, and was evidently intended for the keeping of some treasure, possibly of the monastery, or of the university. It is known that the university chest during the thirteenth century was deposited in a secret place within the Church of St. Frideswide, and this, doubtless, was the spot. The *Choir* is of the same character as the nave. The piers are more massive, and the style of the carving of the capitals differs. We are told that we have distinct evidence here that this is part of Ethelred's church, that the sculpture is Saxon, copied from Saxon MSS., that it has been worn by weather which could only have been done during the ruinous condition of the church prior to its Late Norman restoration. Possibly this may be true, and the carving is certainly peculiar, but at present we cannot quite agree to accept this view. The triforium is Late Norman, and the roof is a fine example of fan-tracery begun in the fifteenth century. Wolsey changed the appearance of the clerestory, and introduced Perpendicular details.

The *East End* is modern, and is a fine conception of Sir G. Scott based upon early models. The *Reredos* is a fine modern work, and the altar, lectern and throne are also new. Turning to the north we enter the *North Choir Aisle*, where we stand upon debatable ground. Perhaps we are in the Early Saxon church built for St. Frideswide, or the later Saxon church of Ethelred. Authorities differ, and it is impossible to decide. At anyrate, there in the east wall are the remains of the three Saxon arches which lead to the apses discovered on the outside. And here, too, is the noted *Shrine of St. Frideswide*, of which Mr. Ruskin said that every stone was worth its weight in silver, if not in gold. It has been gradually collected from odd corners of the precincts, as the shrine was destroyed by Henry VIII. The carved foliage is very beautiful,

Oxford Cathedral

and when this base of the shrine was complete and crowned with the jewelled cover, beneath which reposed the relics of the saints, it must have been very imposing. There is a curious story in connection with these relics. When the tomb was destroyed these were carefully preserved in secret by "the faithful," and in the meantime the body of the wife of Peter Martyr, a Protestant professor, was laid near the saint's shrine. As this poor lady was an ex-nun, in the time of Mary and Cardinal Pole her body was cast out into a cesspool, and the relics of the saint restored to their place of honour. In Elizabeth's time the saint's bones were again removed. The queen ordered the decent re-burial of the remains of Peter Martyr's wife, and while this was being done the sacred box containing the relics was produced, and "the married nun and the virgin saint were buried together, and the dust of the two still remains under the pavement beneath our feet inextricably blended."[1] The exact spot is conjecturable, but a brass has been placed where the mingled remains are supposed to lie.

The *Lady Chapel* is on the west of the choir aisle, and is of Early English construction. It was added about 1250, when the present piers and vault were built. The east wall, as we have said, is manifestly earlier, and is part of one of the earlier Saxon churches. The east window is restored Decorated. The west arch is round-headed, and shows that this part of the chapel was the east aisle of the north transept. There are extensive remains of colouring. Here is the remarkable "Watching Chamber," supposed by some to be a later shrine of St. Frideswide, and by Professor Willis and others to be the chamber where watch was kept for guarding the gold and jewels which adorned the actual shrine. It has three stages, and is very beautiful Perpendicular work. In this chapel there are some interesting monuments—Sir George Nowers (1425) (with good example of armour); Prior Guymond (?) (1149), or Prior Alexander de Sutton (1316), with Decorated canopy and effigy; Lady Montacute (1353), the supposed founder of the Latin Chapel; Robert Burton, author of *Anatomy of Melancholy* (1639). Some "Morris" windows have been inserted here designed by Burne-Jones, very beautiful in themselves, but perhaps scarcely in keeping with their surroundings. The St. Cecilia window is extremely fine. The *Latin Chapel* is mainly Decorated work of the time of Edward III., the western parts being earlier. The vault has some richly-foliated bosses, on which appear the water-

[1] Froude, *Hist. Engl.*, vi. 468.

lily and the roses, and heads surmounted with crown and mitre. The east window has strange Venetian tracery, but some excellent modern glass designed by Burne-Jones and representing incidents in the life of St. Frideswide. The other windows have some fine old fourteenth-century glass; the north-east window is modern. The woodwork is very fine; it is later than the chapel, and was not designed for it. The cardinal's hat, supported by angels on one of the carved poppy-heads, shows that this was prepared for Wolsey's choir. Some of the work is much older. In this chapel the writer used to listen to the lectures of the divinity professor, and was often distracted from the discourse by the architectural beauties around him. Beautiful vistas may be obtained here of " long-drawn aisles and fretted vault," and he became very conversant with the history of St. Frideswide as depicted in the fine east window.

The *North Transept* is similar to the nave in style. The north window is a modern restoration, and the glass is not very pleasing modern work. Here is the Perpendicular tomb of a monk, Zouch (1503), and some good brasses in the aisle. The north aisle has Norman vaulting. The windows are restored Perpendicular, and the glass is modern. The window at the west end of the aisle was refashioned by Dean Brian Duppa in his usual barbarous manner, but it has some good Flemish glass by Van Ling representing Jonah and the Gourd, with Nineveh in the background.

Crossing to the south side of the church we pass several monuments in the vestibule at the west end and reach the *South Aisle*, which is later in style than the north. At the west end is a Burne-Jones window, representing " Faith, Hope and Charity." The south transept preserves its Late Norman character, but has been shorn of its length. On the east side is the Chapel of St. Lucy. At the back of the wall on the south is the slype, and above this the vestry. One of the windows here is said to be Saxon. *St. Lucy's Chapel* is Norman, and is now used as a baptistry. The east window has flamboyant tracery and some fine old glass. Several monuments of distinguished Cavaliers who died for the Royal cause in the Civil War are in this part of the church. The *South Choir Aisle* resembles that on the north. The south windows are in the Norman style, but are modern imitations. The glass of the east window was designed by Burne-Jones and portrays St. Catherine. It was erected in memory of a daughter of Dean Liddell. The monument of Prince Leopold, brother of the king, formerly a student of Christ Church, has a pathetic interest, and the tomb of Bishop King, Oxford's first bishop (1557), is a fine piece of Perpendicular work. The window to his memory is on the south and shows a representation of the Abbey of Oseney, where his episcopal throne was first established, before it migrated to the Church of St. Frideswide.

DIMENSIONS

Extreme length	. . .	175 ft.
Length from screen to reredos	.	132 ft.
Extreme breadth	. . .	108 ft.
Height of spire .	. . .	144 ft.

DATES OF BUILDING

Saxon—East wall of Lady Chapel and north choir aisle, and possibly window in south transept.

Norman—Nave, choir, transept, aisles, door of chapter-house, St. Lucy's Chapel.

Early English—Lady Chapel.

Decorated—Latin Chapel and several windows.

Perpendicular—Cloisters, windows and vault of choir.

BRISTOL CATHEDRAL

BRISTOL, the great western port of England, has a history which tells of the ancient glories of English seamanship. From this port sailed the first Englishman who landed in America, Sebastian Cabot, who was born in Bristol, and was the first to discover that which is now known as the United States. A Bristol chronicle states, "this year 1497, on St. John the Baptist's day, the land of America was found by the merchants of Bristowe, in a ship of Bristol, called *The Matthew*, the which said ship departed from the port of Bristowe the 2nd of May, and came home again 6th August following." It was a Bristol ship which brought home the real Robinson Crusoe (Juan Fernandez) from his island home. Very famous were the great merchants of Bristol, such as William Cannynge, who founded the noble Church of St. Mary Redcliffe, whom his king, Henry VI., delighted to honour, and styled "his beloved and honourable merchant." Vast was his fleet—his shipping, amounting to 2470 tons, was seized by the victorious Yorkist monarch—and vast were his commercial enterprises, whereby he made Bristol a large and flourishing port.

But we must go back to earlier days. In Saxon times the port was famous, or infamous, for its slave-dealing, which the coming of the Conqueror scarcely suppressed. Here Harold's three sons made a vain attempt to rescue the kingdom from his iron grasp. A famous Norman castle destroyed in the Civil War was built here, where Stephen was kept a prisoner. Pleasanter visits were frequently paid by other monarchs. The city was besieged and taken by Henry Bolingbroke, and Shakespeare in *Richard II.* tells of the beheading of four supporters of the luckless king in the city market-place. Here, too, five martyrs were burnt, and in the first year of Elizabeth's reign a mass of roods and images shared the same fate. The imposition of the ship-money tax was so distasteful that the Royal cause was not very popular at Bristol. The citizens opened their gates to the troopers of Cromwell, who held it from 1642 to the following year. Prince Rupert stormed the place, and held it till it was wrested from him in 1645. The

" Bloody Assize " of Judge Jefferies left its mark on this western port; six prisoners were executed, and hundreds sent across the sea to serve in the plantations. The darkest spot in the history of Bristol is the story of the Reform riots of 1831, sometimes called "the Bristol Revolution," when the dregs of the population pillaged and plundered, burnt the bishop's palace, and were guilty of much vandalism. Of the old churches we shall write subsequently. The old quaint houses are very attractive, especially the old Norman hall and Tudor windows of the house of Edward Colston, one of Bristol's merchant princes, Cannynge's house, with its fine Perpendicular roof, and the old Hospital of St. Peter.

THE HISTORY OF THE SEE

Bristol was one of the sees founded by Henry VIII. in 1542, after the destruction of the monasteries. There is, however, in the British Museum, a MS. copy of a Papal Bull of 1551, for the refounding of the see, directed by Pope Paul IV. to Cardinal Pole. In 1836 the Sees of Bristol and Gloucester were united, and remained so until 1897, when they were again separated.

The church has a history long before it became a Cathedral. It was the church of the monastery of Augustinian canons, founded in 1142 by Robert Fitzhardinge, afterwards Lord of Berkeley, on the site of Augustine's oak (so tradition says), where Augustine met the British bishops in conference and offended them by his haughty demeanour. The consecration of probably the chancel took place six years later. In 1155 Fitzhardinge received from the king the forfeited estates of Roger de Berkeley, and was thus enabled to extend his building operations, which were continued until the time of his death in 1170. The church consisted of a nave with north and south aisles, a central tower with north and south transepts, a presbytery with north and south aisles, and a processional path. The choir had a square ending, and consisted of three bays, the altar being at the east of the second bay, the last bay forming a *via processionum*. The chapter-house and vestibule are also Norman. The Early English builders erected the Elder Lady Chapel, Bristol Cathedral being rich in Lady Chapels, and possessing two. Abbot John (1196-1215) or his successor, David, was doubtless the builder. Later Early English work is evident in portions of the north and south transepts and in the Berkeley Chapel, but much of the work of this period has been destroyed. Serious complaints were made at this time concerning the conduct of the monks, and sundry visitations were made and orders issued for the reform of the monastery. During the Early Decorated period the roof and east window of the Elder Lady Chapel were added, and a little later (1306-1332) Abbot Knowle reconstructed the choir and choir aisles. With his work came the beginning of Perpendicular aspiration, and it is an earnest of the course of the later English Gothic which first manifested itself in the choir of Gloucester. Bristol nearly had the lucrative honour of receiving the body of the murdered King Edward II., slain at Berkeley Castle. But for fear of offending his patrons Abbot Knowle declined to have the burial here; hence the corpse was taken to Gloucester, where it caused a great concourse of pilgrims, and brought many offerings. Knowle's successor, Abbot Snow (1332-1341), was made a mitred abbot, and had a seat in Parliament. He continued the work of his predecessor, erected a chantry, and built the Newton Chapel. Soon after his death terrible misfortunes happened to the city and monastery. The Black Death invaded the land, and so great were its ravages that in Bristol the living were hardly able to bury the dead, and few monks survived the awful malady. The effects were disastrous. For over a hundred years no building was attempted, and the monastery was in a deplorable condition. In the time of Abbot Newbury (1428-1473) the great tower was begun, and finished by his successor, Hunt (1473-1481), who re-roofed the church. Abbot Newland (1481-1515) rebuilt the upper part of the abbey gateway in Perpendicular style, and began to rebuild the ruinous nave. As the power of the town increased the citizens often had disputes with the monks over rights of fairs and markets and other matters, and the burghers of Bristol were not more submissive than those of other places. Hence the usual quarrels arose and disturbed the peace of the city. Some of the succeeding abbots wrought some minor improvements, but in 1543 a most drastic remedy was applied to the ruinous nave. It was entirely pulled down, and not rebuilt until recent times. The monastery was dissolved like other similar institutions, and Paul Bush became the first bishop of the new see founded by Henry VIII. For a brief space during Mary's reign the old worship was restored, and Her Majesty and Philip bestowed costly gifts of copes and altar frontals and vestments. But in Elizabeth's reign all "relics of Popery" were ordered to be destroyed, such as the rood-lofts, tabernacles for images, and scripture texts and the table of the commandments to be painted in large characters on the wall. Beyond purloining the lead from the roof neither the besiegers nor the besieged did much damage to the church during the Civil War.

On the site of the destroyed nave some houses were erected, but after the great riots these were taken down. The building seems to have been kept in fairly good order. Edward Colston, the benefactor of Bristol, repaired the pavement. Sundry restorations were taken in hand during the last century, and finally in 1865 it was decided to undertake the stupendous task of rebuilding the nave. The work was begun in 1868 and finished in 1888. Since then the Elder Lady Chapel and the tower have been restored, and the church is now complete. It contains much of unusual value and interest, and the completion of the nave is a triumph of nineteenth-century achievement.

THE EXTERIOR

As we have said, the whole nave is new work, and therefore need not be examined very closely. The *West Front* is flanked by two towers, which bear the honoured names of Bishop Butler and Edward Colston. The style is an imitation of fourteenth-century work. There is a crocketed gable above the door, a rose window of good design, and some delicately-carved work surmounted by a cross. The face of the towers has three storeys; on the first a large window; on the second some lancets; and above two windows with louvres, the heads of which have crockets and finials. There are pinnacles at the four corners.

On the *South Side* we see the remains of the monastic buildings. The north and east walks of the cloisters alone remain, except a few traces of the western walk, and the north is a restoration. We will visit the east walk from the Cathedral. Passing round to the *North Side* we notice the *North Porch* built in 1873. We have often noticed the figures of the four great doctors of the church— SS. Gregory, Ambrose, Jerome and Augustine. They appear in the sculptures of many of our cathedrals. A great storm of indignation arose at Bristol when it was proposed to place these figures here, and the four Evangelists were substituted. We can pass over the modern work, which is not wholly satisfactory, and notice the interesting character of the eastern portion. The north transept has some remains of Norman work in the north wall. The north window is modern in memory of Colston, and replaces

an Early English window.   The building adjoining is the Elder
Lady Chapel, which is Early English work of the early thirteenth
century.   The east window is Decorated and is rather earlier than
the choir built by Abbot Knowle (1306-1332).   The battlemented
parapet is, of course, a later addition.   The buttresses of the chapel
are Decorated, and there are curious little flying buttresses connecting
the two pinnacles.   The Lady Chapel at the east end of the
Cathedral is of the same date as the choir, and has a large, noble
and graceful window.   Passing round to the south we see the outside of the Berkeley Chapel, of Decorated design, and adjoining it
the sacristy and external walls of the Newton Chapel, chapter-
house and modern vestry.   Here, too, is the old churchyard.   The
Central Tower is Perpendicular and was constructed by Abbot
Newland (1481-1515) or his successor, Abbot Elliot (1515-1526).

THE INTERIOR

Retracing our steps, we enter the Cathedral by the north porch
and view the new *Nave* from the west end.   The slender piers and
fine vaulting are striking, and the work is in many ways very beautiful.   The surface of the walls in the aisles is broken by canopied
recesses for tombs, one only being occupied by a marble figure of
Dean Elliot.   The baptistry is in the south-west or Colston Tower,
and is decorated in memory of Bishop Monk.   Already there are
many memorial windows of good modern glass.

The *North Transept* has some original Norman work in the
core of the buttresses and in the wall below the north window.
Some alterations were made during the Decorated period, probably
by Abbot Snow (1332-1341), and the arch leading to north choir
aisle is Perpendicular work constructed by Abbot Newland (1481-
1515), called "the good abbot."   Either he or his successor,
Elliot, constructed the groined roof, which has on the bosses
sculptured representations of the instruments of the Passion.   The
north window is modern, in memory of Colston.   The well-
known writer, "Hugh Conway" (F. Fargus), has a memorial
here, and also Jane Porter of literary fame, Sterne's "Maria"
(Mrs. Draper), and the parents of Macready, the actor.

The *South Transept* has much Norman work in the lower part
of the walls.   Part was rebuilt in Early English times.   Abbot
Snow (1332-1341) continued the work and constructed the arch
leading to the south choir aisle.   The vault is Perpendicular work by

Bristol
The Central Tower
from S.E.

Abbot Elliot (1515-1526). On the south is a staircase now leading to the consistory court, but which formerly echoed with the tread of the monks as they came here to their midnight services from the dormitory. In this transept there are monuments to Lady Hesketh (1807), the friend of Cowper; William Phillips, the sub-sacrist or verger who prevented the rioters from profaning the Cathedral in 1831; Chantrey's monument of Mrs. Crawford; and most famous of all, *Bishop Butler* (1752), one of the most honoured of English divines, the author of *The Analogy of Religion*. The inscription was written by Southey.

It is deplorable that a beautiful stone screen of Tudor architecture, which separated the choir from the transept, was ruthlessly destroyed in 1860, and another one erected. This also has been removed, and the view of the east end, with its Decorated piers and arches and the rich glass of the windows, is extremely fine. All the work before us was constructed by Abbot Knowle (1306-1332) and is Decorated. The Norman choir had two bays with a third for a processional path. Knowle added two bays to the choir and built the Lady Chapel. The clustered piers have triple shafts which support the vaulting. The capitals on these shafts have very graceful foliage. The piers have no capitals, but the mouldings run round the arches continuously, as is not unusual in Decorated work. The vaulting is what is known as lierne. Iron screen-work divides the aisles from the choir. The reredos is modern, erected in 1899, and has some fine carving. The *Stalls* were originally Decorated, but "restoration" has destroyed much, and little of the old work remains. There are some curious *Misereres* : a fox preaching to geese, a tilting with brooms between a man and a woman, one mounted on a pig, the other on a turkey-cock, the story of Reynard the Fox. The pavement is new, and not altogether successful. The organ is a noble instrument placed on the west side, and has been often reconstructed. The *Throne* is modern and has some fine carving. Passing into the north aisle we notice the peculiar vaulting. It will be seen that the roof of the choir and aisles is the same height, and in order to support the weight of the choir-vault transoms are thrown across the aisles supported on arches, and above a vaulting shaft springs from the centre of the transom. This ingenious plan produces the same effect as a flying buttress and is most ingeniously arranged. The windows have beautiful Decorated tracery and the ball-flower is extensively used in the string-course beneath them. The east window has seventeenth-century glass, said to have been given by Nell Gwynne, more probably by Dean Glemham (1661-1667). It treats of the Resurrection, with Jonah and Abraham's sacrifice as types of the same, the Ascension with Elijah as a type. There are monuments here of Robert Codrington (1618) ; Harriet Middleton (1826) ; Paul Bush (1558), the first bishop; Robert Southey, the poet ; Bishop Westfield (1644) ; Bishop Howell (1649) ; and Mary Mason, wife of the poet, with some touching lines (1767).

Between the aisle and the Elder Lady Chapel are the effigies of Maurice, Lord Berkeley (1368), and his wife, Elizabeth. There is a tablet to the memory of Robert Fitzhardinge, the founder of the Cathedral and also of the house of Berkeley. Some Norman corbels will be noticed in the door leading to a staircase in the third bay.

The *Elder Lady Chapel* is Early English and therefore earlier than the choir, and was probably built by Abbot John (1196-1215); it is therefore, as the architectural details testify, very early work. The east window is Decorated. There are some curious grotesques in the spandrels of the arcade—a hunter-goat blowing a horn and carrying a hare on his back, a ram and an ape playing musical instruments, St. Michael with the dragon, and a fox carrying off a goose. The foliage is what is known as stiff leaved, and opposed to the more natural foliage of the Decorated period. The roof is Early Decorated. The eastern *Lady Chapel*, formerly the chancel of the choir, was built by Abbot Knowle and is Decorated like the rest of the eastern part of the Cathedral. It has a magnificent east window with beautiful tracery. This is a Jesse window, showing the descent of our Lord from Jesse, the father of David, and the glass is in the upper parts of the same date as the stone-work. Above we see the arms of many distinguished families—the Berkeleys, Mowbrays, Beauchamps and others. The glass in the other windows is also of the same period and is of much interest. The parapet under the windows is modern. The reredos is ancient, of the same date as the chapel, and designed by Knowle, but it has been much altered in Perpendicular times. The *Sedilia* have been much restored. A characteristic feature of this Cathedral is the star-shaped recesses designed by Knowle, which are very beautiful. In one of these is Abbot Newbury's tomb with ball-flower ornament; in another Abbot Hunt (1473). Here, too, is Abbot Newland's tomb, and a modern brass to the memory of Bishop Butler, and at the back of the reredos a brass to Bishop Ellicott.

The *South Choir Aisle* resembles the north. It has a very similar east window, and the same curious vaulting. Two very interesting chapels adjoin this aisle. The *Berkeley Chapel* is entered by a richly-ornamented doorway which leads into the old sacristy, with its chests for relics and plate, and a hearth for baking sacramental bread. Abbot Knowle was a student of nature and loved to reproduce in stone the fruits and flowers which he saw growing around him. In the ornaments of the doorway we see the ammonite and medlar. The chapel had two altars, as we see the remains of two piscinæ, beneath the two east windows, separated by a screen. There is an altar tomb of Thomas, Lord Berkeley (1321). The lower part of the tomb is Early English. The other chapel is the *Newton Chapel*, which is Late Decorated and almost Perpendicular in some of its details. The ball-flower has ceased to be used as an ornament. There are many memorials of the Newton family here, and one to Bishop Gray (1834). Returning to the south choir aisle we notice another of the curious recesses adorned with oak leaves, acorns and mistletoe. There are some more Berkeley tombs which furnish interesting studies of the armour of the period.

We now enter the *Cloisters*. As we have said, only the north and east walks remain; the north is entirely new, and the east has been much restored. The vestibule and chapter-house are, however, part of the original Norman building, and the work is of Transitional character. It is oblong in shape. The east wall is modern and has three windows. The north and south walls have beautiful arcades, and above lattice work and zigzag mouldings. The west wall has three rows of arcading. Twelve stone coffins were found here and a curious piece of ancient sculpture representing our Lord wounding the head of Satan and rescuing a child by means of the Cross. Adjoining the chapter-house was the dormitory. The refectory was on the south side of the cloister garth. It still exists after many transformations and is the house of the master of the Cathedral School.

The *Great Gateway* should be visited. The lower part is of Norman character, and was part of the founder's work; the upper is Perpendicular and was the work of Abbot Elliot. He probably renewed the rich Norman ornamentation, so much so that in the opinion of Mr. Godwin, the great authority on Bristol architecture, "the so-called Norman gateway of College Green is no Norman gateway, but a Perpendicular restoration of the old work."

Another gateway, which formerly led to the palace destroyed in 1831, exists, which is part of the original Norman work of the Cathedral. At the south-west corner of the cloister is an Early English doorway, which formerly led to the refectory. It is a sad pity that so much of the old monastery has been destroyed.

DIMENSIONS

Total length	300 ft.
Length of nave	125 ft.
Width of nave	69 ft.
Height	52 ft.
Area	22,500 sq. ft.

PRINCIPAL BUILDING DATES

Norman (1142-1170) — Part of transepts, chapter-house, lower part of gateway.

Early English (1196-1215)—Elder Lady Chapel, parts of transepts and Berkeley Chapel.

Decorated (1306-1332)—Choir, Lady Chapel and stalls.
    (1332-1341)—Newton Chapel.

Perpendicular (1428-1481)—Great Tower, upper part of gateway, roof.

Modern—The nave.

The city has a large number of interesting churches. The noble Church of St. Mary, Redcliffe, one of the finest in England, chiefly fourteenth century; All Hallows' (Norman and Perpendicular); Temple Church (Decorated and Perpendicular); St. Philip's, St. Stephen's, St. John's, are the most important.

WELLS CATHEDRAL

THE beautiful city of Wells entirely owes its origin to the noble church and palace built here in early times, around which the houses and population grew. It is one of the most picturesque in England, situated in the most delightful country, and possessing the most perfect ecclesiastical buildings which can be conceived. History tells us that Ina in 704 built a church here, near a spring dedicated to St. Andrew and known as "The Wells," and Edward the Elder, son of Alfred the Great, formed a bishopric for Somerset and set the bishop's throne here. Three Abbots of Glastonbury became Bishops of Wells, which was richly endowed. The first Norman prelate was Giso, who built some dwellings for the secular canons which were destroyed by his successor, John de Villula, a native of Tours, who erected a palace in their stead. Moreover, he moved the seat of the see to Bath, where he had formerly practised medicine, and Wells was allowed to become ruinous. Bath minster we shall visit presently. There was much ancient rivalry between the two places and sore disputings, which were only partially settled by the conjoining of the title " Bath and Wells." Bishop Robert (1135-1166) had pity on the ruinous state of Wells and rebuilt the church. This took place while Stephen and Matilda were fighting for the crown, and Bishop Robert scorned not to take up arms on behalf of Stephen, and was moreover imprisoned by the adherents of his rival. Almost all of Robert's work has disappeared in subsequent alterations. Jocelyn de Wells (1206-1239) has for many years had the credit of building the main part of this beautiful House of God. It is hard to have one's beliefs and early traditions upset, but modern authorities with much reason tell us that we are wrong, and that another Jocelyn—one Reginald Fitz-Jocelyn (1171-1191)—was the main builder of Wells. Old documents recently discovered decide the question, and moreover the style of the architecture is certainly earlier than the fully-developed Early English of Jocelyn de Wells. The latter, and also Bishop Savaricus (1192-1205) carried out the work, but the whole design and a considerable part of the building are due to Bishop

Reginald. Savarac or Savaricus was concerned with the release of Richard I. from his prison in Germany, and was one of the hostages for the payment of his ransom. He styled himself Bishop of Bath and Glastonbury, and when the monks objected he stormed the abbey and beat and imprisoned them. Jocelyn de Wells found his church unfinished and dilapidated. His was a grand era for church-building; moreover, he was a friend of Hugh of Lincoln and Bishop Poore of Salisbury, both consummate architects. So he set to work to finish and repair Reginald's rising church, completed the nave and added that wonderful west front which is one of the glories of this Cathedral. Bishop Burnell (1275-1292) erected in later Early English style the crypt of the chapter-house, which was itself partly built some time late in the Decorated period, probably by Bishop William de la March, a favourite of Edward I., who is said to have advised the plundering of the monasteries. During the episcopate of Drokensford (1309-1329) the central tower was raised, the choir was begun and the Lady Chapel and chapter-house finished. Dean Godelee at this time was a great builder and seems to have devised these additions. Bishop Ralph of Shrewsbury (1329-1363) continued to perfect the Cathedral, enlarging the presbytery and building the fine east end. He did much work outside his church, founding the college, restoring his palaces and fortifying his palace at Wells. The upper part of the Harewell Tower was built by the bishop of that name (1366-1386). This is the south-west tower. The north-west tower was built later still by Bishop Bubwith (1407-1424). This prelate built the east walk of the cloister, the west and south walks being finished by Bishop Beckington (1443-1464) in the Perpendicular style. Wells was then in its full glory. The church, the out-buildings, the episcopal palace, the deanery all combined to form a wonderful architectural triumph, a group of buildings which represented the best achievement of English Gothic art. It was shorn of some of its glory at the Reformation. The church was plundered of the treasures which the piety of many generations had heaped together; the beautiful Lady Chapel in the cloisters was pulled down, and the infamous Duke of Somerset robbed it of its wealth and meditated further sacrilege.

Amongst these despoilers and desecrators of churches there was a mighty hunger for lead ("I would that they had found it scalding," exclaims an old chaplain of Wells). Once the richest of sees, it would probably have been suppressed altogether, but for the advent of Queen Mary to the throne, who appointed Bishop Bourn and restored the palace. In the Civil War it escaped. Some damage was done, the palace was despoiled, and at the Restoration much repair was found needful. Monmouth's rebellion wrought havoc here. The rebels came here in no amiable temper, defaced the statues on the west front, and did much wanton mischief, and would have caroused about the altar had not Lord Grey stood before it with his sword drawn and thus preserved it from the insults of ruffians. Then came the evils of "restoration." A terrible renewing was begun in 1848, when the old stalls were destroyed and much damage done. Better things were accomplished in 1868, save that the grandeur of the west front was belittled by a pipy restoration, when Irish limestone with its harsh hue was used to embellish it. In the palace, too, modern ideas have effaced much of the refinement of its thirteenth-century beauty.

The Exterior

Fergusson declares that though Wells is one of the smallest it is perhaps, taken altogether, the most beautiful of English cathedrals. Some of the distant prospects are perhaps the best. There is a fine view from the Shepton-Mallett Road. We enter the precincts by Browne's Gate at the end of Sadler Street, and see before us the magnificent *West Front*, a masterpiece of art superior to any in this country or abroad. It is 150 feet in width and 70 feet high. Six deep buttresses project from its face. There are six tiers of sculpture. The doors are small. Not for the living throng, but to the dead was this front dedicated who lie in the cemetery at its feet.[1] Here is the history of God's Church on earth expressing its faith and pointing to the hope of the Resurrection. Its style is Early English and is intermediate between the west front of Lincoln and Salisbury. The upper part of the towers is Perpendicular, that on the north being finished by Bishop Bubwith (1407-1424), that on the south by Harewell (1366-1386). In the lowest tier the sculptures have nearly all gone. In the second are angels in small quatrefoils. In the third subjects from the Old and New Testaments. In the fourth and fifth there are 120 statues of kings and bishops and heroes of English history from Egbert to Henry II: The sixth is called the Resurrection tier. And above are the angels and Apostles, and finally the Lord in glory. It is

[1] Prior's *Gothic Art*.

difficult to identify the statues with any feeling of certainty, though many lists have been published which may, or may not, be correct. There can be no doubt about the excellence of the sculpture, and all authorities unite in praising them as being the perfection of design and execution. Flaxman said of them that in them there is a beautiful simplicity, an irresistible sentiment, and sometimes a grace excelling more modern productions.

The *North Porch* is earlier than the west front and possesses transitional features. The zigzag ornament is used, and shows that Norman traditions have not yet passed away; though Early English foliage appears on the weather moulding. On the capitals on the east side are representations of the martyrdom of St. Edmund, who shared the fate of St. Sebastian and was afterwards beheaded. Mystic animals appear in the panels on either side of the arch—one is a cockatrice. Above, three lancets light the parvise.

The *Central Tower* is 182 feet high, and is Early English as far as the height of the roof. In the Decorated period the upper part was added, which caused much disaster, as the foundations were unable to bear the additional weight. Very skilful treatment was required, as we shall see when we enter the church.

The *Nave* is Early English, but Perpendicular tracery has been inserted in the windows, and the walls of both the aisles and clerestory have been crowned with a parapet of Decorated work. The *North Transept* is rather earlier than the nave, and retains much of the Transitional character. It has two aisles, and is not so richly ornamented as the nave. The windows are pointed and have Perpendicular tracery. Passing on we come to the *Chain Gate*, a very beautiful structure erected by Bishop Beckington (1443-1465) in Perpendicular style. Figures of St. Andrew and other saints appear in the niches. The gallery over the Chain Gate connects the Cathedral with the Vicar's College. After passing under the gate we see the beautiful *Chapter-House*, which is octagonal, we are surprised to find the chapter-house in this position and far removed from the cloisters, but this is accounted for by the fact that secular canons served this Cathedral, and not monks; hence the cloisters were an ornamental appendant rather than the centre of the monastic life. The chapter-house was finished in 1319 in Decorated style under the guidance of Dean John de Godilee, who employed one William Joy as the master-mason. There are some curious gargoyles here. The *Choir* and *Lady Chapel* form a beautiful composition. The western portion of the choir was until recently attributed to Jocelyn.

It is now generally believed to have been the work of Bishop Reginald, Jocelyn's predecessor. The eastern portion is the work of Bishop Ralph (1329-1363), the Lady Chapel was finished in 1326. All this is therefore Decorated, and windows of the same style have been inserted in the earlier western portion. There were two Lady Chapels adjoining the cloisters, but these were ruthlessly destroyed by Bishop Barlow in 1552. The *Cloister* does not possess the usual features of a monastic church. It is unusually large, and there are only three walks, the north being absent. The wall of the east walk is Early English, built by Jocelyn, but the rest was rebuilt by Bishop Bubwith; the west and south walks by Bishop Beckington and finished soon after his death. The style is Perpendicular. The grotesque bosses are interesting. An Early English doorway leads to the palace. Over the west walk is the singing-school, and over the east the library. Beckington's rebus (a *beacon* and a *tun*) occurs in the bosses. The garth is known as "Palm Churchyard" from the yew tree in the centre. Branches of yews were carried in processions on Palm Sunday, and this probably accounts for the prevalence of yew trees in churchyards. The cloisters have been made the receptacle of many monuments removed from the Cathedral. The *Library* over the east walk, built by Bubwith, has about 3000 volumes, and contains the books belonging to Bishop Ken. An Aldine edition of Aristotle has the autograph and notes of Erasmus, and there are several important MSS., the chains which formerly attached the books to the desks, a thirteenth-century pyx-cover, and a crozier of the same period.

The *Bishop's Palace*, unfortunately much restored in 1846, is one of the finest examples of a thirteenth-century house existing in England. It was begun by Jocelyn. The great hall, now in ruins, built by Bishop Burnell (1275-1292) for the purpose of great entertainments, was destroyed by Barlow. The chapel is Decorated. The gatehouse, moat and fortifications were constructed by Bishop Ralph of Shrewsbury. The *Deanery* was built by Dean Gunthorpe in 1475, chaplain to Edward IV. On the north is the famous *Vicar's Close*, which has forty-two houses, constructed mainly by Bishop Beckington (1443-1464), with a common hall erected by Bishop Ralph (1340), and chapel by Bubwith, but altered a century later for the use of the Vicars-Choral. We notice the old fireplace, the pulpit from which one of the brethren read aloud during meals, and an ancient painting representing Bishop Ralph making his grant to the kneeling vicars, and some additional figures painted in the time of Elizabeth.

THE INTERIOR

Few will fail to be impressed by the many beauties of this glorious *Nave*, which we will gaze at from the west end. It is rather narrow, but the proportions are good, and the magnificent clustered columns and enriched capitals, the groups of bearing shafts, grotesque carvings, and the fine vault, all combine to form a noble structure. The curious inverted arches at the east end of the nave are remarkable. These were added early in the fourteenth century to save the collapsing central tower; and so skilfully was the work done that the object of the builders was completely accomplished. The nave has generally been assigned to Jocelyn, but architects have noticed that it is only a little removed from the Norman style, and recent investigators have shown that the greater part is the work of Bishop Reginald (1171-1191). The four eastern bays are assigned to him, and the rest to Jocelyn. A close inspection will reveal several points of difference between the earlier and later work. The heads of a king and bishop between the fourth and fifth piers (counting from the west) mark the change. The difference may be thus tabulated [1]—

EAST	WEST
Masonry in small courses of stone.	The blocks are larger.
Small human heads at angles of piers.	No heads.
Grotesque animals in tympana of triforium.	Foliage and larger heads.
Medallions above triforium sunk in the wall.	Flush with the wall.
Capitals plainer.	More ornamented and richer.

The piers are octagonal with clustered shafts. The capitals are enriched with foliage. Birds, animals and monsters twine and perch among the foliage. The triforium arcade is continuous, and composed of lancet openings. The clerestory windows have Perpendicular tracery inserted by Beckington. The roof is vaulted, with bosses of foliage. The *Music Gallery* stands in the central bay

[1] Murray's *Cathedrals*.

on the south side erected in Perpendicular style, and near it formerly was another gallery supported by two brackets, on which are carved the heads of a king and bishop. The curious and grotesque carvings should be carefully studied. The west end has an arcade of five arches. Above are three lancets with dog-tooth moulding and Perpendicular tracery. The glass was collected by Dean Creyghton on the Continent during his exile with Charles II., and represents the life of St. John Baptist. Its date is 1507. The other windows have the figures of King Ina and Bishop Ralph. The north and south aisles correspond with the nave in their architecture. Perpendicular tracery has been inserted in the windows. Under the north-west tower is the Chapel of the Holy Cross, now used as a vestry, and the opposite Chapel is now used by the ringers. There are two beautiful chantries in the nave—one is Bishop Bubwith's Chapel (1421), with much mutilated east end; the other is Sugar's Chantry, formerly dedicated to St. Edmund. Hugh Sugar, dean of Wells, died in 1489. The fan-tracery of the roof, the niches and the cornice of angels are worthy of notice. The *Pulpit* was erected by Bishop Knight (1541-1547). The lectern is by Bishop Creyghton, who erected the west window, and shared Charles II.'s exile. The *Transepts* are rather earlier than the nave, and are part of Reginald's work. They have aisles, and the capitals of the piers are richly sculptured. In the *South Transept* we see on the west Elias, a woman extracting a thorn from her foot, a man with toothache, the grape-stealers and their fate. On the east there is only foliage and no figures. The Chapel of St. Calixtus is on the east, containing the beautiful monument of Dean Husse (1305), with its finely-carved panels. The subjects are the Annunciation, God the Father, and some ecclesiastics. The other Chapel is that of St. Martin, now a vestry, and has the tomb of a Chancellor of Wells (1454). In the transept are the monuments of Lady Lisle (1464), wife of the Earl of Shrewsbury, and of Bishop William de la Marchia (1302). The *Font* is Norman, and probably the only remaining link with the early church built by Bishop Robert (1136-1166). The cover is Jacobean. The *North Transept* resembles the south. Here we see again a series of strange carvings, amongst which are Moses and Aaron, man with goose, woman with toothache. The reason why so many representations of this distressing malady occur is that the shrine of St. William Bytton (1274) was famous for its cures of persons so suffering. On the east are the Chapels of St. David, with tomb of Bishop Still (1607), and Holy Cross with tomb of

Bishop Kidder (1703). Another tomb is that of Bishop Cornish (1513). The famous *Clock* is here with its tilting knights and human-shaped striker, who perform wondrous things when the expiration of each hour summons them to action. We will not dispel the curiosity of the visitor by any description of the performance, which is popular, and should not be missed.

The *Tower* is of Early English date as far as the roofs, and has a fine fan-tracery vault. As we have said, it was raised in the Decorated period, and the superstructure caused a dangerous settlement, which was counteracted by the inverted arches, and some flying buttresses.

The *Choir-Screen* is Decorated, and has not been improved by modern restorers. Above it is the organ, a modern instrument, which replaces the old organ erected by Dean Creyghton.

The *Choir* is very beautiful, but it is only a shadow of what it was before the evil hand of the restorer rested heavily upon it. It is terrible to contemplate the mischief which has been accomplished here in the fatal restoration of 1848. However, it would have been difficult to efface all its beauties, and some of these happily remain. The three west bays are probably Reginald's work, and were formerly attributed to Jocelyn; the rest is Decorated, and two of the west piers have been converted into this style. There is no triforium, its place being taken by rich tabernacle work. At the east end there are three graceful arches; and above these rich tabernacle work, and a large window of seven lights with Late Decorated tracery. There is a lierne vault. The vandals of the nineteenth century destroyed nearly all of the old woodwork, and substituted canopies of Doulting stone. The pulpit is modern; the throne was erected by Beckington, but has unfortunately been much restored. The *Misereres* have happily been saved, and are very remarkable. They are Early Decorated, and can scarcely be surpassed. Amongst the many curious subjects are a mermaid, griffin and various monsters, two goats butting, cats, peacock, cock, fox and geese, lions, rabbits, etc.

The glass of the east window, and of those on each side of it, is fourteenth-century work (*circa* 1330). The east window is very fine, and is a Jesse window, showing the genealogy of our Lord from the "Stem of Jesse," with figures of kings and prophets, the Virgin, and finally the Crucifixion and the Judgment. In the north-east window is a figure of St. George. The *South Choir Aisle* is of the same character as the choir; the windows are Decorated. Here is the famous monument of Bishop Bytton (1274), who was canonised, and whose tomb was much resorted to by pilgrims, especially by those who suffered from toothache. This is the most ancient example of an incised slab in England. Near the saint lie Bishop Beckington (1464), who did so much for this Cathedral), and Bishop Hervey (1894). Below the effigy is a skeleton-like figure, which was intended to proclaim the moral maxim, *memento mori.* The iron-work should be noticed. Here also are the tombs of Bishop Harewell (1386), Bishop Hooper (1727), and Bishop Lake (1626). In the Chapel of St. John the Evangelist are buried Dean Gunthorpe (1498), the builder of the Deanery, and Dean Jenkyns (1854), who was responsible for the "restoration" of the choir. There is a fine Decorated piscina here. The *Retro - Choir* is very beautiful. Slender piers of Purbeck marble support the fine vault. The carving of the capitals and bosses is very excellent. All is in the Decorated style. The *Lady Chapel* is of the same date and style, finished in 1326. Its shape is pentagonal, and it is of rare beauty. The glass is of the same date as that of the choir, but has been restored. Angels bearing the instruments of the Passion appear in the east

Entrance to Cry[pt]

window, and in the tracery of the other windows are the Evangelistic emblems and heads of patriarchs and saints. At the south-east corner of the retro-choir was St. Catherine's Chapel. The glass is old and rich. There is a monument by Chantrey of John Phelips, and that of Bishop Drokensford (1329), who was bishop during the building of the Lady Chapel, and part of the choir is a graceful structure. At the opposite corner is St. Stephen's Chapel, and then we enter the north-east transept or Chapel of St. John Baptist, which contains Bishop Creyghton's tomb (1672), also monuments of John de Myddleton (1337), Bishop Berkeley (1581), Dean Forrest (1446). The *North Choir Aisle* has the tomb of Bishop Ralph (1363), and an effigy, attributed to Bishop Giso (1088). Bishop Jocelyn caused several of these effigies to be executed, in memory of his predecessors. On the north is a door leading to a vaulted passage, which conducts us to the crypt of the chapter-house. Notice the curious carved heads in this passage. There is a curious stone lantern in the wall near the inner door. This crypt or undercroft is on the same level as the floor of the church, and was used as a treasury. It was finished about 1286, and is Late Early English. There is a massive octagonal pier in the centre, and eight other round piers, which support the vaulting. A piscina in the doorway has a curious sculptured dog gnawing a bone. Here are preserved a cope chest, some stone coffins, and other treasures. Retracing our steps to the aisle, we enter the noble *Staircase* leading to the chapter-house. It is Early Decorated, the door at the upper end being added in the Perpendicular period, when the Chain Gate was erected. Two Decorated windows light the staircase. The *Chapter-House*, octagonal in plan, is entered by a fine doorway composed of double arches. There is a curious boss here, composed of four bearded heads. There is a central pillar, with clustered shafts of Purbeck marble, from which the beautiful ribs of the vaulted roof spring. There are eight windows, the mouldings of the arches being ornamented with ball-flower, and retaining some old glass. An arcade runs round the wall under the windows, with ornamented canopies, and beneath this are the stone benches. Sculptured heads and grotesques appear in the ornamentation of the arches. This chapter-house is later than the staircase, and was probably built by Bishop William de la Marchia (1293-1302), the vault being added after his time, and finished in 1319.

DIMENSIONS

Total length . . .	383 ft.
Length of nave . . .	161 ft.
Breadth of nave . . .	82 ft.
Height of nave . . .	67 ft.
Length of choir . . .	103 ft.
Length of transepts . . .	135 ft.
Height of towers . . .	160 ft.
Area	29,070 sq. ft.

PRINCIPAL BUILDING DATES

Early Norman—Font.

Transition (1174-1191)—Eastern bays of nave, transepts, north porch, and west bays of choir.

Early English (1218-1286)—West front, western part of nave, undercroft of chapter-house, palace.

Early Decorated—Staircase to chapter-house.

Decorated (1293-1363) — Chapter-house, Lady Chapel, central tower, inverted arches, east part of choir.

Perpendicular (1386-1400) — Western towers, gateways, Chain Gate, Deanery.

BATH ABBEY

For some time Bath was the rival of Wells, and hot and fierce was the contention between the monks of St. Peter and the canons of St. Andrew at Wells. The monastery was founded here in Saxon times by Offa in 775. In Early Norman times, John de Villula of Tours, who is said to have practised medicine at Bath, became Bishop of Wells, and, by grant from William II., removed the seat of the bishopric to Bath, and rebuilt the Abbey Church, which now became a Cathedral. But the monks liked not this arrangement. In the time of Bishop Robert (1135-1166), in order to settle their disputes, it was decided that the bishop should be styled "of Bath and Wells." But even this did not produce peace. When Jocelyn died the monks of Bath elected Roger without the consent of the canons of Wells, and both chapters nearly ruined themselves by appeals to the Pope and costly litigation. The church at Bath fell much into decay, and was entirely rebuilt by Bishop Oliver King of Wells (1495-1503). He is said to have seen a vision somewhat resembling Jacob's dream, a ladder reaching from earth to heaven, and a voice saying, "Let an Oliver stablish the Crown and a King build the church." A representation of this dream appears on the west front of Bath minster, and an inscription referring to the Parable of the Trees (Judges ix. 8):—

"Trees going to choose their king
Said, Be to us the Olive(r) King."

The style of the church is Late Perpendicular, and was scarcely

L

completed before the monastery was seized and dissolved. It was left in a sorry condition, roofless and ruinous, until it was restored by Bishop Montague in the seventeenth century. It has been restored in modern times, and has lost that dilapidated appearance which long distinguished it. It is a small and not very interesting building, though it lacks not some striking features, and certainly contains some fine tombs and interesting memorials of the fashionable folk who flocked to Bath in the days of its splendour.

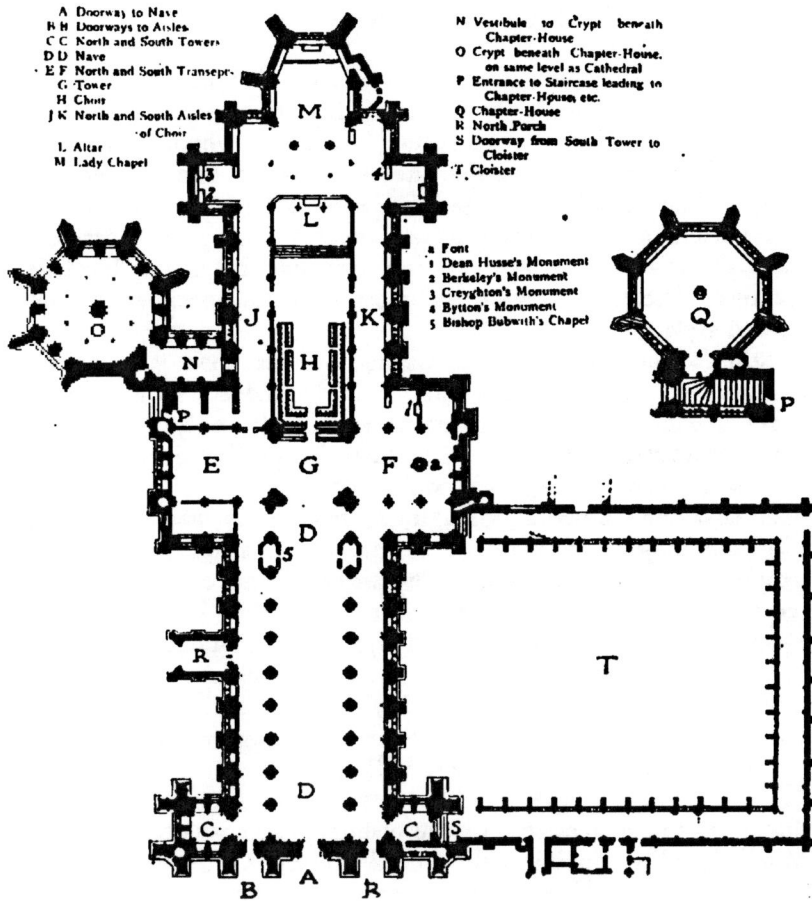

A   Doorway to Nave
B B   Doorways to Aisles
C C   North and South Towers
D D   Nave
E F   North and South Transepts
G   Tower
H   Choir
J K   North and South Aisles
    of Choir
L   Altar
M   Lady Chapel

N   Vestibule to Crypt beneath
    Chapter-House
O   Crypt beneath Chapter-House,
    on same level as Cathedral
P   Entrance to Staircase leading to
    Chapter-House, etc.
Q   Chapter-House
R   North Porch
S   Doorway from South Tower to
    Cloister
T   Cloister

a   Font
1   Dean Husse's Monument
2   Berkeley's Monument
3   Creyghton's Monument
4   Bytton's Monument
5   Bishop Bubwith's Chapel

PLAN OF WELLS CATHEDRAL

EXETER CATHEDRAL

EXETER, the noble city of the west, which proudly bears the motto granted to it by Queen Elizabeth, *Semper Fidelis*— "Always Faithful," has a venerable Cathedral, which was commenced in Norman ·times on the site of a Saxon church, entirely removed. The principal feature of Exeter is its Decorated work. A large portion of the Cathedral was erected during that period; and as Salisbury is the most perfect example of Early English architecture, Exeter represents the most beautiful specimen of the Decorated style.

Southey's judgment on the Cathedral was that "it looked finest when you could only see half of it." Indeed, it is difficult to obtain a good view, and the north side is the only one which presents a favourable prospect. The historian of Exeter Cathedral, Mr. Hewett, wrote: "As we walk round this, we cannot but consider that the Cathedral, though far from lofty, and presenting none of the majestic features of several of its sister churches, is nevertheless a fine composition. The aisles of the choir and nave, intercepted by the stately Norman towers, further broken by the prominence of their chantries, and spanned by flying buttresses richly pinnacled; the large, pure windows, which pierce both aisles and clerestory; the roof, highly pitched, and finished with crest-tiles, form a decidedly graceful and pleasing whole." With this excellent description all visitors will agree.

Glancing back at the early history of the see, we find that Crediton was the ancient seat of the bishop, where was born in 680 St. Winfrid, called Boniface, the apostle of the Germans. There was a monastery at Exeter in the time of Athelstan, which was much plundered by the Danes. In 1050 Bishop Leofric, the favourite of Edward the Confessor, removed his episcopal seat to Exeter, and continued to hold it when William the Conqueror came. Osbern was appointed in 1072, but he contented himself with the old Saxon church, and it was not until William Warelwast (1107-1136), nephew of William the Conqueror, became bishop that the present Cathedral was begun. The Norman work

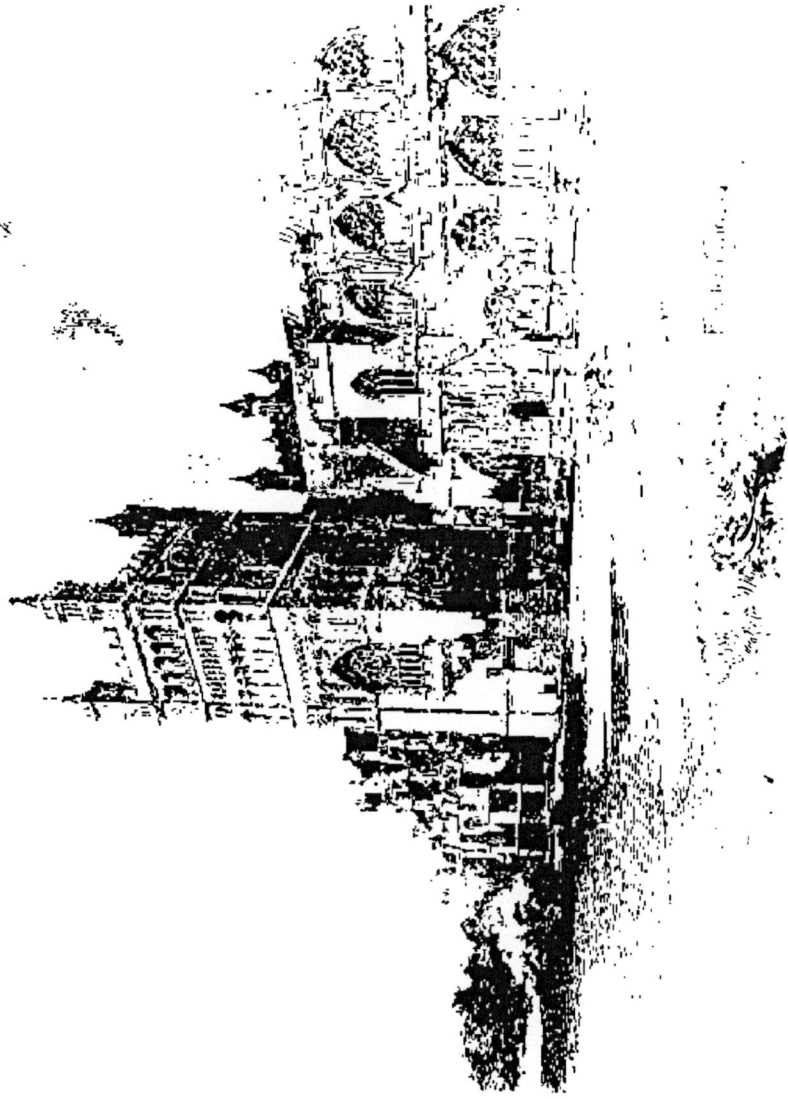

was continued by Bishop Marshall (1194-1206), who is said to have "finished the building according to the plot and foundation which his predecessors laid."

Exeter has suffered many sieges, and during that of Stephen, in 1136, the Cathedral was much injured by fire. The two towers at the end of the transepts are all the portions that remain of Warelwast's building, and one of these (that on the north) has been much altered, until it has assumed the features of Perpendicular style. This was done by Bishop Courtenay (1478-1487), when he transferred here a great bell from Llandaff.

In 1258 a poor man's son, one Walter Bronescombe, though not in priests' orders, was elected bishop, and set to work to rebuild his Cathedral, his labours being continued by his successor. The Lady Chapel with adjoining chapels was partly built by this bishop. His successor, Bishop Quivil, the foe of the Franciscans (1280-1291), finished it, and erected the north and south transepts. The choir, nave, porches and west front were built by Bishops Stapledon (1308-1326) and Grandisson (1327-1369). Stapledon was a great statesman, and in the troubles of the second Edward's reign took the side of the king against the queen and Mortimer, and was murdered by the citizens of London in Cheapside. Grandisson was also a mighty prelate who refused to allow the Archbishop of Canterbury to visit his Cathedral as his ecclesiastical superior. He, with a band of armed men, met the intruding archbishop at the west door and forbade him to enter, and an armed conflict was with difficulty averted. These mediæval bishops were very powerful. They usually built a strong wall with gates around the precincts of the Cathedral, and ruled their clergy, their servants and dependants quite independently of any external control. The conflicts between the clergy and the townsfolk were very numerous, and the struggle severe in nearly all our cities and monastic towns.

When Queen Elizabeth came to the throne, "visitors" were appointed to examine churches and to remove all that savoured of "superstition." Their zeal outran their discretion, and much mischief was wrought in Exeter and elsewhere by their iconoclastic violence. Strange events took place during the Commonwealth period. The Cathedral was divided into two portions by a brick wall, and in one called "West Peter's" an independent preacher thundered forth his declamation, while in the other, "East Peter's," a Presbyterian divine conducted his form of service. Happily the

Restoration put an end to these curious proceedings, and the wall was taken down, and the Church of England service renewed.

We will now examine the west front erected at the close of the fourteenth century. The screen is very remarkable and beautiful, and has three rows of figures of saints and kings and warriors. In the first row appear angels; the second has figures of kings and knights, and the third saints, and figures of Athelstan and Edward the Confessor stand above them. Some of the ancient figures have crumbled away and been replaced by modern sculptures. Bishop Brantyngham was the builder of this screen, who lived in the time of Richard II., and the crowns and armour represented on the figures belong to that period. The figures in the lower row, beginning on the left, are :—

1. Canute.
2. Edgar.
3. Ethelred.
4. Justice, } small figures
5. Fortitude, } above north
6. Discipline, } door.
7. Edward II.
8. Henry III.
9. } Unknown bishops.
10. }
11. Richard I.
12. Henry II.
13. Stephen.
14. Henry I.
15. William I., { a modern imitation.

16. Robert of Normandy.
17. William II.
18. A king unknown.
19. } Bishops.
20. }
21. John.
22. Edward I.
23. Edward III., { over
24. The Black Prince, { south door.
25. Godfrey de Bouillon.
26. Stephen, Count of Blois.
27. Guy de Lusignan.
28. Ethelwold.
29. Alfred.
30. Edward the Elder.

In the upper row, beginning at the left hand, are :—

1. Samuel.
2. Samson.
3. Jephtha.
4. Gideon.
5. Barak.
6. Deborah.
7. Noah.
8. St. Matthew.
9. St. John.

10. St. Jude.
11. St. Bartholomew.
12. St. Matthias.
13. St. Philip.
14. St. Andrew.
15. St. Peter.
16. King Richard II.
17. King Athelstan.
18. St. Paul.

19. St. John.
20. St. James the Greater.
21. St. Thomas.

22. St. James the Less, { a modern statue.

23. St. Simon.
24. St. Luke.
25. St. Mark.
26. St. Augustine.

27. King Ethelbert.
28. St. Berinus.
29. St. Boniface.
30. Kynigils, ⎫
31. Cwichelm, ⎪
32. Kenwalch, ⎬ Kings of
33. Kentwald, ⎪ Wessex.
34. Caedwalla, ⎪
35. Ina, ⎭

The sculpture has been pronounced "remarkable, characteristic and beautiful," but that at Wells and Lincoln is earlier and perhaps better.

Above the screen is a platform on which the bishop used to stand when he blessed the people, and also the choristers and minstrels when they hailed with song the advent of distinguished persons.

The three doorways should be noticed. The central one has a moulding of carved foliage, and on the central boss of the groined roof is a representation of the Crucifixion. The south doorway has two sculptures, the appearance of an angel to Joseph in a dream, and the Adoration of the Shepherds. Between the south and central doorways is the Chantry of St. Radegunde, which we will examine on entering the Cathedral. The north porch was built by Grandisson, and is very beautiful with its triple canopy. The Puritan soldiers have mutilated the Crucifixion scene on the east wall. On the central boss is a well-carved Agnus Dei. Notice the cresting of the roof in a *fleur-de-lis* pattern, which somewhat relieves the long, unbroken stretch of leaden roofing.

We now enter the Cathedral. Though the nave is less lofty than many, it is most beautiful, and the richness of the architectural details abundantly atones for the lack of height, which is 70 feet. The roof springs from slender vaulting shafts and is studded with beautifully-carved bosses, representing foliage, animals, strange figures and heraldic shields. The murder of Thomas à Becket occurs in one of these bosses. Clustered pillars of Purbeck marble support the roof and separate the nave from the aisles. Notice the sculptured corbels between the arches, which are peculiar, and the exquisite carving of the leaves and figures. In the triforium on the north side is the *Minstrels' Gallery*, the most perfect in England, where the musicians played on high festivals, or on the occasion of some Royal visitor. The figures are represented as playing on various instruments—cittern, bagpipes, flageolet, violin, harp, trumpet, organ, guitar, some unknown wind instrument, tambour and cymbals. The heads of Edward III. and his queen, Philippa, support two niches. This gallery is a very beautiful example of mediæval art.

Instead of the usual triforium we have a blind arcade, the height of which is much less than in most cathedrals, but above this there is a very lofty clerestory. The windows of the nave are Decorated, and have a great variety of most beautiful and elaborate tracery. They are arranged in pairs, one window corresponding to its opposite. The glass of the west window, erected in 1766, is a great eyesore, and spoils the beauty of the stone tracery.

We have abundant evidence that this noble nave was constructed almost entirely in Norman times, and subsequently transformed into the Decorated style, just as Winchester was changed from Norman to Perpendicular work. Disturbances of masonry in both north and south walls indicate the position of Norman pilasters, and outside flat buttresses of Norman type are observed which correspond to the position of these. We gather that the nave was finished in Norman times by Bishop Marshall, and that Stapledon (1308-1326) began the transformation, which was carried on and completed by Grandisson (1327-1369).

Nor must the work of our modern men be disregarded. The nave was in a very dilapidated state. The Purbeck marble columns were fallen into decay, and hideous high pews disfigured the view. Sir Gilbert Scott in recent times most judi-

Detail of Minstrels' Gallery

ciously restored the Cathedral, and made it again one of the finest in the land.

We will now examine the chapels and monuments in the nave. On the left of the west door is the *Chapel of St. Radegunde*, which contained formerly the body of Bishop Grandisson; but in the time of Queen Bess the tomb was plundered and his remains scattered no one knows whither. St. Radegunde was a Frankish princess, the wife of Chlotar, the son of King Clovis. Notice the carved figure of our Lord on the roof, His hand outstretched to bless, and the holes in the stone for suspending lamps.

On the north side is the Chapel of St. Edmund, which is earlier than the nave itself, and was connected with it by Bishop Grandisson.

The following monuments in the nave should be examined:—

North Aisle—

Tablet memorial of Lieutenant Allen, and window to memory of one of the Earls of Devon.

Brass memorial of men of North Devon Regiment slain in Afghan war (1880-1881), with regimental flags.

Memorial of 9th Lancers who died in India.

Tablet to the musician Samuel Wesley.

South Side of Nave—

High tomb of Hugh Courtenay (d. 1377), second Earl of Devon, and of his Countess, Margaret (d. 1391), a connection of Edward I. The effigies have been much mutilated.

Brass to memory of General Elphinstone, V.C. (d. 1890).

Brass to Hugh, second Earl of Devon.

Window to Thomas Latimer.

Window to Dean Cowie.

We now pass into the north transept. The Norman towers at each end of the transepts were originally separated from the church. Bishop Quivil, however, wishing to enlarge the building, took down the massive walls which divided the interior of the towers from the body of nave, and constructed arches to sustain the sides of the tower. The original Norman walls remain, and in the north transept one Norman window and two narrow, circular-headed doorways. Quivil also erected the two galleries. On the east of north transept is *St. Paul's Chapel*, used as a vestry for lay choral vicars; there are here some interesting old tiles with heraldic devices, and amongst them the arms of Richard, Duke of Cornwall, brother of Henry III. Near this is the *Sylke Chantry*, founded in 1485 by William Sylke, sub-chanter, whose skeleton effigy proclaims the message—*Sum quod eris, fueram quod es, pro me, precor, ora.* An interesting mural painting has been discovered representing the Resurrection.

The old clock is very remarkable, which is about 700 years old. The historian of the Cathedral thus describes it :—

" On the face or dial, which is about 7 feet in diameter, are two circles : one marked from one to thirty for the moon's age; the other figured from one to twelve twice over for the hours. In the centre is fixed a semi-globe representing the earth, round which a smaller ball, the moon, painted half white and half black, revolves monthly, and by turning on its axis shows the varying phases of the luminary which it represents. Between the two circles is a third ball, representing the sun, with a *fleur-de-lis*, which points to the hours as it daily revolves round the earth."

The maker of the clock was a believer in the old-fashioned astronomy which recognised the earth, and not the sun, as the centre of the solar system. Below the clock is a door leading to the tower, which contains the great bell called " Peter," which is only exceeded in weight by the Great Tom of Oxford. It was brought from Llandaff by Bishop Courtenay at the end of the fifteenth century, and weighs 12,500 tons. It was cracked on 5th November 1611, " from a too violent ringing in commemoration of the Gunpowder Plot."

We now enter the south transept, which is similar to the north. The monuments here are interesting. There is the supposed tomb of Bishop John the Chaunter (1185-1191), but is of later date ; a sixteenth-century monument of Leofric, the first Bishop of Exeter ; a mural tablet to the memory of Sir Peter Carew, who played an important part in the rebellion of the Devon men, caused by the changes introduced into the Prayer-Book at the Reformation, when they besieged Exeter and well-nigh gained an entrance. Sir John Gilbert has a monument, a relative of Sir Walter Raleigh, one of the brave discoverers of the Elizabethan age and founders of our maritime supremacy. The colours of the Cornwall Light Infantry hang here, which were carried at Waterloo and in the Indian Mutiny.

The Chantry of the Holy Ghost in the south-west corner of this transept is a Norman structure. It has a font which was first used at the baptism of Henrietta, daughter of Charles I., who was born in Exeter in 1644. The Chapel of St. John the Baptist, on the east side, is similar to that of St. Paul in the north transept. Bishop Oldham, whose chantry is in the south choir aisle, erected the screen of this chapel. Beyond the Chapel of the Holy Ghost is the chapter-house. The cloisters were destroyed by the Puritans. The chapter-house has been recently restored. Notice the Early English character of the arcade (thirteenth century) in the lower part; the upper part has Perpendicular niches. The Chapter Library has about 8000 volumes.

Retracing our steps we approach the choir, entered by a door in the beautiful screen supporting the organ. This was the old rood-screen, on which formerly stood the rood or figure of our Lord on the Cross. It was erected in the fourteenth century. The rose and thistle in the carvings were inserted later, in the time of James I., to mark the Union of England and Scotland under one monarch, but these have happily been removed, and probably the worthless paintings belong to the same period. The organ was built by Loosemore in 1665 (one of the oldest in England), rebuilt in 1819, and has been so much renovated that very little of the old work remains.

The choir is remarkably fine. The style is now Decorated. The original Norman choir extended to the third arch. Bishop Marshall completed this by adding four more bays. Then came the builders of the early fourteenth century who transformed the Norman pillars and other details, and converted the choir into Decorated work. The bishops who accomplished all this were De Bytton (1292-1306) and Walter de Stapledon (1306-1329) and Bishop Grandisson (1327-1369). The last dedicated the high altar in 1328. The bosses of the vaulted roof are worthy of especial examination, so remarkable are they for the delicacy of the carved foliage. The choir has been carefully restored in recent years, and the stalls, pulpit and reredos are modern, and were designed by Sir Gilbert Scott. Notice the interesting old misereres, which are very remarkable, and probably the oldest and most curious in England. The foliage denotes the Early English period, and they were probably designed by Bishop Bruere (1224-1244). Notice the mermaid and merman on the south side, the elephant, knight slaying a leopard, a minstrel, etc. The lofty bishop's throne was erected by Stapledon, and is said to have been taken down and hidden away during the civil war period. The painted figures represent the four great building bishops—Warelwast, Quivil, Stapledon and Grandisson. The sedilia by Stapledon are very fine. Notice the carved lions' heads, and the heads of Leofric, Edward the Confessor and his wife Editha. The east window is Early Perpendicular, inserted by Bishop Brantyngham in 1390, and contains much old glass. The tombs in the choir are:—

On North Side—

> Bishop Stapledon (holding a crozier and a book).
> Bishop Marshall (d. 1206).
> Bishop Lacey (d. 1455), to which tomb pilgrimages used to be made on account of the reported miracles wrought there.
> Bishop Bradbridge (d. 1578).

On South Side—

> Bishop Chichester (d. 1155).
> Bishop Wolton (1594).

Entering the north choir aisle we see the Chapel of St. Andrew, renovated by Stapledon, having an upper chamber containing the archives, the Fabric Rolls, MSS. of Roger Bacon, Leofric's book of Saxon poetry, and many other valuable treasures.

Next in order we see the Chantry of St. George, or Speke's Chantry (Perpendicular style), containing the monument of Sir John Speke, who endowed this chantry for the good of his soul. When the Cathedral was divided into two portions in the days of the Puritans, a doorway was made through the east window as an entrance to "East Peter's." At the east end of this aisle is the Chapel of St. Mary Magdalene, erected originally by Bronescombe, transformed by Quivil, but has Perpendicular screen. The east window has good fifteenth-century glass. Notice the noble monuments of Sir Gawain Carew (1589, restored in 1857), his wife and nephew, Sir Peter Carew (*see* p. 172). The latter is remarkable as a very late example of cross-legged effigy. The monuments in this north choir are—a cross-legged effigy of Sir Richard de Stapledon, brother of the bishop (d. 1330). [It need not be stated that this fashion of crossing the legs has nothing to do with the Crusades] ; effigy of Bishop Carey (d. 1626) ; a tablet to Robert

Hall, son of the bishop; tablet to Canon Rogers (d. 1856); an emaciated sepulchral figure; Elizabethan tomb of Anthony Harvey (1564), who gained great wealth from the dissolution of monasteries.

Passing behind the high altar we come to the ambulatory, or "procession path." The style is Early Decorated. Notice the ancient Bible-boxes and the two Jacobean tablets. The windows contain good modern glass.

The Lady Chapel was entirely transformed by Bishop Quivil (1280-1291) into the Decorated style. The bosses in the east bay show the Saviour's head and the emblems of the Evangelists. The reredos was erected by Grandisson, but only the central portion is ancient, the rest has been severely "restored." This chapel contains the tombs of: —

1. Bishop Peter Quivil (d. 1291), a slab with the inscription —*Petra tegit Petrum nihil officiat sibi tetrum.*

2. Bishop Bartholomaus Iscanus (d. 1184), a bearded figure, of military type.

3. Bishop Simon of Apulia (d. 1223). This effigy, when compared with the last, shows the advance of art made in a century.

4. Bishop Bronescombe (d. 1280). The canopy is older than the monument, and is Perpendicular.

5. Bishop Stafford (d. 1419). A fine monument, much defaced.

6. Sir John and Lady Doddridge. Sir John (d. 1628) was one of the judges of James I., called by Fuller the "sleepy judge, because he would sit on the bench with his eyes shut to sequester his sight from distracting objects." The dress of Lady Doddridge is remarkable.

In the south choir aisle we see first the Chapel of St. Gabriel, similar to that of St. Mary Magdalene on the north. This was built by Bishop Bronescombe, whose patron saint was St. Gabriel. The colouring of the roof has been carefully restored. Some early glass is in the windows. Then we enter Bishop Oldham's Chantry, or the Chapel of St. Saviour. This bishop died in 1519. His chantry resembles the Speke Chantry in the opposite aisle. Notice the effigy of the bishop, with the owls in the panels, referring to the first syllable of his name, "old," or "owld." The bishop was a Lancashire man, and in that county *old* is usually pronounced *owld*.

The third chapel in the south choir aisle is that of St. James, built by Bishop Marshall, and renovated by Bishop Bronescombe in very Early Decorated style. It contains a beautiful monument, raised in the fifteenth century to the memory of Leofric, first Bishop of Exeter. There are two cross-legged effigies in this aisle, which are usually said to represent Crusaders.

With this chapel our tour of the Cathedral closes. Of some of the great men who have been Bishops of Exeter we have already spoken. The names Warelwast, Marshall, Bronescombe, Quivil, Stapledon, Grandisson, have often been mentioned, and of others whose tombs still adorn their mighty resting-place. Others there are whose memory remains. Miles Coverdale, the well-known reformer; Joseph Hall, the famous theologian; John Gauden, the supposed author of the *Eikon Basilike* (though modern scholars have come round to the belief that the book was really written by Charles I.); the learned Seth Ward; Trelawny, one of the seven bishops committed to the Tower by James II.; Phillpots and Temple, have all added lustre to the See of Exeter.

The city of Exeter is full of interest. The old Guild Hall and scanty remains of Rougemont Castle should be visited, and fifteen miles away is the noble collegiate Church of Ottery St. Mary, which well repays a minute examination. In construction it somewhat resembles the Cathedral of Exeter, and the main part of the building belongs to the fourteenth century.

DIMENSIONS

Total length, 383 ft.; length of nave, 140 ft.; breadth of nave, 72 ft.; height of nave, 66 ft.; area, 29,000 sq. ft.

PRINCIPAL BUILDING DATES

1107-1200—Part of towers in transept and core of walls of nave; 1224-1244—stalls; 1258-1291—Lady Chapel and transepts; 1308-1369—choir, nave, porches and west front; 1390-1519—east window, part of chapter-house, Oldham's Chantry, Speke's Chantry.

TRURO CATHEDRAL

TRURO is one of the oldest towns in England. The courts of the Duchy of Cornwall are held here, and it once enjoyed the privilege of a mint. In the time of Elizabeth it had jurisdiction over the port of Falmouth. Norden, in his survey of England, in 1574, wrote of Truro :—" There is not a towne in the west part of the shire more commendable for neatness of buyldinges, nor discommendable for the pride of the people." It showed its loyalty by furnishing a large body of soldiers for the king in 1642, commanded by Sir Ralph Hopton.

In 1876 the See of Truro was formed, and a new Cathedral was built, Mr. Pearson being the architect. It is one of the most important modern ecclesiastical buildings in England, and is a fine imitation of the Early English style at its best period. The south wall of the old Church of St. Mary, which formerly stood on this site, has been incorporated in the new Cathedral. The newness of this Cathedral and the entire absence of any historical traditions and associations will perhaps hardly tempt travellers to journey so far west to see the creation of modern architects and builders. The whole plan of the Cathedral has not yet been completely carried out, and the church still lacks its towers. Whether our modern architects can build so surely and so well as our ancient monks and priors time will show ; but reports speak none too well of the substantial nature of all that has been done at Truro.

M

GLOUCESTER CATHEDRAL

GLOUCESTER is a very venerable city. It was a Roman station, and was known as Glevum. Remains of the old Roman wall of the city exist in various places, under the house, 36 Westgate Street, under a furniture shop (Messrs. Lea) in Northgate Street, at "Symond's Arms," in Hare Lane. Roman pavements and pottery, coins and altars have also been found, and the four straight streets crossing in the centre are the modern forms of the old Roman roads which intersected the city, forming *insulæ*, as the sections were called. It was an important place in Saxon times, and Bede called it one of the noblest cities in the land. The first monastery was founded by Osric in 681 for monks and nuns. Of the history of this we shall treat presently. The Danes, of course, ravaged and burnt the city. Saxon and Norman kings loved the fair city of the west. We seem to see a procession of monarchs who held their courts here—Alfred, Athlestan, Edgar, Hardicanute, Edward the Confessor, and then the stark Conqueror, who here ordered the compilation of that important survey, the *Domesday Book*. "In the reign of Rufus," wrote a great historian, "everything that happened at all somehow contrived to happen at Gloucester." Here Anselm was consecrated Archbishop of Canterbury. It is famous for lampreys, for which Henry I., when feasting here, acquired a liking, which unhappily proved fatal to him, as he died of a surfeit of them. Here Henry II. held a great council, and Henry III. was crowned, "who loved Gloucester better than London." The Statutes of Gloucester were passed here in an Edwardian Parliament, and the murdered king, Edward II., found here his last resting-place. Numerous Parliaments were held here, and monarchs visited the city. In the Civil War period Gloucester was held by the Parliamentarians, and subjected to a protracted siege, which was eventually raised by the advent of Earl of Essex. The city retains many of its old houses. The house of Robert Raikes, the founder of Sunday Schools, is a fine old building. The Deanery, formerly the prior's lodging, has many interesting associations. Here Henry VIII. and Anne Boleyn sojourned. The inns are famous, especially "New Inn," which was used by

the pilgrims to the shrine of Edward II., and "The Old Raven." Colonel Massey, the governor during the siege, sojourned at 154 Westgate Street. Before the dissolution of monasteries there were many religious houses, and the friars were numerous; there were colleges of Grey, White and Black Friars, some remains of which still exist. There are several interesting churches—St. Mary de Crypt, a cruciform building of twelfth century, with some Decorated and Perpendicular work; St. Mary de Lode, built on the site of a Roman temple, with an old chancel and tower; St. Michael, from the tower of which the curfew sounds each night; St. Nicholas, of Norman construction.

HISTORY OF THE CATHEDRAL

Gloucester was one of the sees founded by Henry VIII.; its episcopal life, therefore, does not extend further back than 1541, when the last Abbot of Tewkesbury became the first Bishop of Gloucester. The story of the minster, however, carries us back to very early times. The first Abbey, as we have said, was founded by Osric, nephew of King Ethelred, in 689, and was designed for both monks and nuns. It was not long-lived, and in a century was deserted and fell into decay. The Mercian kingdom was much distracted, and confusion reigned until Beornwulph restored the ruined walls of St. Peter's Abbey, and introduced secular canons, who seem to have lived as they pleased, and loved not discipline. So Canute in 1022 turned them out and established Benedictine monks. These did no better. Their abbot, Eadric, was a waster of the goods of the Abbey, and the pious chronicler saw in the destruction of the monastery by fire the vengeance of God for their sins. Then Bishop Ealdred of Worcester, who brought back the Black monks of St. Benedict, began to build a new church. Then came Abbot Wulfstan from the Worcester Monastery in 1072, and Abbot Serlo, a worthy monk of Mont St. Michel, who found desolation, an almost empty monastery, a poor, mean building, and began to raise that glorious pile which we see now. It was dedicated in 1100, when there was a mighty concourse of bishops and great men. A remarkable sermon was preached here by Abbot Fulcher of Shrewsbury, prophetic of the death of the cruel king, Rufus. Abbot Serlo sent to warn him, but in vain, and soon the news of his death in the New Forest rang throughout the country.

Fire frequently played havoc with the minster. In 1102 it suffered much, and again in 1122, when "in Lent-tide the town was burnt while the monks were singing their Mass, and the deacon had begun the Gospel *Præteriens Jesus*," and the fire came in the upper part of the steeple, and burnt all the monastery and the treasures except a few books and three Mass robes. Again in 1179 and 1190 fires raged. The Early English builders set to work to repair the damage, and the church was re-dedicated by Walter de Cantilupe, Bishop of Worcester, in 1239. The monks were now very busy building, and in 1242 they had finished the stone vaulting of the nave, which replaced the old Norman wood vault; in 1246 the south-west tower was completed, and they had begun to rear for themselves a new refectory. Yet another fire in 1300 wrought havoc in the cloisters, and deprived the monks of their dormitory. Abbot Thokey was a noble prelate who did much building, erected some of the beautiful Decorated windows in the aisles and choir triforium, and was the means of enriching his Abbey "beyond the dreams of avarice." When Edward II. lay dead, foully murdered at Berkeley Castle, unlike the time-serving Abbot of Bristol, who feared the anger of Queen Isabella and her party, he boldly demanded the body of the dead king and gave it honoured burial in his minster. Then arose that strange cult, the worship at the dead king's shrine. Thousands came from far and near, and their offerings so enriched the monastic treasury that the monks were able to adorn and beautify their church and monastery, and make it one of the glories of English architectural achievement. The fearless abbot felt himself too old to carry on the work; so he resigned in favour of his friend, Abbot Wygmore (1331-1337), who began to erect that "veil of stone" which covers the old Norman work, and is such a characteristic feature of Gloucester.

The south transept was the first recased, a noble screen erected, and the work was carried on by succeeding abbots. Abbot de Stanton (1337-1351) constructed the vaulting of the choir and the stalls on the prior's side, which Abbot Horton completed on the abbot's side, together with the altar and choir and north transept, and also began the great cloister, which Abbot Froucester finished. The west front, south porch and two western bays of the nave are Abbot Morwent's work (1420-1437). The tower was built by Abbot Seabrooke (1450-1457), and Abbots Hanley (1457-1472) and Farley (1472-1498) built the Lady Chapel.

At length the day of dissolution came. Abbot Malvern, the

Cathedral from S.E.

Herbert Railton

GLOUCESTER

last abbot, was offered the bishopric which Henry VIII. had just founded; but he declined, and died of a broken heart. The continued progress of adornment was checked by the appropriation of much of the wealth of the monastery by the king, and the building began to fall into decay. It did not suffer much during the Civil War, in spite of the long siege. The Lady Chapel was mutilated and defaced, and some other damage done, but the burghers seem to have acted well, took a pride in their church, and suffered it not to be destroyed. There have since been frequent " restorations," and some damage done by destructive architects; but, on the whole, Gloucester has escaped with less scars than many of our cathedrals, and retains much of its original beauty and delicate attractiveness.

THE EXTERIOR

The plan is cruciform, and consists of a nave with two aisles; north and south transepts, with apsidal chapels on the east side of each; a tower rises at the crossing. The eastern portion consists of choir with aisles, forming a processional path, with four apsidal chapels opening from them, and a Lady Chapel. With the exception of the Lady Chapel this plan is exactly the same as that of the original Norman church built by Abbot Serlo. We approach the Cathedral from the south-east and obtain a good view of its beauties across the close. The *West Front*, built by Abbot Morwent (1420-1437), is not very rich or striking when compared with many others. There is a large Perpendicular window, and another on each side, and a rather small doorway. The flanking buttresses are crowned with pinnacles, and a cross crowns the centre of the embattled parapet. The pierced buttresses, designed so as not to darken the west window, and the parapets of open-work below and above, are distinguishing features. The south aisle is Abbot Thokey's work, and is very beautiful with its fine Decorated work. The buttresses are very massive, and are surmounted by figures, and the windows deeply recessed.

The *South Porch* is rich Perpendicular work, built by Abbot Morwent. The figures are modern, and represent SS. Peter and Paul, and the four Evangelists, Osric and Abbot Serlo, the founders of the earlier and Norman Church—SS. Jerome, Ambrose, Augustine and Gregory—against whose figures the fanatics of Bristol manifested such unreasonable hate. There is an upper chamber or parvise. The doors are contemporary with the building. The *South Transept* shows the remodelling of the Perpendicular period. Norman work may be seen in the arcading, the turrets, and traces of an original window ; while the capping of the turrets, the windows and battlement belong to the Perpendicular style.

Passing on to the east we notice the beautiful lofty choir. The main part of the walls are Norman, and we notice the unusual polygonal radiating chapels, which are part of the original Norman plan. The windows are Decorated and Perpendicular, inserted in Norman openings. The great east window is the largest and finest in England. The *Lady Chapel* was originally Early English work, built in 1225, but it was rebuilt in 1457-1499, during the rule of Abbots Hanley and Farley. It has four bays, each bay being filled with a lofty Perpendicular window. There is a passage beneath the chapel, which was necessary in order to reach the northern side. The chapel is one of the most beautiful in England. The central *Tower* is remarkable for its grace and grandeur. The present one is the work of Abbot Seabrooke (1450-1457), and belongs to the Perpendicular period. The bells are ancient, and happily were saved, when the monastery was dissolved, from the greedy hands of the commissioners of Henry VIII. The monastic buildings are on the north side, which we shall examine later. There is a fine view of the Cathedral from the north-west. On the north-west is the Deanery, formerly the prior's lodging, a very interesting house ; and between it and the north aisle is a passage, the old Norman slype communicating between the cloisters and the close.

THE INTERIOR

Entering by the south porch we note its Norman character. The old Norman wooden roof has been replaced by a stone vault, and Decorated windows of the time of the second Edward have been inserted, but otherwise there has been little change. The west end, with two bays of the nave, is Abbot Morwent's work (1420-1437). He destroyed two western towers or turrets, which were built in 1222-1243 in place of two similar Norman structures. The height of the Norman piers is unusual, leaving a small space for the triforium and clerestory. The zigzag and double cable moulding appear on the main arches. Abbot Serlo was the builder of the original nave. The stone vault was erected by the monks in the thirteenth century (1242), when the clerestory was altered in the

NAVE PILLARS FROM THE WEST

Early English style by Abbot Foliot (1228-1243). Morwent inserted Perpendicular tracery in these windows. The remains of coloured decoration were discovered during the restoration. We have mentioned the numerous fires which wrought havoc here. Traces of the fire may still be seen in the reddened surface of the piers. The contrast between the Norman piers and the Perpendicular piers at the west end is noticeable, also the disappearance of the triforium in the last bay and the lierne vault. The west window contains some modern glass inserted in memory of Bishop Monk (1856). There is a curious series of grotesque heads on the arches of the nave showing the mummeries of gleemen. The story of the *North Aisle* is similar to that of the nave. We have the same Norman work and the Perpendicular western bays of Abbot Morwent. Perpendicular tracery fills the Norman windows which have zigzag mouldings, and the vault is Norman. The monks' entrance to the cloisters is at the west end of the north wall, and is richly ornamented in Perpendicular style. Another Perpendicular doorway, called the Abbot's Door, is at the east end of the wall. The history of the mythical King Lucius is the subject of the west window. There are memorials of Bishop Warburton (1779), the friend of Pope, a learned divine; Flaxman's monument of Sarah Morley and Thomas Machen (1614).

The *South Aisle* retains some of its Norman style, but was remodelled by Abbot Thokey (1306-1329) in the Decorated style. The ball-flower ornament is much used on the windows. The vault is Decorated work erected by Thokey, and the windows have been more effectually transformed than in the north aisle. There are monuments to John Jones, M.P. for Gloucester at the time of the Gunpowder Plot, with his deeds and documents; Sir G. O. Paul (1820), a prison reformer; Dr. Jenner, the discoverer of vaccination. The Chantry of Abbot Seabrooke (1457), the builder of the tower, is at the east of this aisle, much mutilated. The chantry has been restored. The effigy it a good study of ecclesiastical dress of the period. Near at hand are the effigies of a knight and his lady, supposed at one time to represent one of the Bohun Earls of Hereford, but they are now declared to be members of the Brydges family, perhaps Sir John Brydges, who fought at Agincourt, more probably a descendant of his. We notice the SS. on the collar, and the study of the armour shows that at that time chain armour was being supplanted by plate armour. On north side of entrance to transept we see a canopied bracket with remains of blue colouring. Entering the *South Transept* we see the first part of the Cathedral which was recased, and may be said with truth to be the birthplace of the Perpendicular style. This example is quite the earliest which can be traced, and was finished in 1337 when the treasury of the Abbey was being filled by the offerings of pilgrims at the shrine of Edward II. This part of the church has therefore peculiar interest. The designer was Abbot Wygmore (1329-1337). All the walls are covered with the panel work, which is the "sign-manual" of the Perpendicular style. The clustered shafts form very beautiful groups. On the south is a large Perpendicular window, and below it a passage behind an open arcade. Two doorways should be noticed, one called the *Confessional*, with figures on each side said to represent angels, and the other, now blocked up, with a grotesque monster over it. The angel-guarded door is sometimes called the Pilgrims' Door, by which they entered to worship at the shrine of King Edward. Another story is that penitents entered beneath the monster emblematical of sin, and returned by the other door protected by the guardianship of angels. The curious *Prentice's Bracket*, said to be the memorial of a master-builder and his 'prentice, was probably intended as bracket for a lamp. The roof is a lierne vault without bosses. The flying arches or buttresses which support the tower are very graceful. The effigies of Alderman Blackleech and his wife (1639) are remarkable as studies of the costume of the period. Other monuments are to the memory of Richard Pates (1588) and Canon Evan Evans (1891). The *Chapel of St. Andrew* is on the east side, adorned with paintings by Gambier Parry. Above this is the east window, which has some beautiful old glass contemporary with the remodelling of the building. On the north is the curious Chantry of Abbot John Browne (1510-1514), dedicated to St. John Baptist because of the similarity of the initials. The floor has some intesting tiles and the reredos has been painted.

In the *North Transept* we see the further development of the Perpendicular style in the recasing by Abbot Horton (1351-1377). Here is the remarkably interesting *Reliquary*, of Early Decorated work, said by some to be a lavatory. The carved foliage is very beautiful and also the figures, though mutilated. A chapel is at the east side of this transept, similar to that in the south transept, dedicated to St. Paul. A door opens to the north choir aisle. At the entrance from the transept there is a curious desk which was

THE CHOIR, LOOKING EAST

used by a monk appointed to check the pilgrims as they went to the shrine of Edward. The chapel was repaired in 1870, and the niches supplied with figures of SS. Peter, Paul and Luke. A good Perpendicular doorway is on the north side, with carved angels in the moulding. The *Chapel of St. Anthony* is on the south of this transept, now used as a vestry. There is a curious painting here of St. Anthony rescuing a female from the mouth of hell. The transept has a monument of John Bower (1615), which bears the words: "Vayne, Vanytie. All is Vayne. Witnesse Solomon."

The *Screen* supporting the organ was erected in 1823 and replaced an earlier one. The story of the screens is a long one which Mr. St. John Hope has told so well that we need not repeat it. It appears there were two screens, one called the *Pulpitum* and the other a stone screen supporting the rood-loft. But these have disappeared, and we have instead an early nineteenth-century structure which need not be described. The original organ was built at the time of the Restoration, and some of the pipes bear the monogram of the Merry Monarch. The *Choir* is remarkable for its extreme beauty. From the lofty traceried roof down to the elaborately-tiled floor the walls are covered with richly-carved panelled work, broken here and there with delicate screens of stone. Behind this veiled work of stone stand the old Norman walls and piers. This casing was done by Abbots Staunton (1337-1351) and Horton (1351-1377). The lierne vault is one of the finest in England, with its multitudinous ribs, and ranks with King's College Chapel, Cambridge, and Westminster. The vaults of the tower and choir both belong to the same period. The *Stalls* were erected by the builders of the choir and have fine canopies. The *Misereres* are curious and well carved. Some of them represent hunting scenes, St. George slaying a giant, etc. Before us is the grand *East Window*, the finest in Christendom. Its date is 1345-1350, and is part of Abbot Horton's work. The Coronation of the Virgin is the subject, and the figures consist of angels, apostles, saints, kings and abbots. The arms of Edward III., the Black Prince, and the lords of Berkeley, Arundel, Warwick, Talbot and others appear, who took part in the campaign against France when Creçy was fought. It is thought by some that the window is a memorial of that famous victory. The clerestory windows retain some of their old glass, which is of the same date as that of the east window, but has been restored. The *Reredos* is modern, de-

N

signed by Sir G. Scott. The Birth, Burial and Ascension of Our Lord are represented. The floor of the presbytery is paved with some remarkable old *Tiles*, which record the names of some of the abbots, the arms of knights, and other interesting devices. The sedilia are adorned with modern sculptured figures, and the restoration has been accomplished with much care and taste. There are five principal historic *Monuments* in the choir. Near the altar is the canopied tomb of Osric, the founder of the first Abbey, said to have been erected by Abbot Parker (1515-1539). Guided by the description of the tomb told by Leland, Dean Spence opened the cenotaph and found the grey dust and bones of this ancient benefactor. Near at hand is the beautiful *Tomb of King Edward II.*, murdered at Berkeley Castle. It was erected by Edward III. The effigy is of alabaster, and the features are thought to have been reproduced from a waxen mask taken after death. The tomb is a forest of pinnacles and rich tabernacle work. It has been much restored at various times, but the extreme beauty of the work has in no way been impaired. The white hart, chained and collared, the badge of Richard II., is painted on the pillars. The Chantry of Abbot Parker, or Malverne (1515-1539), has a much mutilated effigy of this, the last Abbot of Gloucester. Vine leaves and grapes adorn the screen, and the base has some heraldic devices and the emblems of the Passion. On the south side is a projecting bracket which Leland tells us marks the grave of Abbot Serlo, the founder of the Norman Church. The bracket is Perpendicular, the effigy Early English, both much mutilated. The figure has a model of a church in his hand, and therefore denotes that the abbot was a founder, but the Early English character of the effigy points to it representing a later abbot than Serlo, and possibly Abbot Foliot (1243).

The *North Choir Aisle*, or ambulatory, is original Norman, the windows being filled with Perpendicular tracery. At the north-east corner is Abbot Boteler's Chantry (1433-1450). The old tiles are interesting, amongst which we see some representing the arms of the Boteler or Butlet family (three cups). The decoration of the chapel is all Perpendicular work, screens, windows and reredos. This last is very fine, and has some well-carved figures of the Apostles. Here is the effigy of Robert, Duke of Normandy, eldest son of William I., whose wild youth was atoned for by his prowess in the Crusades. He, however, had to endure twenty years' imprisonment, inflicted by his father. The effigy was probably made

THE LADY CHAPEL

not long after his death. The chest on which it rests is fifteenth-century work. The effigy was hacked to pieces by Cromwell's soldiers, but the fragments were put together by Sir Humphrey Tracy, and replaced in the Cathedral.

The *Ante-Chapel*, or vestibule, leading to the Lady Chapel, is the meeting-place of the old and new work, and is ingeniously contrived. The Norman apse is pierced by a doorway and two Perpendicular windows. It is separated from the Lady Chapel by an open-work screen, which is very beautiful, and has a fine lierne vault. This, and the Lady Chapel, are the work of Abbots Hanley and Farley, who presided over the Abbey during the last half of the fifteenth century. The *Lady Chapel* ranks with Ely as the largest in England, and certainly it is a triumph of Perpendicular architecture. It has lofty Perpendicular windows, which seem to produce the effect of a wall of glass with panelled tracery. The head of each panel is much ornamented, and panel work, with niches, covers the walls. The lierne vault is very fine, and the bosses carved with beautiful foliage. At one time the walls were painted, and traces of colour remain. The east window has much old glass, which is also visible in the heads of the other windows. There is a very poor modern reredos, which might be removed without much regret, as it hides a very interesting, though much mutilated, mass of rich tabernacle work. The altar rails belong to the time of Laud, who was dean here, and are said to be the first introduced into churches. Many of the original tiles remain, and bear inscriptions: *Ave Maria grā plē, Dñe Jhū Miserere*. There are two side chapels, with fan-tracery vaulting. In the north chapel is the monument of Bishop Goldsbrough (1604). There is an upper chapel, or oratory, and the same arrangement obtains on the south side. This chapel has a monument of Th. Fitz-williams (1579). The marks on the walls of these upper oratories show that the love of recording names by visitors in historic places is not confined to modern times, and dates as far back as the sixteenth century.

Returning to the entrance, we follow the ambulatory to the south, which retains its northern features. *St. Philip's Chapel* is at the south-east corner, and has been restored in memory of Sir C Codrington, Bart. (1864). There are Norman arches, and four-teenth-century tracery inserted in the windows. The spacious chests for copes are interesting records of the rich ecclesiastical vestments in use in former times.

The *Triforium* is unusually fine, and now extends over the north and south choir aisles, but not over the east end. That part was removed when the choir was reconstructed, and in order to connect the severed portions of the triforium together, the Whispering Gallery was constructed. This part of the church retains its Norman features, and is full of interest. The first chapel on the south has Decorated windows, with ball-flower ornament. There is a double piscina. A very ancient painting of a Doom or Last Judgment, discovered in 1718, is a very remarkable example of early art. It was probably painted towards the end of the reign of Henry VIII. The view of the choir is very beautiful, and the way in which the later builders cased the Norman work with a veil of stone can best be observed from the triforium. The next chapel (south-east) is Norman, with later windows inserted. There are some fragments of an old choir-screen stored here.

The *Whispering Gallery* is built out at the back of the great east window, and in its construction old Norman stone-work has been re-used. It happens to possess the curious acoustic property of the famous gallery of St. Paul's, London. The next chapel is over the ante-chapel of the choir, and has a stone altar, with the usual five crosses carved on it. The north-east chapel has a Decorated window, and the north-west a double piscina of the same period.

We will now descend to the *Crypt* (entrance in south-east transept), which is very Early Norman, founded before 1085. The walls and piers are very strong and massive, the former being 10 feet thick. There is a central apse, an ambulatory, out of which radiate five chapels. The half columns in the ambulatory have been strengthened and recased in later Norman times. The chapels have little of interest except their own intrinsic architectural merits. There are some good piscinæ, and some memorial slabs.

The *Monastic Buildings* are some of the finest in England, especially the cloisters, which are remarkable for their excellent preservation and for the beauty of the fan-traceried vault. It is thought that this kind of vaulting, peculiar to this country, originated here. The outer walls are Norman, and have been recased with Perpendicular panelling. This work was begun by Abbot Horton (1351-1377), and finished by his successors, Abbot Boyfield (1377-1381) and Abbot Froucester (1381-1412). The south walk possesses a very interesting feature in the *Carrels* or studies of the monks. The glass of the windows is modern. The passage or slype, of Norman date, at the west end, was the main entrance

CARREL IN SOUTH CLOISTER

to the cloister from the outer court. At the north end was the door to the refectory. A window has been placed there instead, but Mr. Hope points out "the iron hooks on which the doors were hung." Little of the refectory, which was on the north of the garth, remains, except the south wall, preserved by the cloister, and part of the east end. The action of the fire of 1540, which destroyed this noble hall, is observed on the walls. In the north walk are the monks' lavatories, the most perfect in England; opposite is the *Manutergia*, or recess for towels. This walk was reserved for novices, and Mr. Hope shows us the tables for games which they played scratched on the stone bench, the "Nine Men's Morris" and "Fox and Geese" being their favourite pastimes. The east walk gives entrance to the chapter-house. The doorway is Norman, with zigzag ornament. The chapter-house is Norman, with a Perpendicular east end. At the west end is a Norman doorway and an unglazed window (the corresponding one being covered up when the south-east staircase was added), and three Norman windows. Traces of fire may be seen here. The seats of the monks under the arcading may be traced. The vault of the Perpendicular part is finely groined, and there is a large Perpendicular window at the east end. The names of several illustrious leaders under William I. appear on the walls.

The *Locutorium*, or monks' parlour, lies between the chapter-house and the north transept of the church. This passage is often erroneously called the "Abbot's Cloister." Here the monks met to converse when talking was prohibited in the cloister. Above is the vestry and library. The latter is a long room, of Perpendicular character. The library at Gloucester has had many migrations and vicissitudes; the books of the old monastic library were dispersed. A new collection was begun in 1624 by Bishop Goodman. The books have been stored in the chapter-house, and elsewhere, and have now found a permanent resting-place. Its principal treasure is Abbot Froucester's *Lives of the Abbots of Gloucester to 1381.* This copy was lost at the beginning of the nineteenth century, and discovered again at Berlin, and restored to the library. The dormitory has been destroyed. It probably stood on the north of the chapter-house. The remains of the infirmary and little cloisters are on the north of the cloister.

The Cathedral close was surrounded by a wall. Some of the gateways remain. St. Mary's Gate, on the west, is a fine thirteenth-century structure; the Inner Gate, of fourteenth-century work, leading to Miller's Green, the site of the old Abbey Mill and outhouses; the south, or King Edward's Gate, built by Edward I., of which only fragments remain; and the Westgate Street Gate. The Deanery, as we have said, has many interesting features, and remains of the work of eleventh, twelfth, thirteenth and fourteenth centuries. The Bishop's Palace is modern, built on the site of the abbot's house, erected in the early part of the fourteenth century. Previous to that period the abbot lived at the present Deanery.

DIMENSIONS

Nave, length	174 ft.
Nave, width	34 ft.
Nave, height	68 ft.
Transepts, length	46 ft.
Transepts, width	34 ft.
Choir, length	140 ft.
Choir, width	33 ft.
Lady Chapel, length	90 ft.
Lady Chapel, width	25 ft.
Tower, height	225 ft.
Total length	407 ft.
Area	30,600 sq. ft.

PRINCIPAL BUILDING DATES

Norman (1089-1100)—Piers, arches, triforium of the nave, walls and vault of north aisle and pilasters of south aisle, walls of choir and presbytery, chapels and ambulatory, north transept, west end of chapter-house and abbot's cloister.

Early English (1242)—Vault of nave.

Decorated (1307-1329)—Windows and vault of south aisle, south transept, windows of ambulatory and chapels.

Perpendicular (1337-1500)—Windows of nave and north aisle, casing north transept, choir and presbytery, Lady Chapel, cloisters, tower, west end, south porch, and east end of chapter-house.

A B West Doorways
  C Nave
D E North and South Aisles
  F South Porch
  G Choir
H J North and South Transepts
  K Ambulatory
  L Lady Chapel
  M Presbytery
  N Abbot Boteler's Chapel
  O St. Philip's Chapel
  P St. Andrew's Chapel
  Q Abbots' Cloister
  R Chapter-House
  S Site of Refectory
  T Cloisters
  U Lavatory
  W The Deanery

1 Font
2 Osric's Monument
3 King Edward II.'s Tomb
4 Abbot Seabroke's Chantry
5 Reliquary
6 Robert, Duke of Normandy's
    Monument
7 Abbot Parker's Monument

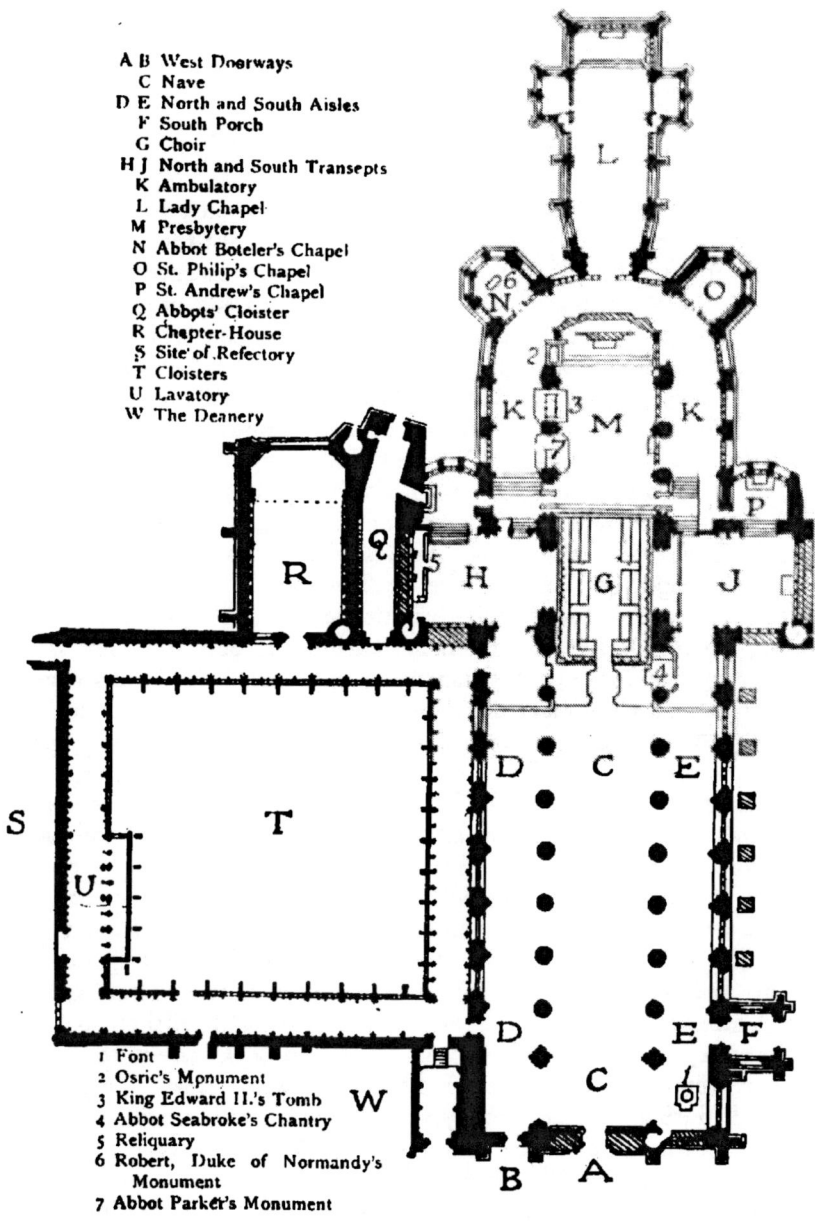

PLAN OF GLOUCESTER CATHEDRAL

HEREFORD CATHEDRAL

THE story of the See of Hereford takes us back to very early times, to the days of the British, and shows the connection and identity of the Church of England of the twentieth century with that which existed even prior to the landing of Augustine. The see was in existence in the sixth century, and was subject to the Archbishop of Caerleon. Legends tell us of Dubricius, who crowned King Arthur at Cirencester. One Bishop of Hereford represented the old British bishops at the famous conference with Augustine, when, by his want of tact and haughty demeanour, the Roman missionary alienated the native British Church. A very tragic event enhanced the glories of the see. King Offa slew Ethelbert, King of the East Angles, who was a suitor for his daughter's hand, and buried him at Hereford. On the night of the funeral, "a column of light, brighter than the sun, arose towards heaven," according to the monkish chronicler, and miracles were wrought at the tomb of the martyred monarch. This distressed Offa, who tried to expiate his crime by erecting a noble monument, founding the monastery at St. Alban's, and devoting costly gifts to the church of Hereford. One Mildred, Offa's viceroy, built "an admirable stone church," dedicated to the martyr Ethelbert. This was rebuilt by Bishop Ethelstan in 1012. Then followed sad times when the Welsh tribes invaded the land and destroyed the city and church by fire. When the Normans came Bishop de Losinga (1079-1095) began to rebuild the ruined church, and the work was continued by his successor, Raynhelm (1107-1115). During the troubles of Stephen's reign Hereford suffered much. The Cathedral was deserted and desecrated, and Bishop Robert de Bethune, a worthy prelate, was forced to seek safety in flight. Stephen entered the Castle of Hereford with great pomp, and occupied during service the episcopal chair, which still remains. On his return he cleansed and repaired the building. Then we see Gilbert Foliot, Bishop of Hereford, the stern opponent of Becket, who preached the sermon at Canterbury, when Henry II.

did penance for the murder of the archbishop. Bishop William de Vere (1189-1199) is said to have built much, removed the apsidal terminations at the east end, and made other alterations. His work was continued by the erection of the Early English Lady Chapel. Probably he built the Palace. Bishop Giles de Bruce (1200-1215) took part with the barons against King John, and was a very warlike prelate, who allied himself with Prince Llewellyn, and destroyed the castle of Earl Mortimer, an adherent of the king. He was driven from his see, but afterwards made peace with John, and died at Gloucester when he was returning to his see. Writers commonly assign to him the building of the tower, on the ground that his effigy has a model of the church in its hand. But this effigy was erected long after his death, and cannot be taken as any evidence of the truth of the statement. The profusion of ball-flower ornament certainly points out that the tower belongs to the fourteenth and not to the thirteenth century.

Peter d'Acquablanca in Savoy (1240-1268) was one of the foreign favourites of Henry III., who fought in the Crusades. He was a simoniacal prelate who tried to gain the See of Bordeaux, and was much ridiculed when, after paying the money, the Archbishop of Bordeaux was found to be alive. He was expelled from England, but returned, and then went off to Ireland to collect tithes. Unfortunately King Henry visited Hereford during his absence, and found that no clergy were there, and the church in ruin and decay. He therefore wrote a strongly-- worded remonstrance to the absent bishop, who returned in time to be seized by Simon de Montfort and put into prison, while his hoards of wealth were divided amongst his captors. He died soon after this. His tomb remains, but his heart is buried in Savoy, his native land. He is said to have rebuilt the north transept.

Thomas de Cantilupe (1275-1282) was a noted bishop, who attained to the honour of canonisation, and was, moreover, Chancellor of England. He was by no means a meek-spirited saint, excommunicated an earl for capturing his game, and made another lord walk barefoot to the altar of the Cathedral, after chastising him for interfering with his tenants. On his death in Italy his flesh was buried at Florence, his heart at Ashridge, Bucks, and his bones at Hereford. Various miracles were said to have been wrought at his tomb. His successor Swinfield (1283-1317), built, or began, the eastern transept, the clerestory of the choir, the central tower above the roof, and probably the nave aisles. Adam de Orleton (1316-1327) espoused the cause of the queen against Edward II., and involved Hereford in the troubles of that disastrous time. He is said to have instigated the murder of the king; at anyrate he captured the fugitive monarch, and Hugh Despenser, the king's favourite, was brought here and hanged. He obtained from the Pope a grant of the tithes of two Berkshire parishes, Shinfield and Swallowfield, for the repair of his Cathedral. The fifteenth century saw several additions to the fabric, the cloisters in 1418-1448, the great west window by W. Lochard, the precentor, some chantry chapels which we shall notice later, and the enlargement of the north porch. At the Reformation an ardent reformer, Edward Fox, was appointed bishop, and Hereford, like other cathedrals, was despoiled of its valuables and treasures. Fox's successor, Skip, was a liturgical scholar, and helped in compiling our liturgies. Another learned prelate was Francis Godwin (1617-1633), the author of the Lives of English Bishops (*de Præsulibus Anglicæ*). At the Civil War period Hereford suffered the usual misfortunes. Both bishop and people espoused the cause of the king. The city was taken and retaken without much damage being done, until Lord Leven with the Scottish army besieged it in 1645, when the church suffered considerably; and when, by the treachery of the governor, Colonel Birch, the city was again taken, it was plundered and the Cathedral ransacked. Brasses were torn up, monuments defaced, old windows broken, the library pillaged, and when the dean courageously preached to the riotous soldiers on their sacrilege, they levelled their muskets at him, and were scarcely restrained from firing.

Injudicious "restorers" have worked their wicked will on the fabric; amongst these was Bishop Bisse (1713-1721) who spent much money, erected several monstrosities, which have happily been removed, and destroyed the half-ruined chapter-house in order to restore the Palace. In 1786 the western tower fell, and carried with it the west front. Then Wyatt, of evil memory, was let loose on the Cathedral. He made a new west front, shortened the nave, and took down the Norman work in triforium and clerestory, substituting his own designing. Plaster was used unsparingly. The old spire was removed, the roofs lowered, and much other vandalism perpetrated. From 1837 to 1863 continued restoration took place, and in spite of the havoc which has been wrought the church retains much of its ancient and interesting character, and is well worthy of accurate study.

HEREFORD CATHEDRAL FROM THE WYE

THE EXTERIOR

A good view is obtained from the close on the south side. On the banks of the Wye is the Palace and College of Vicars Choral; on the east was the old castle, one of the strongest on the Welsh marches. The *West Front* is an erection of Wyatt's, and need not be noticed. Formerly there was a great tower here, which fell in 1786 and destroyed the old west front. The *Central Tower* is very fine. The abundance of ball-flower ornament proclaims its Decorated style. The date is about 1300. It has two stages. The pinnacles are modern. As we have said, a wooden spire which once capped it has been removed. On the west side there is a noble *Porch* of Perpendicular style, built by Bishop Booth in 1530. There is a parvise in the second storey with Perpendicular windows. This porch joins on to an inner one of the Decorated period. Octagonal turrets containing staircases stand at the angles. The iron-work of the doors is excellent modern work. The walls and windows of the aisles are Late Decorated, about 1360. The clerestory is Wyatt's construction, who destroyed the original Norman work. The *North Transept* is worthy of attention. The buttresses are very massive. It was built about 1285 for the reception of the shrine of Bishop Cantilupe. The windows are very lofty, of three lights under triangular-headed arches. The window on the north is similar, but double. On the east side there is an aisle, with triforium windows of three lancets, and above the clerestory windows are triangular.

The Lady Chapel is fine Early English work, and belongs to the first half of the thirteenth century. We notice especially the tall and graceful lancets and elegant arcades of interesting arches.

The east end was rebuilt in 1850. On the south is the Audley Chapel. It is difficult to approach the south side, as walls and gardens prevent easy access. The *Vicar's Cloister*, connecting the Cathedral with the College of the Vicars Choral (incorporated in 1396), is Perpendicular work. The oak beams are finely carved. The quadrangle of the college is well worthy of notice. The *Bishop's Cloister* is on the south of the nave. Two walks remain, and the west walk is partially restored and contains the library. Their style is Perpendicular. The chapter-house was pulled down by Bishop Bisse; only the double doorway remains. We notice the grotesque heads over the windows, the richly-groined roof, and the Lady's Arbour, a small room in the tower at the south-east angle, which may possibly have obtained its name from the Virgin, our Lady. The Chapels of SS. Katherine and Mary Magdalene, of Norman construction, formerly stood against south wall, and some remains are evident.

The Interior

We enter the nave by the north porch, and proceeding to the west end we notice the grand Norman piers and arches. Wyatt's hand was heavily laid upon this structure, and the triforium, clerestory and vault are all his handiwork. Moreover, he took away one bay entirely. The view eastward is very impressive. The arches are adorned with the billet and other Norman mouldings, and are remarkable for their richness. The *Font* is curious and of Late Norman design. It has figures of the Apostles, and at the base projecting lions. The aisles are Late Decorated, except the lower part of the walls, which is original Norman. The chief monuments in the nave and aisle are, on the south:—Sir Richard Pembridge (1375), who fought at Poictiers. The effigy is a good study of the armour of the period. The right leg is a restoration. Two unknown figures of ecclesiastics. On the north—Bishop Booth (1535), the builder of the porch; a fine tomb, protected by original iron-work.

The *Screen* is a magnificent work, designed by Sir G. Scott. The lectern is modern.

The *Central Tower* has passed through many vicissitudes. The original Norman piers being unable to support the heavy Early English shaft, they were cased with new stone-work, and the Norman arches were blocked up. In Dean Mereweather's time extensive restoration was found necessary. All the parts above the arches is fourteenth-century work. The vaulting has been removed, and the tower is now open to the belfry floor.

The *North Transept* is particularly fine and remarkable, and is Late Early English or Early Decorated (1282-1287). It was built for the shrine of Bishop Cantilupe. The arches are sharply-pointed and unusual. On the west are two windows of two narrow lights under sharply-pointed arches, the tracery of the heads being in the form of three circles enclosing trefoils. On the north is a double window of the same character. On the east is an aisle with clerestory and triforium. Dog-tooth ornament appears in the mouldings. The arches of the triforium are very beautiful, and the diaper of leaf-ornament in the spandrels is effective. The windows above are octofoils.

This aisle contains the remains of the Cantilupe shrine, which was a source of much revenue to the church, derived from the pilgrims who flocked hither. The date of the tomb is 1287, and the details are worthy of study. It is made of Purbeck marble. The lower part has fifteen figures of Knights Templar, of which order the bishop was Provincial Grand Master. The details of the armour are very exact. Curious monsters appear at the feet of the knights. The foliage is excellent Early Decorated, retaining some of Early English features. Other monuments are Bishop West-fayling (1602), John Philips, author of *The Splendid Shilling* (1708), Bishop Charlton (1329), Bishop Field (1639), Dean D'Acquablanca (1320), and brasses to Dean Frowcester (1529) and Richard Delamare and his wife (1435). Near at hand is the beautiful monument of Bishop D'Acquablanca (1240-1268), the finest in the Cathedral. (Concerning the unenviable repute of this bishop, *see* the history of the see). The tomb was originally elaborately coloured.

The *South Transept* has much Norman work. The east wall is entirely Norman, and has five ranges of arcades. Perpendicular windows have been inserted in south and west walls, and the lierne vaulting belongs to the same period. Bishop Trevenant (1389-1404) is said to have been responsible for this later work.

The monuments in this transept are :—Sir Alexander Denton and his wife (1566), an altar tomb with alabaster effigies. The latter died with her infant, who is represented as a "chrysome" child, *i.e.*, one who dies within a month of its baptism, and wears its white baptismal robe. Bishop Trevenant, who was responsible for the Perpendicular alterations, is buried here; his effigy has been much mutilated. Masons' marks are observable, and the Norman fireplace is said to be unique.

The *Choir* is full of interest. The main arches and triforium are Norman, the clerestory and vaulting Early English (*circa* 1250). The carving of the capitals exhibits foliage and grotesque heads, and the lozenge ornament appears round the arches. The headings of the pilasters between the piers are Early English. The clerestory windows consist of one lofty pointed window and a small trefoiled one on each side. The reredos was designed by Cottingham, the architect at the restoration in 1850, and represents the Passion of Christ. A curious effect is produced by the central pillar and arches in the retro-choir appearing through the arch at the east of the choir, and presenting a broad spandrel, on which are carved some modern figures of our Lord and St. Ethelbert. The stalls are good Decorated work with rich canopies and some curious misereres, with carvings representing a pair of wrestlers with ropes round their necks, an irate cook throwing a dish at a troublesome guest, etc. Some are modern. The *Throne* is also Decorated, and there is the remarkable old chair already mentioned, on which Stephen is said to have sat on the occasion of his visit here. The *Organ* has some parts of the instrument presented by Charles II. The monuments in the choir are those of—

Bishop Trilleck (1360), an excellent brass; Bishop Stanbery (1474), whose chantry we shall see in the west choir aisle; Bishop Giles de Bruce (1215), with model of church in his hand; Bishop Bennett (1617). We notice the small figure of St. Ethelbert on a bracket on east pier on south side, of fourteenth century.

In the *North Choir Aisle* the wall has Decorated arched recesses, which contain the effigies of Bishop Godfred de Clive (1120) (executed in Perpendicular period); Bishop Hugh de Mapenore (1219); Bishop Richard de Capella (1127). Bishop Stanbery's Chantry (1453-1474) is entered from this aisle, and is Late Perpendicular. It is very richly ornamented with tracery and panelling and shields and has a groined roof. It is a good example of the over-elaborateness of Late Perpendicular work.

The *North-East Transept* is Early Decorated, the original apsidal termination being altered in the latter part of the thirteenth century. Traces of Norman work are still evident. There is a central octagonal pier which supports the vaulting. There are monuments here of Dean Dawes (1867); Bishop Godwin? (1633)

(the tomb is certainly earlier and cannot be his); and the altar tomb of Bishop Swinfield (1316), though the effigy upon it is not his. The ball-flower moulding is plentifully used. Proceeding onwards we come to the *Retro-Choir* or ambulatory, which is Transitional Norman. The chevron and diamond moulding on the ribs of the vaulting point to its Late Norman date. There was evidently an ambulatory and Lady Chapel in Norman times, and the windows on each side of the vestibule show that formerly these walls were outside walls, and the windows were glazed. Here is a monument of Dean Beaurieu (1462), which is of some interest on account of the accurate carving of the dress, and the rebus *boar* and *rue* leaves; and there are some late brasses.

The *Lady Chapel* is remarkably fine, being very rich Early English. Its story is difficult to read, as the architect Cottingham redressed the old stone-work and made complications in 1840-1850. He rebuilt the east gable. Five narrow lancets form the east window, and above are five quatrefoil openings. The glass was erected to the memory of Dean Mereweather, to whom the Cathedral owes so much. The subject is the life of the Virgin. The aumbrey and piscina are reproductions. On the north there is an interesting but somewhat conglomerate tomb. The effigy is supposed to be Humphrey de Bohun, Earl of Hereford, in the reign of Edward III., but the canopy is Perpendicular, and the figures in the arches were discovered elsewhere and placed here, except the two mutilated central ones, our Lord and the Virgin. The others are SS. John Baptist, Cantilupe and Thomas of Canterbury. The Countess of Hereford, Johanna de Bohun (1327), lies here, a great benefactress, whose effigy and tomb are worthy of study. On the south is the *Audley Chantry*, erected by Bishop Audley (1492-1502), who constructed another chantry at Salisbury, whither he was translated, and where he was buried. It has two storeys, and a curious and interesting screen separates it from the Lady Chapel. There are traces of considerable colour decoration. The chapel has five sides, with two windows in the lower and five in the upper storey. The central boss of the vaulting in the upper chamber or oratory has a figure of the Virgin crowned. The window west of this chapel has some good fourteenth-century glass. Beneath the choir is the crypt, of Early English date, and is the only example of a crypt constructed later than the end of the eleventh century. It is called "Golgotha," on account of its being used as a charnel-house.

The *South-East Transept* is similar to its opposite. It has monuments of Bishop Charlton (1369); Bishop Coke (1646); Bishop Ironside, who died in London, 1701, and was buried in a city church, which was destroyed in 1863, and the body brought here. This was the bishop who, as Vice-Chancellor of Oxford, resisted the action of James II. in regard to the expulsion of the Fellows of Magdalen College.

In the *South Choir Aisle* are four Perpendicular tombs under Decorated arched recesses, supposed to represent Bishop William de Vere (1199); Bishop Hugh Foliot (d. 1234); Bishop Robert de Betun (1148); and Bishop Robert de Melun (1167). There is a brass of Dean Frowsetown (1529), an effigy of Bishop Mayew (1516), who conducted Catherine of Arragon to England from Spain; and an effigy of Bishop de Losinga (1096), erected in Perpendicular period. The vestries are of Norman construction; the vaulting is the only example of Norman vaulting in the Cathedral. Here in this south choir aisle is preserved the famous *Map of the World*, as known in 1300. It was designed by Richard de Haldingham, Prebendary of Hereford. This was generally supposed to be the most ancient of its size in the world; but another map has been discovered at Ebstorp, near Hanover, which is larger, more highly coloured, and about the same age. The library of Corpus Christi College, Cambridge, has an earlier map of Henry of Mainz, and there is a small Psalter map in the British Museum. The world is shown to be round; at the top is Paradise, with its rivers and trees, Eve's transgression, etc. Above is the last Judgment with the Virgin interceding for mankind. Jerusalem is in the centre. Rome proclaims itself the head of the world, and Troy the most warlike city. The British Isles have much space, and most of the cathedrals are mentioned. Monstrous animals, birds and fish abound. The monkey appears to live in Norway, the scorpion on the Rhine. There is very much that is strange and curious to be seen in this wonderful map.

The *Library* has a splendid collection of chained books. The building is modern, having been opened in 1897, and built on the site of the old west cloister. There is an ancient copy of the Gospels at least 1000 years old, written in Anglo-Saxon characters, a beautiful twelfth-century MS., a copy of the " Hereford Use " of thirteenth century, Wycliffe's Bible (1420), " Bangor Use " (1400), with a curious charm for toothache inserted in the book, *Decreta Gratiani*, of twelfth century. There are many *Incunabula*, Nicholas de Lyra's Bible and Commentary (1485), *Polychronycon*, by R. Higden, with additions by Caxton (1495); Caxton's *Golden Legend*, a very fine copy.

Here is an ancient *Reliquary*, with representation of the martyr-dom of St. Thomas of Canterbury, a pre-Reformation chalice and paten, taken from the coffin of Bishop Swinfield (1316), and some episcopal rings. This collection of chained books is the finest in England.

DIMENSIONS

Total length (exterior) . .	342 ft.
Length of nave to screen . .	158 ft.
Breadth of nave . . .	31 ft.
Breadth of nave and aisles . .	73 ft.
Height of nave	64 ft.
Height of lantern . . .	96 ft.
Height of tower with pinnacles .	165 ft.
Length of choir to reredos . .	75 ft.
Length of Lady Chapel and retro-choir	93 ft.
Width of central transepts. .	146 ft.
Width of eastern transepts . .	110 ft.

PRINCIPAL BUILDING DATES

Norman (1079-1115)—Main arcade of nave, arcade and triforium of choir, font, east wall of south transept, vestry.

(1189-1199)—Retro-choir.

Early English (1200-1250)—Lady Chapel, crypt.

(1282-1287)—North transept.

Decorated (1300-1360)—Walls and windows of aisles, choir transepts, upper part of tower, stalls and throne.

Perpendicular (1400-1530) — Cloisters, windows in south transept, north porch, Audley and Stanbery Chantries.

Modern—West front, triforium and clerestory of nave, east front, library.

WORCESTER CATHEDRAL

WORCESTER has many points of interest outside its Cathedral. All round the city is historic ground. It was the battlefield of Briton, Roman, Saxon, Dane and Norman. It heard the sounds of fighting in the wars of the barons and in the wars of the Roses, and in the great Civil War Worcester repeatedly suffered, and within its boundaries the great battle of Worcester was fought, the last effort of a dying cause. The half-timbered houses of the Elizabethan and early Stuart times, the interesting churches, and streets that by their names record many a curious custom and phase of old English life, all remind us of ancient times and the manners of our forefathers.

We will walk round the town and note its chief points of interest. We notice the old houses in New Street, the remains of the old city wall, "the Cross," the old centre of civic life, the Guild Hall, designed by a pupil of Wren in 1721; St. Helen's Church, from the tower of which still nightly sounds the curfew. Along Sidbury the tide of battle rolled in 1651, when Charles II. was making his last gallant struggle against the army of the Protector. The old Edgar Gate is near at hand, which leads to the castle and Monastery of St. Mary.

The Commandery in Sidbury was a hospital founded by St. Wulfstan, Bishop of Worcester about 1085, for a Master, Priests and Brethren under the rule of St. Augustine. The house is a wonderful example of mediæval architecture, and is kept in its ancient state by the present occupier, Mr. Littlebury, who allows it to be inspected. Here in 1300 Hugh le de Spencer held a court. The great hall is of Tudor architecture. King Charles I. stayed a night here, and the Duke of Hamilton died here, after wounds received in the fatal battle. "Fort Royal," fortified by Charles I., is seen from the garden, and cannon were placed here at the battle of Worcester; but Cromwell captured the stronghold. Charles II. withdrew with difficulty, and the house in the old Corn Market is shewn where he took refuge, and effected his escape at the back door as Colonel Cobbett, his pursuer, entered at the front. Over the entrance is the inscription : " Love God. Honour the Kinge."

HISTORY OF THE CATHEDRAL

The See of Worcester was first formed in 680, when the unwieldy Diocese of Mercia was divided, and Bosel was its first bishop. The successive Kings of Mercia poured wealth into the episcopal treasury, and endowed the see with many a rich manor. St. Dunstan was bishop here (957-961), and then came Oswald, subsequently Archbishop of York, the reformer of monasteries, who is said to have replaced the secular priests by a community of monks, and built the Church and Monastery of St. Mary on the site of the present Cathedral. This sacred fane was destroyed by the Danes, under Hardicanute, in 1041. Bishop Wulfstan, the second prelate of that name who held the see, was appointed in 1062, a holy, simple and earnest prelate, who, though a Saxon, held his see in spite of Norman opposition and prejudice. He laid the foundations of the existing Cathedral, and some of his work remains in the crypt and monastic buildings. When he saw the workmen pulling down the ruins of the old Church of St. Oswald he wept, saying, " We destroy the works of our forefathers only to get praise . . . We neglect the care of souls and labour only to heap up stones." He was canonised, and many miracles were reported to have taken place at his tomb, to which there was great resort. In 1113 fire destroyed part of the Cathedral, as well as the city and castle. In the troublous times of Stephen, Florence, a monk of Worcester, tells us that when a raid was made on the city the people took their chests and sacks of goods and deposited them in the great church, while all the church goods, the curtains and palls, albs and copes were hidden away in recesses in the walls. The west bays of the nave were built about 1160. In 1175 the " new tower " fell, a misfortune common to so many cathedrals; in 1189 another great fire raged, and the troubles of John's evil reign were felt heavily here, when the city was taken by the king's forces, the church pillaged and the monks compelled to pay a heavy fine, to defray which they even melted down the shrine of the saint. Soon John was buried here, and could do no further mischief.

In 1218 the church was dedicated, when Henry III. and a goodly number of bishops and nobles were present.

In a storm is 1221 the two " lesser towers " fell. Happily the offerings at the shrine of St. Wulfstan, which was soon repaired, were very numerous, and in 1224 the present choir and Lady Chapel were begun by Bishop William de Blois in the Early English style, and doubtless continued by Bishop Walter Cantilupe, uncle of the sainted Bishop of Hereford. He was a sturdy Englishman who upheld the rights of the English Church against the Pope, and was excommunicated by the Roman Pontiff. The work of rebuilding the church gradually progressed. The nave was built in the Decorated style on the north side (1317-1327), and Bishop Thomas Cobham, styled "the good clerk," made the vault of the north aisle; so Leland informs us. The south side of the nave is a little later, about 1360, when traces of Perpendicular work are evident, blended with the Decorated. In this century also was built the Guesten Hall, now, alas! destroyed, the roof of which is now seen in Holy Trinity Church.

Henry de Wakefield was a vigorous builder (1376-1394). During his time the refectory and cloister, the tower, the stone vault over the choir, under the belfry, over the nave, library, treasury and dormitory, the water-gate, infirmary, the stalls in the choir, the west window and the north porch were erected.

At the Reformation Worcester had a very zealous reforming bishop in the person of Hugh Latimer, who was subsequently burnt at Oxford. Under his rule the costly shrines of St. Oswald and St. Wulfstan were destroyed, and the relics buried near the high altar. During the Civil War Worcester fared badly, and terrible scenes took place in the sacred building. In 1642 Cromwell's soldiers under the Earl of Essex entered the town and did after their kind. They pulled down altars, destroyed vestments and furniture, and carried off stores of treasure concealed in the crypt and deposited there for safety. The bishop at this time, John Prideaux, was a vigorous Royalist, who excommunicated freely all who fought against the king. In return the soldiers pillaged his palace, and the poor bishop was reduced to selling his books in order to gain a livelihood. But this was not all the evil that befell the "faithful city." It was besieged four years later from March 26 to July 23, but when the Roundheads gained the day and entered the city they behaved in most becoming manner, and did less damage than the soldiers of the Royalist garrison. But even this was not all. In 1651 was fought the battle of Worcester. We can see Charles II. watching the issues of the fight from the top of the tower, and then the divers fortunes of the fight (to which

WORCESTER CATHEDRAL FROM THE SEVERN

allusion has already been made), the final victory of Cromwell, the capture of 6000 prisoners, who were confined in this sacred building. Then followed one of the most terrible scenes in the war, when the soldiers of Cromwell were let loose on the helpless citizens, and ravaged and plundered without mercy in the streets and lanes and houses of this unhappy city.

At the Restoration of the Monarchy it does not seem that any extensive repairs were immediately undertaken. In the eighteenth century some unfortunate "restoration" was carried out which disfigured the building, and did not materially contribute to its strength. As most of these disfigurements have been removed, we need not record them. A great restoration was begun in 1857 by Mr. Perkins, the architect, and continued by Sir Gilbert Scott, and the church was re-opened in 1874. Opinions differ with regard to the severity of this restoration. Certainly it has destroyed all appearance of antiquity in the exterior of the choir and Lady Chapel, but Professor Willis thinks that we have now a reproduction of its original aspect, as far as that can be determined. However, the attempt to reproduce the original should not be the entire aim of restoration. We want to have the whole story of the building before us, and not its opening chapters interpreted for us, and often mangled and distorted by the modern restorer.

THE EXTERIOR

We approach the Cathedral from the west and obtain a good view. At the foot of the west end the river flows. The *West Front* need not detain us; it is plain and unpretentious. There is a large modern window in Decorated style, and above three lancets, and a cross crowns the gable. The doorway is Norman much restored, and has figures of our Lord in glory, angels and the Virgin and Holy Child. The *North Porch* was built by Bishop Wakefield (1375-1394), and belongs to the period when the Decorated style was merging into the Perpendicular. There is a parvise over it with Perpendicular battlements, and figures of our Lord and the twelve Apostles in niches. Above is a row of small figures. Between the porch and the west front was formerly the charnel-house, built by Bishop William de Blois in the thirteenth century and demolished in the seventeenth. The crypt still exists. The two west bays are Transition Norman. The rest is Decorated work. A small Decorated chapel, called *Jesus Chapel*, juts out

from the aisle on this side. The lower part of the walls of the
north transept is Norman work, but the transept was much repaired
in the fourteenth century and the windows are Perpendicular, and
that in the north wall is a modern antique. Strong flying buttresses
support the main walls on the east of this transept. There is a
choir transept. The east end is plain. The east window is of
Early English design but modern workmanship. The south side
is very similar to the north, but enclosures and buildings prevent us
from a close inspection. The cloisters are as usual in Benedictine
monasteries on the south side, and these we shall enter from the
church. The *Tower* dates from 1374, but the details are modern,
as the tower was very much restored. It is of good proportion,
has two storeys with crocketed pinnacles, a parapet adorned with
lesser spires, and the whole effect is not unpleasing.

THE INTERIOR

We enter by the north porch. The *Nave* covers the same
ground as the original Norman Cathedral, and some remains of the
old building are left. At the west end the door entering into the
north aisle, at the north-east angle of the north aisle, and the great
Norman shafts running up the centre of the second piers from the
west, are pure Norman. The two *Western Bays* are Transition
Norman, and are an interesting study. We see here almost the
earliest advance of Gothic art and the earliest traces of the Early
English feeling which manifested itself for the first time in its
developed form in the choir of Lincoln. It will be observed that
the arches are pointed, but the capitals are Late Norman. The
triforium is peculiar, and has a series of pointed arches over three
round-headed openings, the centre one being much higher than the
rest, and the ornaments are the zigzag, lozenge and curious knots of
carved leafage. The clerestory consists of groups of three windows
under round arches, the tracery at the back being Perpendicular
insertions. The date of this portion is about 1160. The vault
was fashioned by Bishop Wakefield (1375-1394). There are
seven remaining bays. Those on the south are later than those on
the north, and the earlier work is the richer and more beautiful.
On the north the five eastern bays and the pier arches of the other
two are Decorated (1317-1327), while the rest of these two bays and
all the south side are Early Perpendicular. The great west window
is modern, erected in 1865 in Early Decorated style. Sculptured

figures of characters from the Old Testament appear in the tympana of the triforium.

The *South Aisle* has two west bays of Transition Norman work like the nave, quadripartite vaulting, Late Decorated windows, high in the wall on account of the cloister on the other side, and two doorways called the monks' and the prior's. The wall is original Norman. Here is a large modern font. The *North Aisle* has also the two west bays of Transition Norman. The vaulting is Decorated, the work of Bishop Cobham (1317-1321), and the rest of the aisle belongs to the same period. The *Jesus Chapel* opens from this aisle, separated by a modern screen in Perpendicular style. This chapel has been recently restored by the Hon. Percy Alsop, and the scheme of decoration is very elaborate and beautiful. The *Pulpit* is a very handsome and elaborate structure made of marble and alabaster, with some excellent carving.

The principal monuments in the nave and aisles are :—Sir John Beauchamp (1388), much defaced, in alabaster, and his lady, whose head rests on a swan, the Beauchamp crest ; Robert Wylde (1608) and his lady—the sides of the tomb are adorned with sunflowers rising from vases ; Dean Eedes (1608) ; Bishop Thornborough (1641). In the south aisle—an ecclesiastic (late fourteenth century) ; Bishop Parry (1616) ; altar tomb unknown ; Thomas Littleton, judge (1481), learned law writer ; Bishop Freke (1591) ; Sir Henry Ellis, who fell at Waterloo ; Richard Solly (1804) ; Bishop Gauden (1662), the supposed writer of *Eikon Basilike*, a work usually attributed to Charles I. In the north aisle—Earl of Strafford and soldiers of the Worcestershire regiment who fell in India ; Bishop Goldsborough of Gloucester (1613) ; the Moore family (1613) ; and curious effigy of Bishop Bullingham (1576).

Very little ancient glass is left ; the windows of the south aisle have a few fragments, but all the rest is modern.

The *North Transept* is Norman as high as the clerestory and is without aisles. A Norman staircase turret is in the north-west corner. The different coloured stones used in the building is remarkable and gives a pleasing effect. Perpendicular work is evident. In the east wall is a Norman arch recently discovered. Traces of colour are evident above the arch leading to the north aisle of the choir. The north window is a modern insertion. The monuments here are Bishop Fleetwood (1683), Bishop Hough (1743), the Magdalen President who withstood James II., Bishop Stillingfleet and others.

The *South Transept* is somewhat similar to the north. There are some fine Norman window arches now blocked up, and a beautiful Norman arch opening to the Chapel of St. John. The builders of the fifteenth century cased the Norman walls with a screen of Perpendicular tracery somewhat similar to the work at Gloucester. The great organ is placed here. Here is a monument of Bishop Philpott (1892).

We now enter the *Choir* and eastern portion of the Cathedral. The screen is of oak and open metal work designed by Sir Gilbert Scott. A figure of the Saviour is over the centre and a figure of the Virgin looks eastward. This part of the building is certainly the most interesting. It is of Early English design and was begun in 1224, that is four years after Salisbury, and some twenty-four years after Lincoln. Worcester was one of the earliest churches in England in which English Gothic was developed, and therefore has a peculiar interest for us. We notice that the span of the arches is wider than in the nave, and that in consequence the arches rise to a higher level. The triforium is, however, less in height than that of the nave. The piers are composed of clustered shafts of Purbeck marble, and these have curious brass rings which were placed there by Bishop Gifford. The dog-tooth ornament is much used. The whole choir was restored by Mr. Perkins and Sir G. Scott. The *Stalls*, which contain some finely-carved *Misereres*, have seen many vicissitudes. Puritan soldiers destroyed the ancient canopies. The carvings were placed on a hideous screen, at the beginning of the last century, which separated the nave from the choir. The subjects are curious—an old man stirring a pot over a fire, knights tilting, huntsmen, hawking scene, and many others. The *Stone Pulpit* was brought here from the nave; the upper part is Late Perpendicular. The sculpture represents Evangelistic emblems—Heavenly Jerusalem with Tree of Life, Tables of the Law, etc. The *Throne* is modern and is elaborately carved with figures, foliage, animals, birds and Scriptural subjects. It was presented by Bishop Philpott. The modern *Reredos* is of alabaster enriched with gold, mosaic, lapis-lazuli and malachite. Over the altar are statues of our Lord and the Evangelists, and there are figures of Apostles, prophets, David and Solomon and angels. The organ is divided into three separate parts connected by electricity.

There are two Royal tombs; in the centre of the choir is that of King John, who died at Newark in 1216, whence his body was conveyed here for burial. The effigy is the earliest of an English king in this country. The Royal garments are the tunic reaching to the ankles, and over this the dalmatic with wide sleeves and a girdle buckled in front. On the feet are sandals with spurs; on the hands are jewelled gloves, and there is part of a sceptre. The head has a crown, and the face has moustache and beard. The figures on each side are SS. Oswald and Wulstan. Recently the figure has unfortunately been covered with gilt. The tomb on which the effigy rests is sixteenth-century work. The other Royal tomb is that of Prince Arthur, eldest son of Henry VII., who died at Ludlow Castle in 1502. His death was fraught with great consequence to English history. The tomb is a very fine example of Late Perpendicular work, in which the Tudor emblems, the rose and portcullis, are evident. The exterior consists of open tracery, niches and panelled work, crowned with a battlement and pinnacles. Within there is a flat groined roof, a rich mass of tabernacle work at the east end with figures in niches, in the centre a plain altar tomb, and at the west end a small figure of the mourning father, Henry VII.

The *South Choir Aisle* is Early English similar to the choir, as is the rest of this portion of the Cathedral, and therefore this need not be again mentioned. The *Chapel of St. John*, restored by Earl Beauchamp, is very fine. The glass is all modern. Passing into the eastern transept we notice a piscina and aumbries and some remarkable sculptures in the spandrels of the arcade which are reproductions of ancient work. They are supposed to represent the present and future life. The subjects are: Knights fighting with lions and centaurs (the world and its temptations); St. Michael weighing souls, and the devil pulling down the scale; demons torturing souls over flames (purgatory); hell's mouth; a burial (of Adam?); expulsion from Paradise; an angel leading soul to heaven; the Resurrection; angels sounding a trumpet and bearing the Cross and Christ enthroned. Other subjects are monks building, Annunciation, Nativity, Crucifixion, etc. In this transept is the effigy of a knight in full armour of the fourteenth century of ringed mail. The shield has Harcourt arms, and below is the inscription—*Ici gist sur Guilliamme de Harcourt*. Guide books usually point him out as a Crusader because he has his legs crossed. As we have already stated, there is no special signification in crossed-legged effigies. There is a tomb of Sir Gryffyth Ryce (1523), " a noble knight," and his wife, daughter of Sir John St. John, and near Prince Arthur's Chantry the tomb of Bishop Gifford (1302), and Maude de Clifford, wife of Earl of Salisbury, beautifully executed. It is a wonderful study of the dress of the period (1301). Here is a fine statue of Mrs. Digby by Chantrey ; this lady was maid of honour to Queen Charlotte (1820).

The *Lady Chapel*, which has two aisles, is earlier than the west end of the choir. The wall arcade is very rich and beautiful. We notice the brass rings supposed to have been placed round the columns by Bishop Gifford. The east wall is entirely new, and the tracery of the windows is a modern restoration of ancient work. There are some curious grotesque carvings. The *North Choir Aisle* has some beautiful capitals and bosses ; a small oval window of Perpendicular date looks on to this aisle, and was formerly the window of the sacrist's chamber, through which he could watch the great shrines. There is a curious carving under one of the windows.

The principal *Monuments* in the Lady Chapel are :—

A mural slab to the memory of Anne, wife of *Isaac Walton*, the prince of anglers, who probably wrote the inscription : "*Ex-terris.*—M.S. Here lyeth buried so much as could die of Anne, the wife of Isaac Walton, who was a woman of remarkable prudence, and of Primitive Piety. Her great and generale knowledge being adorned with such true humility, and blest with so much Christian meeknesse as made her worthy of a more memorable monument. She died (alas that she is dead !) the 17th of April 1662, aged 52. Study to be like her."

Bishop John Jenkinson (1840) of St. David's.

Prebendary Davison (1834), who wrote his famous work on *Prophecy*.

An unknown lady of the fourteenth century, one of the most beautiful mediæval relics in the Cathedral.

William, first Earl of Dudley (1885).

George William, fourth Baron Lyttelton (1886).

Bishop William de Blois (1236).

Bishop Walter de Cantelupe (1265).

Mutilated effigy of Bishop Brian (1361) or Lynn (1373).

Bishop Cobham (1327).

Bishop Walter de Bransford (1349).

An unknown lady of the thirteenth century.

An unknown knight, *temp.* Henry III.

Last Abbot of Evesham.

The *Crypt* is a very interesting part of the Cathedral, the work of St. Wulstan, begun in 1084. We notice the fine Norman piers with cushion capitals and square abaci. It is apsidal with aisles, and is remarkable for the numerous pillars. Here in this crypt Wulstan assembled a synod in 1092, when were assembled all the wisest men from the counties of Worcester, Gloucester and Warwick. Here used to be preserved the old fourteenth-century doors of the Cathedral, which were said to be covered with human skin, which tradition says was flayed from the body of a man who stole the sanctus bell.

The *Cloisters* are Perpendicular in decoration, though the outer walls are Norman. We pass through the Prior's Door, and notice how perfect the monastic arrangements remain. The vaulting is good lierne, and the bosses are beautifully carved with foliage and other devices. We see the ancient slype or arched passage of Norman character and the *Chapter-House*, with its beautiful central pillar and vaulted roof. It is one of the few Norman ones left, though much altered in the early fifteenth century. Its vault is Perpendicular. A Norman arcade runs round the wall, and the central pillar is Transition Norman. The windows and doorway are Perpendicular and the exterior was coated with masonry of that period. Here are preserved some fragments of ancient vestments, a paten of Bishop Blois', some good bindings and other treasures. On the south is the *Refectory* with Norman crypt. The room is Decorated, *temp.* Edward III., and is now part of the school called the King's School, founded by Henry VIII. A sculptured reredos of great beauty, with traces of coloured decoration, has recently been discovered here. In the west is an interesting lavatory and entrance to the dormitory, both Perpendicular. The dormitory has disappeared, but its foundations have been traced. We return to the Cathedral by the Monks' Door, or go by a vaulted Norman passage to the west front.

In the north-west cloister is a stone inscribed MISERRIMUS, which is said to mark the grave of a non-juror, the Rev. Thomas Morris, or Maurice. Wordsworth wrote the following lines on this subject :—

> " ' Miserrimus !' and neither name nor date,
> Prayer, text, or symbol, graven upon the stone ;
> Nought but that word assigned to the unknown,
> That solitary word—to separate
> From all, and cast a cloud around the fate
> Of him who lies beneath. Most wretched one !

Who chose his epitaph ?   Himself alone
Could thus have dared the grave to agitate,
And claim, among the dead, this awful crown ;
Nor doubt that he marked also for his own
Close to these cloistral steps a burial-place,
That every foot might fall with heavier tread,
Tramping upon his vileness.   Stranger, pass
Softly !   To save the contrite, Jesus bled."

DIMENSIONS

Length (exterior) . . .	425 ft.
Length (interior) . . .	387 ft.
Nave, length	170 ft.
Nave, height	68 ft.
Nave, width	78 ft.
Choir, length	180 ft.
Tower, height	196 ft.
Area	33,200 sq. ft.

PRINCIPAL BUILDING DATES

Norman (1084-1160)—Crypt, chapter-house, and parts of other monastic buildings, west bays of nave with aisles, parts of north and south transepts.

Early English (1224)—Choir with aisles and Lady Chapel.

Decorated (1317-1327)—North side of nave, vault of north aisle.

(1360)—South side of nave.

(1376-1394) — Refectory, cloisters recased, tower, nave and choir vault, library, treasury, stalls and north porch.

Perpendicular—Windows in north transept, Prince Arthur's tomb.

Modern—West window in nave, north window in north transept, east window in nave, reredos, etc.

A North Porch K L Choir Aisles
B Nave M St. John's Chapel, formerly
C North Aisle of Nave Vestry
D South Aisle of Nave N O Eastern or Choir Transept
E F Western or Nave P Q Aisles to Lady Chapel and Altar
  Transept end
 G Tower R Lady Chapel
 H Choir S Chapter-House
 J Altar T Ruins of Guesten Hall
 V Cloisters
 W Refectory, now used as School
  Room

P R Q

N

J

6

K H L M

5

E G F

T

S

C B D 2

V

W

A

3

C D

B

1 Font
2·3 Doorways from South Aisle of
  Nave to Cloister
4 Stairs to the Crypt
5 Stairs to the Crypt from outside
6 King John's Tomb
7 Chantry Chapel and Tomb of
  Prince Arthur

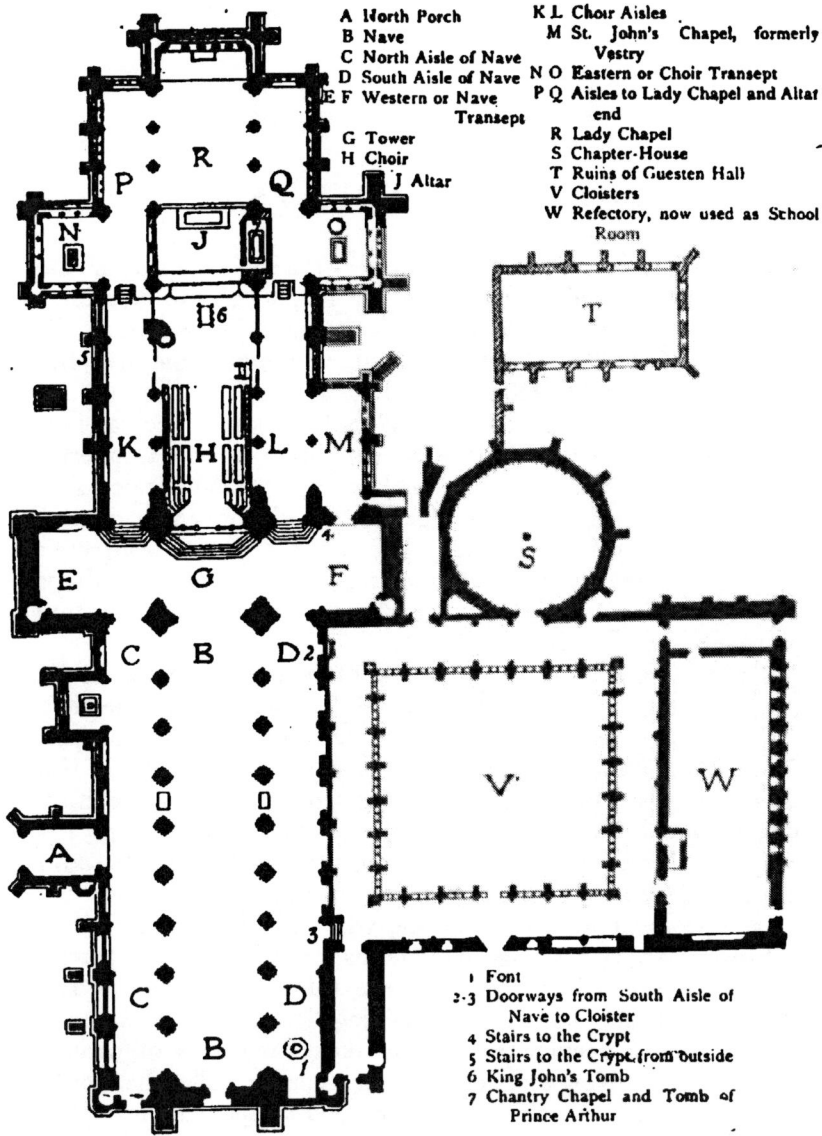

PLAN OF WORCESTER CATHEDRAL

LICHFIELD CATHEDRAL

LICHFIELD has been the victim of Puritan rage and of the over-zeal of modern restorers, but in spite of this it retains much of its ancient beauty and its picturesqueness is evident to all. It is one of the smallest of our cathedrals, but when one sees the three graceful spires of Lichfield, known as the "Ladies of the Vale," the glories of its west front and the richness of the carving, one cannot but retain a warm place in one's heart for this wonderful building which has passed through such strange vicissitudes of fortune. It has been be-pinnacled by our modern Gothic confectioners, who have produced much unnatural "naturalism" in their sculpture ; but if we can forget that much that we see is new, we shall perhaps form some conception of what the Cathedral was like ere innovators and destroyers laid their hands upon it.

The history of the Cathedral is full of interest, and carries us back to the early days of Christianity in England. The heathen King of Mercia, Penda, long withstood the teachers of the Gospel, but when his son, Peada, was was about to marry the daughter of the Christian King Oswi of Northumbria, the latter made it a condition that Peada should be baptised. Forthwith four priests were introduced into Mercia, Diuma became the first bishop (656), and on the death of Bishop Jaruman, the fourth bishop, the famous St. Chad was appointed to the vacant see, who fixed his seat at Lichfield. He was a very holy and humble man, and became the patron saint of the church. Beautiful tales are told of him. Near the Church of St. Mary he built a dwelling for himself and seven brethren. He was deeply affected by the convulsions of nature, and when the wind blew strongly and the thunder rolled he would always retire into the church and pray to God to spare His people ; and when a pestilence broke out and his end was near, angel voices were heard which called him to his heavenly reward. The little Church of St. Chad was near the well that bears his name. Another Saxon church was built by Bishop Hedda (691-721) near the present Cathedral, but this has passed away. The diocese was subdivided at the close of the seventh century, and Hereford, Worcester,

Lincoln and Leicester were all separated from the Lichfield See. In the time of Offa, King of Mercia, Lichfield became an archbishopric, when Higbert was bishop, but this distinction did not last long. At the Conquest William made his chaplain, Peter, Bishop of Lichfield, who removed his seat to Chester. Then Coventry was made the city of the diocese by Bishop Robert de Lymesey (1087-1117). History is silent concerning the church at Lichfield, nor does it tell us with any degree of certainty who built the Norman church which certainly existed here, as its remains were discovered by Professor Willis. It had an apse, of which the foundations lie below the present choir, and also a long, square-ended chapel of twelfth century, destroyed when the Early English choir was built in the thirteenth. Professor Willis compares the building of York and Lichfield, and points out the close parallelism.

Unfortunately the soldiers in the Civil War destroyed all the records; hence we have little to guide us except the history written in the stones of the Cathedral. A Norman prelate, Roger de Clinton, did much for the church, but all his work has perished. The diocese was then called that of Lichfield and Coventry. He died in one of the Crusades.

The Early English builders began to build a new choir about 1200 A.D., of which only the lower part of the three westernmost bays and the sacristy on the south side remain. About 1220 they began to replace the Norman transepts with Early English work, beginning with the south transept and ending with the north. The nave was constructed about the middle of this century and central tower added, and the chapter-house belongs to the same period of architectural activity. In the last quarter of the century the west front was begun. At the end of the century a notable bishop was appointed, one Walter de Langton, Keeper of the Great Seal and Treasurer of England in the reign of Edward I., who incurred the hatred of Prince Edward, afterwards Edward II., and was several times imprisoned by him. He led a very stormy life, but found time to begin the building of the beautiful Lady Chapel at Lichfield, surrounded the close with a wall and a fosse, thus making it a fortress, erected a grand shrine for the relics of St. Chad and built the Palace. This chapel was finished by Bishop Northburgh, who had fought at Bannockburn and been taken prisoner by the Scots, and at the same time the presbytery and clerestory of the choir were rebuilt in the Decorated style.

The church was now complete, and very perfect must it have

been, glorious with the best achievements of true English Gothic art when that art was at its best. Quaint Thomas Fuller describes it as " the neatest pile in England," and tells us that Bishop Heyworth " deserved not ill of his Cathedral Church of Lichfield, which was in the vertical heights thereof, being, though not augmented in the essentials, beautified in the ornamentals thereof. Indeed the west front thereof is a stately fabric, adorned with exquisite imagery, of which I suspect our age is so far from being able to imitate the workmanship, that it understandeth not the history thereof." Quoting a saying of Charles V. of Florence, " that it was fit that so fair a city should have a case and cover for it to keep it from wind and weather," he adds, " so in some sort this fabric may seem to deserve a shelter to secure it." It was also a church rich in relics and costly ornaments, and kings and nobles loved to adorn it with bounteous offerings, while the shrine of St. Chad brought many a pilgrim to fill its treasury when they paid their vows. The fifteenth century made few alterations to the fabric. Dean Heywood built a library, which has now disappeared. Some Perpendicular windows were inserted.

At the Reformation Henry's commissioners carried off a vast store of plate and jewels for " the king's use," and during the Civil War the Cathedral actually endured a siege, the results of which were most disastrous. We have recorded how Bishop Langton surrounded the close with fortifications. The sacred precincts were garrisoned by the Royalists, who awaited the attack of the Parliamentarians, led by Lord Brooke, a fierce fanatic, who longed to pull down all cathedrals as relics of Popery, and extirpate Episcopacy. On St. Chad's day they began the siege, and Brooke prayed in the presence of his men that " God would by some special token manifest unto them His approbation of their design." The " special token " was manifested, but not in favour of the Roundheads; on the second day of the siege a bullet fired by " Dumb Dyott," the son of Sir Richard, one of the leaders of the Royalists, struck Brooke in the eye, and caused his death. This signal act did not save the Cathedral. The spire was struck by cannon balls, and fell, and after three days the garrison made terms of surrender. Desecration and spoliation raged in the once beautiful church. Carved stalls, organ, stained glass windows—all shared the same fate. Images were torn from their niches and broken; tombs were rifled, and the ashes of holy men scattered about with barbarous indecency. Bishop Scrope's tomb yielded a silver chalice and crozier of much value, and a pandemonium of ruthless rage filled the church. Prince Rupert came to Lichfield, and laid siege to the Cathedral, and after ten days turned out the Roundheads. Here the luckless King Charles came, after the disastrous fight of Naseby, and again, when the Royal cause was well-nigh lost, the Parliamentarians besieged the place, and the king's troops were forced to yield.

The Restoration of the monarchy brought about the restoration of the Cathedral, which, according to Fuller, " was now in a pitiful case, indeed almost beaten down to the ground in our civil dissensions." Bishop Hacket, a worthy and zealous man, was appointed to the see, who immediately began the stupendous work, and in eight years completed it, when the church was reconsecrated with much solemnity. King Charles II. gave " 100 fair timber trees " for the restoration, and a poor statue of the monarch was placed at the west end, and the Duke of York gave the large window beneath it. Both have now been removed.

Too soon the ruthless hand of the arch-destroyer, Wyatt, was laid on the luckless Cathedral, who wrought mischief second only to that of the Puritan fanatics. As the canons felt cold, he walled up the pier arches of the choir and closed the eastern tower arch with, a glass screen, removed the altar to east end of the Lady Chapel, patched the piers with Roman cement, hacked away the old stone-work, in order to make this cement stick, and fixed up a large organ screen between the nave and the choir. Roman cement became the passion of the hour. Statues were made of it, old stone-work repaired with it ; arches, mouldings, niches and pinnacles were coated with it. Happily its reign is over. Sir Gilbert Scott began his restoration in 1856. The difficulty of the work was enormous. He endeavoured to imitate the ancient sculpture and stone-work, and restore the Cathedral to the condition of its Early Gothic purity. Though some of the work has been severely criticised, we must take into consideration the difficulties caused by Wyatt and Roman cement which he had to encounter ; we must remember that Gothic revival had not reached its highest development in 1856, and be thankful that so much has been spared to us of this once magnificent Cathedral.

EXTERIOR

When we enter the *Close* we notice that little is left of the fortifications that once made Lichfield into a fortress. Here and there a few traces of the walls remain.   Lichfield was never a monastery, so there are no cloisters.   The view of the Cathedral upon entering the close is very striking and beautiful.   The colour of the stone is remarkable, as it is built of red sandstone.   The three spires are extremely graceful.   A fine view of them is obtained from the south side across the lake.   The two west spires were built by Bishop Northbury (1322-1359), and are Decorated.   The upper part of the north-western one was rebuilt, and there has been some renovation of the other.   The old central tower fell during the siege, and was rebuilt by Bishop Hacket at the Restoration.   The style is Perpendicular, having been built in the fashion of the west tower.

The *West Front* must have been one of the most beautiful in England, and has passed through many vicissitudes.   It was commenced in 1275, and completed by degrees, the work being protracted for more than a century.   The ball-flower ornament in the upper stages points to the later date of the highest part.   There are three principal stages.   In the lowest are three doorways, the wall being covered with a rich arcade of brackets and canopies and statues.   The next stage has three rows of arcading, the lowest extending completely across the front.   The west window divides the two upper arcades.   There are windows in the tower fronts in the third stage, and the wall is covered with rich canopied arcade. The Puritan soldiers did much injury to the statues which filled these niches.   In 1820 the broken figures were restored with Roman cement in a barbarous fashion.   Sir Gilbert Scott in 1877 began to reconstruct the west front, and placed new statues in the niches, and endeavoured to reproduce an exact copy of its appearance in the days of its early beauty.   A study of the figures will not be without interest.

Small figures in central west doorway—on north side—genealogy of Christ according to St. Matthew from Abraham to the Virgin ; on the south, according to St. Luke from Adam to Joseph.   Notice fourteenth-century carving of Our Lord in Glory inside the porch.

North-West Doorway

On North—

1. Ethelbert, angel, with emblem of the Passion.
2. Edwin, orb.
3. Oswald, dove, with letter, and cross in his left hand.
4. Oswy, casket, with key and cross.

DISTANT VIEW OF EXTERIOR

5. Peada, embracing a cross.
6. Wulphere, model of a Saxon church, and a shield.

On South—

1. Bertha, cross in her hand, and her daughter kneeling at an altar.
2. Ethelburga, glass and comb.
3. Hilda, angel hovering over her, and pastoral staff in her hand.
4. Eanfled, priest with letter.
5. Ermenilda, laying down crown.
6. Werburga, pastoral staff, and crown at her feet.

South-West Doorway

The figures represent the two sources of English Christianity, the Celtic and Roman missionaries.

North Side—

1. St. Aidan, pastoral staff, and St. Chad as a boy in St. Aidan's School at Lindisfarne.
2. Finan, pastoral staff.
3. Diuma, pastoral staff and banner.
4. Ceollach, pastoral staff, and mitre at his feet, indicating that he resigned his bishopric.
5. Trumhere, pastoral staff.
6. Jaruman, pastoral staff, and model of a Saxon church.

South Side—

1. Gregory, young Saxon slaves at his feet, in the Market Place at Rome.
2. Augustine, crozier and model of Canterbury Monastery.
3. Paulinus, crozier.
4. Theodore, crozier and scroll.
5. Cuthbert, pastoral staff, and head of St. Oswald in his hand.
6. Wilfrid, pastoral staff, and treading on an idol.

Central Gable

1. Our Lord in Glory, in the act of benediction.
2. Moses, the two tables of stone.
3. Elijah, a book.

4. St. Gabriel, holding a lily, the emblem of purity.
5. St. Uriel, open book.
6. St. Michael, in armour, with spear and shield.
7. St. Raphael, pilgrim's staff.

Highest Stage—South Side—

8. Adam, clothed with skins, and with a lion at his feet.
9. Abel, shepherd's crook and a lamb.
10. Abraham, fire and knife.
11. Isaac.
12. Jacob.
13. Melchisedec, royal and priestly robes and censer.
14. Enoch, prophesying, with uplifted hand.
15. Methuselah, old man's staff.
16. Noah, ark and olive branch.
17. Daniel.
18. Job, staff, and prophesying the Resurrection.
19. Shem.

Middle Stage—Upper Tier—

20. Isaiah, a saw.
21. Hosea, skull at his feet, and scroll, "O death, I will be thy plagues."
22. Jonah, a fish at his feet, and scroll in his hand, "Salvation is of the Lord."
23. Zephaniah, holding a torch and scroll, "The great day of the Lord is near."
24. St. Michael, in armour, with spear and shield.
25. Bishop Hacket, holding the open Bible.
26. Bishop Lonsdale, model of Eton College Chapel at his feet.
27. Bishop Selwyn, his hand resting on the head of a Melanesian boy. Bishop of New Zealand, 1841 to 1867. Bishop of Lichfield, 1868 to 1878.
28. Vacant.

Middle Stage—Lower Tier—

29. Ezekiel, wheel, with Evangelistic emblems.
30. Joel, locust at his feet, and scroll in his hand, "Jehovah is God."
31. Micah, with foot upon an idol; and the words, "Who is God like unto Thee," in a scroll.

32. Haggai, unfinished temple at his feet, and pointing upwards, and scroll, "Go up to the mountain."
33. St. Raphael, a pilgrim's staff, as a messenger of God.
34. Bishop Clinton, A.D. 1129, model of a Norman church.
35. Bishop Patteshull, A.D. 1240, wearing a chasuble, as shown on his effigy in the Cathedral.
36. Bishop Langton, A.D. 1296, model of the Lady Chapel at his feet.
37. Vacant.

Lower Stage of Kings—

38. St. Chad, A.D. 669, pastoral staff, first Bishop of Lichfield.
39. Peada, A.D. 665, embracing the cross.
40. Wulphere, A.D. 657, shield, and model of Peterborough Monastery.
41. Ethelred, A.D. 657, four scrolls, indicating the four subdivisions of the great Mercian Diocese, Lichfield, Worcester, Hereford and Chester.
42. Offa, A.D. 755, archiepiscopal mitre.
43. Egbert, A.D. 827, orb and sceptre. First sole monarch of Saxon Britain.
44. Ethelwolf, A.D. 836.
45. Ethelbert, A.D. 860, crown and sword.
46. Ethelred, A.D. 866, holding a book to his breast.
47. Alfred, A.D. 871, a harp.
48. Edgar, A.D. 958, wolf's head; alluding to tribute of wolves' heads in lieu of money.
49. Canute, A.D. 1017, orb, and looking to the sea; in reference to his rebuke of his courtiers.
50. Edward the Confessor, A.D. 1042, a dove, and a ring in his left hand.
51. William the Conqueror, A.D. 1066, *Doomsday Book* and sword.
52. William Rufus, A.D. 1087, bow and arrow, and hunting horn; alluding to his death.
53. Henry I., A.D. 1100, holding a book.
54. Stephen, A.D. 1135, orb, dove and sword.
55. Henry II., A.D. 1154, sceptre and sword.
56. Richard I., A.D. 1189, with banneret and battle axe.
57. John, A.D. 1199, signing Magna Charta.

58. Henry III., A.D. 1216, model of Westminster Abbey.
59. Edward I., A.D. 1272, the poisoned arrow.
60. Edward II., A.D. 1307, reversed sceptre; alluding to his deposition and murder.
61. Edward III., A.D. 1327, the Garter and sceptre.
62. Richard II., A.D. 1377, orb, cross and sceptre.

Lowest Stage—North to South—

63. St. Cyprian, sword and book. Archbishop of Carthage.
64. St. Bartholomew, knife.
65. St. Simon, saw.
66. St. James the Less, club and book.
67. St. Thomas, the carpenter's square.
68. St. Philip, cross.
69. St. Andrew, a transverse cross.
70. St. John, pen and book.
71. Vacant.
72. Mary Magdalene, the alabaster box of ointment.
73. The Virgin and Child.
74. Mary, wife of Cleophas.
75. Vacant.
76. St. Peter, keys.
77. St. Paul, sword and book.
78. St. Matthew, wallet.
79. St. James the Greater, staff, book and scallop shell.
80. St. Jude, scroll.
81. St. Stephen, stones and the martyr's palm.
82. St. Clement, anchor and open book.
83. St. Werburga, pastoral staff, clasped book and crown at her feet.

NORTH-WEST TOWER

Middle Stage—Lower Tier—

84. Daniel, scroll and flames of fire at his feet.
85. Obadiah, hands lifted up and scroll, " The kingdom shall be the Lord's."
86. Habakkuk, writing the vision.
87. Malachi, fiery oven at his feet and scroll.
88. St. Uriel, a spear.
89. St. Luke, staff with serpent entwined.

90. Queen Victoria.
91. St. Mark, lion at his feet.
92. Dean Bickersteth.
93. Jeremiah, lamenting destruction of Jerusalem.
94. Amos.
95. Nahum, scroll and an Assyrian idol.
96. Zechariah, candlestick and scroll.
97. St. Gabriel, shield and sceptre.
98. Solomon, sceptre and model of the Temple.
99. St. Helena, the cross, and a model of a Basilica.
100. David, harp.
101. St. Editha, foot upon a crown.

North-West Tower—Upper Tier—

102. Eve, a distaff in her hand.
103. Old Figure. This and four others are the only remaining fourteenth-century figures which have survived the wear of time and the violence of the Civil War.
104. Sarah, three cakes in her hand.
105. Old Figure. Fourteenth century.
106. Rachel, crook.
107. Deborah, scroll.
108. Old Figure. Fourteenth century.
109. Hannah, with the boy Samuel at her side.
110. Samuel, anointing horn and scroll.
111. Aaron, scroll.
112. Old Figure. Fourteenth century.
113. Old Figure. Fourteenth century.

St. Anthony over the belfry window on south side of south-west tower.

The west window presented by James II. when Duke of York has been removed and a Decorated window inserted.

Passing round to the north side we see the interesting north doorway, which is a double one, with five orders, and of Early English style (1240 A.D.). The dog-tooth ornament is evident. Carved figures appear in the mouldings. The genealogy of our Lord, beginning with Jesse, is on the east side; on the west St. Chad and the Apostles. Kings and prophets appear on the middle moulding, and angels on the inner. These are good specimens of Early English carving, and are original, though somewhat restored.

Q

A modern figure of St. Anne is in the central niche, and above a figure of our Lord. The figures of SS. James and Jude are examples of the hideous Roman cement work which once was so plentiful here.

Continuing our pilgrimage round the church we see the chapter-house and the Lady Chapel, which has been too much restored with new niches and statues of holy women mentioned in the Bible. The lower row (New Testament) has figures of Priscilla, Anna, Dorcas, Mary of Bethany with box of ointment, Martha with a dish and cloth, Lydia, Phebe and Elizabeth; above Esther, Ruth with corn, Naomi, Rizpah, Deborah, Miriam, Rachel and Rebecca. Passing the so-called mortuary chapels, probably vestries, we notice a noble figure of the Madonna on south side, and though the head has been defaced, and the child knocked away, it remains a beautiful study of fourteenth-century pose and drapery. On the corners of the sacristy are figures of Godefroi de Bouillon and St. Chad. The south portal has been much restored. It is similar to the north doorway, but not so rich in architectural details. On the tympanum are shields with arms of the diocese, and on the west the arms of Lady Catherine Leveson, a benefactress of the time of Bishop Hacket, and an inscription recording her munificence on the east. A row of niches is over the door, formerly filled with figures of Roman cement. Happily they have disappeared. The rose window is very fine.

INTERIOR

We enter the church by the west door, and are struck with the richness and beauty of the view of the nave and choir, the clustered columns with richly-carved capitals, the elaborate reredos of marble and alabaster, and the stained glass of the Lady Chapel. It will be noticed that the choir inclines considerably to the north. This difference in orientation is observable in many churches, and has been interpreted as a figurative representation of the bending of our Lord's head upon the Cross. We believe that this beautiful fancy has no authority, and most probably the inclination was accidental. No records tell us when this nave was built. It is earlier than the west front, and was begun about 1250, at the time when the Early English style was being merged in that of the Decorated. There are eight bays. The piers are octagonal, with many shafts, the capitals enriched with foliage of Early English type. The triforium has two arches in each bay, each arch has two sub-arches, with cusped heads, and a quatrefoil in the tympanum. Dog-tooth ornament is used copiously. The clerestory windows are triangular, with three circles in each, and a trefoil in each circle. Mr. Petit stated, "Nothing can exceed this nave in beauty and gracefulness." The roof was originally of stone. This the besiegers damaged, and after its restoration the stone vaulting was found too heavy for the walls and piers ; hence it was removed, except the portions at the immediate east and west end. Wyatt covered the rest with plaster to imitate the original work. The roof has now been coloured, so that it is impossible to discover any difference between the stone and plaster ceiling.

The *Aisles* are similar in style to the nave, and are very narrow. The wall arcading is very fine Early Decorated work. The windows have three lights, with three foliated circles in their heads. In the north aisle are tablets to the memory of Gilbert Walmesley, the friend of Dr. Johnson and David Garrick ; to Lady Mary Montagu, the introducer of the inoculation for small-pox ; to Ann Seward, the "Swan of Lichfield" (1809), a window ; brass to the memory of officers of the Staffordshire regiment, and its colours. In the *South Aisle* are two curious semi-effigies of ancient date—the heads and the feet are carved, the rest of the body is left a blank in the stone ; a good brass of the Earl of Lichfield (d. 1854) ; and the monument of Dean Addison (1703), the father of a more famous son—the essayist.

We now pass to the *South Transept*, which is earlier than the north, and was begun about 1220. The north transept and chapter-house were built twenty years later. Doubtless for the building of the transepts Henry III. in 1235 and 1238 granted licence to the dean and chapter to take stone from the Royal Forest of Hopwas, south of Lichfield.[1] Both transepts have east aisles. All is Early English work, except the windows. The large south window is Perpendicular, probably inserted by Bishop Blyth (1503-1533). The stone vault is also Perpendicular, erected in place of a wooden one, which served as a model of that at St. George's Chapel, Windsor, according to the order of Henry III. There is some Flemish glass in the south window of the aisle, similar to that in the Lady Chapel. It was brought from Herckenrode. We notice the memorial of one of Nelson's men—Admiral Sir W. Parker. The south window is fitted with good modern glass. In the *North*

[1] *Rot. Lit. Claus.*, 19, Henry III. ; quoted by Britton and Murray.

Transept we see that the style has advanced since the construction of the south transept, twenty years earlier. The arcading here has trefoiled arches. The windows have Perpendicular tracery, and a large north window was inserted in Perpendicular times, but it has recently been removed and the Early English window restored. The curious monument is of Dean Heywood, representing his skeleton. The organ occupies the aisle.

Standing beneath the *Tower*, at the entrance of the choir, we notice the conjunction of styles—the large piers with banded shafts of the Early English of the choir blended with later work of the transept and the Early Decorated of the nave. A modern metal screen of graceful design separates the transept from the choir, and was designed by Sir G. Scott. Above are bronze angels playing instruments of music.

The *Choir*, which succeeded the Norman apsidal choir, was begun in 1200, and the Lady Chapel about 1300, when the choir was lengthened by one bay. Then the Early English choir was removed as far as the third pier east of the tower, and the present choir built in the Decorated style; the upper part of the three western bays was also removed, and a Decorated clerestory added. Thus we have the arches and piers of the first three bays Early English, clerestory Decorated, and three other bays Decorated. Wyatt wrought havoc here, but his plans have now been altered, and the arrangements been made to conform to the original design. It will be observed that the tracery of the clerestory windows is Perpendicular, inserted at the restoration after the siege; only one original being left. There is no triforium, there being only two storeys. The spandrels have cusped circles, and in the older part niches with statues: on south, SS. Christopher, James and Philip; and on north, SS. Peter, Mary Magdelene and the Virgin. The stalls and bishop's throne are modern. The *Reredos* is very magnificent, designed by Sir G. Scott. The pavement contains a veritable history of the Cathedral, while the space before the altar contains Old Testament types of the sacrifice of our Lord. The canopies of the *Sedilia* are ancient and Late Decorated.

The *Choir Aisles* resemble in style the parts of the choir to which they are adjacent. In the north there is Chantrey's monument of Bishop Ryder, and G. F. Watts's effigy of Bishop Lonsdale (d. 1867). The *Lady Chapel* is full of interest, and especially noticeable is the stained glass of sixteenth century, brought from the destroyed Abbey of Herckenrode, having been concealed from the destructive zeal of French revolutionists. The subjects are scenes from the life of our Lord and figures of the benefactors of the Abbey, and are the work of Lambert Lombard, the first, and by far the best, of the Italianised Flemish School of the sixteenth century. The architecture of the chapel was begun by Bishop Langton (1296-1321), and finished by Northburg; the style is Decorated. It has an octagonal apse—an unique arrangement. Beneath the windows is an arcade, resting on a stone bench, and between the windows are niches, which have recently been filled with statues of excellent execution. These are:—St. Werburgh, St. Cecilia, St. Prisca, St. Faith, St. Catherine, St. Margaret, St. Lucy, St. Agnes, St. Ethelreda. The triptych which forms the reredos was carved at Ober Ammergau. The altar rails are of alabaster. Looking back we have a good view of the Cathedral, and note the considerable inclination of the choir. On the south side are the so-called mortuary chapels, which have been restored in memory of Bishop Selwyn, and contain his effigy and some mural paintings recording scenes from the adventurous life of this great missionary-bishop, who did so much to plant the Church in Melanesia. The shrine of St. Chad formerly stood in the retro-choir behind the high altar.

In the south choir aisle is the consistory court, formerly the sacristy. The walls are the oldest part of the Cathedral, being of the same date as the Early English portion of the choir. We notice the old tile and coal pavement, and the old Jacobean choir stalls. Above is the minstrels' gallery, so-called, of Perpendicular work, opening into St. Chad's Chapel, chiefly intended for the exhibition of relics to the pilgrims in the aisle below, and amongst these those of St. Chad. This chapel, formerly used as a muniment room, has been beautifully restored by Dean Luckock, and has good lancet windows, noble reredos of alabaster, old piscina and aumbrey which probably once held the skull of St. Chad. Carved figures in bosses and corbels tell the story of the saint. The old treasury has been beautifully restored, and we see the old aumbreys which once contained such a store of treasures and relics, and some of the cannon balls which wrought such havoc during the siege. There are many interesting monuments in this aisle—notably the famous "Sleeping Children," by Chantrey (1817), daughters of Prebendary Robinson; the monuments of Archdeacon Hodson and his son of "Hodson's Horse" fame, who distinguished himself so much in the Indian Mutiny; Erasmus

Darwin (1802), grandfather of Charles Darwin, a writer of botanical poems; Bishop Langton (1296), much mutilated; Bishop Patteshull (1241), of Purbeck marble; Sir John Stanley (1515), a curious effigy of a knight naked to the waist as if prepared for scourging. It is supposed that he was excommunicated for some offence, and was not ashamed to have his penance recorded on his tomb. Other monuments are those of Archdeacon Moon (1876); Dean Howard (1868); Bishop Hacket, the restorer of the Cathedral after the siege; one of the semi-effigies mentioned above, and at the east end is a curious fourteenth-century mural painting.

We now visit the *Chapter-House*, passing through the vestibule which is of Late Early English design. We notice the beautiful arcading in the latter; on the west side there are seats where, it is said, that the feet of beggars were washed on Maundy Thursday. The dog-tooth ornament is extensively used in the arcading. The doorway to the chapter-house is very fine and is a double one with a figure of our Lord in the tympanum. Clustered shafts are at the sides with capitals carved with foliage. The chapter-house is octagonal, having the north and south sides longer than the others. The central pillar is surrounded by banded shafts with richly-carved capitals. The windows are Early English, with two lights. An arcade of forty-nine arches with rich canopies surrounds the chamber. Traces of mural painting may be seen over the door. All the ancient glass was destroyed, and modern artists are depicting in glass the history of the see. Over the chapter-house is the *Library*. It contains many treasures, in spite of the Puritan destruction, the most valuable being the Gospels of St. Chad (preserved in a glass case in the retro-choir), containing the Gospels of SS. Matthew and Mark and part of St. Luke. It has 700 miniatures. Other treasures are Chaucer's *Canterbury Tales*, which has all except that of the *Ploughman's*, supposed by some to be spurious; Caxton's *Life of King Arthur*, the MS. Household-book of Prince Henry, eldest son of James I., and many rare Bibles. The copy of South's Sermons is interesting, as it belonged to Dr. Johnson, and contains MS. notes for his Dictionary.

DIMENSIONS

Total length	371 ft.
Length of nave	140 ft.

Width of the nave and its aisles . . . 67 ft.
Width of the choir and aisles . . . 66 ft.
Width of the Lady Chapel . . . 29 ft.
Length of the transepts from north to south . 149 ft.
Height of the vaulting . . . . 57 ft.
Height of the central spire . . . 258 ft.
Height of the two western spires . . 198 ft.
Area . . . . . . 27,720 sq. ft.

PRINCIPAL BUILDING DATES

Early English (1220-1250)—Lower part of three west bays of choir and sacristy, south transept.

(1250-1275)—Nave and aisles, central tower, chapterhouse, north and south doorways of transepts.

Decorated (1275-1357)—Lady Chapel, west front, and west spires.

Perpendicular—South window of south transept and vault, north window of west transept, some other windows, minstrels' gallery.

(1661-1671)—Central tower, spire rebuilt.

CHESTER CATHEDRAL

ROYAL Chester is one of the most ancient and interesting cities in the kingdom   It was an important Roman station. It was called the "City of Legions," and the twentieth Legion of the Roman army was stationed here, and left behind it many traces of its occupation.   Saxons and Danes also held the place. The warlike daughter of Alfred the Great, and wife of Ethelred of Mercia, drove out the Danes and rebuilt the walls, but the Welsh again gained the mastery until the first Saxon Edward reconquered it, and later Edgar subdued the Britons, and in 973 was rowed in his victorious vessel on the Dee by eight British chieftains.   William the Conqueror made his nephew Earl of Chester, and for years he and his successors ruled as kings in this corner of England, until Henry III. bestowed the title on his eldest son, and since that time the earldom has always been held by the king's first-born.   Edward I. often came here when he was waging war against Llewellyn and the Welsh, and worshipped in the great church.   Here Henry IV. brought as a captive the luckless King Richard II. and imprisoned him in the castle.   Of Royal visits old Chester had abundance.   The city was famous for its "miracle plays," which were performed in the streets.   Frequently the dread visitor plague made its presence felt, and grass grew in the neglected streets.   Tradition states that the name "God's Providence House" was given to a house in Watergate Street, because that was the only dwelling which the plague passed over. Chester played an important part in the Civil War, and bravely resisted a siege and frequently repelled formidable attacks, and the inhabitants were reduced to great straits and much ruin wrought. The walls of the city are quite complete, and on one of the towers called the Phœnix is the inscription : "King Charles stood on this tower September 24th " (27th it should be) " 1645, and saw his army defeated at Rowton Moor."

Chester retains many of its historical associations, its extensive Roman remains, its walls and ancient houses, its wonderful Rows, "like which there is nothing else in the world," the quaint street names, the interesting churches, all contribute to make Chester one of the most delightful cities in England. Although the great church is ancient, the present see is not. Chester was one of the dioceses founded by Henry VIII. in return for some of the great stores of treasure which he and his courtiers filched from the church. It appears, however, that just after the Norman Conquest there were Bishops of Chester. In 1075 the Bishop of Lichfield removed the seat of the bishopric to Chester, and the Church of St. John the Baptist was his Cathedral. Then Coventry became the centre of the diocese, but the title of Bishop of Chester was frequently used, but fell into disuse in later time, until Henry VIII. constituted the new see.

The church has, however, a very interesting history. Possibly there may have been a Christian church here in Roman times. An old chronicler tells us of an early church dedicated to SS. Peter and Paul, and that in the time of the Saxons it was re-dedicated to St.

ST. OSWALD'S GATE

Werburgh and St. Oswald. St. Oswald we have met before at Durham and elsewhere. St. Werburgh was the daughter of Walphur, King of Mercia, A.D. 660, who, perceiving that his daughter was much disposed to a religious life, caused her to take the veil. Her aunt, St. Ethelreda of Ely, was her spiritual mother, and when St. Werburgh died her body was conveyed to Chester, where a monastic house was built, dedicated to her. The early history of this house is somewhat uncertain. Ormerod, the historian of Chester, states that it continued a nunnery until the time of the Norman Conquest, when secular canons were installed in their stead, but this change took place in the time of King Athelstan (925). Leofric, the husband of Lady Godiva, is also recorded as a great benefactor of the church and monastery. When Hugh Lupus, the nephew of the Conqueror, became Earl of Chester, in the time of William Rufus he founded a new monastery of Benedictine monks, and endowed it with rich possessions. He introduced the famous Anselm, Abbot of Bec, afterwards Archbishop of Canterbury, who made his chaplain, Richard, the first abbot. The Norman church was begun in his time, and some of the features of the Norman Abbey of Bec were introduced at Chester, especially the stone roof of the apse in the south-east of the Cathedral. Some fragments of this church remain in spite of the changes which time has wrought, notably the small arches in the east wall of north transept, and an arch in the canons' vestry, the north wall of the nave, the doorway between the east cloister and the nave, the lower part of the north-west tower and the crypt. Fire played havoc here as elsewhere, and we find Abbot Geoffrey lamenting over the intolerable ruin of his church. This was at the close of the twelfth century, and some reparation was affected, while, during the time of his successor, Hugh Grylle, prosperity dawned upon the Abbey, and the number of monks was soon after increased. Increased wealth tempted the rapacious, and the abbey had to withstand a siege. A noted abbot was Simon de Albo Monasterio, or Whitchurch, who did much for his monastery. He rebuilt the Lady Chapel, enlarged the chapter-house, and began the present choir. The refectory, with its beautiful pulpit, must have been constructed about this time, the close of the thirteenth century, when the king, Edward I., gave grants of venison from his forests for the support of the monks, "who were engaged on the work of building the church." No records tell of any work being done by succeeding abbots until the time of Simon Ripley (1472-1493); but where records are silent the stone-work tells us that in the fourteenth century some beautiful work was accomplished, notably the shrine of St. Werburgh, the sedilia and choir stalls. Simon Ripley was an energetic abbot, and rebuilt the nave, tower and south transept. This south transept was claimed as the Parish Church of the parishioners of St. Oswald, and there were much disputings, but the people had their way, and retained their rights until 1881.

We also find that the usual quarrels took place between the monks and citizens about the rights to hold fairs and markets. Abbot Birkenshawe continued Ripley's work, and completed the west front and part of the west tower. An unfortunate alteration was made at this time. The vault of the cloisters was raised, tradition says, by Cardinal Wolsey, and mars the beauty of the earlier work. Then came the dissolution of monasteries, and the Abbey of St. Werburgh shared the fate of the rest. The See of Chester was created in 1541, the last abbot becoming the first dean, and John Byrde the first bishop. Most of the lands and wealth of the church were seized by the king and his courtiers. But, shorn of its wealth, the Cathedral itself was at this time one of the most beautiful in England. Dire troubles were, however, in store. The waves of the Civil War beat fiercely on Royal Chester; and when, after the protracted siege, the victorious Puritan soldiers entered the city, they defaced the Cathedral choir, injured the organ, and demolished the font, broke all the painted windows, and used the church as a stable. Randle Holme, the historian of Chester, utters a sad lament over the condition of the city which he loved so well, and compares it with Jerusalem, "the beloved citie of God, with not a stone left upon another." Since then the story of the Cathedral has been one of continual reparation and restoration. The exterior of the choir was recased by Bishop Stratford (1689-1707). Bishop Law, in 1818, effected some considerable repairs, and other efforts were made, until at length Sir G. Scott was engaged in 1868, when Dean Howson ruled, and a very "thorough" restoration was made. A modern authority on Gothic architecture states that Sir G. Scott's was "a rebuilding of every external feature of this Cathedral in the style of his own Victorian Gothic." Perhaps this criticism is a little too severe. It must be remembered that the stone of Chester Cathedral was very soft and perishable, that the state of the fabric was so bad that it was almost dangerous, and that the difficulties of the architect were great. However, in spite of what has been done, there is still much to admire, and we will proceed to examine the details of this ancient church.

THE EXTERIOR

To examine the exterior we must avoid the narrow streets in its vicinity, and ascend the old walls of the city, from which we can obtain an excellent view. Starting at the east gate, we get a good view of the south-east of the Cathedral, including the tower, the east side of the south transept, choir and Lady Chapel. We notice the colour of the stone—red sandstone. The plan of the church is cruciform. The *Tower* is Perpendicular in style, and was probably built by Abbot Ripley. Two windows of Perpendicular character look out from each side. It has been much restored, and was only just saved from destruction by this process. Sir G. Scott devised the turrets and pinnacles out of his inner consciousness, and also the parapet; but the effect, though differing, doubtless, from the original design, is not unpleasing. The *Lady Chapel* is a simple and beautiful construction of Early English design. On the south side there are three triple lancets under a pointed arch, separated by buttresses crowned with pinnacles, and a parapet above. The south aisle of the choir is Early Decorated, and there is a modern apsidal termination, with a curious steep roof, almost resembling the spire of a church, which Sir G. Scott constructed, and for which he found justification in the remains of the earlier roof. This example is unique in England, but not unusual in France. The south transept is unusually large, which is accounted for by its being the Church of St. Oswald. There are some curious modern sculptures in a corbel here, representing modern statesmen, and the features of Mr. Gladstone and Lord Beaconsfield are not difficult to discover. Passing along the wall of the city, at the east of Abbey Street we see the north-east view. Near at hand, on the right, is the refectory, and on the left the chapter-house, which is Early English. The north transept is Norman work. The north choir aisle, which extends along the side of the Lady Chapel, is, in its eastern part, Perpendicular; further west it is Early Decorated, while by the canons' vestry we see unmistakable Norman work. In this wall much of the old stone remains, as it has not suffered so much from the weather as on the south side. We see the long expanse of the nave roof, and then pass along Abbey Street, and have a fine view of this north side. Then houses interfere with the prospect. Then we see the old Abbey gateway, a fourteenth-century structure, and the new buildings of the King's School, which occupies the site of the old Palace, and soon stand opposite the *West Front*, which lacks the grandeur of this feature of many cathedrals. It has a large Perpendicular window of good design and rich tracery; beneath it is a Tudor doorway, and canopied niches, and on the south the base of a tower which was never completed. Passing along we have a grand view of the south side.

Chester Cathedral

There is a porch, with a parvise over it, of Late Perpendicular design, with Tudor doorway, and battlements and pinnacles. The vault is modern; the windows of the aisle are Decorated, and those of the clerestory Perpendicular. This concludes our survey of the exterior, and we now enter the Cathedral and examine the principal features of the interior.

THE INTERIOR

Entering by the south porch or the west door, we examine first the *Nave*, which is small and not very striking in appearance. There are six bays, but the southern arcade is much earlier than the north. The piers consist of groups of attached shafts, with capitals of foliage. The southern arcade is Decorated, while the northern is later. The initials S.R. appear on the capital of the first northern pier. These letters stand for Simon Ripley, abbot (1485-1492). He probably built the upper part of the northern arcade, but the lower part is earlier. The clerestory was finished by Abbot Birkenshawe. The last bay eastward is more ornamented than the rest, and has cusped windows in the clerestory and tracery in the triforium opening. This is earlier, and is perhaps more ornate, because the choir included this bay. The roof is modern, and has a good specimen of fan-tracery vault. Some of the bosses are noticeable, and record the benefactors—the Prince of Wales, Duke of Westminster, and others.

Under the south tower is the *Consistory Court*, which is separated from the nave by some curious Jacobean stone-work, and contains some good wood-work of the same period. The south aisle has Decorated windows; the north aisle contains some interesting remains of the old Norman church. The north wall is entirely Norman. A Norman doorway leads to the cloisters at the east end, and at the west there are some remains of the Norman tower built by the nephew of the Conqueror. This is now the baptistry, which has a curious *font*, presented by Earl Egerton in 1885. The dean states that "it came from a ruined church in the Romagna, but it is not known whence it was brought to Venice. It is of a rectangular form, of white marble; and in all probability it was originally a village well-head in early Roman times, and afterwards taken by the Christians and carved with symbols for a font. The work is of the Ravenna type, of the sixth or seventh century." Near here is hung an ancient piece of tapestry, which has been in the Cathedral since 1668. The subject is Raphael's cartoon of Elymas the Sorcerer. The vault of this aisle is modern. The old wall is covered with rich mosaics, representing Abraham, Sarah, Moses, David, Elijah, and other Old Testament characters.

The *North Transept* is small, and is of the same size as the original church, there being no room for expansion on this side because of the monastic buildings. The lower walls are original Norman, the upper Late Norman. A Norman arch, now blocked up, leads to the canons' vestry on the east. The arches of the triforium are very early, and are rude and massive. On the west there are three Norman windows blocked up. Perpendicular tracery has been inserted in some of the windows. That of the north window is modern. The roof is Perpendicular, and on one of the bosses are the arms of Cardinal Wolsey. A conspicuous monument here is that of Bishop Pearson (1686), the author of the famous work on *the Creed*. The initiation of the erection of this magnificent memorial of one of the greatest of English divines was due to an American bishop, Dr. Whittingham of Maryland. The organ-loft is very rich, and the instrument itself is a very noble one, and replete with every modern contrivance. Crossing to the *South Transept*, which until 1881 was the Parish Church of St. Oswald, we notice its great size when compared with that on the north. It was undergoing restoration when we last visited the Cathedral. It has Decorated windows, and Perpendicular in the west aisle. The monuments in the naves and transepts do not possess many features of interest, and may be passed over.

We now enter the *Choir*, and can admire the modern screen, designed by Sir G. Scott, and beautifully executed. The choir is remarkable for the great beauty of the wood-work which it contains, as well as for its architectural merits. The style is that of the transition between the Early English and Decorated. The north side differs from the south, especially in regard to the mouldings. The north side is earlier than the south, the building having been commenced at the east end of that side. The mouldings on the north are bold rounds, while those on the south are shallow and small hollows. The triforium has a series of elaborately-carved cusped arches, and the clerestory windows are light and graceful, with geometrical tracery. The vault is modern, constructed of good English oak. At the east there are figures of the sixteen prophets, and at the west are angels playing musical instruments. There are some curious grotesque corbels, from which the vaulting

THE CHOIR

R

shafts spring. The carving of the *Choir Stalls* is equal, if not superior, to anything in England. These are fourteenth-century work, and rival the noble stalls of Amiens. They have been restored with much accuracy and taste. The carving of the dean's stall should be noticed, as it represents the Jesse tree, surmounted by the Coronation of the Virgin. That representing Jacob's dream is modern. The *Misereres* are extremely interesting and curious, and full of religious instruction, though often conveyed in the way of sarcastic reproof. There are forty-eight, of which three are modern. Some of the most curious are : a pelican feeding her young; St. Werburgh and the stolen goose; a wife beating her husband; the strategy of the fox; stag hunt; Richard I. pulling out the heart of a lion; a fox in the garb of a monk presenting a gift to a nun; various wild men; wrestlers; unicorn resting its head on a virgin's knee, and numerous grotesques. The *Throne* is a handsome modern work, and also the *Pulpit*, presented by the Freemasons of Cheshire, who restored also the ancient sedilia, which, tradition states, came from the old Church of St. John without the city walls. The altar is made of wood grown in Palestine. The oak of Bashan, olive wood from the Mount of Olives, and the cedar of Lebanon, are all used, and the carvings represent palm, vine, wheat, olive, thorn, bulrush, hyssop, myrrh and flax, all of which are included in the *flora* of Palestine. The reredos is a mosaic of the Last Supper. The magnificent candelabra of Italian *cinque cento* work are the gift of the late Duke of Westminster. Over the altar is an arch, through which the window of the Early English Lady Chapel can be seen, and above is a window with Decorated tracery.

The *North Aisle* of the choir is interesting. Traces of Norman work are seen in the base of a massive round pillar at the west entrance, in the inverted capital of a Norman pier, with an Early Decorated pier constructed on it, and the Norman apse is marked on the pavement by a line of dark marble. The canons' vestry is architecturally a very important building, as it contains work of the eleventh, twelfth, thirteenth and fourteenth centuries. The arch in east wall of the transept is Early Norman; the Norman apsidal termination can be traced. It was rebuilt in the Early English period, and made to terminate in a square form, and the doorway from the north aisle is fourteenth-century work. There is an old chest or reliquary here with very good iron-work and lock of the thirteenth century. Re-entering the aisle we can trace the abandonment of the apse and the extension eastward in the Early English period, as shown in the character of the vaulting and in the piscina, which belongs to this period. In Perpendicular times a further extension took place, in order to gain an entrance to the Lady Chapel. The gates of both aisles are old Spanish work of 1558, presented by the late Duke of Westminster.

The *South Aisle* has passed through somewhat similar vicissitudes, but "restoration" has removed some of their traces, and it is now terminated by the apse, the erection of which we recorded when examining the exterior, and which is conjectured to be an exact reproduction of the appearance of this end of the Cathedral in the time of Edward I. The apse has been fitted up as a memorial to Thomas Brassey, the great contractor.

The *Lady Chapel* is of Early English design, and was built about 1266, previous to the present choir. Many alterations were made subsequently, including the removal of the ancient steep and lofty roof and the substitution of a flat roof, and the insertion of Perpendicular windows. Most of these additions have been removed and the Early English character restored. The east window of five lights was designed by Scott, and the original form of the roof has been restored. The vault, which is original Early English, has a boss representing the murder of Thomas à Becket. The mosaics were designed by Sir A. Blomfield. Here the consistory court was held at the time of the Reformation, and George Marsh, the Chester martyr, was condemned to be burnt.

The *Monuments* in the choir and Lady Chapel are to the memory of Dean Howson, Bishop Graham (1865), Dean Arderne, an altar tomb to an unknown person, and the famous shrine of St. Werburgh, of fourteenth-century work, which is of exquisite design and construction. It was richly ornamented by figures. There was a great resort of pilgrims to this shrine in mediæval times. The pavement of the choir is worthy of attention. It is modern; around the lectern are the heads of the twelve Apostles, and of the four doctors of the Church—SS. Ambrose, Augustine, Athanasius and Chrysostom. On the east end are representations of the Passover, and some fragments of tesselated pavement are inserted here which came from the Temple at Jerusalem. The stained glass is all modern. The Cathedral has a rare treasure of the seventeenth century, a carved narwhal tusk, beautifully carved by a Flemish artist. It is thus described by the dean: "The leading subject is the Incarnation of our Lord Jesus Christ, passing on to the exaltation of the Cross. . . . A Jesse tree occupies about 3 feet, and above is seated the Blessed Virgin with the Holy Child. Higher up is the Cross with the figure of our Saviour, whose countenance is full of compassion. . . . St. Michael thrusting down Lucifer with a cross ; the figures of SS. Peter and Paul and the four Evangelists ; St. Anthony of Padua and another monk holding up a cross, and figures of angels, each holding in uplifted hands a cross."

We will now proceed to the *Monastic Buildings*, which are of great importance. They are situated on the north side of the Cathedral, and are approached through a Norman doorway in the north aisle. Turning to the left we see some good Norman arcading. The tombstones of some of the earlier abbots are seen here. The south walk is entirely new, having been restored by Scott. The west walk adjoins a fine Early Norman chamber, probably the great cellar of the abbot's house. The cloisters are Perpendicular work. In the south and west walks there is a double arcade on the cloister-garth side, which contained the *Carrels* or enclosed studies of wainscot, where the monks read or wrote, and on the opposite side are recesses which are not tombs, but *Armaria* or cupboards, where their books and materials for illuminations were stored. In the Perpendicular period the roof of the cloisters was raised, which was not an advantage, as it caused the aisle windows and those of the refectory to be partly blocked up, and the vaulting cuts into the earlier work. The *Lavatorium* is near the entrance to

SHRINE OF ST. WERBURGH

the *Refectory*, an Early English building with Perpendicular windows. It is a noble structure, shorn of some of its length, and now used as a music room. The stone pulpit is remarkably fine, of Early English design, which rivals the famous pulpit of Beaulieu Abbey. In the east walk we see the doorway leading to the *Vestibule* of the chapter-house. It consists of a cusped arch, and three small windows are above it; on the centre one the dog-tooth ornament is used. Both the vestibule and the chapter-house are fine examples of Early English. In the former light, graceful piers support the vaulting without capitals, the mouldings being continued along the piers and vaulting in a very beautiful manner. The *Chapter-House* is a noble chamber. Its shape is oblong, and it was built about 1240. There is a fine east window of five lights; and windows of three lights are on the north and south sides, and have detached shafts. The glass is modern, and represents the chief persons associated with the history of the Cathedral. Here is stored the library, which is not rich in treasures of bibliography. There is a fair collection of the Fathers and liturgical works, a book which belonged to Bishop Pearson and Higden's *Polyolbion*.

DIMENSIONS

Length, 355 ft.; length of nave, 145 ft.; width of nave, 75 ft.; height, 78 ft.; height of tower, 127 ft.

PRINCIPAL BUILDING DATES

Norman (1093-1140)—north wall of north aisle and doorways, part of north-west tower, north transept, part of canons' vestry, cellar in monastic buildings; Early English (1266-1300) —Lady Chapel, choir, part of north choir aisle, chapter-house, refectory; Decorated (1300-1400) — Abbey Gate, south and lower part of north nave, windows of south aisle, part of south transept; Perpendicular (1472-1500)—tower, upper part of north of nave, east of north choir aisle, west front, south porch, part of south transept and some windows; Choir recased (1689-1707).

St. John's Church is well worthy of a visit. It has an important history, and was once the Cathedral of the first Norman bishop. It is mainly of Norman construction. The massive piers are very early (1067-1105), the triforium and clerestory are Transitional. A good history of the church has been written by the Rev. Cooper Scott.

LIVERPOOL CATHEDRAL

LIVERPOOL is a very modern see, the bishopric having been formed in 1880. It has at length been possible to take steps to found a Cathedral, and many architectural problems have to be solved by the citizens with regard to the site and the style of the new church. We trust that these will be solved satisfactorily, and that the Cathedral of Liverpool will be made worthy of the city. If wealth can accomplish this great achievement, there should be no difficulty in this place. The Church of St. Peter is at present used as the Cathedral, but it has no feature of either architectural or historical interest.

MANCHESTER CATHEDRAL

OTHER objects of interest rather than those of history or architecture usually attract the stranger to Manchester. The great centre of modern industry, the city that brings the sea to its walls, that finds employment for tens of thousands, where the pulse of life beats fast—that is the Manchester we all know. But there is another Manchester of quiet and sedate ways, which is not devoid of history, which we will endeavour to read amidst the din and turmoil of this hive of industry. It is difficult to imagine that the parish "was originally a wild, unfrequented tract of woodland, inhabited merely by the boar, the bull, and the wolf, and traversed only by the hunters of the neighbouring country." Under Agricola, Manchester became a Roman station. Camden tells of Roman inscriptions, and many other Roman remains have been found. Edwin of Northumbria came here, and Paulinus brought Christianity and thousands were baptised by him. Two Saxon churches were built, St. Michael's and St. Mary's. Ina and his queen, Ethelburga, sojourned here. The Danes ravaged it, and Edward the Elder re-edified the town in 924. We find that Canute came here, and the historian of the town derives Knot, or Knut, Mill from his name. The Conqueror gave the manor to Roger de Poictiers, but it appears to have been regranted to the Greslie family. It is unnecessary to follow the history of the manor and barony. In 1235 Manchester is said to have had a Deanery, and Peter de Greleigh (Greslie) held the Rectory in 1261. Hugh de Manchester, a favourite of Edward I., went on an embassage to Philip of France to recover certain lands for his king. Other distinguished rectors were William de Marchia (1284), afterwards Bishop of Bath and Wells, and William de Langton, afterwards Bishop of Lichfield, the builder of the beautiful Lady Chapel of that Cathedral; Otto de Grandisson, Geoffrey de Stoke, afterwards Dean of St. Paul's, London. In 1373 Thomas de la Warre was presented to the living, and he obtained Royal licence in 1422 to found a collegiate church, consisting of one warden, eight fellows, four clerks and six choristers. The parishioners cheerfully agreed to build the new church. John Huntingdon, the first warden, built the choir, and several leading families, the Radcliffes, Stanleys, Traffords, Byrons and Strangeways erected chantries. The college was founded at the same time as the residence of the warden and fellows. The right of sanctuary was granted to the collegiate church, the sanctuary men bearing a cross on their hand. The college has a chequered career. In the reign of Edward VI. it was dissolved and its possessions seized. Under Mary it was re-established, together with the chantries in the church. In the time of Elizabeth the college had prolonged disputes with the town, the clergy were beaten by the populace, and one of them stabbed, and the plate and ornaments stolen. In 1578 the charter was renewed. A famous warden was Dr. Dee, who is well known as a dealer in magical arts, and his successor, Murray, was not a very learned divine ; when preaching before James I. from the text, " I am not ashamed of the Gospel of Christ," the monarch said the Gospel of Christ might well be ashamed of him. In 1617 a gallery was erected in the church, which was much dilapidated and the income impoverished. In the time of the Civil War, Richard Heyrick was warden and sided with the Parliament, the Independents setting up a meeting-house at the college. Manchester underwent a siege during the war, and in 1649 the chapter-house and chest were broken into by soldiers and the deeds carried off to London, where it is thought that they perished in the great fire. The college was dissolved. Heyrick was a veritable " Vicar of Bray," and embraced all the opinions in turn of all the parties in that troublous period. The collegiate buildings were in much decay during the Commonwealth period, when Humphrey Chetham, one of the worthiest of benefactors, conceived the idea of converting them into a school and library, and left a large sum of money for this purpose. Chetham's Hospital is quite the most interesting building in the city, which has retained few of its ancient edifices. Lancashire folk were very faithful to the House of Stuart, and in both the rebellions of 1715 and 1745 Manchester took part. The young Pretender was proclaimed here King James III., and the " Manchester Regiment " was formed to fight in the prince's cause, and subsequently many lost their heads, some being stuck upon the Exchange. The Diocese of Manchester was formed in 1847, and has only had three bishops—James Prince Lee, Fraser, and the present Bishop Moorhouse, formerly Bishop of Melbourne.

THE EXTERIOR

Manchester smoke soon causes stone-work to assume a venerable appearance, and although much of the Cathedral is new, its first appearance is one of an ancient edifice. Manchester is a modern see, founded in 1847, but its church, as we have seen, dates back to a very respectable antiquity and has many features of special interest. It stands out well amidst the surrounding mass of modern buildings, of shops and railway stations, and seems to raise the thoughts of all who behold its beauties above the buying and selling in this busy mart of human enterprise.

The present generation of merchants of Manchester and the Cathedral authorities have done much for their Cathedral, and striven to make it worthy of its name and position as the Mother Church of the diocese, and all the resources of modern art have been lavished on the building. We shall see this better in the interior. The exterior also shows that very much has been done in building and decoration. There is first the new *West Porch*, which has just been finished with a statue of Queen Victoria in the niche over the doorway. Just as the burghers of the Middle Ages loved to enrich their churches with the triumphs of architectural art, so do the modern merchants of Manchester strive to adorn their Cathedral with elaborate handiwork. This new piece of work is richly carved. The style follows that of the Cathedral and is mainly Perpendicular. There is rich panel work, an open-work battlemented parapet, and a richly-crocketed pinnacle crowns a turret on the south side. The door itself is a very handsome piece of work. On each side of the main porch there are rooms. The *Tower* stands at the west end above the porch. There is a good west window in the lowest stage with an ogee label richly crocketed. Above is the clock. In former days this clock was not noted for keeping correct time. An old gentleman was observed each morning setting his watch by it. "Excuse me," said a bystander, "that clock is five minutes late." "Sir," he replied, "I have set my watch by that clock for forty years, and right or wrong, I shall go by it for the rest of my life." At each corner of the tower there are three pinnacles. The windows of the church, we observe, as we pass to the south, are all Perpendicular, but there is a pleasing variety in the tracery. The *South Porch* has a parvise, and was built by Mr. James Jardine, a distinguished citizen of Manchester, in 1891. On this side there are several chapels—the Brown Chapel, St. George's, St. Nicholas or Trafford Chapel, Jesus Chapel, the chapter-house with its pyramidal roof, the Fraser Chapel, a new building erected in memory of Bishop Fraser. The battlemented parapet on this side of the church is modern. On the east side is a tiny Lady Chapel with a Decorated east window, which has been reproduced from the earlier design. Proceeding onwards we notice the Ely Chapel, the Derby or John the Baptist's Chapel, the St. James's Chapel, and that dedicated to the Holy Trinity. The *North Porch* is similar in character to that on the south, and was erected in memory of James Craven in 1888.

The Interior

The interior of the Cathedral is full of interest. We enter by the south porch, and we are at once struck by the extraordinary width of the church. On each side of the nave there are two aisles. The outer aisles both on the north and south sides were formerly separated from the rest of the church by screens, and were occupied by chapels or chantries. By a somewhat drastic restoration at the beginning of the nineteenth century these screens were removed, and the outer aisles thrown open. This procedure rendered the church more useful for congregational purposes, though we may regret the disappearance of the historic chapels, a few piscinæ being the only remains. We will commence our pilgrimage at the west end, and from this point view the length of the church, which is shrouded in "a divine religious light," perhaps a little too dim. Most of the windows are filled with modern glass which is generally of beautiful design; but modern glass lacks that transparency which ancient glass has. The sunlight streams through the old glass, and it is quite possible, as at Fairford, to read the smallest print; while modern glass effectually shuts out the light, and at the best too much sunlight is not usually observable in this region of smoky chimneys and polluted atmosphere. The piers of the nave are modern imitations of the original Perpendicular ones, and are lofty and graceful. There is no triforium, and the clerestory is somewhat contracted. The windows have five lights of Perpendicular tracery, and most of them are filled with modern glass. The roof is ancient, but has been much restored.   In the distance we see the handsome choir-screen with the organ over it.   The spandrels of the chancel arch are richly carved with shields in quatrefoils, and above is the Tudor rose.   Shields adorn the spandrels of the main arches.   Above us is the ceiling of the tower, which is a good example of fan-tracery. The modern baptistry is on our right.   Passing the south porch, erected in memory of Mr. James Jardine, we see the extreme south aisle, formerly consisting of chantries separated from the rest of the church by screens.   In a recess east of the porch was the Brown Chapel, and north of this St. George's Chantry (to which saint, together with St. Mary and St. Denis, the church was formerly dedicated) founded by W. Galley in 1508.   At the dissolution of the collegiate institution John Barlow and Edward Smyth, priests of this chantry, received pensions of £6 and £4, 12s. 6d. respectively. Then comes the Trafford or St. Nicholas Chantry, the priest of which received a pension of £5.   The Traffords of Trafford are an ancient Lancastrian family who have held the manor, near Manchester, since the Conquest, and the name of Edmund Trafford appears upon the list of parishioners given in the licence to erect the collegiate church.   A piscina shows the position of the altar of this chantry.   Next follows the Jesus Chapel which has a fine sixteenth-century screen.   It was founded by Richard Bexwick in 1506, being granted to him "to enjoy its privileges by James Stanley, warden, and the fellows."   His daughter Isabel gave it to Francis Pendleton and Cicely his wife, daughter of Isabel.   In 1652 it was in a ruinous condition.   It is now used as the library and vestry.   From this chapel another chapel founded by Ralph Hulme in 1507 opened, but it has been destroyed.   One of this family of Hulme founded in 1691 the Hulmeian scholarships at Oxford.   Next we see the entrance to the chapter-house built by James Stanley (1485-1509), which is good Perpendicular work. Under the arch, which has panelled work in the soffit, there are two doors having four-centred arches, and above panelling.   The Fraser Chapel, erected in memory of Bishop Fraser of Manchester (1870-1885), "a man of singular gifts both of nature and the spirit," who won all hearts and whose memory will ever be venerated in the Manchester Diocese, stands on the south at the extreme east end of this aisle.   It contains an admirable effigy of the bishop, who was buried in the little Parish Church of Ufton Nervet, Berks, where he passed the early years of his clerical life, and for which he had tender memories.   This was a college living to which he was presented by Oriel College. Turning to the north we enter the retro-choir and the Lady Chapel, originally founded by George West, youngest brother of Lord Delaware, who was warden of the college in 1518-1535. The last historian of the Cathedral, Mr. Perkins, considers that West reconstructed a more ancient building, and that the style of the windows inserted in the eighteenth century in imitation of earlier ones point to an earlier date than 1518. This chapel was once known as the Byron Chapel, and then the Chetham Chapel, as it contains several memorials of that family. There is a modern statue of Humphrey Chetham, the founder of Chetham's Hospital (which we shall presently visit), who was born in 1580, and by trade "acquired opulence, while his strict integrity, his piety, his works of charity and benevolence secured him the respect and esteem of those around him."[1] He founded the school, and clothed, fed and instructed twenty-two boys, and, though never married, thus became a father of the fatherless and destitute. At the base of his statue is seated a figure of one of these youths. Near this statue is the tomb of Hugh Birley, a member of a distinguished Manchester family and a representative of the city in Parliament. An ancient organ, more than two centuries old, also is in this aisle. On the north is the St. John the Baptist or Derby Chapel, formerly called the Stanley Chapel, separated by an old screen from the aisle. The Stanleys belong to the same family as the Earls of Derby. The office of warden was held by two members of the Stanley family, both having the Christian name of James. The second James Stanley became Bishop of Ely, and by virtue of his will (he died 1515) this chapel and the Ely Chapel were built. His tomb remains, of grey marble, with a small brass figure of the bishop in his robes, with the inscription :—"Off yur charite pray for the soul of James Stanley, sutyme Bushype of Ely and Warden of this College of Manchestir, which decessed out of this transitore world the xxxi. daye of March, the yer of our Lord MCCCCC. and XV., on whos soul and all Christian souls Jhesu have mercy."

Westward of this Derby Chapel stands the Ducie Chapel, dedicated to St. James, founded in 1507, and next comes the Radcliffe Chantry, dedicated to the Holy Trinity, founded by W. Radcliffe in 1498. The Radcliffes of Radcliffe, near Manchester, were an ancient race, and the ballad of "Fair Ellen," the daughter of one member of this family, who was slain by a cruel stepmother and her body cooked in a pie, is a gruesome legend of old Lancashire.

[1] Baine's *Lancashire*, Vol. II., p. 365.

The east end of the nave is used for services, and there is a fine modern pulpit. Manchester Cathedral possesses some very fine carved wood-work, of which the ancient rood-screen is a good example. The organ is placed above it. On entering the *Choir* we notice the magnificently-carved stalls with rich tabernacle work, and quaint *misereres*. This is the work of James Stanley (1485-1509) afterwards Bishop of Ely, assisted by a Manchester merchant named Beck. The bishop's throne is modern, and also the reredos. The three Patron Saints—SS. Mary, George and Denys—appear in the niches. In accounting for this triple dedication Randle Holme states that to St. Mary was the earlier church dedicated, and that Thomas Delaware, "being partly a Frenchman, and partly an Englishman," selected St. Dionysee, ye Patron Saint of France, and St. George, the Patron Saint of England, as patrons of his new Cathedral. This does not seem probable, and it is more likely that the claim of Henry V. to the crown of France at the time of the founding of the college suggested the additional dedication.

The windows have all modern glass. Formerly there was some curious ancient glass; in the east window of the south aisle, Michael and his angels fighting with the dragon; in the east window of the north aisle, SS. Augustine and Ambrose chanting the *Te Deum Laudamus;* in the clerestory were pictures of the Virgin; and then there were some curious representations of the Trinity. These have all disappeared. Of the modern ones, the most interesting, perhaps, is the Gordon window in the north aisle.

John Huntingdon, the builder of the present choir (1422-1459), lies buried in it, and formerly his tomb was inscribed with the words: *Domine, dilexi decorem domus tuæ,* and there was a brass with this inscription : *Hic jacet Johan Huntingdon Bacc in Decr. Prim. Magister sive custos istius collegii qui de novo construxit istam cancellam, qui obiit ix. mo die xi. bris MCCCCLVIII., cujus animæ proprietur Deus.* We could not discover this brass, but on each side of the Lady Chapel entrance is the rebus of the founder, on one side a man hunting, or the other a tun, which " hieroglyphical quiddity " makes Hunting-ton.

Crossing the street to the north is a profoundly interesting building, known as the *Chetham Library and Hospital,* of which Manchester may be justly proud. Its chequered history has already been partially told, and carries us back to the days when the college of warden and fellows, chaplain and choir-boys, lived here. Now, as we have seen, it is the school, with a noble library attached, founded by that worthy merchant, Humphrey Chetham. As a baron's hall, an ecclesiastical establishment, and a remarkable school, the building presents many features of unique interest, and the grand library is worthy of minute inspection.

DIMENSIONS

Length of nave and choir . . .	172 ft.
Width of nave and aisles . . .	114 ft.
Length of choir and Lady Chapel .	88 ft.
Height of roof	50 ft.
Height of tower	140 ft.
Area	18,000 sq. ft.

PRINCIPAL BUILDING DATES

(1422-1458)—Choir.

(1465-1509)—Nave rebuilt, stalls and canopies, chapter-house, chantries of St. George, St. Nicholas, Jesus, Ducie and Radcliffe.

(1518-1535)—Lady Chapel, Ely Chapel.

Modern—Baptistry, north and south and west porches, Fraser Chapel, throne, reredos and glass.

CARLISLE CATHEDRAL

THIS northern city has had a noted history. It was a town of considerable importance under the Romans, and on their departure was captured by the furious Picts. It has been a city of sieges. Egfrid of Northumbria rebuilt it in the seventh century, and granted it to St. Cuthbert, but the Danes sacked and plundered it. William Rufus again rebuilt and fortified it, but David, King of Scotland, captured the place, and died within its walls in 1153. Two more sieges it again endured, and was at length taken in 1217. Here came Edward I. frequently on his marches to conquer the Scots, and held Parliaments here, and near here he died. A goodly company of nobles hastened here to do homage to his son. After the disaster of Bannockburn Robert Bruce besieged Carlisle, and had his quarters in the Cathedral, which is outside the city walls, but he failed to gain the city. The Bishops of Carlisle were sometimes warlike men, and took the field against the dread invaders from the north. The old castle has seen much of fighting, and it had a notable prisoner in the person of ill-fated Mary Queen of Scots. A long siege, lasting eight months, took place in the Civil War time, and in that time terrible damage was done to the Cathedral, as we shall see. Again, in the rebellion of 1745, "Bonnie Prince Charlie" captured the place, and there was a great flourish of trumpets, or rather bagpipes, until the king's forces came and put an end to the poor campaign. The Cathedral was again used as military quarters, and the prisons of the castle tell the sad story of the fate of the rebels.

The ecclesiastical history of Carlisle reflects its civil history. As we have said, St. Cuthbert of Lindisfarne and his successors ruled over this city and district for many years. When William II. restored the city and raised the castle, one Walter, a noble and wealthy priest, who was left as governor by the king, set to work to build a church and priory. But death stayed his hand, and Henry I. completed the task, and established here a monastery of Augustinian canons in 1121. In 1133, on the advice of Thurstan, Archbishop of York, he established a see here, and Udelulf became the first bishop. The Cathedral, begun by Walter and finished by Henry I., was of the usual Norman character. Its plan was cruciform, and it had a nave with aisles, transepts with a low tower at the crossing. The architect was Hugh, Bishop (1218-1223), formerly Abbot of Beaulieu, Hants, who brought with him to Carlisle the traditions of a splendid style of architecture. In the early part of the thirteenth century the Norman choir was taken down, and rebuilt in the Early English style. Two fires did much damage, especially the one that raged in 1292. The work of rebuilding was at once commenced, and a more imposing plan was projected, but a long time elapsed before it was completely carried out. At length, about the middle of the fourteenth century, the choir was completed in the Decorated style, a new triforium, clerestory·roof and east end being erected. The Late Decorated east window, which was finished at this time, is one of the most beautiful in the world. Fire again injured the Cathedral in 1392, especially the north transept, which was restored by Bishop Strickland (1400-1419), who also rebuilt the tower above the roof, and crowned it with a wooden spire. The monastery was dissolved at the Reformation, and a Cathedral establishment formed, consisting of a dean and canons. In Mary's reign Owen Oglethorpe was made bishop, who, "being a good-natured man and pliable," according to Fuller, crowned Queen Elizabeth, "which the rest of his order refused to do." He was, however, deprived on account of "certain principles of stubbornness instilled into him." The Civil War did terrible damage to the Cathedral. During the siege Puritan soldiers were quartered in the sacred building, "who did after their kind," and, moreover, after the capture of the city, in order to repair the fortifications, they pulled down a great portion of the nave, and used the stones for that purpose. In the rising of 1745 Charles Edward, the Pretender, as we have said, occupied Carlisle, and installed in the Cathedral, as bishop of the see, a Romanist named James Cappoch. When the Duke of Cumberland arrived and recaptured the city, Cappoch allowed himself to be taken prisoner, and was hanged. The church was again used as a barracks, and many of the poor Jacobite prisoners were confined here.

Since then there have been sundry restorations, some very deplorable, one about the middle of the eighteenth century, which were happily effaced, as far as possible, by the work of the middle of the nineteenth. But the hand of the restorers has fallen rather heavily upon the beautiful work of the choir, and destroyed much of its

s

delicate beauty. The architects of 1850 had not yet learned to respect the antiquity of the buildings which fell into their hands to restore, and Carlisle and many other churches have suffered much from their drastic treatment.

THE EXTERIOR

A good view is obtained from the castle. The usual approach is from the east end, whence we observed the grand east window with its beautiful Late Decorated tracery. It is flanked by buttresses, with niches and crocketed pinnacles. In the niches are statues of SS. Peter, Paul, James and John. A floriated cross crowns the gable, and on each side are four similar crosses. In the gable is a triangular window, having three trefoils, and below is a niche with figure of the Virgin. The *Central Tower*, built by Bishop Strickland (1400-1419) on the old Norman piers, is too small for the huge choir, and lacks dignity. Formerly it was crowned with a wooden spire, but this has been removed. There is a turret set at the north-east angle, and in the north side is a niche with the figure of an angel. The lower part of the *Choir* is Early English, with the exception of a Perpendicular window at the west, and a Decorated one in the east bay. The *Clerestory* is Late Decorated, and the windows have flowing tracery. The ballflower ornament is extensively used in the cornice. The sculpture at Carlisle is worthy of notice. Carved heads and curious gargoyles abound. The *North Transept* is nearly all modern. It was rebuilt by Strickland in the fifteenth century, and again rebuilt when the church was restored. There is, however, an Early English window in the west wall. On the east side there was formerly a chapel, which has not survived the repeated alterations. The greater part of the *Nave* was taken down by Cromwell's soldiers. What is left is of unmistakable Norman character. There is some modern imitation work, and late architectural detail. Most of the windows are modern, and also the doorway. The west end is the result of modern restoration. The south side is similar to the north. The *South Transept* preserves the old Norman walls. On the south is a modern doorway with a window over it. On the east is *St. Catherine's Chapel*, a Late Early English or Early Decorated building. The south side of the choir is similar to the north, and presents Early English details of construction. The monastic buildings once stood on the south side of the church, but they have

Carlisle
from S E

been pulled down with the exception of the fratry and gatehouse, the stone being used for repairing the fortifications of the city by Puritan soldiery. The refectory, or fratry, was rebuilt in the fifteenth century, and is now used as a chapter-house. There is a fine reader's pulpit here. The gateway was erected by Prior Slee in 1527. The Deanery is a fine old house, and was formerly the prior's lodging. It was rebuilt in 1507.

THE INTERIOR

The *Nave* was formerly used as the Parish Church of St. Mary, and was filled with high pews and galleries. These have all been cleared away, and it is possible to admire the plain and massive Norman building, which now, alas! consists of only two bays, the rest having been destroyed in the Civil War period. Before that act of vandalism there were eight bays. The work before us, for the most part, belongs to the earliest church, begun by Walter, finished by Henry I. about 1130. Formerly a low ceiling shut out the triforium and clerestory from our view, but this, too, has happily been removed. The piers are low (14 feet high, 17 feet in girth), the arches being semi-circular, some of the capitals having evidently been carved later with some Early English foliage. The triforium consists of plain, open, round-headed arches, and is a little later than the main arcade. The clerestory has in each bay three arches, resting on shafts with carved capitals. The west end is modern. The tattered colours of the Cumberland Regiment tell of the Indian Mutiny, and there is a window in the south aisle to the memory of the men who died in that melancholy time. Sir Walter Scott was married in this nave, when it was a church, in 1797, to Miss Margaret Charlotte Carpenter. The font is modern and also the organ.

The *North Transept* was rebuilt by Bishop Strickland in the fifteenth century, and its north end was again rebuilt in modern times. Here a large modern window of Decorated design has been erected in memory of five children of Archbishop Tait, who died here of scarlet fever when Dr. Tait was dean. In the west wall is an Early English window, which is a good example of plate-tracery. The arch of the choir aisle is Decorated; the roof is modern. Crossing over to the south transept we notice the piers which support the *Tower*. These are Norman, and have additional columns erected by Bishop Strickland when he rebuilt the tower. The latter have foliated capitals, and are in the Perpendicular style. On the capitals of the eastern arch are the badges of the Percy family—the crescent and fetterlock. The most famous scion of this house—Hotspur—was governor of Carlisle. On the western side are the rose and escallop shell, badges of the Dacres and Nevilles.

The *South Transept* is both narrow and shallow, being only one bay in length. The east side is Norman work; there is an arch with zigzag ornament and cushion capitals, opening into the choir aisle. A second Norman arch opens to St. Catherine's Chapel. The window and door on the south are both modern, and have much elaborate decoration, which is scarcely in keeping with the Norman work surrounding it. The triforium and clerestory resemble those of the nave. *St. Catherine's Chapel* stands on the site of a Norman chapel, and is in the Early Decorated style or Late Early English. It was founded by John de Capella, a wealthy citizen, and is now used as a vestry. The screen is Late Decorated, and is of great beauty. The doorway between the aisle and chapel formerly led to a well, now closed. "A similar well exists in the north transept, but has been long covered. Besides supplying water for the use of the church, such wells may have been of special service in border churches, which, like this of Carlisle, served as places of refuge for the inhabitants in cases of sudden alarm or foray" (Murray's Handbooks). The following monuments are in the transepts :—

Robert Anderson, "the Cumberland Bard" (1833); Bishop Fleming (1747): Prior Senhouse (*temp*. Henry VII.); and there is a curious Runic inscription, written in Norse, which, being translated, is: "Tolfihn wrote these runes on this stone."

We now enter the *Choir* by the door in organ-screen. This is one of the finest in England—spacious, lofty, well-proportioned and rich in all its details. The arches of the main arcade are Early English, as the mouldings and dog-tooth ornament testify. These remained after the fire of 1292, and were retained. The piers are Early Decorated, and were evidently built to support the arches after the fire. The capitals were carved later in the Late Decorated period, when the upper parts of the choir, triforium, clerestory, roof and east end were rebuilt. The builders were probably Bishops Welton and Appleby (1353-1395). When the choir was rebuilt in Early English times, the architect determined to enlarge it, and as the monastic buildings on the south prevented any expansion in that direction, the south piers of the choir retained their old position, while the north were moved further northward, and a new north aisle added. Thus the choir and the tower and nave are not quite symmetrical, and there is a blank wall at the north-west end of the choir which is thus accounted for. The details of the architecture of the choir merit close attention, especially the sculpture. Small figures of men, animals and monsters are mingled with the foliage. There are some admirable representations of the seasons, beginning with the second capital on the south, counting from the east end. There is a very fine timber roof, constructed about the middle of the fourteenth century. The scheme of colour decoration is, unfortunately, not original. The *East Window* is one of the finest Decorated windows in the kingdom. The stone-work is new, but it is believed to be an exact reproduction of the original. It has nine lights. The glass of the upper portion is ancient, dating from the reign of Richard II. It represents the Resurrection, Final Judgment and the New Jerusalem. Hell is depicted with the usual mediæval realism. Below is modern glass, representing scenes from the life of our Lord. The *Stalls* are Late Perpendicular, erected by Bishop Strickland, and are excellently carved. The tabernacle work is generally attributed to Prior Haithwaite (*circa* 1433). There are some quaint and curious *misereres*, the carvings representing grotesque monsters, such as dragons and griffins, fables such as the Fox and the Goose, and a great variety of subjects. A Renaissance screen, erected by Salkeld, the last prior, divides the west bay of the presbytery from the north choir aisle. The altar, throne, lectern and pulpit are modern. There is a fine brass to the memory of Bishop Bell (1495) on the floor of the choir.

Passing to the *North Choir Aisle* we notice the Early English character of the arcade and windows. The latter have two lights, and have deep mouldings and dog-tooth ornament. The wall arcade is particularly graceful. The last bay eastward was built when the east window was erected, and is Late Decorated, and in the last bay westward there is a Perpendicular window. The vault was constructed after the fire of 1292. The two sepulchral recesses in the north wall are remarkable. They are of Early English character, and have a chevron moulding which is said to be unique. It is conjectured that the effigy in one of these recesses is that of Silvester of Everdon (1254), and that the other was intended for Bishop Hugh of Beaulieu, who died in Burgundy. In another bay is an aumbrey wherein treasures of plate and other valuables were stored.   There is a late brass to the memory of Bishop Robinson (1416), formerly Provost of Queen's College, Oxford. Archdeacon Paley (1791), the learned divine whose *Evidences of Christianity* is still a divinity text-book at Cambridge, lies buried here.   The curious painting on the back of the stalls, of late fifteenth-century execution, always interest visitors to the Cathedral. They illustrate the lives of St. Anthony and St. Cuthbert, with descriptive verses under each scene, and there is a set of figures of the Apostles with the words of the Apostles' creed traditionally assigned to each.   The *Retro-Choir* is very narrow and is of the same date as the window.   Bishop Law's monument is here (1787), carved by T. Banks, R.A.   The *South Choir Aisle* resembles that on the north.   The two western windows are later than the Early English ones in the opposite aisle.   There are monuments here of Bishop Waldegrave (1869), Bishop Barrow (1429) (or Welton, 1362), Bishop Goodwin (1891), Dean Close (1882).

The screen here is like that opposite by Prior Gondibour, who did so much to decorate his Cathedral, and to whom the paintings are assigned.   The back of the stalls on this side has a representation of scenes from the life of St. Augustine, or, as curious descriptive verses call him, the " gret doctor Austyne."

DIMENSIONS

Length of nave	39 ft.
Breadth of nave	60 ft.
Height of nave	65 ft.
Length of choir	134 ft.
Breadth of choir	72 ft.
Height of choir	72 ft.
Height of tower	112 ft.
Area	15,270 sq. ft.

PRINCIPAL BUILDING DATES

Norman (1092-1130)—South transept, piers of central tower, part of nave.

Early English (1219-1260)—Walls and windows of choir
aisles, part of main arcade of choir, St. Catherine's Chapel.
Early Decorated (1292)—Part of main arcade of choir.
Late Decorated (1353-1395)—Upper part of choir, east end
and roof.
Perpendicular (1400-1419)—Upper part of tower.

NEWCASTLE CATHEDRAL

THE See of Newcastle was created in 1882, as the result of the spiritual expansion of the Church of England which caused the formation of so many new sees. In the days when England and Scotland were separate kingdoms, and when wars between the two countries were not infrequent, Newcastle occupied a position of great strategic importance. Here was a strong castle—the "new castle"—founded by Henry II. on the site of an older structure built in 1080 by the son of the Conqueror. It was the mightiest castle in the north of England, and its keep is one of the finest specimens of Norman military architecture remaining in the country. In this fortress Baliol was brought to do homage for the crown of Scotland to Edward I. The keep is still standing, and also the chapel, a fine specimen of Late Norman architecture. Many Roman remains have been found here.

The Cathedral was formerly the old Parish Church of St. Nicholas. The style is principally Late Decorated. An older church was burned down in 1216. It consists of nave, aisles, chancel and transept. The total length is 245 feet, and the width 128 feet. The transept is Perpendicular in style, and so is the fine tower with spire built in 1474, which is the principal feature of the church. Frequent restorations have taken place and a very extensive renovation was effected in 1876 at a cost of £30,000. Admiral Collingwood, the comrade of Nelson, is buried here.

The Norman Church of St. Andrew and the Church of St. John of the fourteenth century, with an ancient font, are the principal old churches in the town, and also the chapel of 1491 attached to Trinity House. The old Saxon churches of Jarrow and Monk Wearmouth are in the neighbourhood.

DURHAM CATHEDRAL

DURHAM Cathedral is one of the grandest buildings in the world. Standing upon the summit of a lofty hill, which rises abruptly from the River Wear, its position is one of surpassing beauty, and the dignity of the building, its massive walls and towers, and the interesting associations which cluster round the venerable pile, make it one of the most superb edifices in this or any other country.

The story of Durham carries us back to the very early days of Christianity. In spite of the efforts of Paulinus the Saxons of Northumbria were still heathen until Oswald became king in 634, who was converted to Christianity by the monks of Iona, where a monastery had been founded by Columba, an Irish saint. Desiring to benefit his people, Oswald sent to Iona, and under St. Aidan a colony of monks was founded at Lindisfarne, or Holy Island. St. Cuthbert, the Patron Saint of Durham, succeeded, who died in 687. After the lapse of nearly two centuries the coast was harassed by the attacks of the Danes, and the monks fled from Lindisfarne, bearing with them their most precious relics and with these the body of St. Cuthbert. They wandered far and wide with their holy burden; a hundred years elapsed; generations of monks passed away; but the bones of the saint knew no rest. For a long time they tarried at Chester-le-Street, which became the seat of the Northumbrian bishopric; but still the savage Northmen threatened them with danger, and at last in 995 the wearied monks found a shelter on the lofty and impregnable rock where the Cathedral now stands, the abiding resting-place of St. Cuthbert's bones. On the outside of the church there is the figure of the Dun Cow, which is associated with their wanderings. It was revealed to one of the monks that Dunholme was to be their final home; but not knowing where this place was, they were in much distress. However, they heard a woman inquiring about her lost cow, to whom her companion replied that it was at Dunholme. " That was a happy and heavenly sound to the distressed monks," says the chronicler, " and thereupon with great joy they arrived with the saint's body at Dunholme in the year 997." Here they raised a church of boughs to cover their precious treasure and then a stone building, and then Bishop Aldwin "raised no small building of stone-work for his Cathedral church, when all the people between the Coquet and Tees three years were at work, and were paid for their pains with treasure in heaven, than which there was never a dearer or cheaper way to build churches." Around this holy house the city began to grow, which owes its importance and very existence to the monastery.

Troublous times followed the advent of the Conqueror. Exasperated by the tyranny of the favourites of Walcher, the first Norman prelate, the people set fire to the church and slew the bishop. Then followed William de St. Carileph, who founded the present church. He expelled the secular clergy, and introduced the Benedictine rule. For the part he took in the rebellion against William Rufus he was exiled for three years, and lived in Normandy. Animated by the sight of the beautiful churches which there abounded he resolved to erect a more glorious edifice on the rugged hill of Durham, and on his return commenced the work. The foundation stone was laid in 1093. He began to build the east end of the choir, and continued the walls as far as the first arch of the nave. After his death in 1096, the prior and convent continued the building until the advent of Bishop Flambard (1099-1128), who carried on the work and nearly finished the nave, aisles, western towers and doorway. The chapter-house was erected by the next bishop, Galfrid Rufus (1133-1140). Bishop Hugh Pudsey (1153-1195) built the Galilee Chapel. In 1229 Bishop Poore, the builder of Salisbury, was translated to Durham; he discovered the unsafe condition of the eastern apsidal walls of his church, and determined to erect the beautiful Chapel of the Nine Altars, which is such a charming specimen of Early English architecture. He did not live to carry out his design, which was continued after his death under the rule of Prior Melsanby. The priors of Durham rivalled the bishops in their zeal for perfecting their noble Cathedral. Prior Darlington erected a belfry, and Prior Fossor part of the monastic buildings and the west windows of the nave in 1342. Bishop Skirlaw (1388-1405) was the chief builder of the present cloisters. In 1429 the tower was struck by lightning, and was rebuilt under the direction of Prior Bell.

The church was now complete, but like most of our cathedrals it has suffered from the evils of "restoration," and Wyatt, the

Durham Cathedral

destructive architect of the eighteenth century, was allowed to do much damage. We shall notice his handiwork as we examine the details of the building. There seem to have been great disputes between the bishop and the monks, and the peace of this solemn sanctuary was often disturbed by angry quarrels and open violence. Sometimes the Scots made incursions, and on one occasion William Cumin seized the castle and committed great ravages. In the time of Bishop Hatfield was fought the great battle of Neville's Cross, when, by the aid of St. Cuthbert and his banner, the English won the day, and a hymn of thanksgiving is still sung every year on the top of the tower. The choir used to sing on all the four sides, but on one occasion a choir-boy fell, and ever since they only chant the hymn from three sides.

The Bishops of Durham were great men, holding the rank of temporal princes or Counts Palatine. Their courts were independent of the king, and they could coin money and live as they listed. Moreover, many of them were mighty warriors. Bishop Anthony Bek took part in the Scottish wars, and had a vast army of knights and men-at-arms. It was not until the year 1836 that the dignity of Count Palatine was removed from the holders of the Durham See. Cardinal Wolsey was bishop here for six years, but never set foot in his diocese. The monastery was suppressed by Henry VIII., and a dean and chapter appointed. Many learned and good men have held the See of Durham, and the names of the last two bishops—Lightfoot and Westcott—will always be held in esteem.

The Exterior

As we approach the church from the Palace Green we notice the grand Norman building, which is much the same as when Bishop Carileph left it. At the east end there is the Early English Nine Altar Chapel, at the west the Galilee; the upper portions of the towers, the north porch and a few windows are the only additions, and the whole appearance of the church is at once bold, stern and commanding.

The *Central Tower*, the work of Prior Bell, was built in 1471. The Bell Ringer's Gallery divides it into two portions, with two windows in each, the lower ones being glazed and the upper louvred. The panelled work, the ogee-shaped labels and the surmounting parapet proclaim their Perpendicular style.

Two *Octagonal Towers* of Norman character rise at the

north corners of the north transept. The *Western Towers* are Norman as far as the level of the nave roof, the upper portion being added in the thirteenth century, and the pinnacles and parapets at the end of the eighteenth. We have already alluded to the construction of the east end, which replaced the apsidal termination of the original building. The famous rose window is in the gable of the east end, and beneath are nine lofty lancet windows. Notice the sculpture of the Dun Cow in the north angle of the Nine Altars, placed there in 1775.

The *Porch* was built by Wyatt, and we can endorse the decision of Canon Greenwell, Durham's great historian, that "in its present condition it is a most unworthy and discreditable portal for so magnificent a temple as that into which it ushers the worshipper." The woodwork is ancient, and here we see the famous sanctuary knocker, which criminals used when they wished to gain an entrance and secure the rights of sanctuary from mob violence or secular law. Two porters were employed in watching for fugitives, and directly the refugee knocked he was admitted, clad in a black cloth gown, with a yellow cross on his left shoulder, conducted to a chamber near the south door of the Galilee Chapel, and given shelter for thirty-seven days.

At the west end there is the *Galilee Chapel*, of Late Norman work, which covers the west door, over the main entrance. This door, walled up by Cardinal Langley in the fifteenth century, and re-opened in 1845, was made by Flambard (1099-1128). It has thirteen detached cartouches, each having an animal or flower within it, and is adorned with chevron ornament. The window was inserted by Prior Fossor (1342-1374), and contained coloured glass, represented "the Stem of Jesse," which was destroyed at the Reformation. In 1867 Dean Waddington restored the glass, reproducing the old design. The arch-destroyer, Wyatt, actually proposed to remove the Galilee Chapel, and make a carriage drive to the west door; but happily his nefarious design was frustrated.

There are two south doorways; the one opposite the north door, known as the Monks' Door, was erected by Bishop Pudsey, and has fine carvings of floral and other designs upon the arches and columns. The mouldings and sculptures are most profuse, the zigzag and double chevron and diaper being extensively employed. The leaf pattern is observed on the arch, and the iron-work of the door is a fine specimen of Norman workmanship. The other doorway, known as the Prior's Door, is of the same date, but the carving is much decayed.

We will now examine the *Cloisters*, enclosed on the north by the walls of the Cathedral, on the south by the refectory, on the east by the chapter-house, deanery and south transept, and on the west by the dormitory, now, together with the refectory, used as the library, and beneath it the so-called crypt, which was the common hall of the monks. The present buildings were erected by Bishop Skirlaw in the early years of the fifteenth century, the refectory being restored at the Restoration. A stone laver or conduit stood in the centre of the cloister erected in 1432, the basin only remaining.

The *Chapter-House* was a victim to Wyatt's misdoings, and the greater part was pulled down by him. It has, however, been recently restored in memory of Bishop Lightfoot, and is a noble chamber, having an apsidal termination at the east end, an arcade of interlacing arches running round the wall, and round-headed windows.

The library and museum contains many objects of great interest, including a number of Roman altars and tablets, Saxon crosses and carved stones, remarkable for their beautiful scroll-work. There is the famous Ruthwell cross, memorial crosses of the four last Saxon bishops, Hadrian stone from the Roman wall, the monastic dining-table, a remarkable treasure-chest, with five different locks and keys, and—most interesting of all—the remains of St. Cuthbert's coffin, his robes, and other relics taken from his tomb. Amongst these we notice his stole and maniple and pectoral cross. In another case we see three rings of the first Norman bishops, and the crozier of Bishop Flambard. Durham has many interesting MSS., amongst others the Book of the Landisfarne Gospels, brought away by the monks when they fled from Holy Island, which fell into the waves and still retains the stains of sea water; a MS. of the seventh century, which once belonged to the Venerable Bede, and the Bede Roll (1456 and 1468), containing a list of all the religious houses in England and abroad which were asked for prayers for the souls of Priors Ebchester and Burnaby. The roof is remarkably fine.

THE INTERIOR

As we stand at the west door we get a magnificent view of this noble edifice, with its grand Norman cylindrical pillars, 23 feet in circumference, some adorned with zigzag furrows, others lozenge-shaped, with narrow ribs, or spiral, and arches round and carved, with rolls and chevron moulding. The capitals are

T

cushioned, and cut octagonally.   Above is the triforium, composed of large arches, enclosing two smaller ones, with cushioned capitals ; and higher still the clerestory, composed of single round-headed windows, surmounted by the vaulting ribs, adorned with chevrons. This nave and aisles were built by Bishop Flambard (1099-1128).

The roof of stone vaulting was finished in 1133, and Durham is said to be the only Cathedral in England which retains the original stone Norman vaulting over the nave.

The *Sanctuary Chamber*, wherein the hunted fugitives from justice found a shelter, formerly stood near the south door of the Galilee Chapel, but all traces have been removed.   The font is modern, the subjects carved on it representing scenes from the life of St. Cuthbert.   The canopy was erected by Bishop Cosin in 1663.

The internal north doorway should be examined, especially the beautiful foliage-work. In the lozenges and mouldings there are some strange creatures represented— a centaur shooting with bow and arrow, a boy being whipped, a man riding a lion, and other curious subjects.

Before proceeding eastward we will see the Galilee Chapel, which was the Lady Chapel, a beautiful specimen of Late Norman work, erected by Bishop Pudsey in 1175. Lady chapels usually stand at the east end, but no women were allowed to enter churches dedicated to St. Cuthbert, who has been accused of misogyny. We

notice in the nave a boundary stone, beyond which no female foot might go in the direction of the high altar. We mark a change in the style of architecture from that used in the nave. The arches and columns are lighter, with graceful capitals, on which the volute appears. The style is approaching that of the graceful period of Early English. Cardinal Langley (1406-1437) made extensive alterations in this chapel, heightening the walls, erecting a new roof, inserting Perpendicular windows, closing the west door of the church, and making two other entrances. All visitors will approach with reverence and interest the tomb of the Venerable Bede, the great Anglo-Saxon scholar, and the father of English history. His bones were once covered with a splendid shrine, which the iniquitous commissioners of Henry VIII. destroyed. Now a plain marble slab, with the inscription:

"Hac sunt in fossa Bædæ Venerabilis ossa,"

alone marks the grave of this illustrious man. The altar of the Virgin stood in the great western doorway, which was then walled up, of which the stone slab carved with the five crosses, the aumbrey and some colouring alone remain. The builder of this chapel, Cardinal Langley, lies buried here, and his monument remains. Some much-damaged mural paintings mark the site of the Altar of Our Lady of Pity. The paintings are supposed to represent St. Oswald and St. Cuthbert. There is some uncertainty about the origin of the name "Galilee." Most probably it arose from the custom of the monks to go in procession at certain times around the church, and to halt at certain stations in memory of our Lord's appearance after His Resurrection. His last appearance was on a mountain in Galilee; it is therefore not improbable that the place where the procession made its final halt should receive that name. Here in ancient times the consistory court held its sittings, and here the commissioners of Henry VIII. met and destroyed, or appropriated, the rich store of treasures, the vestments, plate and ornaments which had been given to the Cathedral by countless generations of pious benefactors. Again entering the nave in the south aisle, we see the Neville monuments, which have been much mutilated by the Scottish prisoners, or during the Reformation period. Between the fifth and sixth pillars is an altar tomb to the memory of Lord John Neville and his wife Matilda (1386), daughter of Hotspur. The matrix of the brass of Bishop Robert Neville (1438-1457) is in front of this. In the next bay is the altar tomb of Lord Ralph Neville and his wife, Lady Alice (1374), who founded the Neville Chapel. Holes in the pillar show where the iron grating stood which divided the chapel from the rest of the church, and in this enclosure there was "an altar with a fair alabaster table above it, where Mass was daily celebrated." Traces of the colouring which once adorned this beautiful chapel can still be seen.

Leaving the nave, we enter the *Transepts*, which were part of Carileph's work. The large window in the north transept was inserted by Prior Fossor (1341-1374), and is in the Decorated style. Prior Castell in 1512 restored the window, and filled it with coloured glass representing the four doctors—SS. Augustine, Ambrose, Gregory and Jerome. Hence it is known as the Window of the Four Doctors. In the south transept is the large Perpendicular *Te Deum* window, erected about 1450. Some of the glass is ancient, but the greater part was inserted in 1869 in memory of Archdeacon Thorp. Altars stood formerly in the aisles at the north and south extremities of the transepts. Traces of colour may still be seen, and the remains of some brackets which contained sculptured figures. Chantrey's fine monument of Bishop Barrington (1791-1826) stands in the south transept.

The whole of the lantern *Tower* is of the Perpendicular style, and was probably built by Prior Bell (1464-1478). A gallery surrounds the lower stage, supported by grotesque heads. The Tudor flower ornament may be observed on the string-course over the panelling. The screen is modern, and was designed by Sir Gilbert Scott. Passing into the choir, the earliest part of the building, we see the Norman work of Carileph blended with the later Early English style. As we have already noticed, the east end of the Norman church terminated with apses. These were subsequently removed. The whole choir comprehends four pillars on each side, two of them clustered and two round, the latter of which are cut in a spiral form. The roof was new vaulted by Prior Horton, who succeeded in 1289, the ribs of the vaulting being decorated with the dog-tooth mouldings. The work around the altar is all Early English. Clustered pillars divide the nine altars from the choir, decorated with foliage.

In the year 1650 a large number of Scottish prisoners were confined in the Cathedral, who did much damage to the internal fittings. In order to gain fresh air, or for love of mischief, they broke most of the windows, and the holes in the floor in the south transept show where they made their fires for cooking their meals.

Another mark of their presence was the destruction of the wood-work of the choir, which they doubtless used for firewood. At the Restoration Bishop Cosin erected the present stalls. The *misereres* are worthy of remark—lions, mermaids, monsters, apes, peacocks and dolphins being the most striking subjects. The modern lectern and pulpit are both very beautiful, the former being designed after the ancient lectern described in the *Rites of Durham*.

The altar-screen is very graceful and beautiful, and was originally erected by Lord Neville of Raby in 1380, and much restored in 1876. It was originally painted, and the 107 niches were filled with images. The matrix of an immense brass to the memory of Bishop Beaumont (1318-1333) is seen near the altar steps. It must have been one of the largest brasses in England, and resembles the immense one at Lynn, Norfolk. The choir is paved with mosaics similar to those of the Confessor's Chapel at Westminster.

The magnificent tomb of Bishop Hatfield (d. 1381) is on the south side of the choir. He is habited in his episcopal dress. The outer garment is the chasuble, and beneath it the linen alb or surplice. His hands are covered with episcopal gloves, embroidered on the

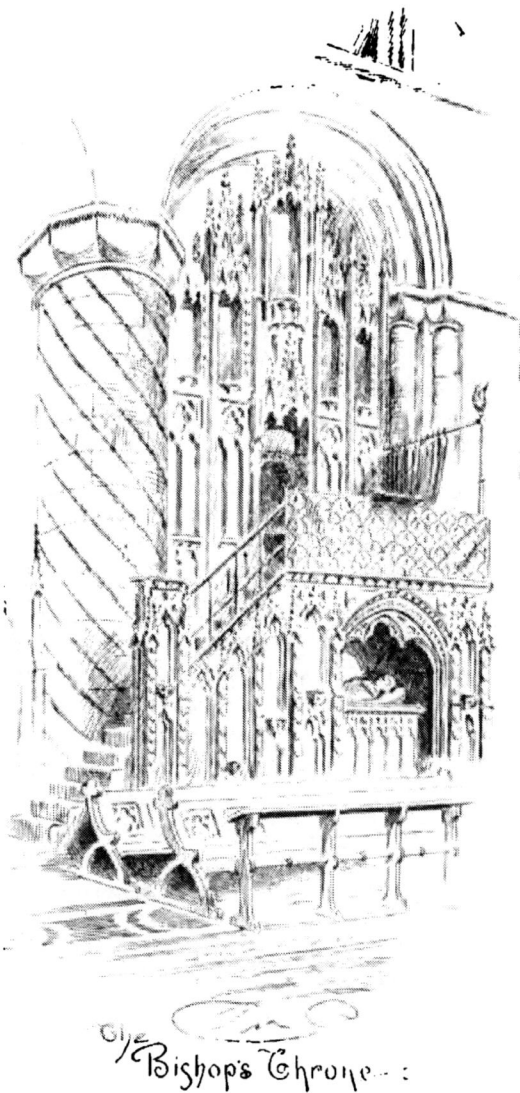

The Bishop's Throne

back ; on his left arm is the maniple. The tomb was originally gilded and coloured. Above is the throne erected by him, the highest in England. The monument of Bishop Lightfoot stands opposite.

The *North and South Aisles of the Choir* are similar in their architectural features to the choir itself, showing the blending of the stately Norman with the graceful Early English work. The monks used frequently to resort to the north aisle, where was a porch having an altar, with a rood and pictures of St. Mary and St. John, where they sang Mass daily. Certain holes in the stone mark the place of the porch, sometimes called the anchorage. Bishop Skirlaw's tomb stood between the third and fourth piers, before the old altar of St. Blaze. His monument has disappeared, but the stone bench remains, erected by him for his almsmen to sit upon. In the *South Aisle* the doorway of the great vestry remains, though the building was destroyed in 1802. The grave cover of the Prior of Lytham, a cell belonging to Durham, is preserved here. Here also stood the famous Black Rood of Scotland, captured from King David Bruce of Scotland at Neville's Cross (1346).

And now we will enter the *Chapel of the Nine Altars*, at the extreme east of the building. It was commenced in 1242, and the architect was Richard de Farnham, probably a relation of Nicholas de Farnham, then bishop. Prior Melsanby (1233-1244) presided over the erection of the building, and the name of the master-mason is preserved on an inscription : *Thomas Moises*. We notice the nine-lancet windows (under each of which stood an altar separated from its neighbour by screens and partitions of wainscot) ; the large rose window, "restored" by Wyatt ; the beautiful arcade, with its trefoiled arches and deeply-cut mouldings, raised on slender shafts of marble, and surmounted by capitals. The altars were dedicated (beginning on the south side) to St. Andrew and St. Mary Magdalene ; St. John the Baptist and St. Margaret ; St. Thomas à Becket and St. Catherine ; St. Oswald and St. Lawrence ; St. Cuthbert and St. Bede ; St. Martin and St. Edmund ; St. Peter and St. Paul ; St. Aidan and St. Helen ; St. Michael, the Archangel.

Forty years were consumed in building this chapel, and the style developed as the work progressed. The north end was finished last, as we see from the noble double-traceried window, one of the finest in existence. The south windows are Perpendicular. Among the monuments are those of Bishop Bury, tutor of Edward III. (1345), and Bishop Bek (1310), and Bishop Van Mildert (1836), the last of the prince bishops.

Behind the high altar is all that remains of the famous shrine of St. Cuthbert, once the glory of Durham, where countless pilgrims came to pay their devotions and offerings, and seek the protection of the saint. The cavities in the floor are said to have been worn by their feet. The grave of the saint was opened in 1827, and the vestments and other relics taken from it are kept in the library, and have already been described.

On the south of the church is *the College*, containing the Deanery and prebendal houses. The gate is an interesting structure, built by Prior Castell in 1515.

THE CASTLE

William the Conqueror in 1072, when Walcher was bishop, on his return from Scotland, ordered the castle to be built, which was continued by Carileph and Flambard. Bishop Pudsey erected a new wall and a hall which bears his name, and Bishop Bek built the hall on the west of the courtyard. Bishop Hatfield rebuilt the keep. Tunstall's Gallery (1530-1558) connects the great hall and clock tower, and his chapel is remarkable for its beautifully-carved stalls. At the Restoration the castle was in a ruinous condition. It had been sold to the Lord Mayor of London. The Scots had plundered it; and Bishop Cosin set to work to rebuild and repair the home of his predecessors. In 1840 the keep was rebuilt, and the castle is now the seat of the University of Durham.

The most interesting *Churches* in the city are St. Mary le Bow (rebuilt 1685); St. Mary the Less (Norman, but much " restored "); St. Oswald (1190, with many subsequent rebuildings); St. Margaret (1154); St. Giles (1112).

About four miles from Durham are the beautiful ruins of Finchale Priory, which was commenced in 1240 and finished about a century later. The Priory was suppressed at the Reformation.

DIMENSIONS OF THE CATHEDRAL

Total length, 470 ft.; length of nave, 201 ft.; width of nave with aisles, 60 ft.; height of nave, 72 ft.; length of choir, 133 ft.; length of Nine Altars Chapel, 131 ft.; height of west towers, 144 ft.; height of central tower, 218 ft.; area, 44,400 sq. ft.

PRINCIPAL BUILDING DATES

Norman (1093-1140)—nave, choir, aisles, west towers, doorways, chapter-house; (1153-1195)—Galilee Chapel. Early English (1238-1275)—Nine Altars Chapel, choir vault. Decorated (1342-1346)—window in north transept and west windows of nave. Perpendicular (1386-1500)—cloisters, dormitory, central tower; (1661-1684)—library.

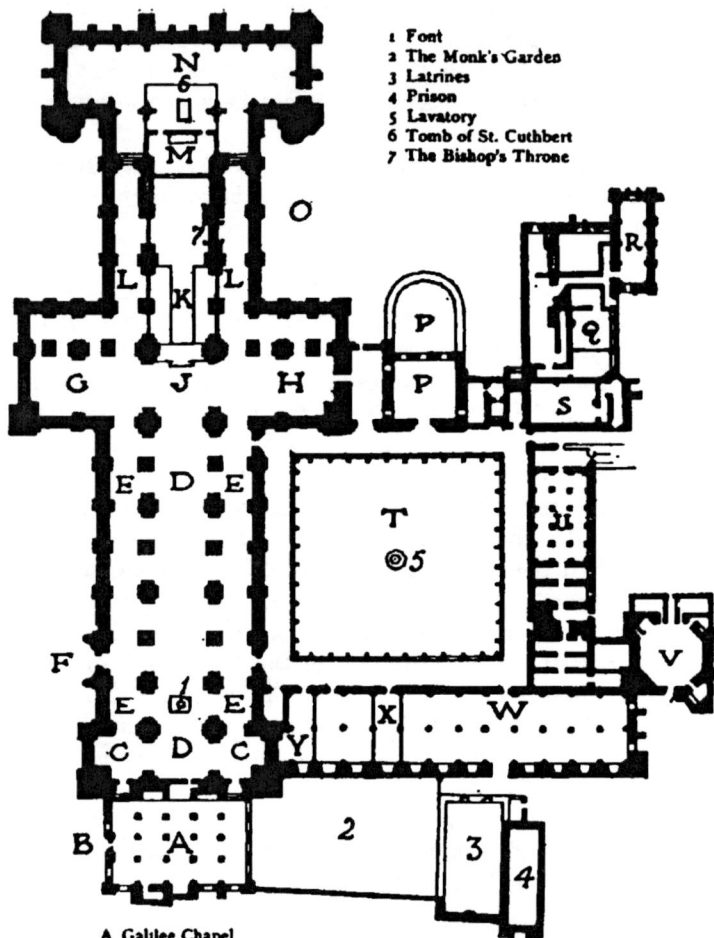

1 Font
2 The Monk's Garden
3 Latrines
4 Prison
5 Lavatory
6 Tomb of St. Cuthbert
7 The Bishop's Throne

A Galilee Chapel
B Entrance to same
C C Western Towers
D Nave
E E North and South Aisles
F North Door (Principal Entrance)
G H North and South Transept
J Tower
K Choir
L L North and South Choir Aisles
M Altar
N Chapel of the Nine Altars

O Site of Old Vestry
P Chapter-House
Q Priory
R Crypt under Prior's Chapel
S Crypt
T Cloister Garth
U Crypt of Refectory
V Kitchen
W Crypt under New Dormitory
X Vestry
Y Treasury

PLAN OF DURHAM CATHEDRAL

RIPON CATHEDRAL

THE historical associations of Ripon carry us back to very early times. Alcfrid, Prince of Deira, was lord of the soil in the seventh century, and in 660 bestowed on Eata, Abbot of Melrose, a portion of the ground at Ripon whereon to erect a monastic foundation. After the expulsion of the Scottish monks the same prince gave the monastery to St. Wilfrid, who, after he became archbishop, erected a church. This was of the basilican type, with which St. Wilfrid had made himself familiar during his sojourn in Italy. With the earlier monastery was associated the holy Cuthbert, who was the Hostillar. Wilfrid was ordained at Ripon, and here he resided when his episcopal seat was usurped by Ceadda (or Chad). The site of the old monastery was on the north-east side of the present Cathedral, bounded by Stammer Gate and Priest Lane. Wilfrid built his new monastery about 200 yards west of the old buildings. There is some doubt about the position of his church. It is the pronounced opinion of the learned that the famous Saxon crypt under the present church is really his work. Did he build an earlier church, and that which stood over this crypt later? Possibly so—but, in all probability, we may conclude that the monastic buildings only occupied the site on the west of Stammer Lane, and that his church stood over his crypt. This church was a very famous one. It is recorded that he brought workmen from Italy, who wrought in the Roman manner. It was fashioned after the model of a basilica, and constructed with wrought stones from the foundation, and had divers pillars and porticoes. It was dedicated to St. Peter, and splendid was the feast of the dedication. Here St. Wilfrid, after all the trials of his wandering life, was buried. For a brief space Ripon enjoyed the rank of an episcopal city, being so raised by Archbishop Theodore, and then for a thousand years the see was in abeyance, until in 1836 another Bishop of Ripon was appointed.

But much happened during this long interval. When the Danes terrified the land, in 995, came Bishop Aldune, bearing the body of St. Cuthbert, and stayed here three months until they set out and found peace at Durham.   Before this Odo of Canterbury, coming into these northern parts, had pity on the desolation of Ripon Church, wrought by the " harrying " of Eadred of Northumbria in 948, and caused a new work to be edified where the minster now is.   After the Conquest hard was the hand of William pressed upon his northern subjects, who liked not his yoke, and all this land was devastated by the Norman conquerors.   But with the Conquest came peace, and soon some building was evidently set on foot here, though the chroniclers are silent.   In later Norman times Archbishop Roger de Pont l'Evêque (1154-1181) began the building of the existing church, incorporating some portion of the older structure.   His work is Transitional, and furnishes a good example of the gradual development of Early English style. Archbishop Walter de Grey (1216-1255) carried on the good work and built the west front with its flanking towers, adorned with lofty spires of timber and lead.   The next alteration was carried out at the end of the thirteenth century, when Archbishop John Romanus determined to rebuild the eastern part of the choir, and for this purpose granted an indulgence of forty days to those who should help forward the work.   This work was in all the glory of the Decorated style.   The Scots made a ferocious raid in 1319, when the people of Ripon took refuge in the church, which suffered much from the attacks of the enemy.   Archbishop de Melton repaired some of this damage, which was chiefly confined to the roofs, screens, stalls, and other wood-work, and Archbishop Thoresby (1352-1373) was very eager to continue this restoration and beautify the minster.   He probably built the Lady Chapel.   A century elapsed, during which the clergy do not seem to have been remarkable for zeal or earnestness, and then the lantern tower was so much shaken and broken that the greatest part thereof had already fallen, and the rest expected to follow, and speedy remedy was found immediately necessary.   Archbishop Booth in 1459 adopted the usual and efficacious plan of granting an indulgence of forty days to all who should assist in re-edifying the steeple.   The work was immediately begun, and a great era of church building was inaugurated.   The canons awoke from their lethargy and worked vigorously.   They rebuilt much of the tower, and then set themselves to entirely rebuild the Norman nave, which was in great decay and ruin.   It was a great work, and nobly done.   The fall of the tower had broken much of the wood-work of the stalls ; so these indefatigable canons made new ones.   It was only the

The Cathedral from Horrible Evening

dissolution of the Establishment which checked their progress, and prevented them from finishing their work. The church was despoiled of all its wealth, and in Elizabeth's time, when Archbishop Sandys applied for an endowment, he could obtain "nothing but fair and unperformed promises." Elizabeth loved not this northern town, the people of which clung to the "old Religion," and took an active part in the rising of 1569. Many of them were hung for their pains. James I., however, restored the constitution of the collegiate chapter, and granted to it many of its old privileges and an assured income. During the Civil War Ripon escaped fairly well, save that the Puritan soldiers broke much of the beautiful glass in the east window, and perhaps were guilty of causing other damage, of which history telleth not. In 1660 the wooden spire, which had suffered by lightning in 1593, fell, and damaged the roof of the choir. This was repaired, and the other wooden spires on the west towers removed lest they, too, should fall. Since then there have been several restorations. In 1861 the church was placed in the hands of Mr. Scott, afterwards Sir Gilbert, who made a very complete renovation of the building, the details of which we will examine when we inspect the Cathedral.

In 1836 an episcopal see was erected at Ripon, and Charles Langley, afterwards Archbishop of Canterbury, became its first bishop.

THE EXTERIOR

Although Ripon is not a Cathedral of the first magnitude or splendour, yet it is a stately structure, and greatly superior to many of our ecclesiastical buildings. It possesses also some features of profound interest, and the story of its building is attractive. Approaching the church from the market-place by Kirkgate we see the beautiful *West Front*, which compares favourably with most others, except perhaps York, Lincoln, Peterborough and Wells. It has much dignity and beauty. It consists of a gable between two square towers. The nave, built by Archbishop Roger, was Late Norman or Transitional, and to this Archbishop Grey added this façade in the best and purest period of the Early English style. In the lowest storey are three deeply-recessed doorways, with detached shafts. Round and hollow mouldings are used, and the dog-tooth ornament, the hall-mark of the Early English style, is plentiful. The doors are old. Above are five-lancet windows, and above them another row of five lancets of unequal height. The dog-tooth is used in the mouldings.   The towers have four stages.   In the lowest is an arcade of trefoiled arches, and above lancets.   Nail-head moulding is used in the string-courses.   When the spires were pulled down in 1660, battlemented parapets were added, and later the pinnacles.

The whole front has been much restored. There is a fine peal of ten bells in the south tower.   There were formerly some old bells, one of which is said to have been brought from Fountains Abbey, but these have all been recast, and their interest has vanished. The nave has six bays, and was built in Perpendicular style in 1503. The south side is earlier than and superior to the north. The arches of the windows are less acutely pointed, and the buttresses have three stages, are crocketed, and have large finials. The pitch of the roof has been lowered since the nave was built.

The *Central Tower* was rebuilt on the south and east sides in Perpendicular times, while the north and west retain Roger's work.   It was formerly capped by a spire.   Returning to the north side we see the north side of the nave, which is later than the south.   There are six buttresses, which project widely and have two stages with crockets and finials, and grotesques.   The arches of the windows both in the aisles and clerestory are very acute, and those of the latter have five lights. From this point we see the original faces of the central tower, built by Roger (1154-1181), which has round-headed windows. The presence of dog-tooth shows the approach of the Early English style. The *North Transept* is also part of Roger's church and the best example of his work; it has round-headed

windows. The parapet is later. We notice two sculptured stones in the north-west buttress, with rich scroll-work, evidently Saxon, and probably taken from Wilfrid's church. The doorway in the north side is remarkable, having a plain trefoil head rising from a corbel-like projection, and is flanked by three receding detached shafts with foliated capitals. The *Choir* has three bays of Transitional Norman work, but the windows are Decorated. The remainder of this side was built late in the thirteenth century and is Decorated. The east end, with its grand window, is very fine. Massive buttresses stand on each side of the front with octagonal turrets. In the north turret there is a small chamber which was probably a reclusorium. The east window is flanked by heavy buttresses. The gable was rebuilt by Scott. The window (51 feet by 25 feet) is a magnificent specimen of Early Decorated work, one of the finest in England. On the south side we see the three eastern windows are Decorated as on the north, but the rest are Perpendicular. On this side is a building which retains some of the earliest Norman work in the Cathedral, probably built by Thomas of Bayeaux, archbishop (1069-1100). This building has three storeys — a crypt, the chapter-house and the Lady Chapel (erected in the fourteenth century), which we shall examine later. The *South Transept* retains much of Roger's Transitional work, but the east side was altered and rebuilt in Perpendicular times. On the south side is a fine doorway contemporary with the transept and resembling somewhat that on the north.

The Interior

Entering by the west door we see a fine and imposing *Nave*, with tall and graceful piers that support without any intermediate triforium a range of lofty windows of elaborate tracery. This nave was constructed in the Perpendicular period, as we have said, and the main arcades stand on the foundation of Roger's earlier church. The latter had no aisles. These the sixteenth-century builders added, taking as their western starting-point the northern and southern extremities of the west tower. Hence the nave is unusually wide (87 feet), and exceeds all other cathedrals except York, Chichester, Winchester and St. Paul's. There are many points of architectural interest. The west bays opening into the tower are Early English. On either side is a lofty thirteenth-century arch, with plain mouldings, and capitals deeply undercut. Above is a blind arcade of four arches enclosed in a circular arch—this occupies the triforium stage ; and the clerestory has a triple window, the centre round-headed, the side ones pointed. The west end, with its ranges of lancets, is most effective. The glass is modern. The next bay shows us clearly the character of Roger's church, and eastward we come to the Perpendicular work of the early sixteenth century, which appears to be earlier than it really is. The traditions of the earlier style lingered on amid the hills and dales of Yorkshire, while the architects and townsfolk of less remote places had developed the more familiar details of the Perpendicular period. The roof is modern. The arch of the tower facing us is part of Roger's church, but there is a curious mass of masonry on the south pier which was erected by the Perpendicular builders, when want of funds or the dissolution of the chapter prevented the completion of the design. The contrast between the materials of the old building and the new in the nave will be noticed. The former is fashioned of yellow gritstone, the latter of white limestone. The aisles are Perpendicular work erected about 1503. The vaulting is modern. In the south aisle is the font, or rather there are two fonts. The earlier one reposes in the corner, and is Roger's work; the later is Perpendicular. Ripon is not very rich in monuments. In this same aisle there is a curious altar tomb with a slab of grey marble, upon which is carved the figure of a lion and near it that of a man kneeling. Tradition states that it covered the body of an Irish prince, who died here on his return from Palestine, whence he had brought a lion that followed him like a dog. There is some old glass, fragments of which have been collected in the window near the font. In the *North Aisle* at the west end is the consistory court. The old *Saxon Crypt* deserves close attention and has occasioned many conjectures and much antiquarian disputing. It is undoubtedly very early, and may with safety be assumed to have been part of St. Wilfrid's church. After descending several steps and passing along passages, which have two niches in the wall, we arrive at a cylindrically vaulted chamber (7 feet by 11 feet), and on the north side is the famous "St. Wilfrid's Needle." Formerly the superstition attached to it was that no unchaste woman could with safety pass through it; now we are told that if a virgin "threads the needle" she will be married within a year. This needle is only an enlargement of one of the niches which were doubtless used for lights. Recent excavations have been made here, which revealed the remains of an altar, a passage round the chamber, and a quantity of bones which were probably relics. It is conjectured that this was a relic chamber, and was built under the church of Wilfrid. It is impossible to touch upon all the interesting problems which this curious chamber suggests, especially as affecting the position and form of Wilfrid's early Saxon church.

The *Transepts* retain, with the exception of the east wall of the southern member, Archbishop Roger's Transitional work, when Norman architecture was slowly developing into Early English. There is a niche on the east side of each transept. A Perpendicular arch forms an entrance to the *North Transept* from the north aisle, and on the north of this is a round-headed window. The triforium has two broad arches in each bay with a central detached shaft, while the clerestory has three arches, the centre round, the others pointed. In the north wall there are three round-headed windows in the highest stage. The mullions in the windows in the second stage are later insertions. On the east is the Chantry of St. Andrew, the Markenfields' Chapel. Outside the aisle is the effigy of Sir Thomas (1497), with that of his lady, and another Sir Thomas lies in the chapel (notice the armour and collar). This family lost its estates in the rising in the time of Elizabeth. Also there is the monument of Sir Edward Blackett of Newby (1718). The *South Transept* resembles the north, except that its east side is Perpendicular. The aisle is called the Mallorie Chapel, and there is a tablet to the memory of Sir John Mallorie of Studley, who defended Skipton Castle for Charles I. There are some ancient mural paintings, which may be seen when going to the library.

The *Choir-Screen* is Perpendicular, and has beautiful enriched tabernacle work. Above the door is a representation of God the Father with angels. Above the screen is the organ. The *Choir* is a delightful architectural study, as the work of three periods are blended here—Transition Norman, Decorated and Perpendicular. The three western bays on the north are Roger's work, Transitional Norman. The three bays opposite were injured by the fall of the tower and renewed in Perpendicular style. The rest of the choir was renewed in the Decorated style of the fourteenth century. The three bays on the north resemble the work in the transept. The group of vaulting shafts is very fine. The triforium openings are glazed like the clerestory. A change was made in Perpendicular times. Before the triforium arches opened into the aisles, but the roof of these was lowered in 1459, and the openings filled with glass.

There is some of Roger's work in the other bays, the earlier work being altered and converted into that of the Decorated style. In the clerestory there is tracery on the inner side of the opening as well as the outer. The foliage of the carving is very beautiful. The roof is modern, but some very interesting ancient bosses have been re-inserted. Some of the subjects are :—the Good Samaritan, the expulsion from Paradise, the Virgin with lilies, the crucifixion (modern), a bishop, a king, an angel. The east window is remarkably fine, one of the best Decorated windows in England. All. the old glass was destroyed by Cromwell's soldiers, and the modern glass is but a sorry substitute.

The wood-work of the *Stalls* is for the most part of excellent fifteenth-century execution. Rich tabernacle work rises at the back of the stalls. Several of the eastern canopies are modern. The finials are curious; some represent an elephant and castle with figures of men fighting, and a monkey. The *misereres* are interesting; the carvings represent many curious grotesques, fables and Scripture subjects. We notice Samson carrying the gates, Jonah and the whale, fox and geese, lion and dogs, griffins and rabbits, etc. The *sedilia* should be noticed. They have been restored, but much old work remains of Late Decorated style. A close examination of the grotesques should not be omitted. The pulpit and lectern are modern.

The *North Choir Aisle* follows the architecture of the choir. Here once stood the famous shrine of St. Wilfrid. The *South Choir Aisle* is very similar to the opposite one. Here is a lavatory, and a piscina at the east end marks the site of a former altar. Above the west bay was a chantry chapel, now used for part of the organ. There is a monument in this aisle to Dean Fowler (1608). On the south is the *Chapter-House* and *Vestry*. The *Crypt* below formed part of the Early Norman church existing here before the rebuilding by Archbishop Roger. It is generally attributed to Thomas of Bayeaux (1070-1100). The vault is supported by square pillars with plain capitals. The windows have a double splay, which is a sign of almost Saxon work. The east end is apsidal. This crypt was formerly filled with bones. There are some interesting stone coffins preserved here.

Returning to the *Chapter-House* we notice the stone benches where the canons once sat in conclave. The vaulting is very fine, of Late Transitional work, almost Early English. This chamber was built by Roger. An arcade runs along the north wall. The windows are circular, the piers round, and have circular bosses and capitals. Some curious fifteenth-century alabaster carvings are preserved here, the subjects being St. Wilfrid, the Coronation of the Virgin and the Resurrection. The *Vestry* is evidently of the same date as the chapter-house, and once formed part of the same building, the partition wall being much later. It has an apse with the remains of an altar and the treasury occupied the apse on the south.

Above these chambers is the *Lady Loft*, the date of which is uncertain; it was probably built about 1330, and is Decorated in style. It is strange to find a Lady Chapel in this position. The room is now the library. It possesses some interesting incunabula and a few MSS.

DIMENSIONS

Total length	270 ft.
Length of nave	133 ft.
Breadth of nave	87 ft.
Height of nave	88 ft.
Length of choir . . . ·	95 ft.
Height of tower . . .	110 ft.
Length of transept . . .	130 ft.
Area	25,280 sq. ft.

PRINCIPAL BUILDING DATES

Saxon—Wilfrid's crypt.

Norman (1070-1100)—Portions of chapter-house, vestry and crypt below.

Transition (1154-1181)—Three bays of north side of choir, portions of nave, piers adjoining west and central towers, transepts.

Early English (1215-1255)—West front and west tower, vaulting of chapter-house and windows.

Early Decorated—Two eastern bays of choir and east window.

Perpendicular—South and east sides of central tower, east side of wall of south transept, two bays south side of choir, nave.

Ripon has some other important and interesting ancient buildings. There is the *Hospital of St. Mary Magdalene*, rebuilt in 1674, with an old chapel of the twelfth century. The Hospital of St. Anne, founded in the fifteenth century, though rebuilt in 1869, has its old chapel, with piscina and altar stone, and there are many other old houses in this city. Near here is the famous Fountains Abbey.

YORK CATHEDRAL

FEW cities can rival York in interest, dignity and importance. The ancient city of Roman Cæsars, the centre of Saxon Christianity, of Danish supremacy, of mercantile enterprise, the abode of kings, the seat of an archbishopric that long contended for supremacy with Canterbury, York may well claim a foremost place in English history, and possesses features of peculiar interest. Professor Freeman stated that " Eboracum (York) holds a place which is unique in the history of Britain, which is shared only by one other city in the lands north of the Alps (Treves)." Here the Emperor Constantius died, here Constantine the Great was crowned. Bishops of York were present at the Councils of Arles (314), Nicæa and Sardica, and when the Christian faith died out, killed by Pagan Saxons, Paulinus taught again the lessons of the holy Cross, and baptised Edwin, the king, in a little wooden church which stood on the site of the present Cathedral. Then Christianity died down, killed by the onslaughts of fierce Paganism, until at length, under the influence of Oswald and the monks of Iona and Lindisfarne, the Cross again triumphed. There was much contention between the Roman faction, led by Wilfrid, and the upholders of the native church, as regards customs and observances, and the influence of Wilfrid predominated. Wilfrid was a great builder, restored the Cathedral at York and erected large churches at Ripon and Hexham. The Danes overran Northumbria, and under their rule York increased its importance and became a large and flourishing city.

Then came the Norman Conquest, and we find Ælred, Archbishop of York, crowning William at Westminster, but his people liked not the change of rulers and rebelled. The Conqueror came and ruthlessly crushed the revolt, and after his wont erected a castle to overawe his subjects. Again they rebelled; the king swore deep vengeance, and terrible was the punishmet inflicted on the northern kingdom. He appointed Thomas of Bayeaux archbishop, who set about repairing the ruined church, and built a new nave with side aisles and transepts, using the old church as a choir for the new. For years the question of the supremacy of York or Canterbury disturbed the ecclesiastical affairs of England, and on one occasion at a council the Metropolitan of York, finding his brother of Canterbury occupying the seat of honour at the right of the Papal legate, gravely sat down on the latter's lap. In the reign of Henry II. came Roger de Pont l'Evêque, who built the new choir and crypt, removing the remains of the old Saxon church.

The people of York have ever been eager for fighting, revolt and riot. Sometimes we find them killing Jews; now disputing with the monks of St. Mary's Abbey, because some offending citizen had escaped their vengeance by claiming the right of sanctuary; now fighting against the Scots, and even rebelling against rulers who were obnoxious to them. Kings of the House of Lancaster were especially hateful, and nowhere in the kingdom did reformers of religion find more bitter opponents.

During the rule of Walter de Grey, archbishop (1216-1255), the Norman transepts were removed and the present ones built, and in the reign of the Edwards the old Norman nave was replaced by the present one, and the chapter-house built. At this period York enjoyed much prosperity. The Scottish wars brought kings here who made it the military and civil capital of the whole country. Parliaments were held here. York Minster saw the marriage of Edward III., and the burial of his infant son. But rebellions against the kings of the House of Lancaster, the famous Pilgrimage of Grace against the reformed doctrines, and other risings, diminished its influence and deprived it of many privileges. York was besieged for six weeks during the Civil War, and suffered much; but happily General Fairfax exercised a restraining influence on his soldiers and prevented them from damaging the Cathedral. Although the citizens at the Reformation rebelled against the "new Religion," at the Restoration they rebelled against the overthrow of Puritanism; and again, when James II. endeavoured to restore Roman Catholicism, they rebelled again, attacked the Roman Catholic prelate whom the king sent to them, wrested from him his silver-gilt crozier, and took it in triumph to the minster, where it remains until this day.

We will now briefly trace the history of the building, which has been rightly called "the King of Cathedrals." In 627 Paulinus built his little wooden church for the baptism of King Edwin. A year later a stone church was begun, which was finished by Oswald and repaired by Wilfrid. In the crypt are

some of the walls of this early church, which show the "herring-
bone" work of Saxon builders. When the Conqueror besieged

Tomb of Archbishop Walter de Grey

York much destruction was wrought on this church.

In 1070 Archbishop Thomas of Bayeaux built the Norman nave
and transepts, and used the old church as the choir. The apse in the
crypt and the core of the tower piers are the remains of this work.

In 1154-1181 choir and crypt were rebuilt by Roger in Late Norman style.

In 1230-1260 the present transepts were built.

In 1291-1324 Norman nave was taken down and the new nave built, and also the chapter-house, vestibule, sacristy and treasury. In 1338 the west front of nave was erected.

In 1361-1400 choir rebuilt and Lady Chapel.

In 1400-1423 central tower built in place of Early English lantern.

In 1433-1474 north and south-western towers built.

The Cathedral was now complete. At the beginning of the sixteenth century the organ-screen was erected, and two disastrous fires in 1829 and 1840 necessitated considerable repairs, and in 1875 some needful restoration of the south transept was carried out.

THE EXTERIOR

The *West Front* is "more architecturally perfect as a composition and in its details than that of any other English cathedral," and is unquestionably the best cathedral façade in this country. The lower part, with the entrances and lower windows, belongs to the Early Decorated period. Above the windows the work is Late Decorated, and the towers above the roof Perpendicular. Numerous niches cover the surface. It is doubtful whether they ever contained statues. The principal entrance is divided by a clustered pier, and above it is a circle filled with cusped tracery. Over the whole doorway is a deeply-recessed arch, and over that a gable with niches, one of which contains the statue of an archbishop, supposed to be John le Romeyn, who began the nave in 1291, and other niches have figures of a Percy and a Vavasour, who gave the wood and stone for the building. The favourite ball-flower ornament of the Decorated style is seen on the gable, and the mouldings in the arches have figures representing the history of Adam and Eve. Above the entrance is a large eight-light window, pronounced by many to be too large even for York Minster, containing very elaborate and beautiful tracery, and over it is a pointed gable. On each side of the west window are buttresses covered with panelling and niches. The noble towers, rising on each side of the west front, have buttresses similarly adorned, and each three windows, and over the second an open battlement forms a walk along the whole front. The towers have battlements and pinnacles. The south-west tower (1433-1457)

Chapter House

was injured by fire in 1840; and the north tower (1470-1474) has the largest bell in the kingdom.

The *Nave* is divided into seven bays by high buttresses, on the south side crowned with pinnacles. It was evidently originally intended to connect them with the clerestory wall by flying buttresses to support a stone vaulted roof. But the builders were alarmed by the great span of the roof and substituted a wooden vault. Hence the flying buttresses were not needed. There are some curious gargoyles. The north side is plainer, as formerly the Palace would conceal any elaborate carving. The style is Decorated.

The *South Transept* (1216-1241) is of Early English design. The central porch is not remarkable, though the clustered shafts are very fine, ornamented with dog-tooth ornament. On each side are lancet windows, and above similar windows; higher still a large rose window, and in the gable a cusped triangular light. Arcaded buttresses with octagonal turrets rise on each side. Extensive restoration took place in 1871, when the old clock was removed.

The *Choir* and *Lady Chapel* are Perpendicular work. The four eastern bays, constituting the Lady Chapel, are earlier than the later ones of the choir, and vary in detail. The triforium passage in the former is outside the building, and the windows are recessed. Strange gargoyles, with figures of apes and demons, adorn the buttresses. The east end is mainly filled with the huge window, the largest in England, which does not leave much space for architectural detail. Above it is the figure of Archbishop Thoresby, the builder of this part of the Cathedral. Panelling covers the surface of the stone, and below the window is a row of seventeen busts, representing our Lord and His Apostles, Edward III. and Archbishop Thoresby. There are two aisle windows; buttresses adorned with niches separate the aisles from the central portion, and others, capped with spires, stand on the north and south of this front.

The *Chapter-House* (Early Decorated) is octagonal, and connected with the north transept by a vestibule, which shows by its architectural details that it was built after the completion of the chapter-house. These constitute the finest examples of Decorated Gothic in England. Buttresses project at each angle, crowned with pinnacles. Curious grotesque gargoyles are seen, and amongst them some strange-looking bears. The roof is in the form of a pyramid, and there is a battlement surrounding it.

The *North Transept* (1241-1260) is a beautiful specimen of Early English work. The five long lancet windows, called the "Five Sisters," surmounted by the seven lancets in the gable, are most effective.

The *Central Tower* is the largest in England, and is in the Perpendicular style (1410-1433). It is 200 feet high. It has windows ornamented with ogee gables, and its surface is covered with niches and panelling. A pair of narrow buttresses support each angle of the tower, decorated with panelling. This tower is one of the greatest achievements of the fifteenth-century builders, and is one of the finest in the world.

THE INTERIOR

The Nave.—The first impression on viewing this nave is a sense of its magnitude. Archbishop Romeyn and his builders determined to build a vast church which would eclipse all other rivals. They would have large windows, high, towering piers, a huge, vaulted roof, and everything that was grand and impressive. Edward I. was then fighting with the Scots, and made York his chief city. It was immensely prosperous, and the ecclesiastical treasury was replete with the offerings of knights and nobles, kings and pilgrims. Nowhere should there be so mighty a church as York Minster. In order to have space for large windows they made the triforium unusually small, which is formed only by a continuation of the arches of the clerestory windows. The design for the stone vaulted roof was never carried out. The builders feared that the great weight of a roof with so large a span would be too much for the walls, so a wooden vault was substituted. The piers have octagonal bases, and consist of various sized shafts closely connected. The capitals are beautifully enriched with foliage of oak and thorn, and sometimes a figure is seen amidst the foliage. We notice thirty-two sculptured busts at the intersection of the hood moulding with the vaulting shafts. Coats of arms of the benefactors of York appear on each side of the main arches. The clerestory windows have each five lights. The old roof was destroyed by fire in 1840. The present one has a vast number of bosses representing the Annunciation, Nativity, Magi, Resurrection, besides a quantity of smaller ones. The whole scheme of decoration is most elaborate.

The west window is a noble specimen of Decorated work, with its curvilinear tracery, one of the finest in the kingdom. It has been entirely restored. There are eight lights. It was glazed by

Archbishop Melton (1317-1340). Niches and arcading cover the west wall. The pinnacles are carved with figures of men and animals, and also the brackets of the niches. The aisles have stone vaulting, windows Decorated like the west window, carved panels and arcading work. Over the north doorway are some sculptured figures of doubtful signification. The walled-up door which led to the Chapel of the Holy Sepulchre has a headless figure of the Virgin. Here is a tomb of an archbishop of Late Perpendicular work, with Tudor flower cornice. All the other monuments have been destroyed. Over the south aisle door are three sculptured representations of David killing the lion, Samson and the lion with Delilah cutting his hair, and a man and woman fighting. The glass of the windows should be especially noticed. Most of it is either Decorated or Early English.

The *South Transept* is the earliest part of the present Cathedral (1230-1241). The finest view is obtained on entering by the south door. The extraordinary magnitude of the transepts, the five lancets with their old glass, and the beauty of the Early English architecture, are most striking. The triforium is not dwarfed as in the nave, but assumes large proportions, whereas the clerestory is small. The former consists of semicircular moulded arches, with dog-tooth ornament, each enclosing two pointed arches, and subdivided into two similar arches. Five pointed arches in each bay constitute the clerestory, with sculptured heads. Clustered shafts of stone and Purbeck marble form the piers. The vaulting is of wood of the fifteenth century, and the bosses are curious. A mermaid and merman, a monk and a nun, look down upon us; an arcade of pointed arches lines the walls. Chantry chapels were formerly in the east aisle. On the south was Ludham's Chantry, archbishop (1258-1265). It contains the large modern monument of Dean Duncombe. Next we see the Chapel of St. Michael with the tomb of its founder, Archbishop Grey (1216-1255), the builder of this transept, and near it the monument of Archbishop Sewal de Bovill (1256-1258).

The *North Transept* resembles the south, but differs in details. Especially noticeable is the profusion of dog-tooth ornament, the magnificent lancet windows, called the "Five Sisters," with the five smaller ones over it. These are the largest ancient lancets in England.* Curious grotesques are seen in the triforium moulding. The monuments here are :—(1) a brass to the memory of soldiers

* We must except Lord Grimthorpe's modern innovations at St. Albans.

slain in India; (2) Archbishop Harcourt's tomb (1808-1843); (3) a skeleton memorial of Thomas Huxby, treasurer (1418-1424); (4) Archbishop Greenfield's tomb (d. 1315), which lies before the place where the altar of St. Nicholas stood; (5) effigy of Dr. Beckwith (d. 1847).

In 1829 a disastrous fire occurred in the Cathedral, caused by a lunatic incendiary named Martin. He hid himself on the night of the fire behind the tomb of Archbishop Greenfield. There is a curious doorway leading to the vestibule of the chapter-house of Decorated style.

Entering the *Vestibule* we notice the exact place where the Early English builders finished their work, and the Decorated style begins. The difference between the styles in the chapter-house and vestibule shows that the former was erected first. It has a wall arcade, and above are windows of curious tracery, filled with beautiful old glass. The shafts of the arcade support trefoiled arches, with a cinquefoil ornamented with a sculptured boss. Each boss and capital is beautifully carved with foliage, amidst which the heads of men and dragons appear. The glass is Early Decorated, and contains representations of Royal personages.

The *Chapter-House* is one of the most beautiful in England. The entrance is an arch, divided into two arches by a canopied pier, which bears a mutilated statue of the Virgin and Child. Clustered shafts, with capitals, are on each side of the doors, which have remarkably good scrolled iron-work. The chamber itself is very magnificent. It is octagonal, and in each bay there are six canopied stalls under a five-light window. The window tracery is superb. Clustered shafts support the vaulted roof. Everywhere we see richly-carved stone-work, the finest in any cathedral, the foliage of maple, oak, vine, and other trees. Here are pigs and squirrels feeding on acorns, men gathering grapes, birds, and coiled dragons and reptiles. The grotesques are most curious and interesting. In 1845, unfortunately, the building was restored, and the painted figures of kings and bishops were destroyed, a poor tiled floor laid down; but, in spite of all, it can still maintain its proud boast :—

> " *Ut Rosa flos florum,*
> *Sic est Domus ista Domorum.*"

[" As the Rose is the flower of flowers, so is this House the chief of Houses "].

The *Choir-Screen*, erected in 1500, is good Perpendicular work,

x

and has figures of kings from William I. to Henry VI. The rebus of the master-mason, Hyndeley (a hind lying) occurs in the capitals. The canopies are richly carved. There is an ogee pediment, and a niche with angels on each side, with censers. The Tudor flower is used as an ornament, and plaster angels by Bernasconi were added in 1810. The organ was erected in 1632.

The Choir and Lady Chapel.—The Lady Chapel, occupying the four east bays, was built in 1361-1405, the choir in 1407-1420.

THE CRYPT

The style is Perpendicular, though it follows the design of the nave; yet the builders endeavoured to improve upon the earlier work and remedy its defects. They were eminently successful, and produced one of the most stately and magnificent choirs in England. The roof is made of wood, like the nave, and has a large number of foliated bosses. A disastrous fire in 1829 destroyed all the old carved stalls and *misereres*, and the modern substitutes are fairly successful. The altar-screen is a good reproduction of the ancient one, and the reredos was designed by Street, with reliefs by Tinworth. The lectern was given by T. Cracroft in 1686.

The differences in the style of the clerestory windows in the east and west portions will be readily noticed. Only in the western part is the Perpendicular style fully developed. The east window is the largest window in England, retaining its original glazing, but in actual size it is surpassed by that at Gloucester. Its height is 75 feet, and breadth 32 feet, and each compartment is a yard square. The artist of the glass was one Thornton, of Coventry.

The Altar of the Virgin stood under this window, and here was a chantry, founded by the Percys. There is a curious ancient carving, much mutilated, of the Virgin and Child. Archbishop Bowet's Chantry (1407-1423) was at the east of the south aisle, and his tomb is here, the finest in the Cathedral, though much mutilated. There are many monuments in the choir, which are too numerous to mention—the second son of Edward III. (d. 1344), Archbishop Savage (d. 1507), Archbishop Sterne (1689), Archbishop Scrope, beheaded by Henry IV., to whose tomb there was great resort by pilgrims.

The *Crypt* was mainly discovered after the fire of 1829. It has fine Norman piers, part of Roger's Cathedral (d. 1181), and contains some "herring-bone" work of Saxon architecture, the remains of Edwin's church. The vestry has some very interesting antiquities : an old Installation Chair, used at the consecration and enthronement of the archbishops ; an old treasury-chest ; Prayer-Book and Bible, presented by Charles I. ; an old chained Bible ; two *misereres*, left after the fire ; a pastoral staff of 1686 ; the famous Horn of Alphus, presented before the Conquest, the title-deed to several acres of land held by horn tenure ; chalices and patens of the fourteenth and fifteenth centuries ; episcopal rings, and the bowl of the Cordwainers' Company, formerly belonging to. Archbishop Scrope.

The vastness of York Minster, with its forest of clustered pillars, its unrivalled ancient stained glass, its importance as the metropolitan church of Northern England, combine to make this splendid Cathedral one of the most interesting in the kingdom.

OTHER OBJECTS OF INTEREST IN THE CITY

St. Mary's Abbey, in the Museum Gardens, founded by Earl Sward in 1050. The present buildings were erected, after a fire in 1137, in 1270, and the Abbey grew to become one of great wealth and importance. The style is Decorated. On the site of the abbot's house is the *King's Manor*, or *Royal Palace*, now used as a Blind School. Near at hand is the *Multangular Tower*, which formed part of the old Roman wall, and *St. Leonard's Hospital*, founded by King Athelstan in 936 A.D., and rebuilt by Stephen. The *Museum* is worthy of a visit, and the *Hospitium* of the old Abbey, which now contains a good collection of Roman antiquities and carved stones from the Abbey.

St. William's College (College Street), the famous abode of the chantry priests of the Cathedral, founded in 1460, is now a series of cottages.

The city walls should be visited, and the old gates—Mickelgate, Walmgate, Monkgate, and Bootham Bar. The hall of the Merchant Adventurers' Company is interesting, and Clifford's Tower, the keep of the Conqueror's castle, celebrated for the Massacre of the Jews in 1190. Many of the churches are ancient, and have beautifully-carved doors and interesting old glass. The Church of St. Mary the Younger has a Saxon tower.

DIMENSIONS

Total length	486 ft.
Length of nave	262 ft.
Breadth of nave and aisles . .	104 ft.
Height of nave	99 ft.
Length of choir	224 ft.
Length of transept . . .	223 ft.
Height of central tower . .	198 ft.
Height of western towers . .	196 ft.
Area	63,800 sq. ft.

For Building Dates *see* page 312.

A B C 3 Western Doorways
D D Nave
E E Aisles
F North Transept, with its
  Aisles J and K .
G South Transept, with its
  Aisles J and K

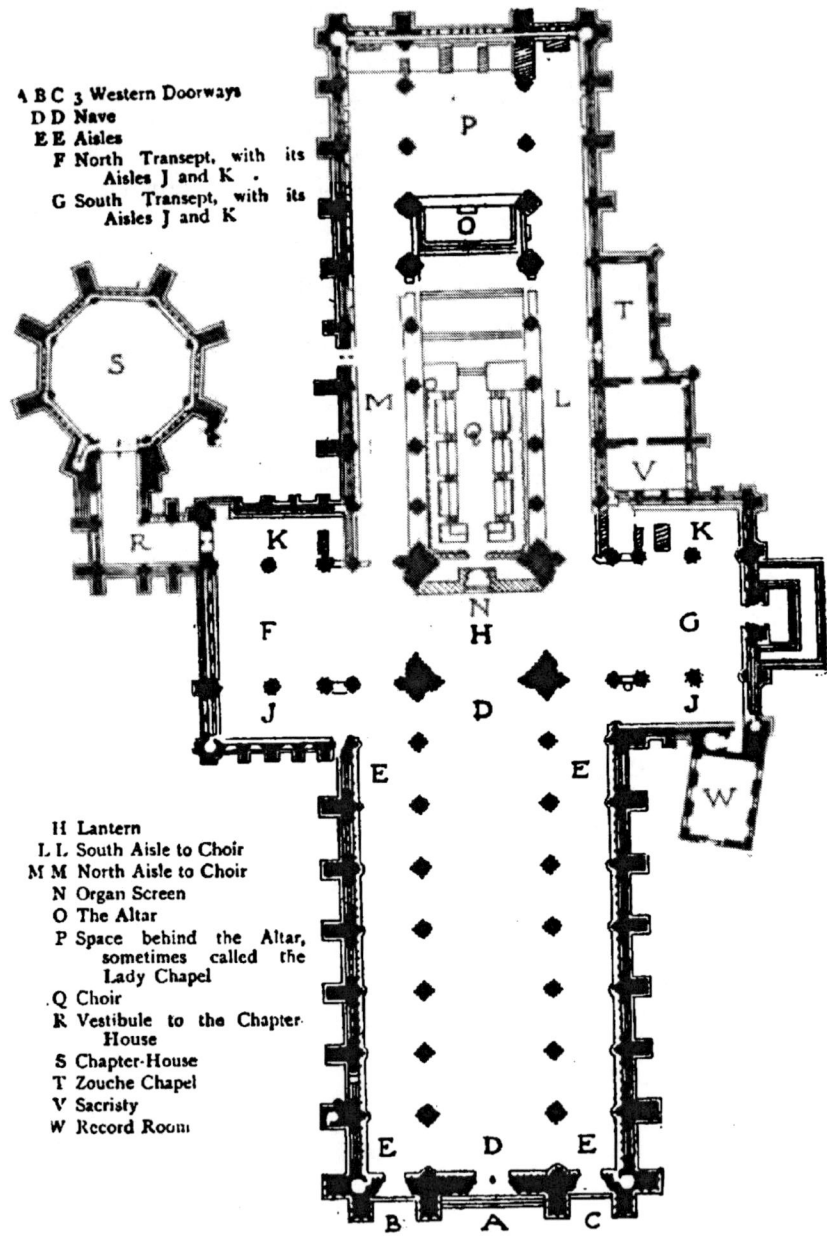

P

O

T

S

M

L

Q

V

R

K

K

F

G

N
H

J

D

J

E

E

E

E

W

H Lantern
L L South Aisle to Choir
M M North Aisle to Choir
N Organ Screen
O The Altar
P Space behind the Altar,
  sometimes called the
  Lady Chapel
Q Choir
R Vestibule to the Chapter-
  House
S Chapter-House
T Zouche Chapel
V Sacristy
W Record Room

E

D

E

B

A

C

PLAN OF YORK CATHEDRAL

BEVERLEY MINSTER

ALTHOUGH Beverley is not a cathedral, its Minster is certainly worthy of being ranked as such, and perhaps some day, when our dioceses are again divided, it may have a bishop of its own. Of John of Beverley's foundation want of space forbids us to write, or of the great Æthelstan, who conferred great privileges on the place. Ælfric and Archbishop Aldred were great builders, and did much for the Minster; but in 1188 a great part of the church was destroyed by fire. The nave seems to have escaped without much serious injury, and the monks set about repairing the east end and building a central tower; but, after the manner of towers, this one fell, and reduced the eastern arm of the church to ruins. Then came the era of the great Gothic builders, and early in the thirteenth century the monks began to rebuild the east end of the church, the tower, and one bay of the nave, and nobly did they accomplish their undertaking. They accomplished a work which caused their Minster to rank with the best achievements of Early English Gothic art, and we must look to Salisbury or the choir of Lincoln to find anything equal to it. For many years the old Norman nave remained. Nearly 100 years passed away, and then a new era of building dawned. At the end of the first quarter of the fourteenth century the monks set to work to rebuild the nave. Quickly the work progressed, until the Black Death, which seems to have been especially virulent in monasteries, laid low many of the builders. The noise of the chisel ceased, until at length the monks resumed their work, and built that crowning glory of their Minster, the noble west front. Such was the history of the building of Beverley Minster. Since that time little has been done, except to preserve the exquisite workmanship of these early builders. The church suffered from neglect, and from the evil genius and vile taste of the Georgian architects; but happily all their monstrosities have been removed by Sir Gilbert Scott, who restored the Minster to its ancient beauty.

The *West Front* is one of the finest examples of the Perpendicular style in England. It consists of two towers, flanking a large window, above which is a high gable, and below a deeply-recessed door.   The window has nine lights.   The whole front is panelled, and the buttresses are ornamented with various tiers of

niche-work of excellent composition and most delicate execution. These niches are about to be filled with figures. We enter the Minster by the north porch, which is a fine piece of Perpendicular work, with a parvise over it.   On entering the building we are struck with its great loftiness and the consummate beauty of its architectural

BEVERLEY MINSTER

details. As we have said, the *Nave* is later than the choir, with the exception of the first bay adjoining the tower. That one bay is Early English; the rest is superb Decorated work. The ball-flower moulding is conspicuous in the latter, the dog-tooth in the former; but there seems to have been some attempt to assimilate the later work with the earlier. The west end is Perpendicular, and the west window is a fine example of the work of that period. The glass is modern. There is some beautiful arcading in the aisles, that in the north aisle being more developed Decorated than that in the south. The tomb of the "Sisters of Beverley" in the south aisle should be noticed. It belongs to the Decorated period, and possesses many features of interest. History is silent as to the names of these sisters, who are supposed to have been benefactors to the townsfolk. The tracery of the windows in the aisles should be noticed, as it is remarkable for its gracefulness and variety. The only relic of Norman work in the church is the font, near the south door, which is of a somewhat late character. The *Transepts* are of noble Early English construction. Tall lancets shed light upon the exquisite architectural details displayed here. Each transept has double aisles. The arcading of the triforium is curious, but effective. In the tympanum of each trefoil arch there is a quatre-foil and two semi-arches, which are completed by similar ones under the next arch. The effigy and monument of a priest in the north transept (fourteenth century) have some exquisite carving, and afford an excellent study of ecclesiastical vestments. The *East End* of the church is entirely composed of Early English work, and without doubt contains some of the best and most perfect architectural achievements of the thirteenth century. The piers are composed of eight massive columns. There is no triforium gallery, a very exquisite arcade taking its place, similar to that in the transepts, consisting of trefoil arches, ornamented with dog-tooth. Purbeck marble is extensively used throughout the choir. The screen is modern. The choir stalls and *misereres* are scarcely surpassed by any in England. They belong to the sixteenth century, and the designs represented on the latter are extremely quaint and curious. Few churches have such a superb *Altar-Screen* as Beverley. It is Early English, but has been much mutilated and robbed of its images, which now have been replaced by good modern sculpture. It has also been decorated with glass mosaic work. Near it, on the north, is the famous *Percy Tomb*, which is well known to all students of architecture. It is very beautiful

Decorated work, and is generally considered to have no equal. It was erected about 1338, and is to the memory of Lady Eleanor Percy, the wife of the first Lord Percy. The carving is quite superb, the details of the figure-sculpture being worthy of the closest attention. In the gable is a figure of the Almighty receiving the soul of the deceased, who is represented as being held up by a sheet supported by two angels. The east transepts and retro-choir possess also some fine Early English work, and is similar to that which has been described. In this retro-choir stood the shrine of St. John of Beverley, which was watched by a monk stationed in the watching chamber over the altar-screen. Notice the frith-stool, seated in which the person who sought sanctuary could defy the approach of his enemies and escape the justice which doubtless he deserved. Beverley was a noted place for sanctuary, and the records relating to this privilege are full of curious interest. The *Staircase* leading to the chapter-house, now destroyed, is remarkably fine, and is certainly a very beautiful feature of this wonderful church. The great east window is Perpendicular, and has some ancient glass. On the north is the Percy Chapel, founded in the fifteenth century; in it lies the body of one of the Earls of Percy, who was cruelly murdered at the close of that century.

Percy Shrine
Beverley Munster

WAKEFIELD CATHEDRAL

THE See of Wakefield was created in 1888. The enormous increase of the population of England and the growth of the Church's work have necessitated the multiplication of bishoprics and the division of many of the ancient enormous dioceses. This is one of the sees which it was found necessary to form. The old Parish Church of All Saints was converted into the Cathedral, but it possesses few of the associations and architectural beauties of our ancient minsters. It is, however, a fine parish church. It was consecrated by Archbishop William de Melton of York in 1329, but almost wholly rebuilt in the fifteenth century. Its main features are, therefore, Perpendicular. It consists of a chancel and large nave, with aisles. There is a clerestory, but no triforium. At the west end there is a tower, surmounted by a fine spire, rebuilt in 1860, the total height being 247 feet. A heavy screen separated the nave from the chancel of Jacobean style, and the organ and font belong to the seventeenth century. The whole building was restored by Sir G. Scott at a cost of £30,000.

On the bridge across the Calder there is a beautiful little chapel or chantry, dedicated to St. Mary (30 feet by 24 feet). This was built and endowed by Edward IV. in memory of his father, Richard, Duke of York, killed at the battle of Wakefield in 1460. It was restored in 1847. Near here was fought the famous battle between Queen Margaret, wife of Henry VI., and the Duke of York, whom this chantry commemorates. Wakefield was an ancient seat of manufacture, foreign weavers being established here by Henry VII.

Wakefield Cathedral.

LINCOLN CATHEDRAL

THE city of Lincoln has a history of profound interest. The first view of its mighty minster rising above the lower houses of the city is most impressive, and the whole place teems with historical association. Professor Freeman states that Lincoln has "kept up its continuous being through Roman, English, Danish and Norman conquests." Before the advent of the Romans it was a British stronghold, and bore a Celtic name—Lindum; and when the conquering legions came they made it one of the chief towns of the empire, and honoured it with the rank of a "colony"—hence *Lincoln*, "the colony of Lindum," thus preserving its ancient name, and adding the title of its dignity. The only existing Roman gateway in England is here, and the remains of a basilica, mosaic pavements, altars, sepulchral monuments, testify to the greatness of Roman Lincoln. The Anglo-Saxons wrought much havoc, and devastated the city. Here came St. Paulinus in 627 A.D., and converted the Pagan Saxons to Christianity. The fierce Danes attacked Lincoln and made it their chief town, the principal member of their League of the Five Towns (Leicester, Stamford, Derby, Nottingham and Lincoln). Before the Norman Conquest it ranked fourth among the cities of England. Then came William the Conqueror, who raised a castle and made it the base of his operations against the northern counties. Lincoln soon was raised to a position of great ecclesiastical pre-eminence, when Remigius of Fécamp became the first Norman bishop, and ruled the vastest diocese in England, extending from the Humber to the Thames. The city was in the eleventh and twelfth centuries one of the greatest trading towns in the country, the resort of traders both of land and sea. Here King Stephen was vanquished and carried off a prisoner to Bristol. Here King John received the homage of William the Lion of Scotland. The din of wars and battles has often been heard in the streets of Lincoln; in the Wars of the Barons against the young King Henry III., the Wars of the Roses, and above all in the great Civil War, when the city was stormed and sacked by the Roundheads. Here Edward I. summoned his first Parliament. Here kings have held their court and worshipped in the minster, and here a most formidable insurrection arose in consequence of the arbitrary acts of Henry VIII. and the destruction of the monasteries. The Bishops of Lincoln have

Y

been men of great power and influence, and have played prominent parts in the history of England.   Such prelates as St. Hugh, Robert

The Potter Gate & Tower
of Lincoln Cathedral

Grosseteste, and many others have conferred honour on the see over which they presided.

History of the Cathedral

. The first Cathedral of Lincoln was built by Remigius, the earliest Norman bishop, on the removal of the see from Dorchester-on-the-Thames about 1074. Previous to this Paulinus had preached here, and converted its prefect, Blaecca, who built a church of stone, which was probably on the site of St. Paul's Church, the name being corrupted from Paulinus. Stow village was the seat of the Lindsay Diocese until the Danish invasion. Then Dorchester was the bishop's residence until Remigius transferred his throne to Lincoln, and built a church "strong as the place was strong and fair as the place was fair, dedicated to the Virgin of Virgins." This church was ready for consecration on the founder's death in 1092 A.D. It was cruciform, with a semi-circular apse at the east end. The parts remaining are the central portion of the west front with its three recesses, a fragment of the first bay of the nave, and the foundations of the apse beneath the floor of the choir. It was a massive stern Norman building.

The third Norman bishop, Alexander, called "the magnificent," after a disastrous fire in 1141, restored the Cathedral "to more than its former beauty." This Alexander was a nephew of Bishop Roger of Salisbury, and during his time raged the war between Stephen and the Empress Maud. The adherents of the latter held the Castle of Lincoln; so Stephen seized the Cathedral and used it as a fortress. The chroniclers tell us that Alexander "remodelled the church by his subtle artifice," and made it the most beautiful in England. All that remains of his work are the three western doorways inserted in the arches built by Remigius, the intersecting arcade above the two side recesses of the west front, and the three lower storeys of the west tower, with their elaborately-ornamented gables facing north and south. These were all in the Late Norman or Transition style.

A terrible earthquake wrought much damage in 1185, and grievous was the condition of the church after this deplorable visitation. But happily in the following year the famous St. Hugh of Avalon, near Grenoble, was made Bishop of Lincoln by Henry II. He determined to restore the ruined House of God, and began to build in 1192. Freeman states that "St. Hugh was strictly the first to design a building in which the pointed arch should be allowed full play, and should be accomplished by an appropriate system of detail." Before his death in 1200 he built the choir and aisles and east (or smaller) transept, with a portion of the east wall of the great transept. All architects praise this beautiful work, the first development of the Early English style, the earliest building of that style in the world.

The great transept was completed and the nave gradually carried westwards in the Early English style during the successive

episcopates of William de Blois, Hugh de Wells and Robert Grosseteste (1203-1253). Of the nave, Freeman wrote: "There are
few grander works in the style of the thirteenth century than Lincoln nave, few that show greater boldness of construction and greater
elegance of detail." To the same period we may assign the two
western chapels, the arcaded screen wall of the west front and its
flanking turrets, the Galilee Porch and the vestry, the two lower
storeys of the tower, and chapter-house. During the rule of
Grosseteste, the two lower storeys of the tower were built. This
Grosseteste was a remarkable man, of great learning and ability,
defended the rights of the English Church against the claims of
the Papacy, and reformed many abuses in his diocese.

Great sanctity was attached to the body of St. Hugh, which
caused many miracles. It was buried according to the wishes of this
holy and humble-minded man in an obscure corner of the Cathedral.
In such honour were his remains held that it was resolved to trans-
port them to a more distinguished place; hence it was decided to
erect a large and costly shrine, and the beautiful "Angel Choir"
was erected for its accommodation. This magnificent structure was
built in 1255-1280, and belongs to the period of Transition between
the Early English and Decorated styles, just when Gothic architecture was touching its point of highest development. It is simply
perfect in its proportion and details. The translation of the body of
St. Hugh was performed with much pomp, and the ceremony was
attended by the highest in the land, King Edward I. himself being
one of the bearers of the revered saint's remains. The cloisters
and vestibule belong to the Decorated period, 1296 A.D., of which
they present a small but beautiful example. The "Bishop's Eye,"
the large circular window of the south transept, was erected in
1350. About the same period much was done to adorn the interior.
John de Welbourn, treasurer of the Cathedral, 1350-1380, set up
the beautiful choir stalls, erected the vaulting of the central and west
towers, with the internal panelling of the latter, and the row of
niches and regal statues over the great west door. The three western
windows and the upper stages of the west towers belong to a closely
subsequent period. In these works we see the transition from the
Decorated to Perpendicular style. Some of the chantry chapels are
purely Perpendicular.

At the Reformation great spoils of treasure were carried off by
the infamous Commissioners of Henry VIII., who purloined a
goodly store of jewels and nearly 9000 oz. of precious metals.

They plundered the gold shrine of St. Hugh and the silver shrine of Bishop Dalderby, and left the Cathedral bare of all the treasures which the piety of centuries had accumulated. The people of Lincoln liked not these proceedings, and there was a formidable insurrection, during which the church was used as a garrison. The advent of the Royal troops and the execution of some of the leaders and several abbots suppressed the revolt. A reforming bishop of evil memory, Henry Holbech, further desecrated the church, destroying images and monuments, so that in 1548 there was scarcely a whole figure or tomb remaining. Further terrible destruction took place in the Civil War, when the soldiers broke the beautiful glass windows, tore up the brass memorials of the dead, wrecked the Palace, and even threatened to pull down the Cathedral, but were happily stayed from their mad enterprise by the intercession of the Mayor, Mr. Original Peart, with Cromwell. After the Restoration Bishop Fuller set to work to repair the destruction which vandalism had caused, and although the hand of the "restorer" has been felt on the fabric of this noble building, Lincoln still maintains most of its ancient features, and remains one of the most interesting cathedrals in the kingdom.

The Exterior

We will now walk round the building and note its chief architectural features. Standing at the west end we will examine first the imposing *West Front*. The central portion with its three recesses are parts of the earliest Norman church of Remigius. It will be noticed that the middle arch has been subsequently raised and pointed. A band of curious sculpture runs across the front, representing scenes from Bible history. They are of Norman character. Noah and the ark, the Deluge, the expulsion from Paradise, scenes from the life of our Lord and Hades are the most curious. The doorways are later than the recesses, and were inserted by Bishop Alexander, "the magnificent," who also built the arcade of intersecting arches above the two side recesses, and the three lower storeys of the towers, in the style of Late Norman. The rest of the screen is Early English work, erected 1200-1250. Bishop St. Hugh had sketched the outline of the new church, and his successors carried it out. Amongst them Bishop Grosseteste did much good work, and his portion is distinguished by the lattice-work ornament which appears in the gable of this front, proclaiming

Lincoln Cathedral and
Exchequer Gate.

its author. There is a row of Royal statues (William I. to Edward III.) above the central door, which were erected by the treasurer, John de Welbourn (1350-1380). The statue of St. Hugh surmounts the south turret, and the Swineherd of Stow [1] the north turret. The three large windows belong to the time of Henry VI., and at this time the towers were completed, which are Perpendicular work, above the Norman three storeys.

Turning to the south side of the church we see the unique chapel and consistory court, and the curious grotesque popularly known as "the Devil looking over Lincoln." Heavy buttresses support the nave, and flying buttresses connect these with the clerestory. The *Galilee Porch* was built in 1230, and is cruciform. The name Galilee is attached to chapels at Durham and Ely, and we have already referred to the most probable conjecture with regard to its origin.[2] A profusion of dog-tooth ornament appears here, the characteristic moulding of Early English period. The muniment room is above the porch. The *Central Tower* is the finest in England, as it is the highest (271 feet), though the spires of Salisbury and Norwich exceed this altitude. Formerly it was capped by an immense timber spire, blown down in the first year of the sixth Edward's reign. Lincoln has suffered from falling towers as have other cathedrals. The two lower storeys were built by Grosseteste in Early English style on the fall of its predecessor in 1237. The lattice-work ornament so freely employed in the work of this bishop is observable here. The upper storey was begun by Bishop Dalderby in 1307 and finished in 1311 in the Decorated style. The timber spire covered with lead rose to a height of 524 feet, and was destroyed by a tempest. Storms and tempests have beat upon this tower for centuries, and occasionally have wrought mischief, but this has been from time to time remedied, and it remains the grandest and most majestic in the world. It is the abode of the famous "Great Tom of Lincoln," the fourth largest bell in the kingdom, recast in 1835. It weighs over five tons, and is 21 feet 6 inches in circumference. The *Choir* is the work of St. Hugh, the earliest example of Early English. In the *Presbytery* we see the style developed to his most perfect form, and merging into the Decorated period. The south doorway is especially worthy of notice, with its fine sculpture and splendid tympanum representing the Last Judgment. The Russell and Longland Chapels (Perpendicular) are on each side of this door-

[1] This swineherd is said to have given a peck of silver pennies to the building of the Cathedral.　　　[2] Page 291.

way. We notice the magnificent Decorated window of the Angel Choir, on the north side the Chapel of Bishop Fleming (Perpendicular), a doorway of good design; and then we see the chapter-house with its flying buttresses and pyramidal roof. On the north side is the cloister garth and Deanery. The cloisters are usually on the south side, and this position is uncommon. Lincoln was not a monastic church, being served by secular canons, and therefore had no necessity for a cloister court. However, this was built in the thirteenth century, the colonnade on the north side being erected in 1674 by Sir Christopher Wren, together with the library over it, which we shall visit presently. By an act of vandalism the old Deanery was pulled down in 1847 and the present house built, which is devoid of many of the interesting associations of its predecessor. The Cathedral close was surrounded by a wall and protected by strong gateways. Two of these remain, the "Exchequer Gate," opposite the west end, and the "Potter Gate." The old Bishop's Palace on the south of the close was destroyed during the Civil War, and quite recently a new episcopal residence has been erected near the ruins of the ancient house.

THE INTERIOR

As we have already stated, the nave of Lincoln was designed by Bishop Hugh in the Early English style, gradually carried westward by his successors, and completed before the death of Grosseteste in 1253. It consists of seven bays. Eight circular shafts of Purbeck marble surround each pier. The mouldings of the arches are deeply cut. Above is the triforium, consisting of two arches, each divided into three sub-arches. Clustered shafts with capitals carved with foliage support the arches. Above each main triforium arch in the clerestory are three lancet windows, and the roof is a fine specimen of English vaulting. Sir Gilbert Scott says that this nave "exhibits an Early English style in its highest stage of development: massive without heaviness, rich in detail without exuberance, its parts symmetrically proportioned and carefully studied throughout, the foliated carving bold and effective, there seems no deficiency in any way to deteriorate from its merits"—an opinion with which few visitors to Lincoln will be inclined to differ.

Under the towers will be noticed the Norman character of the first bay, which is part of the original church of Remigius. The west window, in its present form, is Perpendicular, and was inserted in the place of an earlier one. The *Font* also belongs to the time of Remigius, and is a fine example of the Norman period. It is of black basalt, square in shape, and has been recently placed upon three steps of Derbyshire marble. Grotesque monsters are carved on the sides of the font. The aisles have lancet windows, and below a beautiful arcade of trefoiled arches, the south side being more elaborate than the north. The bosses have figures carved on them. On the north-west corner is the Morning Chapel, having a central column of Purbeck marble supporting a stone vaulted roof. Here is the pastoral staff of Archbishop Benson of Canterbury, who, when Chancellor of Lincoln, restored this chapel. Opposite to this chapel, in the south-west, is the consistory court. None of the old glass has survived in the nave, and most of the shrines and tombs have been destroyed. The fanatics of the Reformation and Cromwell's soldiers left little of the sepulchral brasses and gorgeous tombs and effigies which once were here. A marble slab, carved with Scriptural subjects, is supposed to represent the tomb of the founder, Remigius. The memory of Dean Hoywood (d. 1681), the founder of the library, is recorded on a tablet, and three slabs preserve the names of Bishops Smyth (d. 1514), Alnwick (d. 1449), and Atwater (d. 1521). The *Pulpit* is seventeenth-century work, and the lectern is a memorial of Dean Butler (d. 1894).

The great transept contains some of St. Hugh's work. He devised a beautiful double arcade, and his work ends half-way on the east wall in north transept, and half-way the east wall in south transept, measuring from the centre of the building. The rest was built by his successors in the Early English style. The magnificent circular windows at the north and south ends are very striking, and extremely beautiful. The former is known as the *Dean's Eye*, the latter as the *Bishop's Eye*, which, with the gable and window above, is in the curvilinear style, and was erected about 1350. The Dean's Eye was placed there about 1220, and has some exquisite ancient glass of that period representing our Saviour in Glory. In the east of this transept are six chapels, dedicated to SS. Nicholas, Denis, James, Edward the Martyr, John the Evangelist and Giles.

The stone screen before the Chapel of St. Edward should be examined, with its curious sculpture. Before the Reformation there seems to have been some laxity of conduct among the chaplains and choristers, who were accused of playing games in the church, and here in one of these chapels we see nine holes, which were probably used for the favourite pastime of "Nine Men's Morris."

In the south transept there are the slender remains of the once famous tomb of Bishop Dalderby (d. 1320), to which there was great resort of pilgrims in mediæval times.   His shrine was destroyed at the Reformation.   This bishop built the upper part of the tower.

The *Screen* is good Decorated work, and consists of arches ornamented with figures of ecclesiastics and grotesques.   It has been somewhat severely handled by fanatical destroyers, but, in spite of mutilation and restoration, it remains a noble example of the workmanship of the period.   The organ stands above this screen. The doorways on each side of the screen are Early English, and are very beautiful.

Entering the *Choir*, we see the earliest known example of pure Lancet Gothic or Early English, free from the trace of Norman influence.   It was built by Bishop St. Hugh.   The first stone was laid in 1192.   The perfection of the ornament is wonderful.   This part of the church suffered severely from the fall of the tower in 1237, and many traces of the disaster may still be seen.   Screens divide the choir from the aisles, and were erected to strengthen the building.   The *Choir Stalls* are very fine, and were erected by Treasurer Welbourn in 1370.   The carving is most elaborate and beautiful, and the *misereres* are extremely curious and interesting. Behind each stall is a list of the Psalms which, according to the constitution of Lincoln, each prebendary is bound to repeat daily. The pulpit and bishop's throne are fairly modern.   The brass lectern bears the date 1667.   The *Reredos* was restored about the middle of the eighteenth century, but contains some thir-teenth-century work.   A very interesting feature of the north side is the *Easter Sepulchre*, fashioned for the deposition of the consecrated elements of the Eucharist from the evening of Good Friday until the morning of Easter day ; during which time it was watched by a quasi-guard.   Three figures of sleeping soldiers appear in the carving.   The style is Decorated.   This tomb has been very doubtfully assigned to Remigius.   There are the monuments of Katherine Swinford, third wife of John of Gaunt (d. 1403), from whom King Edward is descended in a direct line, and of her daughter, the Countess of Westmoreland (d. 1440), much mutilated by the soldiers.   In the *North Aisle* of the choir the beautiful double arcade work of Bishop Hugh is seen on the wall.   In the *South Aisle* are the remains of the *Shrine of Little St. Hugh*, the Christian boy with whose crucifixion the Jews were charged in 1255.   The style is Decorated, but the shrine was mutilated by the soldiers in the Civil War. The great chronicler, Henry of Huntingdon, also lies buried here.

The eastern transept is part of Bishop Hugh's church. In each arm, on the east side, there are two apsidal chapels, with arcading round the walls. The style of the construction resembles that of the choir. On the south of the north arm is the so-called *Dean's Chapel*, the use of which can only be conjectured. The iron-work of the door is worthy of notice, and also the faded paintings of some Lincoln prelates, by Vincenzo Damini (1728). It is sad to see the fragments of the tomb of Grosseteste, to whom the Cathedral of Lincoln and the whole Church of England owe so much, stored away in one of the chapels. Respect for his memory and gratitude for his work might suggest the restoration of this tomb. The southern arm of this east transept has been much altered, and most of the present work is later than the choir. In one of the chapels the sub-dean was murdered by one of the vicars in 1205. Here is the tomb of Bishop Kaye (d. 1853). The screen and lavatory of the choristers' vestry are beautiful examples of Decorated work.

The Angel Choir

We now enter the *Angel Choir* (1256-1280), pronounced by Sir Gilbert Scott to be "the most splendid work of that period which we possess, and did it not lack internal height, I do not think it could be exceeded in beauty by any existing church." It is the latest portion of the main fabric, and was built when the Early English style was developing into the Decorated. The piers are beautiful clustered shafts, with carved capitals of Purbeck marble. The east window of eight lights is very fine (the glass is modern), and is said to be the noblest example of Geometrical Decorated in the kingdom. The choir takes its name from the carved angels in the spandrels of the triforium, which exhibit combined grace and dignity. The famous *Lincoln Imp* can with difficulty be distinguished on the north side, above the most eastern pier. Early English glass fills the east windows of the north and south aisles. On the north of the Angel Choir is the *Fleming Chantry*, which contains the double effigy of the bishop (d. 1431), the founder of Lincoln College, Oxford, first in his episcopal robes, and then of his corpse in a state of decay. Bishop Fleming exhumed and burnt the bones of Wyclif. Opposite this chantry is the *Russell Chantry*, founded by Bishop Russell (d. 1494), Chancellor of Richard III., and near this the Chantry of Bishop Longland (d. 1547).

Here in the Angel Choir stood, in former days, the rich shrine of St. Hugh, plundered at the Reformation, and a monument of Queen Eleanor, the beloved wife of Edward I., who caused to be erected the famous Eleanor crosses at every place where her body rested, as it was borne to its final resting-place at Westminster. This monument was destroyed by Cromwell's soldiers, and recently a modern copy of the original has been erected. The Burghersh monuments are worthy of careful study. The family played an important part in history, and held high honours. Also we notice the tombs of Nicholas de Cantelupe (much mutilated), the artists Peter De Wint (d. 1849) and W. Hilton (d. 1839) ; Bishop Fuller's memorial of St. Hugh, Bishop Fuller (d. 1675), Bishop Gardiner (d. 1705) and Sub-Dean Gardiner (d. 1732), Bishop Wordsworth (d. 1885), Dean Butler (d. 1894), Bishop Sutton (d. 1299) and Robert Dymoke (d. 1735), whose family held the office of King's Champion.

The *Cloisters* were erected in the thirteenth century, with the exception of the north colonnade, which was built by Sir Christopher Wren. Over this is the *Library*, which contains many treasures : an original copy of Magna Charta, a letter of Edward I. ; a chalice of Bishop Grosseteste (1254) and his ring ; Bishop Sutton's ring and chalice and paten (1299) ; a Roman mile-stone (260 A.D.). Of books there is a large collection, including a MS. copy of the Vulgate (1106), other valuable MSS., and many versions of the Bible in English. The old desks are curious and interesting.

Lincoln Cathedral

The beautiful *Chapter-House* is of Early English design, and was completed about 1230. It is ten-sided, and has a central pillar girt with Purbeck marble shafts, and a stone vaulted roof; lancet windows, filled with good modern glass enlighten the chamber, two in each side. An arcade runs round the walls beneath the windows, and in the carving we see the tooth ornament. There is a very ancient Chair of State here, which is said to have been the throne of Edward I. when he held his Parliament in this room.

[My grateful thanks are due to the Very Reverend the Dean of Lincoln for the great assistance which he has kindly rendered me in investigating the history of his Cathedral.]

DIMENSIONS

Total length	482 ft.
Length of nave	252 ft.
Breadth of nave with aisles	80 ft.
Height of nave	82 ft.
Length of choir	158 ft.
Length of presbytery	72 ft.
Height of central tower	271 ft.
Height of west towers	200 ft.
Area	44,400 sq. ft.

PRINCIPAL BUILDING DATES

Norman (1074-1092)—Central part of west front, fragments of first bay of nave.

(1123-1183)—West doors, arcade of west front, three lower storeys of west towers.

Early English (1192-1253)—Choir and presbytery, nave, transept to west chapels, turrets and screen of west front, Galilee, vestries, two lower stages of tower and chapter-house.

(1255-1296)—Angel Choir, cloisters.

Decorated (1307-1380)—Upper storeys of tower, "Bishop's Eye," stalls, statues over west door, upper stages of west towers.

(1450-1500)—Chapels.

(1674)—North colonnade of cloister and library.

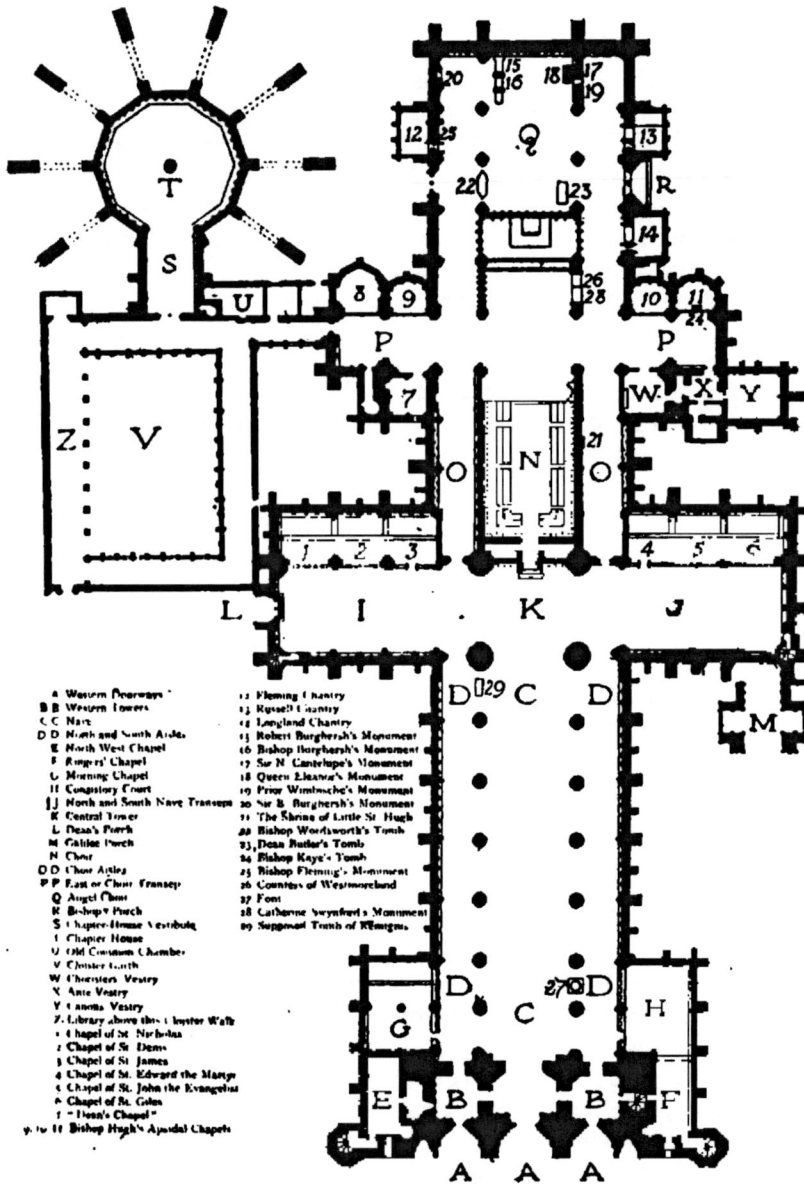

PLAN OF LINCOLN CATHEDRAL

A Western Doorways
B B Western Towers
C C Nave
D D North and South Aisles
E North West Chapel
F Ringers' Chapel
G Morning Chapel
H Consistory Court
I J North and South Nave Transepts
K Central Tower
L Dean's Porch
M Galilee Porch
N Choir
D D Choir Aisles
P P East or Choir Transept
Q Angel Choir
R Bishop's Porch
S Chapter-House Vestibule
T Chapter House
U Old Common Chamber
V Cloister Garth
W Choristers' Vestry
X Ante Vestry
Y Canons' Vestry
Z Library above the Cloister Walk
1 Chapel of St. Nicholas
2 Chapel of St. Denis
3 Chapel of St. James
4 Chapel of St. Edward the Martyr
5 Chapel of St. John the Evangelist
6 Chapel of St. Giles
7 "Dean's Chapel"
8 to 11 Bishop Hugh's Apsidal Chapels

12 Fleming Chantry
13 Russell Chantry
14 Longland Chantry
15 Robert Burghersh's Monument
16 Bishop Burghersh's Monument
17 Sir N. Cantelupe's Monument
18 Queen Eleanor's Monument
19 Prior Wimbush's Monument
20 Sir B. Burghersh's Monument
21 The Shrine of Little St. Hugh
22 Bishop Wordsworth's Tomb
23 Dean Butler's Tomb
24 Bishop Kaye's Tomb
25 Bishop Fleming's Monument
26 Countess of Westmoreland
27 Font
28 Catharine Swynford's Monument
29 Supposed Tomb of Remigius

SOUTHWELL CATHEDRAL

THE ancient and interesting Church of St. Mary, Southwell, became a Cathedral in 1884, when the bishopric was founded, and the building is worthy of its high honour. In the time of Henry VIII. it nearly attained that rank, Southwell being one of the sees which that monarch proposed to found out of the spoils of the monasteries, but his good intentions were not fulfilled. For centuries it was in the large Diocese of York, and was esteemed as the Mother Church of the district, and enjoyed many rights and privileges.

With the exception of a few fragments, no part of the present church dates further back than the twelfth century. There was an early Saxon church here, which was probably founded by Paulinus when he converted the wild folk of Nottinghamshire and Lincolnshire to the Christian faith. Then came the savage Danes, who swept away all traces of Christianity. The next church is said to have been built by the Saxon King Edgar, in 960 A.D., which was one of much importance before the Conquest; and in 1061 Aldred, Archbishop of York, founded prebends here, and built refectories for the canons. In the time of Henry I. it was raised to the dignity of Mother Church of the district, and the church was entirely rebuilt in the Norman style. When Walter de Grey was Archbishop of York (1216-1255), he was very energetic in improving the condition of his diocese and in erecting churches. He rebuilt the nave of Southwell, granting an indulgence of thirty days' pardon to all who should assist the work. John de Romeyn, sub-dean, whose son was afterwards Archbishop of York, assisted him in the work. There is a close resemblance between the nave of York Cathedral and the earlier choir of Southwell, and it is not improbable that the latter served as a model for the former. There is also a very close resemblance between the chapter-house of the two Cathedrals, which are evidences of the same designer and workmanship. Archbishop John de Romeyn was doubtless the architect of both buildings.

The community of clergy at Southwell consisted of the prebendaries, who formed the chapter, the vicars-choral and chantry priests and choristers.   The prebendaries had much power and many privileges.   They held property, and each had a large house, hunted in neighbouring forests, and lived as country gentlemen as well as canons of Southwell.   At the Reformation they surrendered their goods to Henry VIII., who contemplated making Southwell a Cathedral.   He despoiled the church of vast quantities of plate and other valuables.   In 1574, however, the college, like other similar institutions, was seized by the unscrupulous advisers of Edward VI.   In Mary's reign it reverted to the Crown, and she restored the college to its former owners and uses, and this arrangement was happily left undisturbed by her successors. During the Civil War Cromwell's soldiers stabled their horses in the nave of the church.   Charles I. stayed in the town at the "Saracen's Head," and here he delivered himself up to the Scotch commissioners, who stayed at the Palace.   Cromwell wished to destroy the nave, but was stayed in his fanatical design by the intercession of one of his officers.   The story is told of the wife of a hunted Royalist, named William Clay, registrar of the minster, hiding herself in the parvise, or room over the porch, and there giving birth to a child, while the soldiers lived in the church.   A general pillage took place in the church at this time ; the font was destroyed, lead torn from the roofs, brasses from the tombs, and every vestige of an image swept away.

The College of Southwell has suffered in many other ways, sometimes from the carelessness of the prebendaries and their lack of zeal, sometimes from the effects of unwise and revolutionary legislation.   In 1846 its position as a peculiar ceased to exist. Southwell is now a Cathedral with a diocese of its own, and if the ecclesiastical commissioners and the friends of the Church could see their way to granting an adequate endowment and means for carrying on its great work, Southwell would be able to maintain the dignity of an important see, and fulfil its mission to the Church and nation.

EXTERIOR

The finest view of this noble minster is obtained from the north-west corner of the churchyard.   We notice the general Norman character of the building.   The massive western towers, capped with spires, the lantern tower, the north transept and beautiful chapter-house, the noble roof, all combine to form a magnificent example of dignified and noble building.

The *West Front* has been altered in character from its original Norman work. We see a huge Perpendicular window with an embattled parapet over it, an alteration made in the fifteenth century. The windows in the lower stages of the towers are modern imitation of Norman work. The towers have seven stages, and the sixth is enriched with fine arcading composed of intersecting arches. The present spires are modern imitations of the originals destroyed by fire in 1711. These were immediately restored, but removed in 1802, and have now again been replaced. The old Norman doorway is remarkably fine. It has five orders, the zigzag and filleted edge roll being the chief mouldings.

Passing to the south side we see the wall of the nave pierced by apparent Norman windows, but these are modern imitations. The most western window in the north side is the only original Norman window; the rest are copied from it, and were erected in 1847.

Four Perpendicular windows were inserted in the fifteenth century. There is a row of small square windows above which light the triforium, and the clerestory has a curious series of circular windows which are unique in this country. The roof is high pitched, having been erected in modern times by the architect Christian, and the parapets are Perpendicular in style.

The south doorway should be noticed, of Norman workmanship with zigzag string-course over it. Near here are the remains of the old Palace. The banqueting hall has been recently restored. The kitchens belong to the time of Henry VI. On the east of the transepts there were formerly apsidal chapels, which were removed when the present choir was built in the Early English period.

The *Choir* is a noble specimen of Early English work and "seems to be an emanation from Lincoln," wrote Sir Gilbert Scott, which it much resembles. We notice the extensive use of the dog-tooth ornament. Lancet windows give light to the interior. Two flying buttresses support the walls on the south side, and were added subsequently in the Decorated period to help them to bear the weight of the vaulted roof.

The *Chapter-House* is on the north side, and was built in the Decorated period during the reign of Edward I., when York was extremely prosperous and profited by the presence of the court. The resemblance between the chapter-houses of York and Southwell is very striking, and both were evidently designed by the same

z

architect. This one is octagonal, and has windows of three lights with trefoil and circular ones in the heads. The roof is modern. A vestibule connects it with the church. An Early English wall with an arcade of lancets connects the vestibule with the north transept. The *North Porch* is good Norman work, and has a parvise which is very unusual in a porch of this date. This parvise was the scene of the story of the hiding of Mistress Clay in the troublous times of the Civil War. The inner doorway is very fine with its zigzag and beak-head moulding.

THE INTERIOR

We now enter the church by the west door, and looking down the nave (1110-1150) we are impressed by the massive appearance of the interior. The piers are rather short, only 19 feet high, six on each side, with square bases and round capitals. The triforium is large, and above is the clerestory with its unique plain circular windows. The Norman mouldings, zigzag, billet, hatchet, etc., are easily recognised. The present roof was erected in 1881.

The *Font*, erected in 1661, is a poor substitute for the one destroyed by the soldiers of Cromwell. The *Pulpit* is modern; the figures represent the Virgin and Child, King Edwin and his queen, Augustine and Paulinus. The second pillar from the east on the south side is called Pike's Pillar, and retains faint traces of a mural painting of the Annunciation; the nave aisles have some good vaulting. A plain stone bench runs along the walls. This was common in old churches, and was the origin of the saying, " let the weakest go to the wall," where they could sit and rest, as the days of pews were not yet. The only original Norman window which remains is at the west end of the north aisle. Formerly there were several chantry chapels in the aisles, but all have been destroyed. The marble slab in the north aisle marks the site of one.

The *Tower* is a lantern, and also has a peal of bells. The chimes were given by Wymondesole in 1693. This tower is part of the original Norman church, and was built in 1150. The cable moulding round the four large arches should be noticed. It is composed of a series of double cones.

The *Transepts* are beautiful specimens of the work of Norman builders, and are full of interest. Originally there were apsidal chapels on the east side of both transepts. One has been destroyed,

Southwell
Central Tower &
N Transept

but the arch which connected it with the church can be seen in the wall, with its zigzag and cable mouldings. The Norman chapel on the east of the north transept has been replaced by a Late Early English building which will repay careful study. There were formerly two altars here, as the piscinæ and aumbreys show. The old Norman arch is replaced by two pointed arches of unequal width. The windows are later insertions, and belong to the Decorated period. There is an upper storey, formerly the treasury, now the library. The chapel has been recently restored, and is a most interesting architectural study. Returning to the north transept we see a curious tympanum over the belfry doorway, with strange carving representing the teaching of Psalm xci. 13 : "The lion and the dragon shalt Thou tread under Thy feet." Other interpretations are given of this subject, but this is the one usually accepted by scholars. It is also said by some to be Saxon, but this is incorrect. There is a very similar sculpture in the church of Charney Bassett, Berks. Here is the fine alabaster tomb of Archbishop Sandys (d. 1588). He is represented in his episcopal robes, and the details of his dress are important, as they show what the vestments of a bishop really were in the time of Elizabeth, a point often disputed by English Churchmen of to-day. The east arch of the central tower has some curious sculptured capitals hidden by the organ which belong to the twelfth century. Beginning on the south side, the subjects are lamb and dove, Triumphal Entry into Jerusalem, Nativity or Resurrection, Last Supper, bishop saying Mass, the Blessed Trinity, and the Virgin and Child.

A stone *Screen* of rich Decorated work separates the transept from the choir, over which is now the organ (a modern instrument). The screen is richly ornamented, and a noble specimen of the work of the period. There are three arches opening to the space beneath the tower, separated by slight piers of clustered shafts, the capitals carved with foliage of a Late Decorated character. The walls of the screen support the old rood-loft, access to which is gained by two staircases.

Entering the *Choir* we see on each side of the doorway three prebendal stalls with *misereres*, on which are carved some foliage. The bishop's stall was once occupied by Cardinal Wolsey. The choir, as we have said, was built by Archbishop Grey in Early English style (1230-1250). There are six arches, with piers of eight clustered shafts. The dog-tooth moulding is conspicuous in the arches, and on the vaulting of the roof. It will be noticed that the triforium and clerestory are blended together. The east window consists of two rows of lancets, the lower ones containing old glass brought from Paris in 1815, where it was formerly in the Chapel of the Knights Templar. The Baptism of our Lord; Raising of Lazarus (Francis I. is to be seen in a crimson cap); Christ entering Jerusalem (Luther is near our Lord, Louis XI. and the Duke of Orleans); the Mocking of our Lord (the figure of Dante appears).

The *Sedilia* were erected in 1350, and are good Decorated work. They have the unusual number of five seats on the same level. The arches are ogee-shaped, and are richly carved. The sculptured figures are remarkable, and represent the Creation and the Redemption. Beginning at the east we see the Father holding the world (two groups uncertain), Joseph's Dream, the Nativity and Flight into Egypt.

The *Lectern* belonged to the monks of Newstead Abbey, who threw it into the lake to hide it from the commissioners of Henry VIII. Its date is about 1500. The choir aisles had several altars, as we see from the piscinæ and aumbreys which are left. We will now visit the *Chapter-House*, and pass through the vestibule which leads to it, entering by a beautiful doorway in the north aisle. The transition between the Early English work of the choir and the Decorated style of the chapter-house is very gradual. The doorway, with its two arches and shafts of Purbeck marble, is remarkably fine. There is a small cloister court, with a stone-covered well. In the vestibule we see the walls covered with beautiful arcading of lancet arches of an Early English character. The capitals are beautifully carved with foliage. There is a curious boss of sculpture representing a secular priest shaking the regular monk by his hair, which figuratively depicts the supremacy of the former in the church of Southwell.

The *Chapter-House* (1285-1300) is described by Ruskin as " the gem of English architecture," and all architects agree in singing the praises of this noble building. It much resembles that of York, but is smaller and perhaps more beautiful. It is octagonal, has no central pillar, and is remarkable for its fine sculpture. The historian of Southwell says : " The foliage everywhere is most beautiful : the oak, the vine, the maple, the white-thorn, the rose, with a vast variety of other plants, are sculptured with exquisite freedom and delicacy ; and no two capitals or bosses or spandrels are found alike. Everywhere we meet, in ever-changing and ever-charming variety, with some fresh object of interest and admiration. Figures are introduced amid the foliage, heads with branches issuing out of their mouths, birds and lizard-like monsters. In the capitals a man reclines beneath a tree, puffing lustily at a horn, or a goat is gnawing the leaves, or a bird pecking the berries, or a pair of pigs are grunting up the acorns, or a brace of hounds just grabbing a hare. All this is the work of no mere chiseller of stone, but of a consummate artist; than whom it may be doubted whether any sculptor, of any age or country, ever produced anything more life-like and exquisitely graceful." The entrance doorway is remarkably fine and is worthy of close study. The main arch is divided into two by a slender shaft, and over them is a quatrefoiled circle, of beautiful design. The leaf ornament is largely used, both in the smaller arches and in the main arch. Filleted rounds and hollows are the other mouldings used.

Southwell once contained the shrine of a Saxon saint—St. Eadburgh, Abbess of Repton (d. 714). "The Pilgrim's guide to the Saints of England" (a MS. in the British Museum, written in 1013) states that "the shrine of St. Eadburgh is still at Southwell," but no trace of it can now be found. There are several incised monumental slabs in the minster which have been cut and set in the floor. There is a Latin inscription to the memory of William Thorton, a chorister of the church, and the humble epitaph of William Talbot, who was a shining light in his day and died 1497, is of pathetic interest :—

> " Here lies William Talbot, wretched
> and unworthy priest, awaiting
> the resurrection of the dead under the sign of the Cross."

[My thanks are due to the kindness of Archdeacon Richardson, Rector of Southwell Minster, for his kindness in explaining to me the interesting features of his church. I am also indebted to the works of Mr. Dimock, Mr. Livett and Mrs. Trebeck for much valuable information.]

DIMENSIONS

Length, 306 ft.; breadth, 61 ft.; length of transept, 123 ft.; height of central tower, 105 ft.; height of west towers and spires, 150 ft.

PETERBOROUGH CATHEDRAL

THE towns and cities of England owe their origin to various causes. Some arose around the walls of great castles, some as trading centres or harbours, some clustered around the palace of a bishop, and others sheltered themselves beneath the shadow of a monastery.

Peterborough, or Medeshamstede, is of this last class. It is a monastic town, and owes its existence to the great fenland Monastery of St. Peter, the minster church of which is now this beautiful Cathedral. Peada, the son of Panda, King of Mercia, first founded a monastery here in 654, of which Saxulph was the first abbot. The Pagan Danes came in 870 with fire and sword, and wrought fearful havoc in all this region, burning the holy house of Medeshamstede, and slaughtering the monks. For a hundred years the monastery lay in ruins; then came the religious revival under the rule of Dunstan and King Edgar. Monastic houses increased in number greatly, and Bishop Ethelwold of Winchester began to rebuild the waste places of the ruined Saxon Medeshamstede, and constructed a minster, some foundations of which still remain. The Abbey flourished for nearly a century, but sad misfortunes befell. Hereward the Wake, the hero of Kingsley's story, the gallant "last of the English," was making his last brave stand against William the Norman, and in conjunction with the Danes attacked the Abbey, and wrought much destruction. Fires and robbers were also occasionally dread visitants, and at last, in the time of Henry I., a great fire destroyed the whole buildings. The then abbot was John de Sais, who set to work immediately to erect a new monastery. This was in 1117. Then was begun the glorious minster which is the pride and glory of the fenlands. Subsequent abbots continued the work. Abbots Martin de Vecti and William de Waterville completed the transepts and tower and part of the nave, which was finished by Abbot Benedict (1177-1193). There is a striking uniformity of design throughout all this Norman work, which shows that the builders followed one plan, and imitated the work of their predecessors. The western transept, however, shows

360

evidences of the coming change, and when we come to the beautiful west front we find unmistakable Early English work. This part was probably finished in 1238, in the time of Abbot Walter of St. Edmunds, when the church was dedicated by Bishop Grosseteste of Lincoln. Abbot Robert de Lindsay, who liked not the windows of his monastery " stuffed with straw " to keep out wind and rain, filled many of them with glass, and built the lavatory in the cloister. Gradually the erection of the monastic buildings was being completed, and refectory and infirmary added, and Prior Parys built the Lady Chapel and one of the steeples at the close of the thirteenth century, which also saw the removal of the Norman windows from the aisles and the substitution of Early Decorated ones. This was a time of much splendour and magnificence for the Abbey, when Godfrey was abbot, and King Edward often visited it and received aid for his Scottish wars. This Godfrey built the large gateway. A century later the abbot was endowed with the privilege of a mitre, and thus took his seat in the House of Peers; and during this fourteenth century the lantern tower was erected with an octagon framed of wood, the triforium windows changed into the Decorated style, and the west front improved by the erection of the spire and the central porch. During the fifteenth century we hear sad complaints of the relaxation of the discipline of the monks, who too often frequented taverns and " the vulgar company of dancers and ballad singers." Abbot Kirton was a notable man, who built, or rather finished, " that goodly building at the east end of the church, now commonly known by the name of the new building," begun by his predecessor Ashton; and his rebus—a *kirk* and a *tun*—appears on the grand gate, now leading to the Deanery. At this time several Norman windows were filled with Perpendicular tracery. We see Cardinal Wolsey visiting the Abbey, and on Maundy Thursday washing the feet of poor persons, and the luckless Catherine of Arragon being buried here in 1535.

Then came the dissolution of monasteries, and Peterborough shared the fate of the rest. Whether it was on account of the subservience of the abbot, or because it contained the ashes of his queen, Henry VIII. spared the church, and made it a Cathedral, the last abbot being the first bishop. The burial of Mary Queen of Scots in 1587 is the next historical event which was here witnessed. We can imagine the scene of the torchlight procession bearing the executed body of the frail but fair queen into the church, and the last solemn obsequies of that sad and stormy life. Cromwell's

soldiers " did after their kind," and Dean Patrick tells us of " the
rifling and defacing " that ensued :—

" The next day after their arrival, early in the morning, they
break open the church doors, pull down the organs, of which there
were two pair.

" Then the souldiers enter the quire, and their first business was
to tear in pieces all the common-prayer books that could be found.
The great bible indeed, that lay upon a brass eagle for reading the
lessons, had the good hap to escape with the loss only of the
apocrypha.

" Next they break down all the seats, stalls and wainscot that
was behind them, being adorned with several historical passages out
of the old testament.

" When they had thus defaced and spoilt the quire, they march
up next to the east end of the church, and there break and cut in
pieces, and afterwards burn the rails that were about the communion table.   The table itself was thrown down, the table-cloth
taken away, with two fair books in velvet covers ; the one a bible,
the other a common-prayer book, with a silver bason gilt, and a
pair of silver candlesticks beside.   But upon request made to
Colonel Hubbert, the books, bason and all else, save the candlesticks, were restored again.

" Now behind the communion table there stood a curious piece
of stone-work, admired much by strangers and travellers : a stately
skreen it was, well wrought, painted and gilt, which rose up as high
almost as the roof of the church, in a row of three lofty spires, with
other lesser spires growing out of each of them.   This now had
no imagery work upon it, or anything else that might justly give
offence, and yet because it bore the name of the high altar, was
pulled all down with ropes, lay'd low and level with the ground.

" Over this place, in the roof of the church, in a large oval yet
to be seen, was the picture of Our Saviour seated on a throne ; one
hand erected, and holding a globe in the other, attended with the
four evangelists and saints on each side, with crowns in their hands,
intended, I suppose, for a representation of Our Saviour's coming to
judgment.   This was defaced and spoilt by the discharge of muskets.

" Then they rob and rifle the tombs, and violate the monuments
of the dead.   First then they demolish Queen Katherin's tomb :
they break down the rails that enclosed the place, and take away the
black velvet pall which covered the herse : overthrow the herse

itself, displace the gravestone that lay over her body, and have left nothing now remaining of that tomb, but only a monument of their own shame and villany. What did remain [of the herse of Mary Queen of Scots] that is, her royal arms and escutcheons which hung upon a pillar near the place where she had been interr'd, were most rudely pulled down, defaced and torn.

"In the north isle of the church there was a stately tomb in memory of Bishop Dove, who had been thirty years bishop of the place. He lay there in portraicture in his episcopal robes, on a large bed under a fair table of black marble, with a library of books about him. These men soon destroy'd all the tomb.

"The like they do to two other monuments standing in that isle.

"In a place then called the new building, and since converted to a library, there was a fair monument, which Sir Humprey Orm (to save his heir that charge and trouble), thought fit to erect in his own life time, where he and his lady, his son and wife and all their children were |lively represented in statues, under which were certain English verses written :—

> " *Mistake not, Reader, I thee crave,*
> *This is an Altar not a Grave,*
> *Where fire raked up in Ashes lyes,*
> *And hearts are made the Sacrifice, &c.*

"Which two words, altar and sacrifice, 'tis said, did so provoke and kindle the zealots' indignation, that they resolve to make the tomb itself a sacrifice : and with axes, poleaxes, and hammers, destroy and break down all that curious monument, save only two pilasters still remaining, which shew and testifie the elegancy of the rest of the work.

"When they had thus demolished the chief monuments, at length the very gravestones and marbles on the floor did not escape their sacrilegious hands. For where there was any thing on them of sculptures or inscriptions in brass, these they force and tear off.

"Having thus done their work on the floor below, they are now at leisure to look up to the windows above.

"Now the windows of this church were very fair, being adorned and beautified with several historical passages out of scripture and ecclesiastical story; such were those in the body of the church, in the isles, in the new building, and elsewhere. But the cloister windows were most famed of all, for their great art and pleasing variety. One side of the quadrangle containing the history of the Old Testament; another, that of the new; a third, the founding and founders of the church; a fourth, all the kings of England downwards from the first Saxon king. All which notwithstanding were most shamefully broken and destroyed. Yea, to encourage them the more in this trade of breaking and battering windows down, Cromwell himself, (as 'twas reported,) espying a little crucifix in a window aloft, which none perhaps before had scarce observed, gets a ladder, and breaks it down zealously with his own hand.

"But before I conclude the narrative, I must not forget to tell, how they likewise broke open the chapter-house, ransack'd the records, broke the seals, tore the writings in pieces, specially such as had great seals annexed unto them, which they took or mistook rather for the popes' bulls.

"Thus, in a short time, a fair and goodly structure was quite stript of all its ornamental beauty, and made a ruthful spectacle, a very chaos of desolation and confusion, nothing scarce remaining but only bare walls, broken seats, and shatter'd windows on every side.

"Many fair buildings adjoyning to the minster, were likewise pulled down and sold by publick order and authority, such were the cloysters, the old chapter-house, the library, the bishop's hall and chapel at the end of it: the hall was as fair a room as most in England; and another call'd the green-chamber, not much inferior to it. These all were then pull'd down and destroyed; and the materials, lead, timber and stone exposed to sale, for any that would buy them. But some of the bargains proved not very prosperous; the lead especially that came off the palace was as fatal as the gold of Tholouse; for to my knowledge, the merchant that bought it, lost it all, and the ship which carried it, in her voyage to Holland."

And thus the church continued for some time ruined and deso-late. A relative of Cromwell, Oliver St. John, was granted the possession of it, and converted it into a parish church. The Lady Chapel was pulled down in order to obtain material for repairing the main building; the painted boards of the ceiling they found useful for making the backs for the choir. At the Restoration Dean Cosin was recalled, and since that time many alterations and much reparation have been undertaken, though often with more zeal than good taste. Dean Tarrant (1764-1791) collected the frag-ments of stained glass, and placed them together in two windows at

Scarborough Church

the east end. Dean Kipling removed the octagon, and erected four hideous turrets, which no longer disfigure the tower. Dean Monk (1822-1830) did much for the Cathedral, though little of his work remains. Since then the tower has been rebuilt (finished in 1886), much internal decoration added, and the west front rendered secure. Much controversy has raged about the restoration of this west front. Experts on both sides have expressed divers opinions, the relative merits of which it is difficult to decide. Certainly to take down a building stone by stone and rebuild it again is not legitimate restoration. But whether it was possible to make the north gable secure without this drastic treatment it is for experts to decide, and it is presumptuous for others to express an opinion or attempt to arbitrate when these experts puzzle us with the variety of their judgments.

THE EXTERIOR

We enter the precincts by the western gateway, built by Abbot Benedict in Norman style, but subsequently altered at the end of the fourteenth century. There is a Late Decorated arch, and two arcades of the same date built over the Norman wall; but the Norman arcades proclaim its ancient origin. The upper room was the home of the Peterborough branch of the Spalding "Society of Gentlemen," who advanced learning and published papers at the beginning of the eighteenth century. Previously it was the Chapel of St. Nicholas. On the left of the close is an old building, also erected by Benedict, the remains of the Chapel of St. Thomas of Canterbury. The old Grammar School, founded by Henry VIII., utilised the building until recent years. The style of the present building is Decorated.

Immediately before us we see the noble *West Front*, " the pride and glory of Peterborough," the finest portico in Europe. With the exception of the porch, the style is pure Early English. On the north and south are two lofty turrets, flanked at the angles with clustered shafts and crowned with spires. Between these are three pointed arches, supported by clustered shafts, six on each side, with floriated capitals. The central arch is narrower than the rest, but its mouldings are ornamented with crockets and dog-tooth. A string-course runs along the top of the arches, and the spandrels have trefoils, quatrefoils and niches with statues. Above the string-course is a series of trefoiled arches, some of which have statues. Between the three gables are pinnacles much ornamented. The gables have circular windows of beautiful design and a cross at the apex; they are ornamented with dog-tooth and have niches with statues—St. Peter in the centre, with SS. John and Andrew on either side. The turrets on the north and south have six stages panelled with arches. The spires are good examples of the difference between those of the Early Decorated and Perpendicular periods. The south spire is connected with the pinnacles of the tower by clustered pinnacles springing from an arch; these are decorated with crockets, and the spire belongs to the early fourteenth century; whereas the spire on the north has no such connection, and is Early Perpendicular.

We now notice the *Porch* with parvise over it. This was built late in the fourteenth century in order to give additional strength to the west front and act as a kind of buttress to the piers of the central arch. The design is very beautiful. The entrance has an obtuse arch, and above a Perpendicular window with elliptical arch. Buttresses empanelled with niches stand on each side. It has a stone vault of good design. One boss is curious, representing the Trinity. The attitude of the Saviour shows that the figure was designed by a freemason, and bears witness to the antiquity of that fraternity. The parvise is now a library.

A Late Perpendicular gateway at the north-east, erected by Abbot Kirton, whose rebus appears over the side door, leads to the Deanery. It has a Tudor arch, with the arms of the see in spandrels, and is ornamented with Tudor rose and portcullis, and Prince of Wales's feathers. Here is the old burial-ground, and a fine view of the Cathedral is obtained from the north-east. The Norman character of the building is evident, though there have been many changes. The Norman windows in the clerestory have been filled with Perpendicular tracery. The low Norman aisles have been raised, the windows taken out and replaced by thirteenth-century substitutes in the lowest range and by Decorated ones in the triforium. Below this the old Norman arcade remains. A good Norman door, called the Dean's Door, is in the centre of this north wall. An Early English parapet crowns the aisle walls, and a Decorated one surmounts the clerestory, which is continued in the *North Transept*, where similar alterations have taken place, and Perpendicular tracery inserted in Norman windows.

The central *Tower* was rebuilt in 1884. The necessity for continued rebuilding and restoration at Peterborough is much to be deplored. Probably the cause is the draining of the fens, which makes the clay to contract and thus produces insecure foundations. It has some good windows. We have already recorded the history of the previous structures. As much of the old work as possible was preserved in the rebuilding of the present tower.

Walking around the church we come to the east of transept, where formerly stood the Lady Chapel, pulled down at the Restoration by the townspeople, and its materials sold in order to provide funds for restoring the church after Puritan destruction. Notice the marks of the gable of Lady Chapel in the transept wall. The thirteenth-century builders pierced the Norman wall with lancets.

The east end of Peterborough is rather peculiar. There remains the old Norman apse, with Decorated windows inserted, and this is surrounded by what is called the *New Building*, though it is 400 years old, formed by extending the walls of the choir and building a square end to the Cathedral. This was erected by Abbot Kirton. His work possesses the best features of Perpendicular style. It is richly ornamented, and when we examine his work we cannot say that the glories of Gothic achievement had quite departed. We see the twelve buttresses, each terminated with a seated figure, usually said to be one of the Apostles.

On the south-east of the Cathedral are the ruins of the infirmary of the monks, always a pleasant place in a monastery. It is a thirteenth-century building, and consisted of a hall, with aisles and a chancel. The aisles were used as cells or couches for the sick monks, and the religious services of the infirmary were performed in the chancel. On the south are the remains of the monastery. Only the south and west walls of the cloister court remain. There is a good thirteenth-century doorway and Perpendicular lavatory. The south view of the Cathedral is very fine. Passing through the cloisters, which once echoed with the tread of the monks, or saw them poring over their tomes and writing their beautiful MSS., we retrace our steps to the west front and so enter the Cathedral.

THE INTERIOR

As we enter we notice the distinctive character of the Norman work of which this Cathedral is a notable and excellent example. In the extreme west there is a blending of the two styles of Norman and Early English, but the monks of Peterborough clung tenaciously to their old ideas and to Norman and Romanesque models, and right up to the end of the twelfth century built in this style, not from any desire to imitate the work of their predecessors (as some writers assert) but from an obstinate adherence to conservative tradition. Even when the glorious tide of English Gothic was rising, and they could no longer resist the flood, they clung to the old zigzag mouldings. It is evident from the construction of the third column that they intended to end their church there; but happily the thirteenth-century brethren decided to rear the noble twin-towered front and the perfect portico. Some of the later columns show Transition work; on one side we see a Norman base or capital, on the other an Early English.

There is a grand uninterrupted view of the whole length of the Cathedral from west to east. It will be observed that the tower arch is Decorated, and this adds to the beauty of this view. Before leaving the west we notice some dog-tooth carved in wood, which is somewhat rare. The south end of this west transept is the baptistry, the font of which has a thirteenth-century bowl. The north end is now used as a vestry. The west window has Perpendicular tracery.

The nave has ten bays with Norman arches; the triforium has likewise Norman arches, but each of these has two sub-arches. The windows of the clerestory have Perpendicular tracery. The *Ceiling* is intensely interesting, and is original Norman work. It has various figures within lozenge-shaped medallions, viz. :—Agnus Dei, SS. Peter, Paul, Edward the Martyr, Edward the Confessor, Moses, and other kings, archbishops, bishops and allegorical and

NORTH-WEST TRANSEPT

grotesque figures. As we have seen from the exterior, the walls of the aisles have been raised, and later windows inserted. The roofs of the aisles were vaulted by Norman builders. The visitor may discover for himself some mason marks in the south aisle.

As at Norwich the *Choir* begins with the two east bays of the nave, which was the original arrangement, and not unusual in Benedictine minsters, and extends over the space under the tower, and besides the apse occupies four bays east of the tower. The gates are good modern iron-work. The erection of a screen is in contemplation. Two pillars have been placed in position; but the scheme presents difficulties which have not yet been solved. The piers are alternately round or polygonal. This portion was the earliest part of the Cathedral, and was constructed by Abbot de Sais (1114-1125). The hatchet moulding is conspicuous. The triforium arches are double, like the nave, and the clerestory has triple arches, the centre one being the highest. The apse is particularly fine. The Decorated style is evident in the windows, which were inserted in the fourteenth century instead of the old Norman ones, and the hanging tracery of graceful design was then added. The roof of the choir is late fourteenth-century work except at the east end where the roof is flat. Here Cromwell's soldiers discharged their muskets at the figure of our Lord in glory, which they deemed to be an idol. This ceiling was decorated in 1884 by Sir Gilbert Scott. The bosses of the rest of the roof are curious. Nearly all the old glass was destroyed in the Puritan desecration; the remaining fragments have been placed in the two highest east windows. The fittings of the choir are modern, except an ancient lectern of fifteenth-century date given by Abbot Ramsay and Prior Malden, as the inscription testifies, though it is now scarcely legible. The choir stalls are remarkably fine, and as the carved figures contain a history of the Cathedral written in wood, it may be well to record their names. We will begin with the dean's stall and proceed eastward :—

1. St. Peter, the Patron Saint.
2. Saxulph (656), first Abbot, afterwards Bishop of Lichfield.
3. Adulph (971), Abbot Chancellor to King Edgar, afterwards Bishop of Worcester, and Archbishop of York.
4. Kenulph (992), Abbot, afterwards Bishop of Winchester.
5. Leofric (1057), Abbot.

6. Turold (1069), Abbot, appointed by William the Conqueror.
7. Ernulph (1107), Abbot, afterwards Bishop of Rochester.
8. Martin de Vecti or Bec (1133), Abbot. During his time the choir and transept aisles were finished, and solemnly dedicated.
9. Benedict (1175), Abbot, Keeper of the Great Seal for Richard I. He built the greater part, if not all, of the nave.
10. Martin de Ramsey (1226), Abbot.
11. John de Caleto or Calais (1249), Abbot, one of the King's Justices. He built the infirmary, and probably the refectory and part of the cloisters.
12. Richard de London (1274), Abbot. He built the north-western tower.
13. Adam de Boothby (1321), Abbot.
14. William Genge (1296), first mitred Abbot.
15. Richard Ashton (1438), Abbot.
16. Robert Kirton (1496), Abbot. He built the Deanery Gateway, and the new building; his rebus, a church on a tun, carved in stone, is to be seen on most of his work.
17. John Towers (1638), Bishop, previously Dean.
18. Thomas White (1685), Bishop. He was one of the seven bishops committed by James II.; and also one of the seven non-juring bishops.
19. William Connor Magee (1868), Bishop, afterwards Archbishop of York.
20. Simon Patrick (1679), Dean, afterwards Bishop of Chichester, and finally of Ely.
21. Augustus Page Saunders (1853), Dean.
22. John James Stewart Perowne (1878), Dean, afterwards Bishop of Worcester.

The upper figures on the north side represent the following :—

1. Peada (655), King of Mercia, founder of the monastery.
2. Cuthbald (675), second Abbot.
3. King Edgar and his Queen.
4. Ethelfleda.
5. Brando (1066), Abbot.

6. Hereward, the Saxon Patriot (1070), nephew of Abbot Brando, and knighted by him.
7. John de Sais (1114), Abbot. He commenced the building of the existing choir.
8. Hedda (d. 870), Abbot murdered by Danes.
9. Robert de Lindsay (1214), Abbot, with model of west front.
10. Godfrey of Crowland (1299), Abbot. Gateway.
11. William Ramsay (1471), Abbot.
12. William Parys (1286), Prior, builder of Lady Chapel.
13. St. Giles, with hart.
14. Hugo Candidus, historian of Abbey.
15. Henry de Overton (1361), Abbot.
16. Queen Catherine of Arragon.
17. Dean Cosin, afterwards Bishop of Durham.
18. Simon Gunton (1546), historian of the church.
19. Herbert March (1819), Bishop.
20. George Davys (1839), Bishop.
21. Dean Monk, afterwards Bishop of Gloucester and Bristol.
22. Dean Argles (1891).

Much history is also contained in the carvings of the pulpit and bishop's throne. The altar has a marble canopy over it, which is a magnificent piece of work, but perhaps hardly suitable for its position. The mosaic pavement is remarkably fine. We now pass into the *Choir Aisles*, which have Norman vaulted roofs, and formerly had apsidal ends, but these were removed when Abbots Ashton and Kirton built the *New Building* or square end to the church, or perhaps earlier, as there are some aumbreys and double piscinæ of the thirteenth century, and also on the south wall some painted shields and a scroll border of the same date. The windows are later insertions as in the nave. Traces of the old entrance to the destroyed Lady Chapel may be seen in the north wall.

We have noticed the building of the ambulatory called the New Building from the exterior of excellent Perpendicular work. Perhaps the most striking features of the interior is the fan-tracery of the roof, the curious bosses, the rebuses of the two Abbots Ashton and Kirton, and the monuments. The principal ones in the choir and aisles are a modern memorial stone of Catherine of Arragon (the old tomb was destroyed by the Puritans, of which fragments have been discovered); the tablet in memory of Mary Queen of

Scots; Archbishop Magee's marble monument; Sir Humprey Orme's mutilated tomb; several abbots' tombs and tablets to bishops; Late Saxon tombs of two Archbishops of York, and the famous Monks' Stone which popular tradition associates with the massacre of the Peterborough monks by the Danes in 870. Recent investigators have assigned a later date, and attribute it to Norman work, but we are inclined to favour the Saxon theory.

We will now visit the *Transepts*, which are of Norman character. Norman fish-scale ornament and cable and saw-tooth mouldings are plentiful. In both north and south transepts there is an eastern aisle separated by pillars and forming several chapels, which are divided off by Perpendicular screens. The Morning Chapel occupies the aisle of the north transept, formerly the Chapels of SS. John and James, and here is preserved two pieces of old Flemish tapestry, and portions of the old nave screen, and ancient tiles. In this transept are some interesting Saxon coffin lids. In the south transept are the Chapels of SS. Oswald and Benedict. In the former the relics were kept. Here Abbot Sutton's heart was buried. The window is modern. A pre-Reformation inscription is carved round the edge of a stone much worn by time. The old chapter-house, now a music-room, is on the west of this transept. It is Late Norman. A Perpendicular doorway has been inserted here instead of the old Norman door.

A very interesting discovery was made here during the alterations a few years ago, and that is the remains of the actual original Saxon church which was sacked by the Danes, rebuilt by Bishop Ethelwold and visited by King Edgar and Dunstan, and then destroyed by fire. Evidences of this destruction were not wanting when the discovery was made. The east wall of the chancel stood just where the piers of the aisle of the transept stand. The church was cruciform. This discovery is of great interest and importance.

Old Scarlett's memory must not be forgotten, the aged sexton, who lived ninety-eight years, and buried two queens in the Cathedral, dying in 1594. The painting is a copy of the original made in 1747. The well-known rhymes beneath are :—

> "You see old Scarlett's picture stand on hie,
> But at your feet there doth his body lye;
> His gravestone doth his age and death-time show,
> His office by these tokens you may know.
> Second to none for strength and sturdye limm,
> A scarbabe mighty voice, with visage grim,
> He had inter'd two queens within this place
> And this towne's householders in his live's space

Twice over ; but at length his own turne came,
What he for others did for him the same
Was done ; no doubt his soul doth live for aye
In heaven : though here his body clad in clay."

DIMENSIONS

Total length of interior . .	426 ft.
Nave, length	228 ft.
Nave, width	35 ft.
Transept, length . . .	185 ft.
Transept, width . . .	58 ft.
Height of interior . . .	78 ft.
Area	41,090 sq. ft.

PRINCIPAL BUILDING DATES

Norman (1117-1193)—Choir, transepts, central tower (rebuilt in 1886), nave, ceiling of nave, chapter-house.

Early English (1214-1295)—West front, font, infirmary, refectory and part of cloisters, north-west tower, windows and parapet in aisles of nave.

Decorated (1299-1400)—Large gateway, west porch, roof of choir, south-west choir, parapet of clerestory, inserted windows.

Perpendicular (1400-1528) — New building, north-west spire, north-east gateway, Perpendicular tracery in windows, and west window.

A West Front or Portico
B Western Transept
C Nave
D North Aisle
E South Aisle
F Choir
G Central Tower
H Presbytery
I Retro-Choir or
  New Building
J Site of Lady Chapel
K North Transept
L South Transept
M Chapter-House (now Music-
  Room)
N Cloisters—
   (a) Chapel of St. John
   (b) Chapel of St. James
   (c) Chapel of St. Oswald
   (d) Chapel of St. Benedict
   (e) Chapel of SS. Kyneburga
      and Kyneswitha
   (f) High Altar
(The dotted lines represent the foundations
of the Saxon Church built in 972 A.D.)

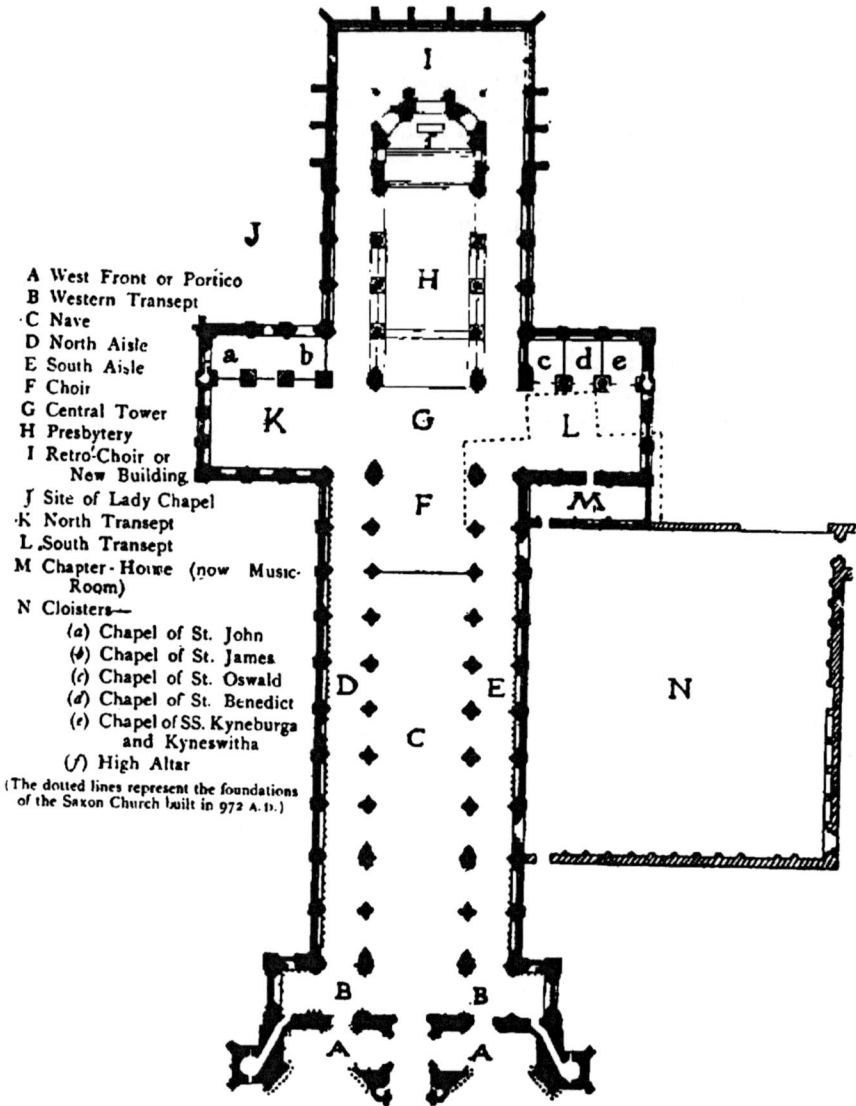

PLAN OF PETERBOROUGH CATHEDRAL

ELY CATHEDRAL

E LY is one of the monastic towns of England, and owes its existence to the famous church and monastery which were built here in Early Saxon days. The patriotic monkish chronicler of Ely, who compiled the *Liber Eliensis*, wishing to add glory to his church, states that in 607 St. Augustine founded a church at Cratendune, a mile south of the present site. The first monastery on the Isle of Ely was founded by St. Etheldreda, daughter of Anna, King of the East Angles. She received the Isle of Ely as her dowry from her first husband, an Earldorman of the South Girvii or Fenmen, and when she married Egfrid, afterwards King of Northumbria, feeling the call to a religious life, she left her court and retired to the lonely isle, and there founded a monastery, of which she was the abbess. As was not unusual at that time, the house was a double one, for both monks and nuns. St. Wilfrid assisted her considerably in carrying out her plans, but no fragment of this early church and monastery remains. The saintly queen died in 679, and was buried in the nuns' resting-place. Some years later her body, placed in a marble sarcophagus, was translated to the Saxon church. In 870 the isle was ravaged by the Danes, who destroyed the church and monastery, slaying both monks and nuns, plundering the town, and returned loaded with the spoils of the pillaged island. Some of the monks who escaped returned to their ruined house, and King Alfred is said to have confirmed them in their possessions. King Edgar, by the advice of Dunstan, Archbishop of Canterbury, and Ethelwold, Bishop of Winchester, reorganised the monastery under the Benedictine rule, restored to it all its lands, and made Brihtnoth the first abbot.

The Norman Conquest brought many troubles to the Isle of Ely. The monks espoused the cause of Hereward, "the last of the English," the hero of Charles Kingsley's romance, and here he made his last great stand against the Norman invaders; but the monks "did after their kind," and surrendered to the Conqueror in 1071. Little harm was done to the monastic buildings by the

377

warriors of either side, and twelve years later the building of the present Cathedral was begun by Abbot Simeon, brother of Walkelin, Bishop of Winchester. He commenced with the transepts, some parts of which still declare themselves to be his work. Abbot Richard (1100-1107) continued the building, and finished the east end, where the body of St. Etheldreda was conveyed and reburied before the high altar.

Ely was now raised to the dignity of a bishopric, the revenues of the abbot being used for the endowment of the see, and henceforth the prior was the head of the monastery. The building of the church proceeded gradually. The nave was growing by degrees during the twelfth century, and Bishop Riddell (1174-1189), by his energy, did much towards its completion and that of the great west tower. The isle was much disturbed during the troublous time of Stephen's reign, and the bishop took the part of the enemies of the king, who exacted heavy fines from the prelate and his monks. Bishop Eustace (1198-1215) accomplished much, and erected the beautiful Galilee Porch. In 1235 the building of the noble presbytery was beugn by Bishop Northwold (1229-1254), and here, in the presence of King Henry

ARM OF ABBOT'S CHAIR

III. and his court, the shrines of the founders and of three other abbesses were removed, and the whole church in ground plan completed as we see it to-day.

Having finished their church, the monks turned their attention to their domestic buildings, and to the Lady Chapel, which stands here in an unusual position. It was erected by Alan de Walsing-

WEST TOWER FROM DEANERY GARDENS

ham (the sub-prior) in 1321, and finished in 1349. In 1322 a sad calamity happened—the central tower fell, and caused much destruction. But the catastrophe called forth the constructive genius of Alan de Walsingham, a prince among architects, who built the beautiful octagon and lantern tower, which add so much

grace and beauty to the building. The superb Lady Chapel, with its marvellous sculptured work, the sub-structure of St. Etheldreda's shrine, and Prior Crauden's Chapel —a perfect gem of beauty and originality — are all Alan de Walsingham's work. The monks elected this great builder Bishop of Ely, but the Pope refused to ratify the election. He is admirably described on his tomb as the *Flos Operatorum*, or " flower of craftsmen."

In this period Decorated windows were inserted in the triforium of the presbytery, the outside walls being raised for this purpose, and flying buttresses added. The Cathedral then appeared externally much as we see it to-day. The Perpendicular style finds few examples in Ely except in some of the smaller chapels and one or two windows.

The Assumption of the Blessed Virgin Mary. Lady Chapel.

At the Reformation the monastery shared the fate of similar institutions, and a dean and chapter were appointed. The fact that the bishop occupied the place of the abbot of the monastery is observable in the position of the bishop's seat, which is south of the entrance to the choir. He has not a throne, which most bishops

have in their cathedrals.   Ely was spared much destruction in the
Civil War.   The Parliamentarians pulled down some of the cloisters,
and broke a few windows, but the Cathedral fared better than most
others at the hands of Cromwell.   It has suffered, however, from the
fancies of "restorers."   In 1770 the ritual choir, with the stalls,
was moved from under the octagon to the extreme east end, to be
again moved to its present position in 1847.   About the same time
the massive Norman stone screen, which for eight centuries had
stood across the nave, was ruthlessly destroyed, and the roof of the
upper hall of the Galilee Porch removed, and the western opening
of the tower arch filled with a modern window.   Wyatt's destructive hand was only just restrained from working further mischief,
though some authorities make him responsible for the removal of
the screen and the destruction of the roof of the Galilee.   A vast
amount of money has during the last century been spent upon the
fabric, and happily the restorers have been, in the main, governed
by good taste and sounder architectural knowledge than that of their
destructive predecessors.

THE EXTERIOR

As you ascend the hill from the station you will undoubtedly
be struck by the external appearance of this magnificent pile.
Professor Freeman remarked that the first glimpse of Ely over-
whelmed us, not only by its stateliness and variety of outline, but
by its utter strangeness and unlikeness to anything else.   Its huge
western tower, its beautiful but curious central octagon, are quite
peculiar, and the general view, especially from the north-west,
is extremely fine, and can never be forgotten.

We will begin our survey, as usual, with the *West Front*, which
has been much altered, but remains a very imposing structure.   It
will be noticed that the north side differs from the south, and either
was never completed or fell into decay.   They both belong to the
Late Norman or Transitional period.   The *Galilee Porch* is a perfect
gem of exquisite architecture.   It has been pronounced "the most
gorgeous porch of this style in existence, combining the most
elegant general forms with the richest detail."   The style is Early
English, and is the work of Bishop Eustace (1198-1215), who was
ordered by the Pope to excommunicate King John, and had to fly
from England in consequence.   It will be seen that this porch is
one of the earliest examples of good Early English work, and for

its excellence and perfection rivals the choir at Lincoln. There is a profusion of dog-tooth ornament. The doorways are most graceful. The main arch is divided into two cinquefoiled sub-arches, separated by a slender shaft, and in the head there is very beautiful tracery. The walls are covered with arcading, of lancet-shaped arches cinquefoiled. In the interior there is a beautiful double arcading, similar to that which we have seen at Lincoln.

The *West Tower* is earlier than the porch, and its lower stages are Transition Norman. The upper stages are Early English,

ELY CATHEDRAL FROM SOUTH-EAST

except the highest octagonal stage, which is Decorated. Bishops Riddell and Northwold were the builders of earlier stages, and the octagonal summit was built during the bishopric of John Fordham (1388-1425). This magnificent tower has been a source of continual anxiety to the monks and masons of Ely, on account of the great weight of the superstructure, and continual repairs and strengthening operations have been needed.

The *North Side* of the nave preserves its Norman character, but Perpendicular windows with ogee arches have been inserted. Formerly the Church of St. Cross stood on this side, erected by

Walsingham, but it fell into decay and was pulled down in 1566. We can still see the walled-up door in the north wall of the Cathedral which led to this parish church. Norman mouldings

THE OCTAGON AND LANTERN FROM NORTH-WEST

(such as the billet) may be seen round the arches of the windows in the clerestory. The curious and beautiful *Octagon* is a striking feature of Ely. It consists of an eight-sided tower crowned with an octagonal lantern, the dimensions of which are much smaller than those of the tower which supports it. Decorated windows of large size occupy the sides facing north-west, north-east, south-west and south-east, which are narrower than the other sides. Turrets crowned with pinnacles stand at each corner of the lower tower, and quadrangular turrets at each corner of the lantern, which is made of wood. The whole has been recently restored with the greatest possible success.

The *North Transept* is Norman. Some Perpendicular and Decorated windows have been inserted, and the north-west corner, which fell in 1699, was rebuilt by the builder of St. Paul's, London, Sir Christopher Wren, who inserted the Renaissance door in the north side.

The *Lady Chapel* has been pronounced to be one of the finest specimens of Decorated architecture in the kingdom. It is the work of Walsingham, and was finished in 1349. The east and west windows are later insertions, but belong to the same century. The building is oblong, and is enriched with much beautiful carving; niches destitute of figures appear in the buttresses, and at the east and west ends. The tracery of the side windows should be noticed.

The *Presbytery* is fine Early English work, built by Bishop Northwold (1229-1254), and has been scarcely altered by succeeding builders. The windows are double lancets in each bay, and in the clerestory three lancets under an arch, the centre one higher than the others. The arrangement of the east end is as follows:— In the lower stage three tall lancets with dog-tooth moulding, above them five lancets of unequal height, and in the gable three lancets of the same height. Buttresses carved with niches stand on each side, and flying buttresses springing from the side buttresses support the roof. Alterations have been made in the triforium in order to increase the light in the church.

The *South Transept* is Norman, with some later windows inserted. Notice the curious Perpendicular window on the south side. The *Cloister Court* was on the south side of the church, but was destroyed by the Commissioners of Cromwell. Two doorways are remarkable, named the *Monks' Door* and *Prior's Door*, both Late Norman work, and enriched with much carving. The tympanum over the Prior's Door contains a representation of our Lord in glory.

THE INTERIOR

We now enter the church at the west end, and are struck by
2 B

the noble character of this magnificent Norman work. It consists of twelve bays (there were thirteen before the central tower fell). The two eastern bays were finished by Abbot Richard (1100-1107), and the rest completed by Bishop Riddell (1147-1189). The earlier character of the five bays nearer the central tower is discoverable. The ceiling was painted forty years ago by Mr. le Strange and Mr. Gambier Parry, whose artistic work can also be seen at Gloucester. The subjects are the Creation, the Fall, Noah Sacrificing, the Sacrifice of Isaac, Jacob's Dream, Marriage of Ruth, Jesse, David, Annunciation, Nativity, Adoration of the Shepherds and Magi, the Lord in Glory. We see also representations of the patriarchs and prophets, and in the medallions at the sides the heads of the human ancestors of our Lord. The west window was inserted at the close of the eighteenth century and filled with modern glass (when the roof of the upper hall of the porch was re-

ST CATHERINE'S CHAPEL

moved), thus effectively blocking the view of the three great lancets, 40 feet further west, through which, up to that time, the setting sun must day by day, through so many centuries, have flooded the nave with its evening light.

At the west end, under the tower, we notice the strengthening of the original pillars with additional Perpendicular work. The arches of the tower, though Norman, are pointed, showing that they were erected at the end of that period, and the richness of ornament and detail of the southern portion of the west transept bears out the same conclusion. *St. Catherine's Chapel* is in the south corner, rebuilt in the old style, and the font is modern.

The *Nave Aisles* have arcades of Norman arches, and the chevron moulding appears about them in several parts where it has not been cut away. In the south aisle is an interesting memorial of Ovin, the steward of St. Etheldreda, which has been recovered from a neighbouring village. It is part of a cross, with the inscription on the base—"*Lucem tuam Ovino da Deus et requiem. Amen.*" (O God, give light and rest to Ovin. Amen).

The *Octagon* would require a volume adequately to record its many beauties and perfections. We have already described its construction. It is pronounced by all architects as the gem of the Cathedral, and one of the most beautiful buildings in the world. The vault is of wood, and a remarkable series of paintings appears on the boarding. The Crucifixion and the Apostles are here represented. Large corbels have sculptured scenes of the life of St. Etheldreda. The vault has been painted by Mr. Gambier Parry.

IN SOUTH AISLE OF NAVE LOOKING TO NORTH TRANSEPT

The *Transepts* were the portions of the church first begun by Abbot Simeon when he first commenced the present Norman Cathedral. The lower part of the walls and part of the triforium were built by him and finished by Abbot Richard (1100-1107). The arcading in the south transept is Transitional, and the upper windows Late Decorated.

CARROL IN CLOISTER

Perpendicular windows have been inserted in the north transept. There are three chapels at the east of the north transept, one of which bears the name of St. Edmund, and is divided off by a wooden screen of the middle of the fourteenth century. The east aisle of the south transept is walled off and used as the library, and the west as the vestry.

A modern oak screen of graceful design, replacing a massive Norman screen ruthlessly destroyed in 1760, separates the octagon from the *Choir*, which we now enter. It will be remembered that the central tower fell and carried away three bays of the choir. Hence the work of these bays is later than the more eastern portion forming the presbytery, which was built by Bishop Northwold (1229-1254) in Early English style. The choir was erected by Bishop Hotham (1316-1337), and is a noble specimen of Decorated work. Between the choir and presbytery are fine Norman piers of the earlier choir. On the bosses of the roof we see figures of St. Etheldreda and the Virgin. The east wall is pierced by lancet windows, which are grouped in a most perfect manner. The stalls are splendid examples of Decorated work, and the *misereres* have some curious grotesques. The fifty carved panels of scenes from the Old and New Testament are by Abeloos of Louvain, a modern wood-carver. The lectern is modern, and also the reredos. Of this eastern part Freeman says :—" Nowhere can we better study the boldly clustered marble pier with its detached shafts, the richly foliated capitals with their round abaci, the yet richer corbels which bear up the marble vaulting shafts, the bold and deeply cut mouldings of every arch great and small. Lovelier detail was surely never wrought by the hand of man."

On each side of the presbytery are some ancient monuments of especial interest. On the south side, beginning at the west, we see Bishop William de Louth (1298), a fine tomb of Early Decorated character ; Bishop Barnet (1373), translated from Bath and Wells (the effigy has been lost) ; Tiptoft, Earl of Worcester, with his two wives, one of whom was the sister of " the King-maker," Earl of Warwick (this earl was one of the victims of Edward IV., and lost his head in 1470. He was a great patron of learning and art, and Fuller exclaims, " The axe did at one blow cut off more learning than was left in the heads of all the surviving nobility ") ; Bishop Hotham (1337), much mutilated. On the opposite side are the monuments of—Bishop Northwold (1254), which affords a good illustration of the ecclesiastical dress of the period (at the foot of the tomb is an interesting representation of the martyrdom of King Edmund, who shared the fate of St. Sebastian. Northwold was abbot of St. Edmundsbury before he came to Ely, hence the origin of the carving) ; a shrine, believed to be that of St. Etheldreda, of

Decorated design, probably constructed by Walsingham about 1340; Bishop Kilkenny (1286), who died in Spain, his heart being buried here; Bishop Redman (1505), a fine Perpendicular structure.

At the end of the north aisle is the chantry of Bishop Alcock (1500), a fine Perpendicular work in good preservation, though the figures which once adorned it were destroyed at the Reformation. He founded Jesus College, Cambridge, and built Ely Palace. On the east is the inscription, "*Johannes Alkoc Epus Eliensis hanc fabriciam fieri fecit* 1488." In this aisle are the supposed arm of Northwold's chair, which he brought from his abbey (the sculpture represents the wolf with St. Edmund's head in his paws), and the tombs of Bishop Marson (1771), Bishop Patrick (1707), and Basevi, architect of the Fitzwilliam Museum, Cambridge.

In the retro-choir are the monuments of Bishop Allen (1845), Canon Fardell (1819), Cardinal Louis de Luxembourg, Bishop, 1444, and an early muniment chest.

At the east end of the south aisle is Bishop West's chantry (1534), a beautiful chapel in the Late Perpendicular and Renaissance style. The carving is very elaborate, with delicate tracery. This Bishop was the champion and chaplain of Catherine of Arragon, Henry VIII.'s queen. Above his tomb, in seven small niches, are deposited the bones of six Saxon bishops and of Earl Bryhtnoth, killed by the Danes in 991, who exclaimed when he died, "God of Nations, I thank Thee for all the joy I have had in life." Here are the tombs of Bishops Woodford (1885), Sparke (1836), Keene (1781). In the south aisle are—an ancient gravestone of Norman date, representing Michael carrying to heaven the soul of a bishop, with the inscription, "*St. Michael oret pro me*"; Bishop Hotham (1337), Canon Selwyn (1875), Dean Steward (1557), last prior and first dean of Ely; Bishop Gunning (1684), author of *The Prayer for All Conditions of Men*; Bishop Goodrich (1554), a zealous reformer, destroyer of images and shrines, compiler of "Duties to God and Neighbour," in the *Catechism*; Bishop Heton (1609), Dean Tyndall (1614), and other monuments.

The *Lady Chapel* is a superb structure, with its beautiful sculptured work, one of the finest specimens of Decorated architecture in the kingdom in spite of the cruel mutilation to which it was subjected at the Reformation. It was completed in 1349, but the east window is a little later and shows evidence of the approach of the Perpendicular period. An arcade of sculptured canopies runs round the walls, of extremely delicate carving. The mythical history of the Virgin and of Julian the Apostate appear in the spandrels, and the bosses of the roof have some sculptured figures representing the Crucifixion, Ascension, Annunciation, the Virgin crowned, the Virgin and Elizabeth, and some which cannot be distinguished.

[My thanks are due to the Dean of Ely for his kind assistance in interpreting the history of the Cathedral which he knows and loves so well.]

DIMENSIONS

Total length	517 ft.
Length of nave	230 ft.
Breadth of nave	78 ft.
Height of vault	70 ft.
Length of transept	190 ft.
Diameter of octagon	65 ft.
Height of west tower	215 ft.
Area	46,000 sq. ft.

PRINCIPAL BUILDING DATES

1083-1189—Transepts, nave, lower stages of tower, monks' and prior's doorways.

1189-1254—Galilee porch, presbytery, upper stages of tower.

1316-1349—Lady chapel, octagon, choir, windows of triforium of presbytery, buttresses, Prior Crauden's Chapel, stalls.

1388-1534—Highest stage of tower, chapel and some windows.

1699—North-west corner of north transept and doorway.

1 Prior's Doorway
2 Alan de Walsingham
3 Altar Tomb of Bishop Woodford
4 Bishop Redman's Monument
5 Bishop Kilkenny's Monument
6 St. Etheldreda's Shrine
7 Bishop Northwold's Tomb
8 Bishop Allen's Tomb
9 Canon Mill's Monument
10 Cardinal Luxembourg's Tomb
11 Bishop Gunning's Monument
12 Tomb of Tiptoft, Earl of Worcester
and his Two Wives
13 Bishop Barnet's Tomb
14 Bishop Goodrich (brass)
15 Dean Tyndall (brass)

A Galilee Porch
B West Tower
C South-West Transept
D St. Catherine's Chapel
E E Nave
F G North and South Aisles
H J North and South Transept
K Octagon
L Library
M Lady Chapel
N N North and South Choir
O Choir   Aisles
P Presbytery
Q Site of Chapter-House
R Site of Refectory
S Cloister Garth
T St. Edmund's Chapel
  or Northwold Chantry
V Bishop Alcock's Chapel
W Bishop West's Chapel
X Vestry

16 Bishop William de Louth's Tomb
17 Bishop Hotham's Tomb
18 Sir Christopher Wren's Doorway
19 Monk's Doorway

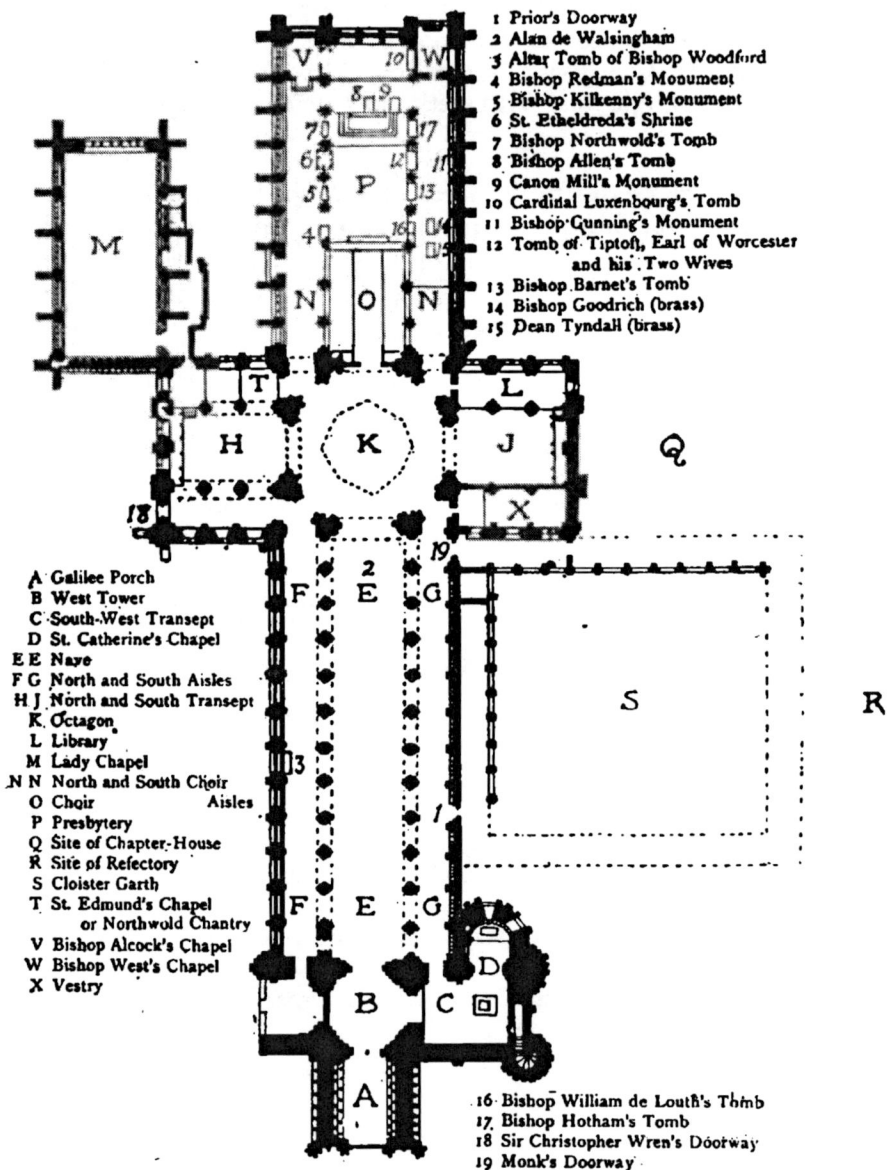

PLAN OF ELY CATHEDRAL

NORWICH CATHEDRAL

NORWICH, the capital of East Anglia, is a delightful city, beautifully situated on the winding Wensum and full of the charm of the associations of mediæval times. The hill on which the castle stands carries our thoughts back to Saxon days, to King Uffa in the sixth century. Saxon, Dane and Norman held sway here. It was also the city of the Dutch. The cruelties of Alva sent Flemings and Walloons, who came with their silks and threads and worsteds and implements, and made the textile manufactures the glory and fortune of the county. Here kings kept their Christmas feasts, and in no less royal fashion did the old Dukes of Norfolk, when Norwich was the gayest of episcopal cities. Very independent were the turbulent burghers, who often contended with the monks and bishops for rights and privileges, as when in 1272 they quarrelled over the tolls of a fair, and sacked the Cathedral, and in 1549 when Kett the tanner raised his formidable rebellion, which was with difficulty subdued. Few cities can rival Norwich in the interest of its associations and the treasures of antiquity which here abound.

The Cathedral—Its History

The See of Norwich was created in Norman times, Dunwich, Elmham and Thetford having previously been the episcopal seats. In the time of Rufus there was a general transference of bishoprics to the larger towns, in accordance with a decree of a church synod, hence in 1094 Norwich had the honour conferred on it by Bishop Herbert de Losinga, who two years later commenced his Cathedral. This bishop obtained his preferment by simony, and it is said built the church in expiation of his crime. Beginning at the east end " he finished the church as far as the altar of St. William,"[1] which was on the north side of the present screen. This included the choir and transepts with the two chapels and two bays of the nave. His successor, Bishop Eborard, finished the nave. Herbert

[1] *Registrum Primum.*

393

built also a Bishop's Palace, and a monastery of Benedictine monks was attached to the Cathedral. A curious scene was witnessed here in 1144 when a number of Jews were tried for the ritual murder of the boy saint, St. William of Norwich, in Thorpe Wood, whom they cruelly tortured. The houses of the Jews were plundered, and in memory of the miracle-working boy a chapel was built on the scene of his murder, and a shrine erected in the Cathedral.

Fire played its usual destructive part here, as elsewhere, in 1171, and the church was repaired and perfected by Bishop John of Oxford in 1197. In the Early English period there seems to have been little progress, except the building of the Lady Chapel at the east end by Walter de Suffield (1244-1257), which was destroyed in the time of Queen Elizabeth. The entrance only remains.

Very stormy times befell the Cathedral at the end of the thirteenth century. The city was sacked by the revolting barons in 1266, and a few years later a dispute arose between the citizens and the prior about the right of tolls to a fair held in the Tombland at Whitsuntide, which were of much profit to the monastery. It was the same story which is told of many towns, the quarrels of the burghers and the ecclesiastics. In 1272 the disputants fell to blows, and some of the citizens were slain. They arrested some of the men of the monastery for murder, and an interdict was hurled by the prior against them. Moreover, he imported three barges-full of mercenaries who plundered the burghers' houses and killed and wounded many. Reprisals followed. The citizens stormed the Priory and Cathedral, routed and slew the monks and their mercenaries, set fire to the buildings, and pillaged the church. Such violence against the Church was then unheard of, and dire punishment was inflicted on the citizens of Norwich. The Pope excommunicated them, Henry III. deprived them of their liberties, and ordered 3000 marks to be paid towards the restoration of the Cathedral. New gates and gatehouses were erected by order of the Pope in order to prevent the renewal of such sacrilege, and St. Ethelbert's Gate was built at the close of the thirteenth century to guard the precincts. History concludes that the violence of the fierce prior was the main cause of the trouble, and not the obstinacy of the people. The work of restoration was immediately begun and the church reconsecrated in 1278 in the presence of King Edward I. and his queen and a grand assembly of bishops, knights and nobles, when Bishop Middleton was raised to the see. His successor, Bishop Ralph de Walpole, began to rebuild the cloisters, which were continued by Bishop Salmon, and form some of the largest and most beautiful in the country. Their style is mainly Decorated, but there is some Perpendicular work constructed in Bishop Wakering's time, who was a great persecutor of the Lollards (1416-1425). The chapter-house was erected by Walpole.

In the time of Edward IV. troubles sore oppressed the diocese. Bishop Anthony, who was of a violent and imperious spirit, rendered himself very obnoxious to the monks, and was poisoned by his servants, and six years later the Black Death is said to have carried off 50,000 inhabitants. This was in the time of Bishop Bateman, buried at Avignon, a mighty prelate who compelled the powerful Lord Morley to do penance in the Cathedral for killing the bishop's deer.

The lofty spire was blown down by a fierce hurricane in 1361, and rebuilt by Bishop Percy, who rebuilt also the clerestory. His successor, Henry de Despencer, was a very warlike prelate, who ruled with an iron hand. He crushed the revolting peasants in 1381, and fought in the Netherlands for Pope Urban VI. against the adherents of his rival, Clement. The vicissitudes of prelates were great in those days; both he and his successor, Totington, were imprisoned by the king. Bishop Alnwick (1426-1449) began to alter the west front, and Bishop Lyhart put in the large west window and built the rood-screen and vaulted the nave. During the rule of Bishop Browne (1436-1445) the quarrel between the burghers and the monks again broke out, and the former besieged the monastery, for which conduct the king deprived them of their rights and liberties. A fire occurred in 1463, caused by lightning striking the spire, and did much damage to the presbytery, which was restored by Bishop Goldwell (1472-1499), who also finished the spire. Fire again did much damage in 1509 during the rule of Bishop Nykke or Nix (1501-1536), whose reputation was not so unblemished as his name (*snow*). The transept roof was destroyed, which Nykke rebuilt in stone. The dissolution of monasteries soon followed in 1538, and Norwich shared the fate of the rest. The Cathedral foundation was renewed; the last prior being made the first dean. The church suffered from the usual acts of spoliation and desecration at the hands of the Commissioners of Edward VI. and the Puritans. Dean Gardiner (1573-1589) destroyed the chapter-house and the beautiful Lady Chapel. Bishop Hall (1641-1656) thus alludes to the misdeeds of the Puritans :—

" It is tragical to relate the furious sacrilege committed under the authority of Lindsey, Tofts the sheriff, and Greenwood; what clattering of glasses, what beating down of walls, what tearing down of monuments, what pulling down of seats, and wresting out of irons and brass from the windows and graves; what defacing of arms, what demolishing of curious stone-work, that had not any representation in the world but the cost of the founder and the skill of the mason; what piping on the destroyed organ pipes; vestments, both copes and surplices, together with the leaden cross, which had been newly sawn down from over the green yard pulpit, and the singing books and service books were carried to the fire in the public market place; a lewd wretch walking before the train, in his cope, trailing in the dirt, with a service book in his hand, imitating in an impious scorn the tune, and usurping the words of the Litany; the ordnance being discharged on the guild day, the cathedral was filled with musketeers, drinking and tobaccoing, as freely as if it had turned ale-house."

The citizens joined eagerly in the work of spoliation and burned in the open market, by order of the court of assembly, "Moses and Aaron, and four Evangelists that came from the Cathedral, and some other superstitious pictures."

The Restoration of the Monarchy caused the restoration of the Cathedral. A new organ and church plate were presented, and since that time much restoration has taken place, which has greatly enhanced the glory and beauty of this ancient House of God.

THE EXTERIOR

We enter the Cathedral precincts by the Erpingham Gate, built by Sir Thomas Erpingham, a knight who fought at Agincourt, and is mentioned by Shakespeare (*Henry V.*, Act IV). The style is Early Perpendicular. Notice the figures of saints in the arch moulding, the donor's kneeling figure in the niche above the arch, his arms and those of his two wives on the buttresses, and the word *Yenk* (think) on the shafts. The other gates are that of St. Ethelbert, Early Decorated, much restored, built by the citizens in expiation of their sacrilege in 1272, and the Bishop's Gate leading to the Palace, built by Bishop Alnwyck in Early Perpendicular style.

Entering by the Erpingham Gate, on the left is the Grammar School, formerly the Chapel of St. John the Evangelist, founded by Bishop Salmon in 1315. Below was a charnel-house, now

EXTERIOR VIEW OF NORWICH CATHEDRAL

used as a gymnasium. The porch was added by Lyhart at the end of the fifteenth century. Here Nelson was educated, and George Borrow and many other distinguished men.

The *West Front*, in spite of its noble window, is far from being a satisfactory compilation. The injudicious restoration of 1875 has had much to do with this. Portions of the original Norman work remain in a great part of the wall, two side doors, arcades and windows above. The main doorway was erected by Bishop Alnwyck, who seems to have cased the old Norman with Perpendicular work—an arch of the old work was uncovered by Dean Goulburn. The same bishop left money for the great Perpendicular window of nine lights, which was erected by Bishop Lyhart. We can see the result of perverse modern restoration by comparing the present front with those shown in earlier illustrations, and discover that the towers flanking the great window have been cut down and shorn of their cupolas, and also the turrets at the extreme north and south have suffered a like deprivation, and some inelegant pinnacles erected instead, while the battlemented parapet has been removed, and some ridiculous little round windows inserted. Certainly the efforts of modern architects have not been crowned with success.

The best view of the long nave is obtained from the upper close, or from the cloister garth. The wall is divided into three storeys. Behind the cloisters some late windows have been inserted in the aisle. Above the cloisters we see a Norman arcade with Norman windows over it, which have been blocked up; above them a row of Perpendicular windows, with a battlemented parapet, and above this a row of Norman windows, and parapet added later. Two Perpendicular windows were inserted at the west end by Bishop Nykke. Norman buttresses divide the windows. The north side resembles the south, and is enclosed by the bishop's garden.

The south transept is Norman, but it has been recased with new stone, and pyramid caps set on the turrets in imitation of Norman work, instead of some Perpendicular turrets which these replaced. Why will architects and restorers thus destroy the history of a building written in stone by trying to imitate what they imagine to have been the original form? On the east is the dean's vestry, formerly a chapel. The chapter-house and ancient slype have been destroyed, also an apse-shaped chapel on the east side of the south transept.

The *Choir* in its lower storeys resembles the nave, with its Norman arcade, windows, and inserted Perpendicular windows, but is has a lofty clerestory of Late Decorated style supported by flying buttresses, erected by Bishop Percy, when the fall of the spire destroyed the old Norman clerestory. Carved figures surmount the summits of the exterior buttresses. There are projecting Chapels of St. Mary-the-Less (Decorated), St. Luke and the Jesus Chapel (Norman).[1] The Lady Chapel was destroyed by iconoclastic Dean Gardiner, as we have mentioned, who regarded Lady Chapels as relics of Popery. The north front is very similar to the south, and needs no separate description.

The chief glory of Norwich is its *Tower* and *Spire*. The tower is a very fine example of Norman work. At the four corners are noble Norman buttresses, crowned with crocketed pinnacles, added in Early Perpendicular times, when the fall of the old wooden spire had carried away the original Norman ones. On the surface of each wall are three Norman arcades, and in the upper and lower three of the arches have been pierced with windows, and above are two rows of small circular windows. The spire is Perpendicular work, erected by Bishops Lyhart and Goldwell towards the end of the fifteenth century. May it long escape the fate of its predecessors, one of which was blown down in 1361, and the other struck by lightning, on each occasion causing considerable damage to the church.

The *Bishop's Palace* is on the north, founded by Bishop Herbert, but subsequent alterations have left little of the original structure. Some of the original vaulting is in the basement, and the ruin in the garden is the remains of the great hall built by Bishop Salmon in 1318. In the chapel are monuments to Bishop Reynolds (1661-1676) and Bishop Sparrow, a learned divine, who assisted in the revision of the Prayer Book in 1661.

There was a curious open-air pulpit, with a cross over it, somewhat similar to Paul's Cross in London, on the north, in what was known as Green Yard. Galleries were erected around it, and good accommodation provided for the mayor and his officers, with their ladies, who came in summer time to hear the sermons.

THE INTERIOR

The view of the nave from the west end is magnificent. A

[1] The restorers have been very busy here, and most of the windows are imitations of Norman work.

long vista of Norman arches, and beautiful expanse of vaulted lierne roofing, is most impressive. A fine screen, with organ above it, prevents a full view of the whole interior, but this detracts nothing from the grandeur of the view.

The nave has fourteen piers on each side, divided into seven bays, two arches to each bay. The lower arches, and those in the triforium, are about equal. Each pier has several shafts attached. A lofty shaft runs up the face of the main arch to support the roof. The zigzag and billet mouldings will be observed on the arches. The clerestory is Norman, and has triple arches. The first Norman prelate, Herbert, built the nave as far as the two most eastern bays, and his successor, Eborard, finished it. The old Norman roof was destroyed by fire in 1463, when Bishop Lyhart, who loved to display his punning rebus, a stag lying in water, erected the lierne stone vaulted roof, which is a noble specimen of its kind. The bosses are very interesting, and contain a full epitome of Bible history from the Creation to the Descent of the Holy Spirit, and include the terrors of Hades and the Final Judgment. One boss is absent, and through the hole in the roof it is conjectured that on Whitsunday a white pigeon was released and a burning censer swung, as an eyewitness testifies to a similar representation in old St. Paul's. There is a somewhat similar custom in Florence at the present time.

We notice in the west the large window erected by Lyhart, with modern glass, and the Norman arch over the door. The north aisle has Decorated windows inserted in the Norman walls. A reconstruction of the roof was made in the fifteenth century, when the walls were raised and Perpendicular

A Bay
N. side of
Nave.

2 C

windows added, and the slope of the roof changed into one much less steep. The *South Aisle* differs little from the north. In the centre was Bishop Nykke's Chapel, which he devised for himself, to perpetuate a not very desirable memory. Here we have Late Perpendicular work in the vaulting and windows. Few monuments or brasses escaped the destructive hands of the Puritans. In the aisles there are a few—the altar tomb of Sir T. Wyndham and four wives; Dean Prideaux (d. 1724), a distinguished divine, the author of *The Connection between the Old and New Testament*, Sir John Hobart, Attorney-General to Henry VII. (1507); Bishop Parkhurst (1574).

The *Choir* occupies the space between the two last arches of the nave, being shut off from it by an interesting stone *Screen*. The lower part of this structure is ancient, having been erected by Bishop Lyhart in Perpendicular style. The upper portion was added about 1830. Two altars stood near the central door, one dedicated to the boy saint of Norwich, St. William, slain by the Jews. The scanty remains of these altars mark the site of two chapels, over which were the rood-loft and organ, destroyed by the iconoclastic Puritans, whose sacrilege and abominable riotings have been already mentioned in the records left us by Bishop Hall. At the Restoration Dean Croft endeavoured to remedy the result of their evil deeds, and fashioned a new organ which, with additions and improvements, remains and stands over the screen.

Modern taste has removed some of the obstructions erected in times when the ideas of beauty and fitness were defective, and the alterations and improvements of the east end were not concluded till a few years ago. The stalls are very good Perpendicular work, fashioned at the time when the art of wood-carving had attained its highest development. The *misereres* are specially worthy of examination. The old popular legend is often repeated concerning them, that if one of the monks fell asleep during service, and caused the bench to fall, he was condemned to severe penance. This idea has no foundation in fact, as the raised seat was designed, as its name implies, out of *pity* for the infirmities of the brethren, and not for any idea of punishment. The bishop's throne and pulpit are modern, and the lectern is good Decorated work.

The presbytery was damaged on two occasions by the fall of the tower, and these accidents obliged subsequent repairs and alterations, which were constructed in the style then in use. Hence we have blended with the old Norman work the Decorated clerestory of Bishop Percy (1355-1369), and the Perpendicular roof of Bishop Goldwell, erected a century later. The lower arches were altered by the same bishop into the Perpendicular style, and his name is preserved in the canting rebus—gold and a well. The old Norman triforium remains. The vaulting of the roof is curious. Between each pair of clerestory windows is a niche, and from the heads of these spring the ribs, which form a beautiful example of lierne vaulting. The eastern termination is the original Norman apse, built by Bishop Herbert. The old bishop's throne is particularly interesting, chiefly from its position in the centre of the apse, with the presbyters' seats on each side. This idea was probably derived from Rome, where this position was not uncommon, though unusual in this country. The bishop's throne at Torcelli is a well-known example of this use. The present altar is modern, and also the present floor, designed by Sir Arthur Blomfield.

The following are the principal *Monuments* :—

A slab marks the resting-place of Bishop Herbert, the founder; Goldwell's Chantry and tomb; Bishop Wakering's tomb (d. 1425); Bishop Overall (d. 1619); Sir W. Boleyn (d. 1505).

The *North Transept*, built by Herbert, has good Norman arcading, and a vault erected by Nykke. The clerestory resembles the nave. There was at the east an apsidal chapel dedicated to St. Anne, but it is now closed and used for baser purposes. A processional path runs round the presbytery. On the north side is a curious bridge, which was connected with the Reliquary Chapel, now destroyed, situated on the exterior of the church. This bridge

Ancient Bishop's Throne

was an ante-chapel to that in which the relics were stored, and is adorned with mural paintings. Probably relics were exhibited here for the worship of the pilgrims, who went in procession along the path below.

The curiously-shaped *Chapels*—the *Jesus* and *St. Luke's*—with their Norman arcading are next seen. In the former there is some mural painting much restored — a facsimile of the ancient picture — and over the chapel is a museum. The latter is a parish church for the precincts. The windows are sham Norman, having been inserted in the last century. There is a mutilated font of fifteenth century, carved with Crucifixion and Seven Sacraments. Above it is the treasury. Here is a curious oil painting accidentally discovered by Professor Willis, which was part of a reredos, converted into a table after the Puritan outbreak. It is sometimes attributed to an Italian artist of 1370, but there is no reason to suppose that it was not the production of genuine English art of that period. Even Dean Stanley attributes the Eleanor bronze to an Italian, Torel, and Professor Freeman calls De Noyer of Lincoln a "crazy Frenchman," and others ascribe the Exeter chancel-screen to French workmen. This error of attributing pure English work to foreign artists has caused a very unjust depreciation of the skill and genius of our native craftsmen. The subjects of these paintings are the last scenes

Bridge of North Aisle of Presbytery.

of our Lord's life. Other mural paintings are :—On ceiling of
sacrist's room of late thirteenth century—subjects : Virgin, SS.
Catherine, Margaret, Andrew, Peter, Paul, and Richard of Chichester. On south wall of south aisle—SS. Wulstan, Edward the
Confessor, and others.

The Lady Chapel has been destroyed, as we have said, by
Dean Gardiner in Elizabeth's reign, but happily the doorway
remains, the only part of the Cathedral of Early English workmanship. The profusion of the dog-tooth ornament is evident. The
doorway is formed of a double arch, with clustered shafts, and
was built, together with the Lady Chapel, about the middle of the
thirteenth century by Bishop Walter de Suffield. Stone was brought
from Caen and Barnack for the purpose. The destruction of these
Lady Chapels was a sign of the decay in the worship of the
Virgin, which was so extensively followed in mediæval times.

There is another chapel on the south ; that of St. Mary-the-
Less, now used as the consistory court, built by one Bauchun in the
fourteenth century. An ecclesiastical lawyer, Seckington, added
the groined roof in the fifteenth century. The altar has been
displaced by a doorway. The sculptured bosses represent the
legendary history of the Virgin.

We enter the *South Transept* by a Tudor doorway, over which
is some rich open screen work of fifteenth-century design, under the
original Norman arch. This transept, built by Herbert, is fine
Norman work, with good arcading, the vault being added by Bishop
Nykke. This transept has the oldest coloured glass in the Cathedral,
a copy of Raphael's Ascension, erected by Dean Lloyd in 1790.
Here we see the following *Monuments* :—

Bishop Bathurst (d. 1837), by Chantrey ; and memorial tablets
to East Anglian heroes who fell in China and Afghanistan.

The *Cloisters* are extremely interesting and beautiful. We
enter them by the Prior's Door, a fine Decorated work, having four
columns on each side, with archivolt mouldings, in front of which
are seven canopied niches, with richly-sculptured crockets, containing
figures. The Norman cloisters, probably constructed of wood,
were destroyed in 1272, at the time of the citizens' revolt. The
east walk was rebuilt by Bishop Walpole (1289-1299) in Early
Decorated style. His successor, Bishop Salmon, built the south
walk, the windows of which show a great advance in the same
style, the windows having flowing tracery. The west walk has
also Late Decorated work, and the north walk has at the east end

an Early Decorated window, at the west end two Late Decorated, while the other five are Perpendicular in their tracery. This part was finished by Bishop Alnwyck (1426-1436). The slype and chapter-house have both been destroyed. The usual plan of Benedictine monasteries was followed here. The dormitory was on the east side, the refectory on the south, with entrance at south-west corner, and near to this is the monks' lavatory, the kitchen being further west. Carved figures representing the Temptation of Adam and Eve are above this door leading to the refectory. The locutory or parlour of the monks was on the west side of the cloisters and the hospitium, and from this walk the *Monks' Door* leads us back to the Cathedral. The bosses are extremely interesting. In the east walk the subjects are foliage, the four Evangelists, the Scourging, Crucifixion and Resurrection of Christ, and Nebuchadnezzar eating grass. In the south and west, scenes from the Book of the Revelation of St. John; and in the north, legends of the saints—Christopher, Laurence (being burnt on a gridiron); the dancing of Herodias's daughter before Herod, which represents her as tumbling rather than dancing, in accordance with the usual conceptions of mediæval artists.

DIMENSIONS

Length of church	407 ft.
Nave length	252 ft.
Nave to choir-screen	204 ft.
Width of nave	72 ft.
Height of roof	95 ft.
Height of spire (from ground)	315 ft.
Height of tower	140 ft.
Height of spire from tower	174 ft.
Area	34,800 sq. ft.

OBJECTS OF INTEREST IN NORWICH

The *Castle*, of which I have already written.

Guild Hall, parts of which were built in 1407, and contains much that is interesting—portraits of Norwich worthies, regalia, etc.

St. Andrew's Hall, once the Church of the Dominicans, in Perpendicular style, which has passed through many vicissitudes, and has some good pictures.

Norwich abounds in interesting churches—

St. John of Timberhill—Norman font, squint; parvise, principally Decorated.

All Saints—fine Perpendicular font.

St. Michael-at-Thorn—Norman doorway, curious registers.

St. Peter, Mancroft; St. Gregory, Pottergate; St. Giles, St. Helen's, St. John the Baptist, St. Michael-at-Plea.

The Stranger's Hall is well worthy of a visit, and Norwich abounds in objects of the greatest interest.

The old " Maid's Head " hotel is one of the most ancient and interesting hostels in the kingdom.

PRINCIPAL BUILDING DATES

Norman (1091-1145)—Choir, transept with chapels, nave and tower.

Early English (1244-1257)—Door of Lady Chapel.

(1278-1299)—Ethelbert's gate, east walk of cloisters.

Decorated (1299 - 1369) — Chapter-house and cloisters, clerestory of presbytery, Chapel of St. Mary-the-Less, some windows.

Perpendicular (1420-1538)—West front altered, Erpingham Gate, presbytery restored, vault of nave and transepts, spire, screen, stalls, some windows, Bishop's Gate.

(1573-1859)—Chapter-house and Lady Chapel destroyed.

A Great Western Doorway to Nave
B B Smaller Doorways to North and South Aisles
C Nave
D E North and South Aisles
F Staircase, with Entrance Doorway on the outside,
        to the Roofs of Aisle and Nave
G Staircase to the Galleries, etc.
H Choir
J K North and South Transept
L Presbytery
M N North and South Choir Aisles
O Chancel with Altar, etc.
P The Consistory Court or Chapel of St Mary-the-less
Q St. Luke's Chapel
R The Jesus
S Site of Lady Chapel
T Site of Chapter-House
U Dean's Vestry
V Cloister Garth
W Site of Refectory
X The Locutory, now used as Choir School

1 Font
2 Altar Tomb of Sir Thomas Wyndham
3 Altar-Tomb of Sir William Boleyn (Great grandfather
        of Queen Elizabeth)
4 Bishop Goldwell's Chantry
5 Altar Tomb of Sir John Hobart
6 Altar Tomb of Bishop Parkhurst
7 Lavatories
8 Doorway, called the Prior's Entrance, to the East Walk
        of the Cloisters
9 Doorway from South Aisle of Nave to West Walk of Cloisters
10 Tomb of Sir Thomas Erpingham
11 Tomb of Chancellor Spencer
12 Bishop Nykke's Chapel

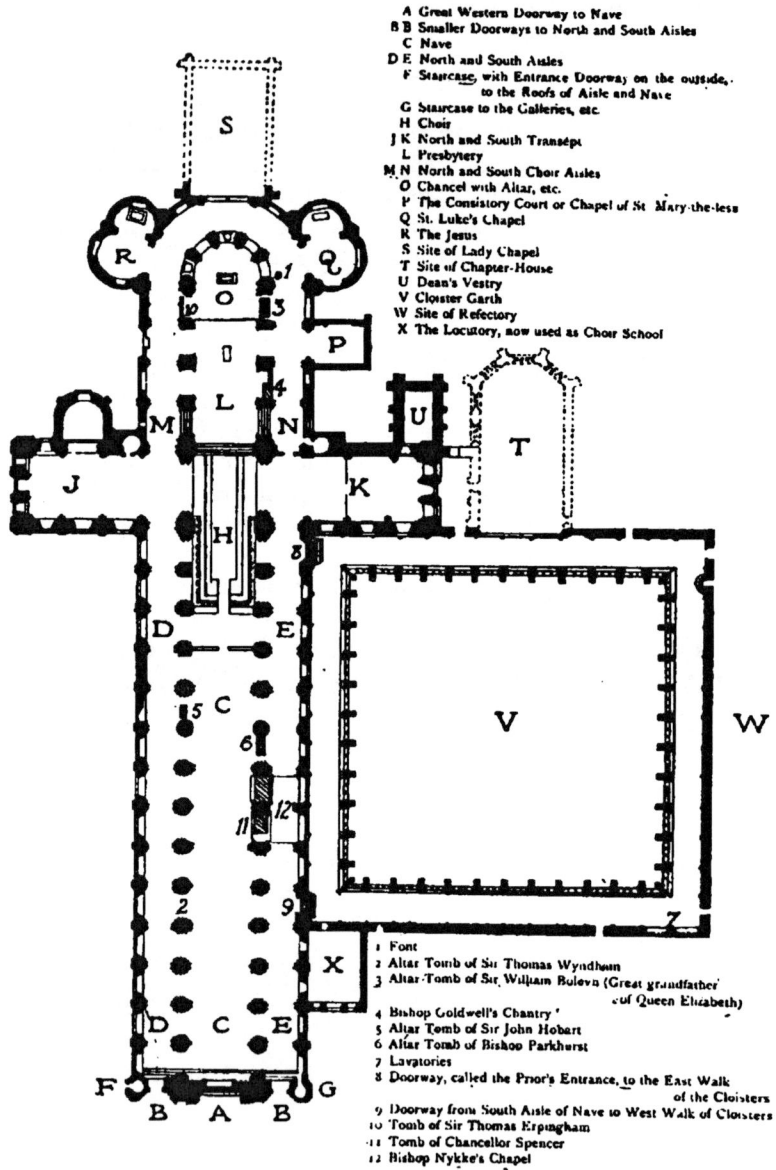

PLAN OF NORWICH CATHEDRAL

ST. ALBAN'S CATHEDRAL

S T. ALBANS, the ancient Verulam, is one of the most ancient towns in England, and is replete with historical associations. It was the home of the British chieftain Cassivellaunus before the Romans came. Boadicea killed many of the people for loving the Romans; and soon came Christianity, and then the record of the slaying of St. Alban, Britain's proto-martyr. It was during the Diocletian persecution that Alban sheltered a deacon named Amphibalus from the fury of the oppressors, and was himself converted to the Christian faith. Alban enabled his guest to escape, and was himself seized and slain, many miracles taking place at his execution. Offa founded a monastery here in 793, near his manor-house — of which the earthworks remain — and dedicated it to the saint, finding the remains of the martyr, which he placed in a reliquary and deposited in the church. The monks introduced here were Benedictine, of which order this was the chief house in the kingdom. The town increased, and Ulsi, the sixth abbot, founded the three churches of SS. Peter, Michael, and Stephen. We need not dwell on the records of Saxon abbots, many of whom were of Royal descent. When the Normans came, Paul of Caen, a relative of Lanfranc, was made abbot in 1077, and rebuilt the church, using the Roman town of Verulam as a quarry. He found much material collected by the last two Saxon abbots, who intended to build a new church, but were prevented by the troubles of the time. The large amount of Roman tiles used in the construction of the building is apparent. Much of his work remains in the eastern portion of the nave and in the tower and transepts. The church was dedicated during the rule of Abbot Richard D'Aubeny, in the presence of the king, Henry I., his court, and a goodly number of bishops, in 1115, and a little later we read of the relics of the saint being deposited in a beautiful shrine and conveyed to a place of honour in the minster. One Ralph de Gobion, seventeenth abbot, plundered the shrine in order to increase the territorial possessions of the Abbey, but his successor, Robert de Gorham (1151-1167), restored the shrine, and built anew some of the monastic buildings. This monastery had the high honour of producing the only English Pope, Nicholas Breakspeare, who was a monk here, and who, in the time of his prosperity, forgot not his early monastic home. The noble west front that once adorned this church, ruined by modern "restoration," was begun by Abbot John de Cella (1195-1214), but the troubles of John's reign prevented him from finishing it. His work was continued by William de Trumpington (1214-1235), who placed a lantern on the tower and rebuilt the west end of the nave. St. Alban's was fortunate in having a historian among its monks. Matthew Paris lived here, and died in 1259. He tells us much in his chronicles about the Abbey he loved so well, of royal visits, of dread plagues, and of the abbots who ruled here. Here came Edward I. on his way to Scotland, here his queen's body lay on its last sad journey, and here one of the Eleanor crosses was raised—alas! now destroyed. There was here a famous school of chroniclers, who did much for the history of England, and amongst them were Roger of Wendover, Matthew of Westminster, Thomas of Walsingham, and many others. A great work was begun in 1256 by Abbot John de Hertford (1235-1260), the successor of Trumpington, and this was the rebuilding and extension of the eastern arm. The apsidal termination was removed, the aisles lengthened two bays, a square-ended central chapel placed at the end, and the Lady Chapel begun. The work lasted until almost the end of the century, and is pronounced to be the most perfect example of the art of the age. A terrible disaster befell the Abbey in the rule of Hugh de Eversden (1308-1326). A great part of the south aisle gave way, two piers, with triforium and clerestory roof and south wall, being involved in a mighty ruin. The abbot set to work to restore the church; he built in the Decorated style, and finished also the Lady Chapel. The usual disputes between the monks and townsfolk raged at St. Albans, as in most places where there was a powerful abbot and a growing town. In Eversden's time the lordly abbot was compelled by the king to give way, but his successor regained all his power over the town. He was a wonderful man, this Richard de Wallingford (1326-1335), who made a marvellous astronomical clock, and could manage to tell the ways of the stars and the course of the sun as easily as he could manage the people of St. Albans. But all disputes did not cease for many a long year, and frequently the abbot's servants and the townsfolk came to blows. The work of restoring the south aisle progressed, and was finished by Abbot

St Albans
from the …

Mentmore (1335-1349), who also repaired the north walk of the cloister, damaged by the fall of the adjoining aisle. Abbot Thomas de la Mare (1349-1396) was the son of a noble house, and a favourite of Edward III. After Poictiers the French King John was brought here, and kept as an honourable prisoner, and afterwards expressed his gratitude to the courtly abbot for his care. Edward III. granted leave to the abbot to fortify his monastery, and walls and gates were much needed a few years later when Wat Tyler and his rebels besieged it and frightened the abbot and caused much damage. The rebels suffered here later when the king came, and some he hanged. Then was the Great Gate, with its prisons and vaults, constructed, which still stands, mightily convincing of the power of the abbot. Nor did he forget his church. He paved all the west part at great cost, and spent large sums on the services. The abbot, John de la Moote (1396-1401), took some part in dethroning Richard II., and it is said that the conspiracy was hatched at the abbot's dinner-table. Here they brought as a prisoner the Bishop of Carlisle, who stoutly defended Richard at Westminster. The rivalry of the Houses of York and Lancaster brought trouble to St. Albans. Here was fought the first battle, and here, in the house of a tanner, Henry VI. was found and conveyed to London. The second battle of St. Albans was fought here in 1461, when the king's party were victorious, and the Abbey was the scene of a great thanksgiving service. Great privileges were granted to the Abbey by Edward IV. Several alterations were made in Perpendicular times. The walls of the nave aisles were lowered and their roofs flattened, so that the backs of the Norman triforia were exposed, and their openings made into windows. Several Perpendicular windows were also inserted. St. Albans played a great part in the introduction of printing, and a press was set up in the Abbey. The earliest book printed here was in 1480, and many other incunabula came from this renowned press. The era of the Reformation is at hand. Cardinal Wolsey was abbot here in 1521. The fate of the monastery was doomed. In 1539 it was surrendered to the king by his creature Abbot Boreman, and the manors, goods and possessions were soon seized by the courtiers. Much damage was done in the church; of course, the beautiful shrines were destroyed. The Abbey church and buildings were granted to Sir Richard Lee, who soon began to uproot and destroy. The cloisters were levelled to the ground. Abbot Boreman did good service in buying the site of the monastery from Sir R.

Lee. Then the townsfolk did nobly. They bought the church from the Crown, and made it the Parish Church of St. Andrew, and moreover established a Grammar School in the Lady Chapel. The eastern ante-chapel was walled up, and a public passage made across the church west of the Lady Chapel. The knives of the schoolboys improved not the ancient stone-work of this once beautiful building. Various attempts have been made in successive ages to keep this Abbey in repair. In 1832 and 1856 much was accomplished, and the story of the reparation of 1870 under Sir G. Scott tells of the triumphs of the skill of modern builders, and their bravery and resolution in saving the fall of the great tower. This mighty mass began to give way, and the architect discovered that some dastard attempt had been made to destroy it, after the dissolution of the monastery, by digging a great hole under one of the piers. The greatest credit is due to all concerned in the hazardous and most difficult task of saving the falling tower. The Grammar School was removed from the Lady Chapel, and much done to restore the building to its ancient beauty. In 1871 it was raised to the dignity of a Cathedral; and surely no church more worthily deserved this honour. In quite recent times injudicious "restoration" has wrought terrible mischief. The west front has been entirely modernised, and much else has been "restored" beyond all knowledge of English Gothic art; but, in spite of all this, St. Alban's remains one of the most interesting buildings in the kingdom, and one can only regret that time has dealt so hardly with this venerable pile.

THE EXTERIOR

As we approach the Cathedral from the south we get a fine view and notice the great length of the building, its great central tower, and large amount of Roman tiles used in the construction. These tiles are $1\frac{1}{2}$ inches thick and measure 16 inches by 12. In addition much flint is used. The piers, arches, towers and staircases are mainly composed of tiles. Originally the building was covered with cement, which has almost entirely disappeared. Its plan is that of a Latin Cross, and originally there were no less than seven parallel apses, all of which have disappeared. The grand *Tower* is Norman. Formerly there were turrets at the four angles, and in the thirteenth century an octagonal lantern was added; but these have disappeared, and the tower is very much the same as it was in Norman times. The embattled parapet is recent. The *West Front* creates sad reflections, and words are powerless to convey a sufficiently strong protest against the evils which have been wrought by the injudicious though well-meaning efforts of modern restorers. The original Norman west front was removed by Abbot John de Cella (1195-1214), who began to erect a new one. It was a magnificent intention, but it was too ambitious for the resources of the monastery, and the levies of Richard I. for his crusading exploits, and the confiscations of John, were too much for the abbot, and put a stop to his enterprise. He intended to build two western towers, but got no further than the foundations. The front would have been 160 feet in width, 40 feet wider than Salisbury. Abbot. William de Trumpington proceeded to finish the work, and rebuilt five bays on the south side of the nave and four on the north. John de Cella's three deep porches are left to us in some small fragments; the rest is modern, and owes its erection to Lord Grimthorpe. The *Nave* shows three periods of architecture. The eastern portion is the work of Paul de Caen (1077-1097). On the south side the three easternmost bays are Norman and were constructed by him. The next five bays are Decorated. These were begun by Abbot Hugh de Eversden (1308-1326), in whose time during Divine service two great piers on the south fell, and all the roof and beams of the south part were ruined. The rebuilding was finished by Abbot Michael de Mentmore (1335-1349). The four remaining bays are the Early English work of William de Trumpington (1214-1235). In Perpendicular times the roof of the aisle was lowered and made flat, disclosing the triforium openings, but in the recent restoration the original pitch has been renewed. On this side stood the cloister court, and against the south wall of the church are seen the remains of the arches of the north cloister walk. Part of the east walk cloister left its marks on the west wall of the south transept, but recent restoration has obliterated them. The south transept is Norman, the work of Paul de Caen, except the south wall, which has been entirely rebuilt by Lord Grimthorpe. The tall lancets are an imitation of "the Five Sisters" of York Minster. Turrets crowned with small caps stand at each angle of the transept. Below the window are the remains of the slype, or passage from the cloister to the monks' burial-ground. The south wall is all that remains of the chapter-house. On the east side of the transept were formerly two apsidal chapels, but all traces of these have been removed. They were destroyed in the time of Edward II. to make room for a sacristy. On the south of the south chancel aisle is a fine Norman arch leading to these apsidal chapels. When they were removed the arch was contracted by the insertion of a pointed arch. A vestry was constructed here in 1846.

This eastern part of the church beyond the third bay from the tower was built in the latter half of the thirteenth century under the rule of Abbot John de Hertford, and completed by Abbot Roger Norton (1260-1290). The Lady Chapel was mainly built under the rule of Abbot Hugh de Eversden (1308-1326), one Reginald of St. Albans being the master-mason. It is in the Decorated style, and was begun as early as 1280. Abbot Wheathampstead (1420-1464) embellished it with much decoration in the Perpendicular style. It was with the ambulatory long separated from the church by a wall, and used as a Grammar School. A public path passed through the building here. The north side of the chapel and presbytery resembles the south. The north door is much later. The most western part of the wall is Norman. The north transept is entirely Norman, the work of Abbot Paul. On the east side were two apsidal chapels, removed in the fifteenth century. The upper part of the north front was rebuilt by Lord Grimthorpe. The north side of the nave preserves its Norman character, both in the clerestory and aisle, except at the west end, where it has been reconstructed in the Early English style.

On the west of the Abbey is the *Great Gateway*, which is an unusually important building. The greater part of the present structure was built by Abbot Thomas de la Mare (1349-1396), but there seems to be some thirteenth century incorporated with it. Here the abbot held his court, and dealt out justice to the townsfolk and received his rents, and transacted other business; and here there were prisons for rebellious clerks and others. The gateway was stormed by Wat Tyler's rebels in 1381, who broke into the Abbey and terribly frightened the abbot and his monks. But vengeance was in store for the rioters, several of whom were imprisoned here and afterward hanged. After the dissolution it was used as the Assize Court, and subsequently as a prison. Then the Grammar School, evicted from the Lady Chapel, found a home here. All the other monastic buildings have been destroyed

THE INTERIOR

We enter the church by the west door, and are at once struck

by its immense length. It is the longest in England, and consists of
thirteen bays. Originally the Norman style prevailed throughout
the building, but in the course of ages numerous alterations have
been made, and its architectural history is somewhat complicated.
The five bays on the north and the three bays on the south are the
work of Trumpington, who left the great piers standing, removed
the Norman arches, triforium and clerestory, and began his reconstruction with all the gracefulness of the Early English style. He
cased the piers with stone-work, which are octagonal and have
attached shafts. The triforium has in each bay an arch enclosing
two sub-arches with a quatrefoil in the head. The dog-tooth appears
in the string-courses. The clerestory windows have two lights.
The roof is modern. It was evidently intended to have a stone
vault, but this was abandoned apparently for want of means. The
work in the aisles corresponds to that in the nave as far as Trumpington's building extends. There is a remarkable juncture of this Early
English work with the Norman on the north side of the nave. This
Norman work is that of Paul de Caen. It is simple and plain, and
not dissimilar from that at Caen, whence the abbot came. On the
south side the five bays next to Trumpington's work were rebuilt by
Abbots Hugh de Eversden (1308-1326) and Michael de Mont-
more (1335-1349), owing to the fall already alluded to. Here we
see rich Decorated work, and though it differs in detail, it follows
the lines of the earlier work on the west. Instead of dog-tooth, we
have the ball-flower alternating with lilies. There is more sculpture,
some of the heads being beautifully carved. The aisle here is similiar
in character to the nave. The cloister court having been on the
south side of this wall, the windows here are high up. The next
three bays on the south side are Norman, and also the nine eastern
bays on the north side. The piers are very massive and are square-
edged. The arches have three orders. The triforium arches are
plain, but less lofty than those of the nave, and the clerestory arches
are of the same character. We will now examine the mural paintings in the nave, which are of Norman date. Upon the west side of
the six Norman piers are examples of the same subject, the Crucifixion,
with St. John and the Virgin. Beginning with westernmost Norman
pier we notice a representation of our Lord, and below is the Annunciation. On the south is St. Christopher, on the next pier is the
same subject, and on the south the figure of St. Thomas of Canterbury. The figures of St. Syth, Edward the Confessor, Coronation
of the Virgin, and the Virgin and Child also appear. The nave

has been shorn of most of its monuments, but on the second pier on the north side is the monument of Sir John Mandeville, the great traveller, with this inscription :—

> "*Siste gradum properans, requiescit Mandevil urnâ*
> *Hic humili ; norunt et monumenta mori.*
>
> > "'Lo, in this Inn of Travellers doth lie
> > One rich in nothing but in memory;
> > His name was Sir John Mandeville ; content,
> > Having seen much, with a final continent,
> > Toward which he travelled ever since his birth
> > And at last pawned his body for yᵉ earth,
> > Which by a statute must in morgage be
> > Till a Redeemer come to set it free.'"

There is another monument which records the undying fame of one John Jones, who wrote a poem on "the Shrine of St. Albans." But time has been unkind to the poet, and his poem no longer exists. The massive stone pulpit was designed by Lord Grimthorpe. An inscription at the west end informs us that in the time of Henry VIII. and Elizabeth, on account of the Plague in London, the Courts of Justice were held in this nave. Dividing the choir from the nave is the fine Decorated screen commonly but erroneously called that of St. Cuthbert, erected about 1350 by Abbot de la Mare. It is not the rood-screen as it is commonly described. That with its great, high, towering rood stood a little further east. This is excellent Decorated work. It has suffered from iconoclastic reformers. Over the screen is the modern organ. The extensions of the screen over the aisles are the work of Lord Grimthorpe. Notice the rich tabernacle work of the screen.

The *South Aisle of the Choir* beyond the screen is all Norman, except the modern vault. Here on the south is the tomb of two famous hermits—Roger and Sigar—who lived in the time of King Stephen, though the tomb is later. Roger lived near Dunstable, and Sigar in the wood of Northaw, of whom it is said that he banished all nightingales from his retreat, as their sweet song prevented him from saying his prayers. Next we notice the Abbot's Door, which is rich Decorated work, built by the fashioner of the screen, Abbot de la Mare (1349-1396). The *Transepts* and *Central Tower* are plain Norman, the work of Paul de Caen. The south wall of the south transept, however, with its Five Sisters' Window, copied from York Minster, was entirely rebuilt by Lord Grimthorpe. The eastern triforium arches are extremely interesting, as they have curious baluster shafts which are recognised as Saxon work. These doubtless are the sole remaining relics of the ancient church built by Offa in 793, and were inserted here by Abbot Paul. The capitals are, however, Norman. The small window on the opposite side was an opening into a watching chamber, whence a monk could keep guard over the treasures in the transept. This chamber was not a reclusorium as the legends tell. On the east side were two apsidal chapels, destroyed in order to make room for a sacristy, which has now shared their fate. The altars of SS. Stephen and John the Evangelist stood here. On the west side are three ancient Jacobean cupboards, fashioned for the distribution of bread to the poor on Sundays. On the south is a fine Norman doorway, brought here from the slype, which is now entered through it. The south wall of this passage is all that remains of the old chapter-house. Here are some Norman arcading, and as the modern verses tell us, " fragments brought together from all sides." We enter the *Choir*, which occupies the three eastern bays of the nave and the space under the tower. The stalls are modern. The ceiling is extremely interesting and dates from the time of Edward III., the painted panels being adorned with the sacred monogram, numerous shields with royal arms supported by angels, the *Te Deum*, and invocations to the Virgin. The Roses of York and Lancaster appear on the lofty ceiling of the tower. The choir pulpit here was given by the English Freemasons. The *North Transept* resembles the south, and is mainly Norman. Here is another Saxon baluster-shafted arch in the triforium, a relic of Offa's church. The old painted ceiling has been replaced by a modern roof. The upper part of the north wall was rebuilt by Lord Grimthorpe, who inserted here a huge rose window which has received some very severe criticism. He has also placed beneath it an inscription which records the fact that he ("Edmund") has built anew the work of Abbot " John " Wheathampstead which had perished while that of Abbot Paul remains. On the east were formerly apsidal chapels, which have been removed, and altars dedicated to the Holy Trinity, St. Osyth, and the Holy Cross of Pity. Near the last is a painting on the wall, the subject being the Incredulity of St. Thomas. On the floor are some remarkable ancient tiles. On the splay of one of the Norman windows a vine is represented, and there is a small Norman door. Bishop Claughton's fine monument is here (1892) and Bishop Blomfield of Colchester (1894).

The presbytery occupies the space between the tower and the

Wallingford screen, and retains its Norman walls as far as the third bay. The rest is the work of Abbot John de Hertford (1235-1260). The style is Early English. Before us is the famous Wallingford screen or reredos, erected by Abbot William Wallingford (1476-1484), which resembles that at Winchester. It was much mutilated, and has very recently been thoroughly restored, and the niches filled with statuary. There is a fine figure of our Lord in the centre, with the Virgin and St. John on either side, surrounded by angels. Below are the twelve Apostles with our Lord in the midst. On either side are figures of saints and kings connected with the history of the Abbey. On the north is the Chantry of Abbot Ramryge (1521), which has some rich Perpendicular work ; the abbot's rebus—*rams* with *ryge* on the necks— may be discovered. Notice the representation of the martyrdom of St. Alban over the door. On the south is the Chantry of Abbot Wheathampstead (1464), which has a fine brass (that of Abbot Thomas de la Mare), and bears his arms (three ears of corn with the motto *Valles habundabunt*). Some attribute this tomb to Abbot Wallingford, but the details seem to point to Wheathampstead. This abbot caused the ceiling to be painted whereon are depicted the *Agnus Dei* and the Eagle of St. John. There are numerous tombs and brasses of other abbots here. The south door has some fine Early English tabernacle work. The architecture of the adjoining *North Aisle* corresponds with that of the presbytery, and through it we pass to the *Saints' Chapel*, which is the work of Abbot John de Hertford and his successors, and may well be described by Sir G. Scott as being " among the finest productions of that period." On the east side of the reredos are some fine modern statues of the Virgin and other saints. Here is the famous *Shrine of St. Alban*, broken and destroyed at the Reformation, and now happily built up again, the fragments having been collected by careful hands from many parts of the building. It was first erected by Abbot John de Marynis (1302-1308), and is of Decorated style. Gorgeous must have been its original appearance ; but though shorn of all its jewels, gold and silver, it remains a noble piece of work. The holes in the panels of the base were intended for the insertion of diseased limbs, in order that they might be healed by the merits of the saint. The carved leafage in the tympana of the canopied niches is admirable. Only two carved figures remain, those of Offa and St. Oswin. On the west we see a representation of the martyrdom of the saint, and at the east his scourging. On the north side of the chapel is the *Watching Tower*, a wooden structure, probably erected by Abbot John de Wheathampstead. This and a similar one at Christ Church, Oxford, are the only watching towers remaining. A monk was stationed here to guard the treasures of the shrine. There are some curious carvings on the frieze. Treasures were preserved in aumbreys which now contain some curios. The famous Humphrey, Duke of Gloucester, son of Henry IV., murdered by order of Queen Margaret (1446), lies buried here in a tomb on the south. The sculpture of the numerous figures is very bold and vigorous. Some painting is observed on the piers, and there is a figure of St. William of York. In the *North Aisle* is part of the *Shrine of St. Amphibalus*, which shares the history of its neighbour, and has been now partially recovered. It belongs to the last half of the fourteenth century. On the sides are the initials of Ralph Whitechurch, sacrist of the Abbey.

The *Ante-Chapel* and *Lady Chapel* have been extensively restored. Indeed, their condition was deplorable. A public path ran through the former, and the latter was used as a Grammar School, and suffered in consequence. The story of the architecture is rather complex. The ante-chapel was begun by De Hertford and finished by his successor, Roger Norton (1260-1290), who continued to build the Lady Chapel, which was finished by Hugh de Eversden (1308-1326). The style is Decorated. The whole of the chapel has been most completely restored by Lord Grimthorpe. The modern carving is exquisite. We now pass to the *South Aisle*, which follows the architecture of the rest of the east end. Here we see an iron trellis screen of thirteenth-century work. There is here some good arcading, and an interesting panel taken from the old ceiling of the north transept representing the martyrdom of St. Alban. At the east end of this aisle was the Altar of St. Mary of the Four Tapers, and numerous other altars existed in the aisles and ante-chapel. In the wall above the old poor box is a curious figure of a pensioner carved by a sexton about 100 years ago.

An ascent of the tower reveals many interesting features of that ancient structure, and helps one to realise the formidable nature of the task which the skilful architect and builders of 1870 accomplished when they saved this massive pile from destruction.

DIMENSIONS

Total length	550 ft.
Length of nave to tower . .	284 ft.
Length of nave to screen . .	215 ft.
Width of transepts . . .	189 ft.
Width of tower	144 ft.
Total area . . .	40,000 sq. ft.

PRINCIPAL BUILDING DATES

Saxon—Baluster shafts of windows in triforium of transepts.

Norman (1077-1115)—Nine bays on north of nave, and three bays on south, transept, and three bays of presbytery.

Early English (1195-1260)—Western end of nave, presbytery, Saints' Chapel with aisles.

Transition (1260-1290)—Foundations of Lady Chapel and ante-chapel.

Decorated—Lady Chapel and five bays of nave.

Perpendicular—South buttresses of choir; windows inserted which have since been removed.

The city possesses many objects of interest :—

The Roman city of Verulamium.

The Churches of St. Michael, St. Peter, St. Stephen.

Sopwell Nunnery.

The old Moot Hall.

And the old inn called the "Fighting Cocks," said to be one of the oldest inns, and the oldest inhabited house in England, but this reputation is somewhat legendary.

NOTE

The Welsh Cathedrals of Llandaff and St. David's should be approached from Gloucester ; and Chester is the most convenient starting-point for St. Asaph and Bangor.

ST. ASAPH'S CATHEDRAL

THIS Cathedral, like that of Bangor, is small, but its history is not unimportant. It owed its origin to Kentigern, otherwise called St. Mungo, the founder and Bishop of Glasgow, who, being driven from his northern see in the sixth century, found a refuge here, and enjoyed the protection of Prince Cadwallon. This prince aided him in building a church and founding a monastery here, and fabulous records tell of the amazing number of the monks. His biographer assures us that there was no less than 965 dwellers in this monastery, which number must be an extraordinary exaggeration. When Kentigern returned to Scotland, he left one of his followers, St. Asaph, to act as bishop of the diocese. The chroniclers are silent about the names of the subsequent bishops, until they record the doings of Norman times. In 1143 one Gilbert was consecrated bishop. The church in existence during his rule was burnt down in 1283, during the fierce wars between Edward I. and the Welsh. Anian II. was bishop during that time, and contemplated the transferring of the seat of the bishopric to Rhuddlan; but, on the advice of the Archbishop of Canterbury, he determined to rebuild the ruined church, and most of the present building is his work, or that of his two successors, Leoline and David. The work extended from 1284 to 1350. Owen Glendower, after his fashion, set fire to the church and burned the roof in 1404, and for a century the church remained in a roofless ruined state. Bishop Redman, in 1490, began to rebuild and restore the ruined church. He raised walls, erected a new roof, added the east window, and placed in the choir the stalls and a throne. Bishop Owen Jones, in 1631, made some further alterations, and repaired the steeple and belfry. Then came the disasters of the Civil War, when terrible desecration ensued, principally caused by a wretch named Miller, who turned the Palace into a wine-shop, and the church into a stable and cow-house, and the font into a hog-trough. Since the Restoration there have been several learned and devout prelates, amongst others, Isaac Barrow, William Beveridge, Thomas Tanner, author of *Notitia Monastica*; Samuel Horsley;

but they were more learned in theology and their books than in the study of the correct principles of architecture. Hence they disfigured the church, and destroyed many of its most interesting features. In 1780 the choir was remodelled, a plaster ceiling erected, and much further damage done. " Oh, *Restoration !* what evils have been wrought in your name."

The church is cruciform. At the west end is a large Decorated window, and a deeply - recessed doorway of six orders, with buttresses on either side, which have crocketed pinnacles ; a wooden cross surmounts the gable. It will he noticed that the shafts supporting the arch of the doorway have no capitals, the wave moulding making a complete sweep round the arch, with no capitals intervening. This arrangement we shall notice in the church. The great central tower was the latest addition to the mediæval church, and was constructed late in the fourteenth century. The embattled parapets was added in 1714. It is 93 feet high. The nave consists of five bays, and at once we notice the same peculiarity observable in the west doorway. The mouldings are carried up the piers and round the arches without any break. They are very plain, and of two orders, and are of the Early Decorated style, the work of Bishop Anian. Formerly there was a clerestory, but during one of the tasteless restorations a ceiling was erected, which shuts it out from view. The windows of the clerestory were in the Perpendicular style, and exist still in the south. Grotesque carvings appear on the brackets supporting the roof. The windows of the aisles have been much restored, and are in the style of the Early Decorated. The south transept was once the Lady Chapel, the consistory court and chapter-house. The windows are of five lights, and were finished about 1336. Here is a much mutilated effigy of a bishop, which is of great beauty, especially the figures of censing angels. It is supposed to represent Bishop Anian.

The north transept has the monument of Bishop Luxmore (1830). In the south aisle are some monuments of the relatives of Mrs. Hemans, the poetess, and a tablet has been erected to the memory of that lady, who died in 1835. Under the central tower stand the old finely-canopied stalls. The throne is modern.

The style of the old choir was almost entirely changed at the eighteenth-century " restoration." It was of Early English design, and Sir G. Scott wisely resolved to restore it to its primitive form. This proceeding was somewhat drastic, but such was the condition of the choir, and so severe was the treatment it received in 1780, that perhaps no other course could with advantage have been taken. He discovered the old sedilia, and the door leading to the old old chapter-house. The east window has entirely modern tracery, and the reredos is modern. Bishop Barrow's tomb outside the west door is worthy of notice.

The Bishop's Palace is a large modern building. At the foot of the hill is the parish church. From the summit of the tower of the Cathedral a fine view can be obtained of the Vale of Clwyd, with the Castles of Denbigh and Rhuddlan, and a long line of sea coast. Robert Montgomery sang sweetly of this wondrous view :—

> " Thy heart might beat
> In thrilling answer to the strain I sing,
> Hadst thou beside me, from the sacred tower,
> Beheld this beauteous vale."

BANGOR CATHEDRAL

THE early Bishops of Bangor are shadowy beings. We read of Bishop Daniel in the sixth century, concerning whom the records are misty, although he was canonised. Godwin says that there were no bishops here before the Norman Conquest. At any-rate Hervey, or Harvé, was consecrated bishop in 1092, but he was so rigid in his discipline, and so severe upon the Welsh, that they rebelled, murdered his brother, and threatened him with a like fate. So he fled for refuge to the court of Henry I., and was ultimately appointed to the See of Ely. The early Celtic church was destroyed by the Normans in 1071. A second church was at once built, and here, in 1188, Archbishop Baldwin preached the Crusades, and so moved the heart of the Bishop of Bangor that he joined the army of Crusaders to rescue the Holy City from the Saracens. This church was destroyed in 1211 by a great fire. It was, however, partly restored, and again fell a prey to destruction in the wars of Edward I. and the Welsh. Bishop Anian, however, seemed to have been a favourite of the king, who helped him to rebuild his church. This bishop baptised the first Prince of Wales, born at Carnarvon Castle. He also drew up the Bangor Use, or Service Book, which ranked highly among the Cathedral uses of the mediæval church.

During the wars of Owen Glendower in 1402 the church was completely gutted, and for nearly a century it lay in ruins. A new church was begun by Henry Deane in 1496, who finished the choir, and the Cathedral was completed by Bishop Skeffington, Abbot of Beaulieu, Hants, who was appointed to the See of Bangor in 1509. The style of the architecture was therefore entirely Perpendicular. Though the body of this benefactor was buried in his Hampshire Abbey, his heart was conveyed for sepulchre to the church he loved so well. The church suffered at the Reformation, when the see was held by Bishop Bulkely, who cared not for his church, and sold its store of vestments, plate, ornaments, and the bells given by his predecessor. Bishop Rowlands, in 1598, put a new roof on the church, and gave four new bells. In the Civil War it suffered much; the soldiers destroyed all the wood-work and broke the glass. At the Restoration the church was renovated and beautified, and Brown Willis gives a good account of "its lightsome" appearance. In the early nineteenth century some terrible "restorations" took place, and the church was divided into two portions, one for the Welsh and the other for the English service. The general appearance of the church was stunted and low, and was much inferior to many parish churches, possessing neither dignity nor beauty. In 1866 a very thorough restoration was undertaken by Sir G. Scott, which practically amounted to a rebuilding. He, however, carefully collected all the old materials found built up in the wall, and from these he endeavoured to reconstruct the church as it originally stood.

The plan of the church consists of a west tower, a nave with aisles, a central tower, transepts and choir, and on the north a muniment room, and above it the chapter-house. The *West Tower* was built by Bishop Skeffington (1509-1533), and is a good example of Late Perpendicular work. It has three stages, and is 60 feet high. The door is of the usual character of the style, and above it is the inscription:—"*Thomas Skevynton, episcopus Bangorie hoc campanele et ecclesiam fieri fecit, Aᵒ Partus Virginei, 1532.*" In each of the other stages there is a window of three lights. The *Nave* has six bays, and the Perpendicular style is evident in the arches, octagonal piers and characteristic bases. The windows in the south aisle are Decorated, and those in the north Perpendicular. The masonry of the walls seems to have survived the various fires and other accidents which befell this ill-fated Cathedral, and probably are the remains of Bishop Anian's work. The font was probably erected by Skeffington, and is good Perpendicular. The *Transepts* have been almost entirely rebuilt, and the Perpendicular work, which was much decayed, was replaced by Decorated, authority for which was discovered by Sir G. Scott in the fragments of old stone-work built up in the walls. Some very fine thirteenth-century piers stood at the crossing until an unfortunate restoration in 1824, when they were replaced by imitation Perpendicular. These have now been removed, and new piers and arches constructed in accordance with the conjectured design of the originals. There was no central tower in the Perpendicular church, but the relics of earlier work prove that the original church had such a tower. Hence Scott added this to his design, and when completed it will enhance the dignity of the building.

The *Choir* has had a chequered history, which, as Sir G. Scott states, is of a threefold nature. The Norman choir had an apsidal termination. This apse was removed, and the length of the choir or presbytery greatly increased in Early Decorated times. After the destruction wrought by Owen Glendower, Bishop Deane (1496-1500) restored it, and the main object of Scott's restoration was to make the present choir conform to the condition in which Bishop Deane left it. The Civil War brought much destruction to this excellent work of the Perpendicular period, and decay had also left it marks upon it ; but during the recent restorations all has been again renewed, and all that we see conforms as nearly as possible to that produced in the days of Henry VII. Cromwell's soldiers left none of the fittings untouched. The stalls were destroyed. Now all has been restored, and most of the fittings are new. The modern tiles of the floor are worthy of notice. Some mural paintings have been added at the east end. The tombs on either side are probably those of Bishop Anian (1328), the rebuilder of the church, and one Tudor ap Tudor (1365). In the south transept is recorded the burial of Owen Gwynedh (1169), the son of the last King of Wales, Gryffydh ap Gynan, who also was buried here. A rude representation of our Lord upon the Cross appears over the supposed Royal tomb. In the north transept is a memorial to a Welsh bard, Gronovil Owen (1722).

Sir G. Scott entirely rebuilt the old chapter-house and muniment room on the north side of the choir in the Early Decorated style.

The Bishop's Palace is a large mansion, but has no great architectural merits. The Deanery and some old almshouses and an Elizabethan school are all near the Cathedral.

LLANDAFF CATHEDRAL

THE history of the Welsh sees carries us back to the early days of British Christianity. When the Saxon tribes swept over the land they destroyed the churches and monasteries, and drove the British westward, who found a refuge in the hills of Wales, in Devon, Cornwall and Somerset, and in the regions north of the Mersey, and there the British Church continued to exist and flourish, though the rest of England was submerged in the flood of Paganism. When Augustine came he found in these parts of England a church governed by its bishops, who did not recognise the authority of the Pope, and whose customs differed somewhat from those of Rome. He summoned them to a conference, which was held at a place called "Augustine's oak," where by his haughty demeanour he offended the representatives of the ancient native church, who refused to abandon their accustomed usages, especially in the matter of the time for observing Easter and the forms of the tonsure.

In Roman times Caerleon was a see, which seems to have embraced the whole of Wales. Then there were five principalities, each of which had a bishop. These were Bangor, Llanelwy (St. Asaph's), St. David's, Llandaff and Llanbadarn, afterwards incorporated with St. David's. Judging from the number of the names of saints which occur in Welsh nomenclature, we may conclude that the Welsh Church was famous for its zeal and activity and for the holiness of its members. It sent preachers and missionaries to Ireland, to Brittany, and Cornwall and Devon. It founded colleges and schools, and the great Celtic Church assisted in the conversion of the Northern Saxons of England, and even sent missionaries to the Continent. By degrees the British Church became merged in the English, founded by Augustine, and with the appointment of Norman prelates in the time of the Conqueror, any lingering survivals of ancient customs and usages were lost, and the unity of the church fully established.

The earliest bishop of the See of Llandaff whose name is recorded was St. Dubricius. He is reputed to have founded the see in 612 A.D., but his successor, St. Teilo, seems to have had the chief credit of accomplishing the work. Of course the mythical King Lucius is dragged in as the earliest founder, but we have always neglected the legends connected with him. Of the early Welsh bishops we have no sure information, though there is the famous *Book of Llandaff*, which does not afford much certain knowledge, and is full of inaccuracies. Bishop Urban was consecrated in 1107, conveyed here the relics of Dubricius, and began to rebuild his Cathedral, for which an indulgence was granted by the Archbishop of Canterbury to all who should assist him in the work. Possibly it was finished in his time, but we have no certain information, and the stones of the church can alone tell the story of its building. During the thirteenth century the western part of the nave was erected, and also the chapter-house, which is of Early English design. During the Decorated period the Lady Chapel was added and the presbytery rebuilt, and the walls of the aisles also renewed. The north-west tower was erected in the Perpendicular period by the Earl of Pembroke, uncle of Henry VII. Thus the church was completed. It was not a very beautiful structure, and time has dealt hardly with it. The spoilers at the Reformation plundered it ; decay and desolation reigned in the deserted " long-drawn aisle." Some bishops seem to have attempted to do something, but the whole condition of the church was deplorable. Then the troubles of the Civil War period fell upon this Job-like structure, and in spite of some attempts to improve its condition at the Restoration, and at subsequent periods, it still remained in a ruinous state. Then in 1723, when the taste for Italian models was rampant, the authorities erected an Italian temple-like building at the east end. This happily has been entirely removed during the restorations, which commenced in the middle of the last century, when the church was completely renovated, and all the old portions which had escaped the action of time, or the barbarous efforts of the followers of Christopher Wren, restored to their original state. The work was finished in 1869. Although much of the church is new, on close inspection we can discover some ancient work that lacks not interest.

The *West Front* is very beautiful. The doorway is a fine example of Early English work. It consists of a round arch, with two sub-arches, and in the tympanum there is an episcopal figure, probably that of St. Dubricius. The shafts at the sides of the doorway are Early English. Above them are lancet windows, and in the gable a figure of our Lord in glory. The cross above the gable is modern. The front is flanked on each side by two towers. The north-west tower is Perpendicular, the work of Jasper Tudor, Earl of Pembroke, uncle of Henry VII.; the south-west tower is modern.

The *Nave* consists of five bays, and is of Early English design. There is no triforium. The clerestory windows are lancets, and a passage runs in front of them. We notice the graceful foliage on the pier capitals, of Late Early English design, when the stiff-leaved foliage was giving way to the more natural foliage of the Decorated period. The aisles were rebuilt in the Late Decorated period, but two Norman doorways on the north and south sides were preserved. The choir is of the same character as the nave, but in the presbytery we see some of the Norman work of Urban's church, mixed with that of the Decorated period. Here stood the Italian temple, until happily this monstrosity was removed. The clerestory was destroyed when the temple was erected, but in the restoration of Sir Gilbert Scott it was rebuilt. On the south side we notice the curious blending of the Norman with the Decorated work. One of the most striking features of this Cathedral is the Late Norman arch at the east end. It is very richly ornamented, and has four orders, being adorned with zigzag, roll, and a curious row of flower-like circles. The reredos is modern, and has some fine paintings by Rosetti. The sedilia are modern.

The *Lady Chapel* has a stone vault, the ribs rising from Purbeck marble shafts. The windows are of good design, having two lights with a circle in the head. The east window is modern. The chapter-house is Early English, and is almost unique in having a square plan with a central pier.

Few of the monuments possess much interest. We notice that of St. Dubricius; a brass memorial of Bishop Copleston (1849); Bishop William de Bruce (1287); Bishop St. Teilo; Bishop Bromfield (1393); Bishop Marshall (1496), a skeleton figure of the *memento mori* type; Sir David Matthew, standard-bearer to Edward IV. (1461); Sir William Matthew; Lady Audley. The old reredos discovered during the restoration has been placed in the north aisle of the choir.

ST. DAVID'S CATHEDRAL

FAR away on the most western point of Southern Wales stands the ancient Cathedral of St. David's, the most inaccessible, but the most interesting of the four Welsh Episcopal churches. The see was founded in the sixth century, and was known by the name Menevia. St. David was the reputed founder of the see, concerning whom there are many legends. He founded a monastery at Glyn Rhosyn, which became a fruitful school of saints and Celtic worthies, wrought divers miracles, and through him the Welsh Church extended its influence to Ireland, and also to Scotland and Northumbria. After his death troubles befell the monastery. It was plundered in 645, but recovered from the disaster. Here Asser, the biographer of Alfred the Great, acquired his wisdom. Then the Norse pirates frequently attacked the place, and on one occasion, in 1011, Eadric of Mercia wrought havoc here. But the see survived all these misfortunes, and here came William the Conqueror, who made an offering at St. David's shrine. For a time Welsh prelates continued to hold the see, but in 1115 Bernard, the first Norman prelate, chaplain of the queen of Henry I., was appointed to the see. Although he altered the constitution of the chapter, he made no alterations in the old church. The rebuilding was begun by Bishop Peter de Leia (1177-1198), but it is doubtful whether he personally did much to forward the work, as on account of his unpopularity he spent most of his time in England. However, the work progressed rapidly during his episcopacy, and was finished in the early years of the thirteenth century. After the fashion of cathedral towers, the tower of St. David's fell in 1220, and was immediately rebuilt. But it showed signs of again collapsing, and for centuries was a cause of anxiety, until it was made secure by Sir G. Scott in the restoration of 1866.

The greater part of the present building is Transitional Norman, but there was much architectural activity in later periods. Owing to the fall of the tower and the action of an earthquake in 1248, much rebuilding was found necessary. The thirteenth century witnessed the reconstruction of the north transept, together with the building of the east chapels, which incline at so great an angle, much reparation of the choir, and the commencement of the Lady Chapel and eastern portion of the presbytery. During the Decorated period much work was accomplished. Bishop Martyn (1290-1328) finished the Lady Chapel, and Bishop Gower (1328-1347) did much for the fabric of the Cathedral, and built the noble Palace, which is still beautiful in decay. His work is seen in the upper portion of the walls of the nave and eastern part of the choir and presbytery, the inserted Decorated windows, the eastern chapel of the south transept, the alterations in the corresponding chapel of the north transept, the south porch, the second stage of the tower, and the famous rood-screen. During the fifteenth century and the latter years of the fourteenth century, new roofs were added, the south window in the south transept constructed, heavy buttresses placed against the north wall of the nave, which had shown signs of giving way, and during the early years of the sixteenth century the tower was raised, and a stone vault erected over the Lady Chapel and the chapels behind the high altar.

During the Civil War sad havoc was wrought ; lead was torn from the roof, and this caused the eastern chapels and the Lady Chapel to fall into decay. The once noble Cathedral, in consequence of the treatment which it received during the strife of King and Parliament, and of subsequent neglect, was shorn of its ancient glory, and ruin and desolation reigned. At the beginning of the nineteenth century some efforts were made to improve this state of things, and the west front was rebuilt in a debased and miserable style, and during the course of the century sundry alterations were made, and at length, in 1862, Sir G. Scott commenced a thorough restoration. Vast sums have been expended upon the fabric of the Cathedral, and though the eastern chapels remain in their ruined state, the rest of the building has been repaired and renewed, and preserved from destruction. "It remains," wrote Sir G. Scott, "a wonderfully interesting and valuable landmark in architectural history, taking in the extreme west a position parallel to that held by Canterbury in the extreme east of the island.

THE EXTERIOR

The *West Front* is entirely modern, the work of Sir G. Scott, but it is designed after the fashion of the ancient front which existed before the hideous construction of the early eighteenth-century architect. As we walk around the Cathedral we must remember that nearly all the work is Transitional Norman, although its character is much disguised by later alterations and the insertion of Decorated windows. The *North Doorway*, with its curious ornamentation, is Transitional Norman, but time and weather have destroyed much of its beauty. The walls of the aisles were raised in the time of Bishop Gower (1328-1347), who inserted Decorated windows. The massive flying buttresses were added about 1500 A.D. On this side was the cloister court of the College of St. Mary, the ruined walls of which appear on the north. This college was founded by John of Gaunt in 1377 for the maintenance of a master and seven priests. The *North Transept* has been much altered. During the recent restoration the low Perpendicular roof has been removed, and one with a high pitch erected. The north window was inserted by Butterfield in 1846 in place of one which had been blocked up. A curious building is seen on the east side of this transept, which has three storeys, and is higher than the roof of the main building. It contains the Chapel of St. Thomas the Martyr, built mainly by Sir Richard Symonds in 1329, and above it the old chapter-house, and in the highest storey the treasury. The east end of the church was extensively restored by Scott. The Perpendicular roof was retained, but finding amongst the *débris* the evidence of lancet windows at the east end, Scott reproduced these with excellent effect. The *Lady Chapel*, built by Bishop Martyn (1296-1328), is still in ruins. The south transept has a Transitional Norman west wall, and the rest was built about 1220, after the fall of the tower. Large Perpendicular windows were inserted in the south wall. The old vestry is on the east side. On the south side is the beautiful *Porch*, built by Bishop Gower (1328-1347) in the Decorated style. There is a parvise chamber above. The doorway is remarkable; the sculptures represent the Root of Jesse, with Adam and Eve on the west side and the Patriarch Jesse on the other; above it a representation of the Holy Trinity, with censing angels.

The *Tower* was erected originally by Bishop de Leia, and fell in 1220. It was then rebuilt. Bishop Gower added a second storey in the Decorated style, and above this a Perpendicular storey was raised in Perpendicular times. The wonder is that all this extra weight did not cause the tower to collapse again. It certainly caused continual anxiety, and produced bulges in the neighbouring walls. However, the restoration of Sir G. Scott has secured safety and removed anxiety. The Perpendicular parapet is curious and not very beautiful.

Only one gateway remains, though there were four in the great wall which surrounded the precincts. The *Tower Gate* is a fine structure, flanked by two towers, one of which is octagonal and the other semicircular. The ruins of the *Bishop's Palace*, a magnificent structure, should be visited. It was built by Bishop Gower, and must have been one of the finest residences in the whole kingdom.

THE INTERIOR

The *Nave* is the work of Peter de Leia (1176-1198), and is Transitional Norman. The elaborate carving and the richness of the ornamentation are remarkable, and the colour of the stone adds a wonderful effect. St. David's has many peculiar features, and is unlike any other church in the kingdom. The arches are round, the triforium and clerestory are blended together under one arch. The piers are round and octagonal, with attached shafts. It was evidently intended to vault the nave, but this was abandoned. A Perpendicular roof of intricate and unusual design was constructed about 1500. The capitals afford an interesting study. The west end is modern, the work of Scott. Traces of coloured decoration may be seen on some of the piers of the nave; among the designs are figures of the Virgin, our Lord, and some monarch. The font in the south aisle is, with the exception of the shaft, of the same date as the nave. It is octagonal, and is carved with an arcade of pointed arches. The aisles do not possess any special features of interest. The architectural changes which have taken place there have already been mentioned. In the north aisle is the Transitional Norman doorway, and in the south the Decorated door of Bishop Gower.

The *Rood-Screen* is very remarkable, the work of Bishop Gower in the Decorated style. It is very massive and elaborate, and contains several tombs and monuments, has a groined roof, and is a very unusual and noble structure. The organ, which is modern, stands above this screen. The iron gates leading to the choir are also modern. Before entering the choir we will visit the *Transepts*, which are entered through Late Norman doorways from the nave. The western walls are Late Norman, built by De Leia, the rest were erected after the fall of the tower in 1220. In the *North Transept* the large north window was erected in 1846 in the Decorated style. This transept was dedicated to St. Andrew. On the east side is the Chapel of St. Thomas the Martyr, begun in 1220, refounded by Sir R. Symonds in 1329, and used for a variety of purposes. We notice a fine Early English piscina in the south wall. Above is the library and the old treasury. The *South Transept*, formerly known as the "Chanter's Chapel," had altars dedicated to the Holy Innocents and St. David, and was once used as a parish church. The east side of this transept has passed through several vicissitudes, and has now been restored to its original form.

The *Choir* is entered through the gates of the rood-screen, and occupies the space beneath the tower and half a bay beyond. The presbytery occupies the rest of the space beyond the parclose screen to the east wall behind the altar. All this is the work of Bishop de Leia, or that of his immediate successors, who rebuilt the tower after its fall in 1220. First, we examine the tower itself, and wonder at the marvellous skill of our modern architects and masons who could rebuild from their foundation two out of the four piers, each sustaining a weight of 1150 tons. Rich ornamentation is observed on the east and west arches, one of which is round, the rest pointed. Scott raised the wooden ceiling, and greatly improved the appearance of the interior of the tower. The *Stalls* were erected at the end of the fifteenth century, and are the work of Bishop Tully. There are a number of curious *misereres* with strange grotesques, amongst others — three men in a boat with a fourth rowing, one of the passengers being very sea-sick; a cowled fox offering a wafer to a goose with a human head; a carpenter building a boat, etc. The fox is doubtless a satire on the monks, and possibly also the sea-sick passenger. The *Bishop's Throne* is an elaborate structure erected by Bishop Morgan (1496-1505), and is of great height. It is a blend of the Perpendicular and Decorated styles; probably Bishop Morgan used some older materials in its construction. The *Parclose Screen*, separating the choir from the presbytery, is a peculiar feature of this Cathedral. It is of Decorated design. Passing through it we enter the *Presbytery*. At the east end above the altar are two rows of lancets, the lower lights being blocked, and filled with rich mosaics. The glass in the upper lights is modern, of good design and execution, erected by the Rev. John Lucy in memory of his ancestor, Bishop Lucy (1660-1677). The subjects of the mosaics are the Crucifixion, and figures representing the

Christian and Jewish Churches. The type of our Lord upon the Cross, the brazen serpent, appears below the central figure. Scenes from the life of St. David also are represented. The roof of the presbytery dates from about 1500, and on the bosses and in the panels are heraldic shields. The altar is modern. The floor is paved with old tiles, and the five crosses cut on some of the slabs in the sanctuary show that these stones were formerly altars. On the north of the presbytery is the famous *Shrine of St. David*, to which pilgrims flocked from all parts of Great Britain and Ireland. Kings and queens, nobles and princes came to pay their devotions at this shrine of the great Welsh saint, and bestowed many offerings on St. David's Church. Only the base of the shrine remains, and above this once stood the *feretrum*, which was doubtless covered with gold and jewels. The base is of Late Early English design, and was probably constructed in 1275 by Bishop Richard de Carew. The lowest part consists of three pointed arches with quatrefoils in the spandrels. The two inner quatrefoils communicate with lockers at the back, and were evidently intended for offerings. The upper portion consists of three arches with Early English capitals to the shafts, and under the arches were paintings of SS. David, Patrick, and probably Denis, but these have disappeared.

Another shrine is in the Cathedral, that of *St. Caradoc*, on the south side of the north transept. He was a Welsh saint, who was ordained and ministered in the Cathedral of St. David, and dying in 1124 was canonised by Innocent III. Here too are seen two quartrefoil openings for the reception of offerings.

We need not linger in the choir aisles except to observe the monuments, and will at once pass to the part of the east end behind the altar. This part consists of Bishop Vaughan's Chantry on the east of the presbytery, the ante-chapel, with two chapel aisles, and the Lady Chapel. This part of the church awaits restoration, for which funds are needed. With the exception of Vaughan's Chantry and the ante-chapel, all the building is roofless, exposed to the storms and rains of this exposed headland, and pitifully beseeches a new roof and shelter. Several architectural puzzles are presented by this portion of the Cathedral, which have not yet been entirely satisfactorily solved. Examining first Vaughan's Chantry or Trinity Chapel, we find a very beautiful example of Perpendicular work. The roof is a fine example of fan-tracery, and the whole structure rivals King's College Chapel, Cambridge, or Henry VII.'s Chapel at Westminster. Before the construction of this chapel the space occupied by it was left waste, and was described by Vaughan as *Vilissimus sive sordidissimus locus in totâ ecclesiâ.* A curious recess of Late Norman work has been discovered behind the high altar with beautifully-carved crosses. Above the recess is the figure of an angel, and some relics were found in the cill embedded in mortar, where they had doubtless been placed for the purpose of preservation at the Reformation. Recent discovery has revealed at the east end a beautifully-carved niche and two fine windows. Here are preserved some interesting Celtic crosses. On the south is the Chapel of King Edward the Conqueror, and on the north the Chapel of St. Nicholas. The *Ante-Chapel* has Early English arches with a Perpendicular roof. The *Lady Chapel* in its present form belongs to the transition from Early English to Decorated. Bishop Gower added the sedilia, founded a chantry here, and made sundry other alterations of a Decorated character.

The Cathedral is rich in monuments. The most important are :—

Bishop Gower, south of rood-screen.
Bishop Morgan (1564), south of nave.
Edmund Tudor, Earl of Richmond, father of Henry VII. (1456), presbytery.
Bishop Anselm le Gras (1247), presbytery.
Two tombs of Knights, on each side of presbytery.
A Priest (Decorated period), in presbytery.

Two ancient Celtic slabs, one of which records the name of Bishop Abraham (1078), and is in memory of his two sons.

In the ruined eastern chapels are the monuments of Bishop Vaughan, Sir J. Wogan (*temp.* Edward I.), Archdeacon Hoit (1319), an unknown knight, Bishop Martyn, and the fine tomb of a priest under a beautifully-carved canopy.

SCOTTISH CATHEDRALS

ALTHOUGH the Church of Scotland is Presbyterian, it was not until the stirring events of the Revolution of 1688 that this form of church government was adopted. From that day forward the Church of Scotland knew no bishops, and hence the application of the term cathedral to a church belonging to that communion is a misnomer. The Episcopal Church of Scotland has its cathedrals, but these for the most part are modern. But Scotland still possesses many of its ancient fanes, which are usually preserved with much care and solicitude, and retain much of the splendour of their Gothic architecture, and are rich with historical associations and tradition.

GLASGOW CATHEDRAL

THE Cathedral of St. Mungo in this city has vast treasures of architectural beauty. Its Patron Saint was the contemporary of St. Columba, a devout, miracle-working apostle, who converted the King of the Strathclyde Britons to Christianity and gained a victory for the Cross of Christ over the wild people who inhabited these parts. A cathedral was built here in Norman times. It was begun in 1124 and consecrated in 1192 in the presence of King David of Scotland. Before the century had closed fire destroyed this ancient church. But a new one was immediately begun, and five years later a portion of the building was so far finished that it was fit for consecration. About 1258 the fine Early English choir was completed. It is one of the best works of the thirteenth century in Scotland. The style of architecture followed closely the Early English of the northern type. The windows are deeply moulded on both sides, and the piers are strong and massive without clustering shafts. But Scotland at an early date developed peculiarities in her architecture which differed from English art. We see this in the use of the double lancet and simple tracery, whereas in England the lancets were widened. The influence of French architecture was not yet felt, though there was a distinct difference from the English usage. We see also that the choir has two storeys, the lower or crypt being entirely above the ground. Mr. Watson has recently published a learned work on this double choir, and gives excellent reasons for assuming that the vault of the "lower church" was built at five different periods, extending over half a century. His first period (*circa* 1220) includes only the south-east compartment. Then followed the north and south aisles with the springers of the south middle portion. The lower church was then left unfinished until the upper church had been built. The central portion of the lower church was then vaulted (*circa* 1260), and later still the eastern aisle and chapel. Mr. Watson's conclusions have not been universally accepted, but they are certainly worthy of credence. A few years later the tower and transepts were finished. Bishop Wishart took the part of Bruce as a loyal Scot against Edward I. and his attempted conquest, and suffered a long imprisonment. A disaster happened to the steeple in 1400, when it was struck by lightning. Bishop Lauder erected a stone one. The chapter-house was built by Bishop Cameron in the Perpendicular style. The rood-screen, with its curious sculpture, was the work of Bishop Blackadder, and also the great staircase leading to the crypt or lower church. At the close of the fifteenth century Glasgow became the seat of an archbishopric. Beaton, the nephew of the more famous Cardinal, finding that he lived in times dangerous for prelates, fortified his Palace and stored therein all the plate and precious things he could find, and then carried them off to Paris. The Cathedral happily was spared when the storm of contending forces at the Reformation raged, though it was long disused. The archbishop was in France, and Episcopacy was not in favour. With the advent of James VI. of Scotland to the throne of England Episcopacy was restored, and Spottiswood became Bishop of Glasgow. Then during the civil war Cromwell came here during the Presbyterian rule, but Episcopacy was restored with the monarchy, until it vanished again with the coming of Dutch William.

Much has been done during the past century in the way of "restoration." Two western towers have been bodily removed. The glass is modern and is almost entirely the work of foreign artists. The great east window was the gift of Queen Victoria. From the close we gain a fine view of the necropolis, which abounds in the sculptured tombs and monuments so dear to Scotland's sons.

IONA CATHEDRAL

We must now journey to the ruined shrine of Iona, the cradle of Western Christianity, the place whence flowed the stream of missionary enterprise which watered the dry furrows of northern England as well as Scotland, and caused Christianity to flourish throughout the country. We owe much to this lonely isle where St. Columba landed in 563 and built his rude monastery, the forerunner of the ruined buildings which now greet us. This isle could tell us of many a scene of carnage when the wild Norse pirates came. The Cathedral was begun in the Early English period, and is cruciform. The tower, 75 feet high, has two fine windows. The capitals are beautifully carved, though they are much weather-worn owing to the roofless condition of the church. On the north side are the remains of the monastery; a Norman arcade shows that it is older than the present Cathedral; and on the south is the Chapel of St. Oran, the companion of St. Columba. It is of early date, probably founded in the eleventh century by Queen Margaret when the isles were wrested by Scotland from the Norsemen. Its western doorway is Norman with beak-head ornament. In the *Reilig Oiran*, or cemetery of kings, lie buried forty-eight Scottish, four Irish, and eight Scandinavian monarchs, together with many abbots and monks and chieftains, a veritable Valhalla of the great. The carved sepulchral stones and crosses of Iona are noble examples of early art, the interlacing work sculptured upon them being wonderfully intricate and beautiful. The two most perfect crosses are Maclean's cross and St. Martin's, one of the most beautiful and perfect in Christendom. A nunnery was founded here in Norman times, and traces of Norman architecture are evident in the ruins. In 1208 a colony of Benedictine monks was established here by one Reginald, the heir of the Abbot of Derry, who handed over the nunnery to the guidance of his sister Beatrice. There was a close connection between Iona and Norway, and for a long time the bishopric of the Isles was united with that of the Isle of Man. At the present time the bishop of that island is known as the Bishop of Sodor and Man, Sodor being a corruption of Sud Ja, or southern island, so called by the Norwegian Vikings, who long held rule here. The monastery was destroyed in 1561. Iona was a much-esteemed seat of learning, and was much frequented by pilgrims. It was long regarded as the isle of special sanctity, and kings and warriors from far and near were brought here to be laid in their last resting-place near the sacred tomb of Columba. Few places have so great a fascination as this sacred isle.

BRECHIN CATHEDRAL

BRECHIN has many interesting features, notably its half-finished Cathedral, the famous round tower which was undoubtedly connected with it, or an earlier shrine, and the ruins of the *Maison Dieu* or hospitium founded by William of Brechin in 1256. The old Cathedral was founded by King David of Scotland in 1150. It is a plain and unpretentious building, now used as a parish church, and it has suffered much from restorers and renovators. Its plan was originally cruciform, but some vandals at the beginning of the eighteenth century entirely destroyed the transepts. The west window and doorway are thirteenth-century work. Most drastic treatment did this church receive in 1806, when besides the destruction of the transepts, the aisles were removed, and new and larger ones erected. The renovators were not satisfied with the old arches of the nave ; so they built new and wider ones, and raised the walls, so that one roof could span the whole, and thus eclipsing the clerestory windows. The south side of the nave seems later than the north. Its piers are lighter than those on the opposite side. At the north side of the choir are three lancet windows. The church is disfigured by galleries and pews. The ruins of the chapel of the *Maison Dieu* are small but interesting. An Early English doorway and a few lancet windows remain. The *Round Tower* is the principal architectural feature of Brechin. Ireland possesses many of these curious structures, and besides this one Scotland has only one other, the tower at Abernethy. Its date is about 980. The object of such towers is mainly to provide a place of refuge in times of attack, where the monks could store their treasures and protect themselves. They may also have been used as belfries, and their origin is certainly ecclesiastical. There is no staircase, access to the top being gained by ladders resting on wooden floors. The height is 86 feet, the thickness of the wall near the base 4 feet, and the inner diameter 8 feet. An octagonal spire crowns the summit. There is a doorway on the west which is adorned with rude carvings. Over the doorway is a carved representation of the Crucifixion, and on either side of the door are ecclesiastics, and below are strange creatures realistically carved. These figures are interesting memorials of Celtic art.

ABERDEEN CATHEDRAL

ONE mile north of the large and flourishing city is the quiet, ancient town of Old Aberdeen. Here is the Cathedral of St. Machar, built entirely of granite. It is not remarkable for its sculptured elegance or vast dimensions, but it has an interesting history, and its flat panelled ceiling, adorned with numerous heraldic shields, is a distinguishing feature. The church is small, and is only 200 feet in length. Its Patron Saint was a companion of St. Columba, who journeyed here on his missionary work, and founded a church about the year 597. A second church was begun in 1183, but this was not equal to the ambition of Bishop Cheyne, and was destroyed by him in order to make way for a better. This again was superseded by a church begun by Bishop Kinnimond, in 1357, but the work progressed slowly, and not until the rule of Bishop Leighton (1422-1440) was the nave finished with the north transept and west towers. The roof was added by his successor, Bishop Lindsay, and the central tower and spire by Bishop Elphinstone, who began the ill-fated choir. Bishop Stewart built the chapter-house. The troubles of the Reformation and of the Civil War wrought much havoc. The lead was torn from the roof; the bells were shipped off to Holland and lost at sea. The stones of the choir were used for fortifications by Cromwell's troops; the great tower fell and destroyed the transepts, and all that remains of this church is the nave. The west front is an imposing piece of work. The west window consists of seven lofty narrow openings, with cusped arches at the head. The towers, capped with spires, are very massive in their granite ruggedness. There are five bays in the nave, with round piers, Decorated arches, no triforium, and small clerestory windows. On the ceiling are forty-eight heraldic shields of princes, nobles and bishops who aided in the erection of the church.

King's College, founded by Bishop Elphinstone in 1498, should be visited. The original oak canopied stalls, *misereres*, and lofty open screen in the chapel, are some of the finest work of the period. The influence of the French Flamboyant style is evident in their execution. These beautiful works of art were saved from destruction by the bravery of the Principal, who summoned his people, and protected his treasures from the fury of the barons of Mearns after they had sacked the Cathedral.

DUNBLANE CATHEDRAL

THIS Cathedral is one of the few specimens of Gothic art in Scotland which escaped destruction at the Reformation. Nearly all the building is Early English, except the tower, which is Early Norman. Ruskin wrote his praise of this edifice :—

" He was no uncommon man who designed the Cathedral of Dunblane. I know nothing so perfect in its simplicity, and so beautiful, so far as it reaches, in all the Gothic with which I am acquainted. And just in proportion to his power of mind, that man was content to work under Nature's teaching, and instead of putting merely formal dog - tooth, as everybody else did at that time, he went down to the woody banks of the sweet river, beneath the rocks of which he was building, and took up a few of the fallen leaves that lay by it, and he set them on his arch, side by side for ever."

There was an early church on this site founded by St. Blane. This early church was superseded in 1150 by one erected by King David of Scotland. All that remains of this church is the fine Norman tower. The rest of the church fell into ruin and neglect, until the time of Bishop Clement, who, about 1240, began to build this beautiful church in Early English style. At the Reformation great damage was done, when over-zealous Protestants pulled down the roof and carried off much plate and treasure. For centuries the nave remained in this condition ; the choir and chapter-house were roofed over, in order to form a parish church ; and now a great restoration of the church has recently taken place. A new roof has been erected, after the fashion of the Cathedral church of Aberdeen, with its heraldic devices, and the whole church repaired and beautified.

The west front is Early English in design, with lancet windows, a deeply-recessed doorway, and in the gable a window with the leaf decoration praised by Ruskin. The nave has eight bays, and is Late Early English. The pulpit is modern, and also the screen.

The choir has no aisles, and has six lancet windows, with a large east window. The stall-work of sixteenth-century is beautifully carved, and there are some interesting grotesques. On the west side of the choir is the chapter-house, which is the earliest part of the present church, with the exception of the tower, and has an upper room, possibly used as a treasury or *Reclusorium*. The tower is an important structure, of Early Norman character, and doubtless served the same purpose as the round towers of Ireland and Brechin, affording shelter in case of attack. There are good reasons for believing that originally it was separate from the church. The upper portion was added later. A fine view can be obtained from the summit. There are some interesting monuments in the Cathedral, and in the churchyard is the tomb of the heroine of the song, " Charming young Jessie, the flower of Dunblane."

DUNKELD CATHEDRAL

THE first church was founded by Constantin, King of the Picts, about 800 A.D., and the Culdees were established in a monastery here. In 1107 it became the seat of a bishopric, and a colony of Augustinian canons replaced the former dwellers. A new choir was built in 1220-1250, in the Early English style. During the wars with England, in 1380, it was burnt, but almost immediately restored. The nave was finished by Bishop Lauder in 1465. He was a most munificent prelate, who did much for his Cathedral, began the tower and chapter-house, and furnished the Cathedral with gifts of much valuable church plate. There is a curious story [1] of a Highlanders' raid, and of their entry to the church, and of the bishop's perilous escape to the rafters of his church, in order to escape their hands. On another occasion the church was besieged in the time of the famous Bishop Gavin Douglas, the translator of the *Æneid* (1576). His election to the see was opposed by the Stewarts, the inveterate enemies of his house ; and Andrew Stewart barred the door against him, and fought against him from his stronghold in the tower. Douglas soon gathered his friendly clans together, and forced an entrance. It is uncertain when the nave lost its roof, probably when certain lairds at the Reformation went on their base crusade, plundering and destroying churches, and seizing their goods and valuables.

[1] *Scottish Cathedrals and Abbeys*, by M. E. Leicester Addis.

After the battle of Killiecrankie there was a great fight here, and an asylum of refuge was found here by the people, who fortified their position with the seats, and did much damage. The roof was destroyed, and the nave has been ever since exposed to the storms of wind and rain. The choir is now used as the parish church, having been rebuilt. The nave has seven bays, and measures 120 feet by 60 feet. The piers are of massive Norman character, and there is a somewhat poor triforium and clerestory. The original choir was built by Bishop Sinclair in 1350. The tower, 96 feet high, is Perpendicular, the work of Bishop Lauder (1469), and finished by Bishop Brown in 1501, and is a very good example of the style. The south porch was built by Lauder, but it is now in ruins. The chapter-house is the work of the same bishop. It contains the vault of the Dukes of Athol. Here, near the porch, is buried Alexander Stuart, Earl of Buchan, better known as the " Wolf of Badenoch " (1394), who burned down Elgin Cathedral and devastated the place. Few churches have passed through such stormy scenes as Dunkeld, and its ruined state is a melancholy testimony to the lawlessness of the tumultuous times, which have left their mark upon its desecrated walls.

ST. ANDREW'S CATHEDRAL

Of the once great Cathedral of St. Andrew, the Primatical See of Scotland, few traces are left. Its consecration in the time of Robert Bruce was marked by unparalleled pomp and circumstance. All the most distinguished in Church and State were present, no less than seven bishops and fifteen abbots, the king and well-nigh all the flower of his nobility. It was originally founded by Bishop Arnold (1159-1162). Its plan was cruciform, and was 355 feet in length, and the nave 200 feet, and there was a Lady Chapel at the east end. It had a grand central tower, and six turrets, of which three remain. A fire partly destroyed it in 1378, but it was restored and embellished, and finished in 1440. In 1559 John Knox preached a fiery sermon in the town church, which led the magistrates and inhabitants of the city to plunder the Cathedral and strip it of its altars and ornaments. The whole church was ransacked and left to fall into ruin. Soon the central tower fell, and carried with it the north wall; and since then the church has been used as a quarry. The ruins are picturesque in their decay. All that remain are the east and west gables, part of the south wall of the nave and the west wall of the south transept. The style of these ruins is partly Norman and partly Early English. Under the east window, built up in the wall, is a curious Runic inscription. The Castle at St Andrews is closely connected with the Cathedral, as it was built by Bishop Roger in the thirteenth century as an episcopal residence. The old Castle was destroyed in the fourteenth century, and soon afterwards rebuilt. Here Cardinal Beaton was murdered, who had witnessed the burning of Wishart in front of his Castle. The Bottle Dungeon is a curious place of incarceration, and, besides the towers and walls, there is an interesting subterranean passage which enabled persons to escape from the Castle in time of siege.

ST. GILES' CATHEDRAL, EDINBURGH

EDINBURGH was not raised to episcopal rank until the time of Charles I. The church has a great history, though it is popularly remembered as the place where Jenny Geddes threw her stool at the dean, when the English service book was introduced in the time of Charles I. The first Church of St. Giles was consecrated in 1243, but it was burnt down during the English wars, when most of the city shared the same fate. Indeed, signs of fire may still be detected on the piers of the choir and elsewhere. The church is remarkable for its numerous chapels. On the south of the nave two were built in 1387, but these have been destroyed by drastic " restoration." There are the Chambers's Memorial Chapel, the Preston Aisle, named after one William Preston, who brought from France a relic of the Patron Saint ; the Chapman Aisle, named after Chapman, the " Scottish Caxton," who introduced printing into Scotland, and the Moray Aisle. During the fifteenth century much building was in progress. The choir was lengthened, a clerestory added and the roof raised, and ere the century had elapsed it was raised to the dignity of a collegiate church. The choir is a fine example of fifteenth-century work, and the Gothic crown which surmounts the central tower forms a very distinguishing feature. It is unlike anything else we know. Few scenes and events in Scottish history have not in some way been connected with this church. We see John Knox preaching violently here against the iniquities of the court, and especially of the unfortunate

Queen Mary. Knox was appointed minister of the church. It was divided into three portions—the Great and Little Kirk and the Tolbooth. Then in the time of James I. Episcopacy was restored, and in 1633 Charles I. made St. Giles into a Cathedral. Here Jenny Geddes, as we have said, expressed her displeasure at the new English liturgy by throwing her stool at the clergyman, and commenced the famous riot which had lamentable results. Later on we see the struggle between the Covenanters and the Royal Party, and the head of the Duke of Argyll stuck on a spike on a gable of the Cathedral, the advent of " Bonny Prince Charlie," and all the events of Scottish history seem to be associated in some way with St. Giles'. Its war-worn banners, its monuments of national heroes, all combine to add a peculiar interest to the building. The church owes much of its present beauty to the munificence of Dr. William Chambers, who rescued the building from neglect, and renewed and beautified it. He was one of the firm of the great Edinburgh publishers. Amongst other memorials of recent worthies we find a window to R. L. Stevenson, and in the Moray Chapel a monument to General Wauchope, who was killed gallantly leading his troops in the recent war in South Africa. Although the choir is fifteenth-century work, it differs much from that of the same period in England. In Scotland French influence was much felt in the development of architecture, and the builders inclined more to the French Flamboyant rather than to the English Perpendicular.

The new Cathedral of the Episcopal Church of Scotland at Edinburgh, designed by Sir G. Scott, is one of the finest and largest of our modern Gothic buildings.

KIRKWALL CATHEDRAL

If we journey to the remote Orkneys we shall see a noble Cathedral at Kirkwall, which is of peculiar interest. Until the year 1472 these islands belonged to Norway, and were under the episcopal supervision of the Archbishop of Drontheim in that kingdom. The Cathedral is therefore connected with the rule of Norwegian earls and bishops, and has many features differing from those types which are more familiar to us. It was founded by the Norwegian Earl Ronald in 1137, and was designed and constructed by the Norwegian Kol. Here were buried many

Scandinavian jarls and bishops, but their tombs have disappeared. There is a fine nave of eight bays, which is of the Norman character, and a choir of six bays, screened off so as to form a parish church. The piers are all round and massive, and the arches round-headed, both in the main arcade and in the triforium and clerestory. There is some fine Norman arcading, with intersecting arches on the side walls. The church is dedicated to St. Magnus, and is 226 feet long by 56 feet wide. The original choir ended in an apse, but it was lengthened by Bishop Stewart in 1511, and the west end of the nave was finished by Bishop Reid in 1540. Different coloured stone is used extensively in the building, principally the red and yellow sandstone, and these varied hues add greatly to the architectural effect. The three west doors are particularly fine. The tower has fifteenth-century windows, and the bells were given by Bishop Maxwell at the end of the fifteenth century. Near the church are the ruins of the Bishop's Palace, where King Haco died in 1263, and also the Earl's Palace, which, after the incorporation of the islands with Scotland, was assigned to the bishops for a residence. The church has been much restored during the last century.

GLOSSARY OF ARCHITECTURAL TERMS

Abacus.—The uppermost division of the capital, or head of a column, originally square and plain, in later styles more or less decorated with moulding, and in the Early English and Decorated periods generally circular or polygonal. In classic architecture it supported the horizontal superstructure of the entablature, but in Gothic architecture the arch rises directly from it.

Apse.—The round or polygonal end of a chancel.

Architrave.—The lowest division of the entablature in classic architecture; ornamental moulding round the exterior curve of an arch or round the openings of doors and windows, etc.

Ashlar.—Hewn stone.

Aumbrey or Almery.—A cupboard for containing the sacred vessels.

Ball-Flower Moulding.—Ornament resembling a ball enclosed in a globular flower of three petals.

Baluster.—A small turned wooden pillar, generally circular.

Bay.—The compartment of a church formed by the buttresses or pilasters on the walls, the main arches or pillars, the ribs of the vaulting, or other features which separate the building into corresponding portions.

Campanile.—A bell tower.

Cavetto.—A concave moulding of a quarter of a circle, used in classical and other styles of architecture.

Chamfer.—To cut off angles.

Clerestory or Clear-Story.—An upper storey, or row of windows in a Gothic church; so called to distinguish it from the blind-storey, or triforium.

Corbel.—A projecting stone or piece of timber supporting a weight.

Corbel-Table.—A row of corbels.

Credence.—A small table or shelf near the altar on which the bread and wine were placed before they were consecrated.

Crocket.—A bunch of projecting flowers or foliage decorating pinnacles, arches, etc.

Cusps.—The projecting points in Gothic tracery, or inside an arch; sometimes worked at the ends with leaves, flowers, or heads.

Dog-Tooth Moulding.—Ornaments usually consisting of four plain leaves, arranged so as to form a point.

Dripstone.—Projecting tablet or moulding over heads of archways, windows, doorways, etc.

Fan-Vaulting.—Vaulting in which the ribs rise with the same curve and diverge equally in every direction from the springing of the vault.

Finial.—A foliated ornament ending a pinnacle or gable, etc.

Flamboyant.—A name given to Late Decorated style of architecture from the flame-like wavings of its tracery.

Gargoyle.—A projecting spout, often carved in a grotesque form.

Groin.—The angle formed by the intersection of vaults.

Herring-Bone Work.—Masonry in which the stones are placed aslant, forming a fish-bone pattern.

Jamb.—The side of a window or door, etc.

Miserere.—A projecting bracket on the under side of the seats of stalls, which were made to turn up; the monks were allowed to lean on these brackets during the long services, which were performed standing.

Mullion.—Perpendicular bar between the lights of windows in Gothic architecture.

Nail-headed Moulding.—Moulding in imitation of ornamental nail-heads.

Newell.—The column round which a spiral staircase winds.

Ogee.—A moulding partly concave and partly convex, forming a round and a hollow. Term also applied to an arch formed of contrasted curves.

Orders.—The recesses of a divided arch.

Parvise.—A small room over the porch.

Pilaster.—A pillar, sometimes disengaged but generally attached to a wall.

Piscina.—A basin attached to the wall near the altar of a church, where the priest washed his hands and rinsed the chalice.

Plate-Tracery.—Tracery which appears as if formed by piercing a flat surface with ornamental patterns.

Plinth.—The lowest division of the base of a column, or projecting face at the bottom of a wall.

Presbytery.—The part of a church where the high altar stands.

Reredos.—A screen at the back of an altar.

Rood-Loft.—A gallery over the screen separating the nave from the chancel, on which the great cross or *rood* was fixed.

Sedilia.—The seats for the officiating clergy.

Soffit.—The under side of an arch, cornice, etc.

Spandrel.—The triangular space between arches.

Splay.—The expansion given to windows and other openings by slanting the sides.

Springing.—The point at which an arch unites with its support.

Squint.—An oblique opening in the wall of a church.

Stoup.—A vessel or stone basin formed in the wall, serving as a receptacle for holy water.

String-Course.—A horizontal moulding running along a wall.

Transom.—A horizontal cross-bar in a window.

Triforium.—A gallery in the wall over the arches which separates the body of the church from the aisles.

Tympanum.—The space above the horizontal opening of a doorway and the arch above; the space between an arch and the triangular drip-stone or hood-mould which surmounts it.

INDEX

Lightning Source UK Ltd.
Milton Keynes UK
UKOW040634131211

183664UK00003B/80/P